The Essential Guide to Wireless Communications Applications

ISBN 0-13-009718-7

9 780130 097187

90000

D1411427

Prentice Hall PTR
Essential Guide Series

The Essential Guide to Wireless Communications Applications

SECOND EDITION

Wireless Communications Applications

From Cellular Systems to Wi-Fi

ANDY DORNAN

Prentice Hall PTR, Upper Saddle River, NJ 07458
http://www.phptr.com

Library of Congress Cataloging-in-Publication Data

Dornan, Andy.
  The essential guide to wireless communications applications : from cellular to
WiFi / Andy Dornan.--2nd. ed.
    p. cm.
  ISBN 0-13-009718-7
  1. Wireless communication systems. I. Title: Wireless communications applications.
II. Title.

 TK5103.2 .D673 2002
621.382--dc21

                                                            2002019685

Editorial/Production Supervision: *Donna Cullen-Dolce*
Executive Editor: *Mary Franz*
Editorial Assistant: *Noreen Regina*
Manufacturing Manager: *Maura Zaldivar*
Art Director: *Gail Cocker-Bogusz*
Interior Series Design: *Meg Van Arsdale*
Cover Design: *Bruce Kenselaar*
Cover Design Direction: *Jerry Votta*

 © 2002 by Prentice Hall PTR
A division of Pearson Education, Inc.
Upper Saddle River, NJ 07458

The publisher offers discounts on this book when ordered in bulk quantities.
For more information, contact: Corporate Sales Department, Prentice Hall PTR
One Lake Street, Upper Saddler River, NJ 07458; Phone: 800-382-3419; FAX: 201-236-7141;
E-mail: corpsales@prenhall.com

Printed in the United States of America
10 9 8 7 6 5 4 3 2 1

ISBN 0-13-009718-7

Pearson Education LTD.
Pearson Education Australia PTY, Limited
Pearson Education Singapore, Pte. Ltd.
Pearson Education North Asia Ltd.
Pearson Education Canada, Ltd.
Pearson Educación de Mexico, S.A. de C.V.
Pearson Education—Japan
Pearson Education Malaysia, Pte. Ltd.

To Rachel

Preface

The first cell phone I ever saw was the size of a small television set. It needed an antenna to match, and a battery that now would look more at home in a car. While this could theoretically last ten hours between charges, actually making calls reduced its lifetime to minutes. The cellular network itself was equally primitive, with coverage so poor that I often had to lean out of a window in order to pick up a signal.

The whole system was so unreliable that mobile phones often seemed more like expensive toys than a serious means of communication, and indeed they were often sold as such. Their high cost—a minute's talk time cost around an hour's salary—made them popular status symbols. People would clip phones to their belts as a way to show off how rich and important they were (or believed themselves to be).

I'd bought mine for the opposite reason: My crumbling flat in Notting Hill wasn't able to support a landline, and I reasoned that even an expensive and erratic connection was better than nothing. When the building eventually caught fire, I wasted valuable seconds giving directions to the emergency services operator: Mobile phones aren't mapped to addresses in the same way as landlines, so as far as she knew, I could have been anywhere in the country.

A decade later, I again had to make an emergency call from a mobile phone. This time, the emergency operator was able to determine which part of San Francisco I was in, thanks to equipment that automatically relayed the location of the cellular base station I was closest to. Had I been in Tokyo, it would have been able to do even more, pinpointing my exact latitude and longitude. Such systems are on their way to other parts of the world, prompted both by regulations designed to enhance public safety and by a commercial imperative to offer location-based services. They also raise obvious privacy and security fears, as do several other aspects of wireless networking.

WHAT'S NEW ....

The ability to pinpoint a location to within a few meters is just one of the new technologies that have emerged since the first edition of this book. Though it was published only two years ago, wireless is such a fast-moving industry that a lot has changed in this time.

The idea that people who have telephone wires leading to their homes will willingly rely on a mobile as their primary phone no longer seems absurd. Nor does the idea of surfing the Web while sitting under a tree, or watching TV streamed across the Internet from the other side of the world while riding a bus. As a result, I have totally rewritten much of this book, adding new sections and figures to every chapter.

Other new developments since the first edition include Ultra Wideband, which is still in its infancy but may soon allow very high-speed data transmission over short distances, and T-Rays, a type of link that mixes the qualities of light with those of radio. The most significant is the growth of wireless Local Area Networks (LANs), which now appear to be playing a greater role in the wireless future than many had once thought. Amidst the dotcom and telecom busts of 2001, Wi-Fi (IEEE 802.11b) was a great success story. Its successor could even form the basis of fourth-generation systems, which unlike so much else in the wireless world might actually arrive ahead of schedule.

For computer geeks like me, this is a welcome change. A wireless LAN is something that individual people can set up and tinker with at relatively low cost, not a service provided by a giant corporation and licensed by the government. Of course, most people don't want to construct their own networks, so the technology still has a way to go. I've tried to look at how it will develop, as well as explain the competing standards and what each can do.

Not every change in those two years has been positive for the wireless industry: Though technology advanced, the economy collapsed, and many companies that planned or built wireless networks have fallen into bankruptcy. (I particularly miss Metricom and its Ricochet system.) New sections in Chapters 1 and 7 deal with the realities of the wireless business, which is actually surprisingly resistant to wider economic recession and even depression.

As well as all these revisions, there is one new chapter, examining the possible health risks of wireless communications. Though radiation from a cell phone is unlikely to be the "new smoking" as some alarmists claim, mounting evidence since the first edition suggests that it is not entirely risk-free. I personally have *not* decided to limit my use of cell phones and wireless data devices, but then I also drink beer and ride a bicycle without a helmet (though not at the same time). You may reach a different conclusion. Wireless devices also bring about other safety and social problems: Regardless of any effects from radiation, it's now clear that using a cell phone while driving can kill.

ABOUT THIS BOOK...

Most of us form some kind of picture in our mind when we talk to someone on the phone. We usually still imagine them sitting at a desk or lounging on a sofa, but those pictures are no longer true. Dial a number in some European countries, and the chances are that it will reach a wireless phone. The person you talk to could be sailing in Lake Geneva, trekking across Lapland, or just walking down any city street.

Soon we won't have to imagine. The phone companies are already demonstrating wireless videophones that double as pen-based computers—and that's just the start. The very term cell "phone" is itself becoming outdated, as the latest mobile data terminals are already able to more than just transmit voice. Visionaries predict mobile links as good as those that office computer users enjoy, enabling high-speed Internet access, responsive networked applications, and crystal-clear video.

Even more exciting are the new applications unique to mobile devices: location-based maps, personalized weather forecasts, even real-time medical monitoring. Electronic currency could allow a cell phone to become a virtual wallet, transmitting the equivalent of cash to stores both in the real world and online. Marketers refer to all these applications as the "wireless Web," a somewhat empty phrase. It is both as meaningless and as promising as the "Information Superhighway" of nearly a decade ago.

The Essential Guide to Wireless Communications Applications is designed to look beyond the hype, examining just what is and isn't possible with present-day and future wireless systems. It is primarily focused on the applications, but a proper understanding of these requires a look at the underlying technology. For example, the first version of WAP promoted a backlash among European users because it had been promoted as equivalent to the wired Internet. If the PR people had understood the technology and been more honest, it might have seemed less of a disappointment.

This book is intended for anyone who wants (or needs) to learn about the new wave of wireless networks. It will introduce you to all the most important wireless technologies, then explore their likely impact on both commerce and culture.

STRUCTURE ....

Each chapter is intended to stand alone, though the whole book should also make sense when read from beginning to end. Readers who already know a bit about the technology, or who are entirely technophobic, may wish to skip some parts of Chapters 2 to 5. These explain in detail how the first, second, third, and now fourth generations of cellular systems work, including the type of applications that each is best suited to as well as the financial and regulatory problems in their way.

Chapters 6 and 7 focus solely on the applications, looking at the types of services available from each system today and tomorrow. They also take a look at the hard economics behind investment in mobile systems, and the reason that Europe's telecom carriers have gambled around a trillion dollars on new spectrum licenses and equipment.

The hardware required by a wireless network is surveyed in Chapter 8, from the cellular operators' infrastructure of radio masts to the servers hosting individual WAP and i-mode sites. Chapter 10 investigates mobile phones themselves, considering the different paths that their evolution may take. Some pundits predicting that they will expand to become computers, others that they will shrink to the size of headsets.

As mentioned above, wireless LANs are among the most interesting new mobile technologies, as well as the fastest changing. Chapter 9 takes a detailed look at these, as well as similar systems such as Bluetooth and cordless phones. This is the longest chapter in the book, as well as the one that has changed the most from the first edition.

While terrestrial mobile technologies receive most of the hype, fixed wireless and satellite technologies are also interesting. Chapters 11 and 12 look at these. With fiber and Digital Subscriber Line (DSL) looking less attractive all the time, satellite and fixed wireless could be the best hope that most residential customers have for high-speed Internet access. Satellite networks are particularly exciting, and despite many high-profile failures, new satellite constellations are always on the launch pad. They claim to offer truly global networks, promising access from ocean liners, intercontinental jets, and even the South Pole.

At the end of every chapter is a summary page, highlighting the important information contained within. Each chapter also contains a short a list of relevant Web sites, for readers wanting to learn more. None of these have any connection with this book, but all contain some useful information. There's always a risk that Web sites will change or disappear—one that was listed in the first edition has since been replaced with a hardcore porn site—so I have also added a more conventional bibliography, listing other relevant dead tree books.

Acknowledgments

First and most obviously, I need to thank all the people at the various cell phone and wireless data companies who taught me about their technology and the applications that it makes possible. Though the companies themselves are often shameless liars that will say anything to extract money from customers or investors, many of the people who work for them are honest and helpful. Even after I wrote nasty things about their employers, they went out of their way to explain complicated topics and let me play with the latest gadgets. Without them, this book would contain many more inaccuracies than it undoubtedly does.

I'd also like to thank my family and friends. In particular, Becky understood when I had to spend many long nights writing the first edition, and generally kept me less insane than I would otherwise be. Rachel did the same while I was working on the second edition. Also Dave, always willing to discuss technology and society over a pint or ten. And Alec, without whom I would have been homeless when I arrived in London. All also kept the futuristic vision of a wireless world grounded in today's reality. If Europe has such a great mobile infrastructure, they asked, why can't I use my phone on the Tube (London's subway system) or travel abroad without having to pay roaming charges that cost more than the flight?

Also thanks to the staff (and former staff) of *Data Communications* and *Network* magazines, especially Peter Heywood and Steve Steinke, who got me into this stuff in the first place, and Ellen Terry, who didn't harass me over deadlines in my day job while I was working on the second edition. *Data Communications* ran for nearly 28 years, covering the evolution of computer networks from punch cards to fiberoptics. Though I joined in its twilight phase, the book's editorial ethic still had a profound impact on me. It also nurtured my fascination with the subject matter of the next 400 pages. *Data Comm.* eventually folded into *Network* magazine, which is equally exciting to write for.

Most importantly, I need to thank everyone who read the first edition, particularly those who contacted me with comments or who translated it into other languages. (Thanks to Fabio Freitas, people now assume that I can write in Portuguese!) The best part of writing a book is hearing from readers, whether they are pointing out errors or suggesting improvements.

— Andy Dornan, andy_dornan@hotmail.com

Contents

1 The Wireless World

In this chapter...

Wireless technology is changing the world. Where communication has hitherto relied on cables strung on poles or dug into the ground, we are now able to send voice and data through air and empty space. Without wires holding us back, we will be able to stay in contact wherever we are. New services can be set up in minutes, without spending months negotiating rights of way or constructing tunnels.

The preceding paragraph could have been written a hundred years ago. At the beginning of the twentieth century, wireless technology also promised to revolutionize communications. It did, but it took many decades before it could be combined with another of the twentieth century's new technologies—telephony. A second wireless revolution occurred in the 1990s as wireless transmitters became small and lightweight enough to be built into hand-held telephones. Rather than simply watching TV or listening to radio, the majority of people in some countries were broadcasting signals of their own.

The effects of this second revolution continue into the 2000s, as both wireless technology and telephony converge with the Internet. The result may eventually be a single network for both voice and data, with wireless as the dominant access method. Most information will still travel over high-bandwidth fiberoptic cables for parts of its journey, but the phones and computers through which people actually interact with the network will not require wires.

WHAT'S IN A NAME?

Wireless technology is littered with three-letter acronyms (TLAs). Those that appear in this book are spelled out when first used and sometimes again in later chapters. They are also listed and defined in the glossary.

A few are impossible to spell out; this is because some vendors and standards groups develop a kind of "acronym envy" over the capital letters that acronyms usually use. These people insist that their technologies be capitalized, even though they don't actually stand for anything.

Still more vendors like to take an existing acronym, often one of an official standard, and change or add one letter (often **m**, for **mobile**). This is an attempt by companies to differentiate themselves from the competition, but it has the opposite result—many very similar-sounding products or standards.

The situation is further complicated by the way that certain acronyms change over time. For example, the basic cellular standard in the United States is called **AMPS**, which originally stood for **Advanced Mobile Phone System**. As technology progressed, it began to seem anything but advanced, so the **A** changed to **Analog**. When a digital version was developed, it changed again to the more accurate **American**. All three are still in use.

The terms **cell phone** and **mobile phone** mean almost the same and are often used interchangeably. Technically, **cellular** is a subset of **mobile**, but a large one: Most mobile systems are cellular, and all cellular systems are mobile. In general, the British tend to say **mobile**, whereas the Americans say **cell**. The industry prefers **mobile**, because it implies freedom, whereas **cell** suggests imprisonment. A few companies don't like the term **phone**, because newer devices are more like small computers. For this reason, they are often referred to as **terminals**.

One advantage of cellular/mobile telephony is that it can compete with monopoly wireline phone companies. These monopolies are known by a variety of names, not all of them printable, but are officially called **Incumbent Local Exchange Carriers** (ILECs, or simply incumbents), because they own the telephone exchange. In the United States, they are sometimes called **Regional Bell Operating Companies** (RBOCs), after the Bell system from which they are descended. In most other countries, they're called **Post**, **Telegraph**, and **Telecommunications Authorities** (PTTs), because they used to be (and in some cases still are) run by the country's Post Office.

CUTTING THE CABLES ....

The wireless revolution cuts both ways: It changes the Internet and the phone system, but also requires change in the wireless technology itself. Digitization and Internet protocols enable radio to carry much greater amounts of data than its nineteenth-century pioneers thought possible, all personalized for individual listeners. Instead of poor-quality television programs broadcast to everyone, users may eventually have virtual reality on demand.

By mid-2000, more people in Europe had a mobile phone than had a PC or a car. By the end of 2001, the world's most popular online service was one that could be accessed only through a cell phone, not a computer. Analysts predict that the trend will continue, with wireless gadgets overtaking traditional computers as the dominant Internet access means at some point between 2004 and 2006. Unlike the relatively primitive, text-based Internet phones that appeared in 2000, these new gadgets will allow true Web surfing, as well as location-based services and other enhancements that take advantage of mobility.

This shift from fixed to mobile access could have profound effects on the Internet, which, in its early years, was dominated mainly by the wealthy, the young, and the male. That will change: Mobile phones are more evenly distributed across society, and even the cheapest models are beginning to incorporate some kind of Internet access. Though these cost slightly more to produce, operators often subsidize the manufacturing to promote usage.

And wireless technology isn't just for rich consumers in the West. In the late 1990s, cell phones enabled many people all over the world to make their first-ever calls. In the next few years, they will also be sending their first e-mails—again, wirelessly—and probably from something that more closely resembles a phone than a traditional PC. The Web will become truly worldwide.

Most of the excitement is justifiably about *mobile* wireless, but there are also significant advancements in fixed wireless, which is used to replace local telephone wires. Satellite systems can be either mobile or fixed, with some systems, such as the futuristic Teledesic, planning both. These are aimed both at globe-trotting travelers and at parts of the world that have no communications infrastructure at all. A combination of cellular and satellite technology can often bring telephony and Internet access to areas that would have to wait many years for cables.

Network Philosophies

In the wired world, boundaries between networks are quite clearly defined: Whoever owns the cables or the devices connected to them controls the network. There are generally two types:

- **Wide Area Networks** (WANs) cover a long distance, from several kilometers to the entire world or beyond. They are usually run by telecom companies and carry voice or data for various customers. The Internet and the phone system are both comprised of many WANs. They are often called *public* networks, because they carry traffic for anyone who can pay. (In this case, public does *not* refer to ownership: Whether owned by a government, a traded corporation, or a private individual, a network that carries traffic for others is considered public.) WANs are sometimes divided into subgroups, of which, the most important is the *MAN* (Metropolitan Area Network), a type that covers a city or other region of only a few kilometers. Because radio waves have a limited range, most wireless WANs are MANs. The exceptions are satellite networks, which can cover intercontinental distances.

- **Local Area Networks** (LANs) cover only a short distance, usually 100 m or less. They are usually installed within homes or offices and are accessible only to the residents or employees. For this reason, they are referred to as *private* networks. The *PAN* (Personal Area Network) is a special case of a wireless LAN, with a particularly short range. It can cover a distance of only 10 m and is envisaged as a way to connect devices carried by a single individual.

In the wireless world, the distinctions between LAN and WAN or between public and private networks are less clearly defined. Radio waves don't respect legal boundaries or even physical walls, meaning that private transmissions can spill over into the public space. The first effect of this has been to expose private data to all comers, thanks to unencrypted wireless LANs. In the future, it could change how people access the Internet or make phone calls.

The companies that run wireless networks want people to use the public WAN. Their vision of the future is something similar to that shown in Figure 1.1, where each wireless device has its own separate, long-distance connection. This means that users have to pay the companies for access and that the devices can be used almost anywhere. A cell phone user can travel many miles while making a call, often without the connection being broken.

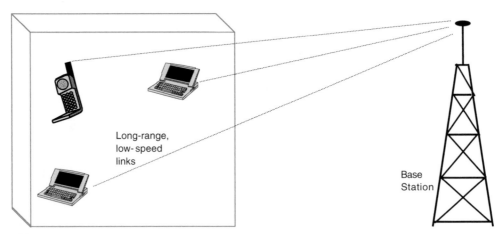

Figure 1.1
Wireless WAN: Devices communicate with base station several km away.

Many people have an alternative vision, shown in Figure 1.2. This uses a small LAN access point within the home or office, connected via a fixed network to the Internet and the phone system. Cordless phones and wireless-equipped computers communicate with the access point, which aggregates all their voice and data together and sends it over a single connection. The advantage of this is that it's cheaper—one connection costs less than many—and can achieve higher data rates, thanks to the shorter range of the wireless signal and the high capacity of the fixed network. The disadvantage is that the phones and computers can't be carried out of range of the access point while maintaining a connection.

For narrowband voice, the WAN philosophy seems to be winning: Many people in Europe have a mobile as a "primary" phone, using it for all calls, even when at home. The same is beginning to happen in North America, though only for long-distance calls. This is partly because the cell phone is more convenient and partly because aggressive competition keeps cell phone charges relatively cheap, whereas fixed telephony is often run by a de facto monopoly.

For broadband data, the situation is reversed. No WAN technologies can yet match the speed of wireless LANs, so many people prefer to set up their own wireless LAN and connect it to some kind of high-speed fixed-access technology. This is usually a cable in the ground, as shown in the figure, but in future may be a point-to-point wireless system, such as a laser beam. It's also possible that the WAN and LAN will converge as mobile operators set up wireless access points of their own.

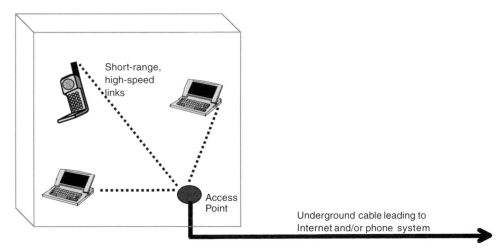

Figure 1.2
Wireless LAN: Devices communicate with access point less than 100 m away.

Cell Phone Generations

The present hype is around *third-generation* (3G) phones, which will provide most of the advanced services planned until at least 2010. But it's worth looking at the other generations and the features they offer:

- **1G.** First-generation phones are *analog*, meaning that they send information as a continuously varying wave form. They can be used only for voice and have highly variable call quality, thanks to interference. Another serious disadvantage is that they are very insecure; snoopers can listen in on calls with a simple radio tuner or can even charge calls to another person's account.

  Almost no new 1G networks are now built anywhere in the world, but the phones to use with them are still manufactured. Europe and Japan both gave them up in the 1990s, upgrading to digital systems. North America is not as far advanced, but it's moving in the same direction: At the beginning of 2002, about 30% of U.S. subscribers relied on 1G phones, down from twice as large a proportion two years earlier. They are more popular in some parts of Africa and South America, thanks to their low cost, but even there, they will soon be squeezed out by second-generation (2G) and even 3G technology.

- **2G.** Second-generation phones convert all speech into digital code, resulting in a clearer signal that can be encrypted for security or compressed for greater efficiency. Most also include some kind of simple text messaging, as well as support for Centrex-style services, such as voice mail and Caller ID. The most popular is the Global System for Mobile Communications (GSM), but several others are used around the world. They can send data, but usually at less than 10 kilobits per second (kbps); by comparison, most modems achieve a real speed of at least 30 kbps. Some data-only devices, such as two-way pagers, are also considered to be 2G, because they send a digital signal at relatively low speeds.

  Most cellular operators are upgrading their 2G networks to higher data speeds, theoretically more than 100 kbps but more realistically those of a fast modem (about 40 kbps or less). These are referred to as *2.5G*, because they are significantly better than existing 2G systems but less advanced than the more futuristic 3G. As well as offering higher data rates, they often use *packet-switching* for data, a more efficient way of sharing a connection between many users. This is the same system used by the Internet, so it makes interconnection between the phone and the Internet easier.

  Some 2.5G upgrades don't try to reach higher data rates, instead adding the capability for specific applications. Wireless Application Protocol (WAP) and i-mode both use a compressed version of the Web to fit into a mobile phone's slow data rate and small screen. Location technologies can find a user's exact position, intended both for emergency calls and for services such as maps.

- **3G.** Third-generation systems will provide a variety of advanced services, including data transfer at up to 2 megabits per second (Mbps) and videoconferencing. Instead of phones, many terminals will be small computers or *PDAs* (personal digital assistants) with built-in Web browsers and possibly other applications, such as word processors, spreadsheets, and address books. They will include small keyboards, handwriting recognition, and, eventually, voice recognition.

  Like many new technologies, 3G has initially been disappointing. The first data rates of the first terminals are only 64 kbps, less than those once envisaged for 2.5G, let alone 3G. Many companies admitted that the expected 2 Mbps would be available only for users standing right next to a base station tower. These initial services are sometimes referred to as *3G lite*. At the other end of the scale, many researchers are working on enhancements to 3G that they claim really will reach the hoped-for data rate and beyond. These are known as *3.5G*.

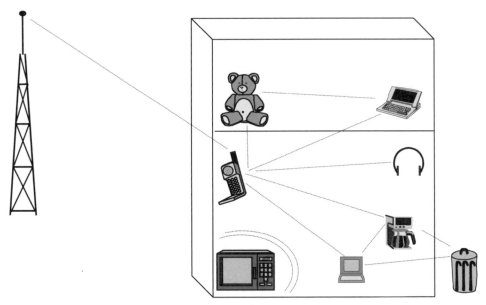

Figure 1.3
Wirelessly networked home.

Many 3G terminals will also be able to link to a PAN, which links all the devices in a very small area, such as a room or even a person's pocket. The most promising technology for this is Bluetooth, which puts a very low-power radio into a single microchip. Bluetooth's designers envisage a chip inside almost all household devices, as shown in Figure 1.3, enabling them all to connect to the Internet via a 3G terminal.

- **4G.** Fourth-generation networks are already in the labs, with Japanese operator NTT DoCoMo planning to offer the first commercial services in 2006. They will offer very high data rates, perhaps as much as 100 Mbps, enabling new services that have not yet been invented. They will also be focused primarily on data, using packet-switching for all traffic and replacing basic voice service with video or even virtual reality.

Many wireless LAN technologies already come close to 4G's hoped-for data rates, though they don't offer the service guarantees or roaming capability that users of cell phones expect. If these can be added to wireless LANs, 4G may actually arrive earlier than expected.

FROM THE 20S TO THE 2000S.............................

As far as the economy is concerned, we've been here before. In 2000, some farsighted stock market analysts compared the 1920s to the 2000s, implying that the economic boom of the 2000s, like that of the 1920s, would result in a huge crash and worldwide depression. So far, the bears have been accurate. The actual similarities are scarier than that, because the two booms also share the same driving technology—wireless.

In the 1920s, wireless was everywhere. Radio was a new technology that, like the wireless Internet today, people believed would change the world. Though investors lost a lot of money, the people developing the technology were ultimately proven right. Companies fell, but radio did change the world, and that change hasn't finished yet.

Moore's Law (named after Intel cofounder Gordon Moore) states that the number of circuits packed into a given area of a silicon chip doubles approximately every 18 months, leading to a similar improvement in processing power. Today's supercomputer is tomorrow's wristwatch. In the late 1990s, the rate of advance actually increased: Mobile computing is accelerating at a rate *faster* than Moore's Law.

The Wireless Economy

The wireless industry got caught up in the Internet bubble of 1998–2000 and in the subsequent crash. Although this means that many people and companies may have made bad investments, it doesn't mean that wireless (or the Internet) has no future. Some companies will go bankrupt, but the infrastructure they build will live on. Unlike Enron and most of the dot-coms, wireless network operators are creating something that is permanent and useful. They may fall, but their legacy can benefit everybody.

Companies such as Iridium and Metricom have already demonstrated this: They were at opposite ends of the mobile networking scale—Iridium built a global satellite network for voice traffic, whereas Metricom built a high data rate system that served just a few cities—but their rise and fall followed similar paths. Both won plaudits for their technology but few customers. Both went bankrupt months after they began service, leaving behind networks so useful that the military or police kept them going even after they'd officially been shut down. Both were eventually bought by new companies for about a hundredth of what they cost to build. With the networks already in place, the new companies hoped to operate them profitably—bad news for the stockholders in the original companies but good news for everybody else.

Many mobile phone operators, particularly in Europe, have spent vast sums of money on licenses to operate 3G networks. Paying so much was probably a mistake for the companies involved, but again, it is good news for everybody else. European governments are using the revenues from these to cut taxes and increase spending on services that benefit their entire population. Perversely, the large amount already spent may actually *encourage* the companies to spend even more on actually con-structing networks. The licenses are nonrefundable and are automatically cancelled if the operators fail to meet an aggressive deadline for network buildout. The only way that the companies can hope to recoup their costs is to build a network and operate it profitably. The odds of doing this may be slim, but like gamblers who refuse to take a loss, they have no choice but to double up and take an even larger gamble.

Some economists argue that companies who follow this path are committing the *Concorde fallacy*—throwing good money after bad. It's named after the plane developed by the British and French governments in the 1970s, which took far longer to develop than originally planned and cost millions of pounds more than estimated. At more than one point during the development cycle, the governments realized that the costs of finishing the project would be more than the potential revenues it could generate. In this case, the rational economic choice was to cancel the Concorde and write off the millions already spent. Economists argue that the same applies to 3G: The costs of actually build-ing a network are more than some estimates of the potential revenues, so the companies should just abandon their licenses and try to invest their money in other, more profitable services.

Concorde wasn't cancelled, for reasons of national pride and to avoid political embarrassment. Similarly, 3G won't be cancelled, because many wireless operators have said that high-speed mobile data is their whole raison d'être. Individual share-holders are free to take a loss and try to find a better investment—indeed, many have done so, hence the fall in the stock prices of companies holding 3G licenses—but companies often are not. In the case of Concorde, the losers were the British and French taxpayers, while the winners were a few transatlantic business travelers and frequent-flying celebrities. In the case of 3G, the losers are likely to be investors in wireless operators and the winners everyone.

Japan's experience during the 1990s shows that wireless technology can make great advances, even during an economic depression. It can even be profitable, as both NTT DoCoMo and many smaller companies have found. Similarly, the U.S. computer networking industry suffered its worst ever year in 2001, thanks to the bursting dot-com bubble. One of the few bright spots was the wireless LAN market, which continued to grow even as the economy shrank.

Visions of the Future

Companies pushing wireless technology often make extreme predictions, such as one prediction that human brains will be wirelessly networked to each other by the year 2030. (This came from British Telecom, back when it still ran a mobile network.) Some of this hype is justified, but much of it isn't. In the late 1990s, the industry was burned by *underestimating* the potential of wireless technology: The first phones to provide even limited Internet access were snapped up so fast when first launched in mid-1999 that many people had to wait a year before they could get one. Analysts repeatedly had to raise their predictions of the mobile phone's popularity in Europe as it became ubiquitous, first in Finland and then in Norway, Sweden, and Britain.

Two years later, mobile technologies were failing to live up to their hype. They arrived late, they didn't perform as expected, and they weren't as popular as most of the cell phone companies had hoped. Their predictions for market growth usually relied on cell phone penetration reaching more than 100%—often 400% or 500%, which would mean people buying and operating four or five cell phones each. The companies envisaged customers maintaining one for business, one for the home, and several for various different social activities.

This hasn't happened: Though a large proportion of cell phone users have bought or owned more than one during their lives, this is only because their previous model has been broken, or stolen, or has become obsolete. People do not buy several different cell phones and keep them all active at once, because a mobile phone subscription usually costs at least $20 per month (and often a lot more). Some critics remarked that this was blatantly obvious: The market for almost anything will stop growing once everybody already has one.

Although some new wireless technologies seem disappointing, these are just the first versions. WAP has been a lot less popular than mobile operators hoped, but it has actually grown faster than the wired Web did in its early years. Some of this growth could be due to hype, but other types of wireless Internet service are popular. As of January 2002, the world's largest Internet Service Provider (ISP) is NTT DoCoMo. It has over 30 million users, more than AOL or any other ISP that offers wireline access. All of these are in one country (Japan), all access the Web via a cell phone, and the majority actually pay for content.

Similarly, the first 3G systems have not lived up to expectations, but they eventually will. GSM, now the world's most popular mobile system, was first developed in the early 1990s. At the time, few customers wanted it, and it was written off as a failure. Today, more than 10% of the Earth's population carries a GSM phone.

Among the more interesting uses for 3G and other wireless technology:

- **Videophones.** Combining a Web cam and a mobile phone with a Palm-type device, these also allow fast access to the Web. They're already here, but not popular. It's likely that they never will be, but the technology exists if people want it.

- **Voice Recognition.** The cumbersome twentieth-century method of entering text into phones will eventually be abandoned as phones gain the ability to recognize and understand human commands, even against the background noise of the mobile environment. In 1999, British Telecom predicted that it would be widespread by 2002. In 2001, the Universal Mobile Telecommunications System (UMTS) Forum predicted some point between 2005 and 2010, which is more realistic.

- **Web Phones.** In 2000, many mobile phone manufacturers said that *everything* they sold would be Web-enabled by 2002. This prediction was largely right, though often using more primitive WAP technology, rather than the true "Web."

- **Retinal Displays.** British Telecom predicted in 1999 that these would be possible by 2003. They will use tiny projectors mounted in the frames of glasses to shine images directly onto a user's retina, allowing access to information services while walking around or interacting with other people. More cumbersome goggles are already available, but they don't permit contact with the real world: Users must immerse themselves completely in virtual reality.

- **Wireless LAN Ubiquitous.** Many analysts predict that wireless LAN antennas will be standard on all computers by 2005. They are already built into most high-end laptops.

- **All Phones Become Mobile.** The difference in cost between mobile and fixed telephony has all but disappeared in some areas. Analysts predict that mobile operators will eventually have to rely on value-added services to make their money. Phone numbers will refer to people, not places. British Telecom predicts that, by 2006, the idea of standing in a fixed spot while making a call might seem rather quaint.

- **Internet on Mars.** NASA is planning to launch a series of communications satellites into Martian orbit, all based on the same standard protocols as the Internet. The network should be running by 2008, then extended outward in the following decades and centuries.

- **Internet Appliances.** Some members of the Bluetooth Special Interest Group predict that, by 2010, it will be rare to find new white goods—refrigerators, dishwashers, and the like—that do not have a built-in Internet connection. The Net will be as ubiquitous as microchips became in the 1990s.

- **Remote-Controlled Cars.** Researchers in government and industry are already working on these: Japan hopes to have one operational before 2015, and in 2001, the U.S. government approved a communications system in dedicated spectrum. Roads will be made safer as powerful traffic computers take over driving, preventing accidents and automatically routing every vehicle via the most efficient path.

- **Holophones.** British operator Orange predicts that, by 2020, mobile phones will be able to project three-dimensional moving images of people and other objects.
- **Mind Reading.** British Telecom predicts that, by 2025, thought recognition will become the standard form of input. Primitive mind-reading techniques were used by computer games in the 1990s, but this technology will be used on a far greater scale. Machines will act as an extension of the user's body. Making a call in a public place will no longer disturb others.

  The same researchers predict that, five years later, this could evolve into a full, direct brain link. People will have wireless data devices hardwired into their brains, allowing instant telepathic communication. Learning will become obsolete because high-speed networks will allow people to access the sum total of all human knowledge as easily as they access their own memories. Such technology raises all kinds of objectionable possibilities, from *Star Trek*'s Borg to a literal thought police.

BUYING A CELL PHONE ....

Back in the real world, choosing a cell phone can be a complicated decision. Beware of slick salespeople offering "free" phones, often with bundled accessories and other freebies, such as televisions or computers. They require you to sign a service contract that lasts at least a year and can be difficult to get out of after that. The companies make up more than the cost of the phone in monthly service charges, and most people end up paying hundreds of dollars.

This isn't to say that all the cheap or free phones are necessarily a bad thing; it's standard practice in many countries for the operators to subsidize the cost of phones, and sometimes the service contracts offered are good value. But it is important to shop around. "Prepay" deals with no contract attached may be better if you need a phone only for emergency use, whereas if you want Internet access, it may be worth turning down the free phone in favor of a more advanced model.

Each mobile operator typically offers many rate schedules and payment plans, seemingly designed to confuse. In general, paying a high monthly line rental leads to reduced per-minute charges. But even for the same monthly fee, there are usually choices, such as how much to pay for different kinds of calls and whether international roaming is allowed. Pick the wrong one and you could end up paying far too much, or you may even find that your phone doesn't work when you most need it.

Posers

Companies like Nokia freely admit that many of their phones are sold on appearance, not features. They target specific models at groups they call "posers" and "yuppies." A case in a fashionable color will often prove more popular than Internet access or long battery life, and visual appearance is expected to become more important as the diversity among users widens. The same applies to other mobile devices; the most sought-after Palm PDAs tend to be those with the most stylish case, not the most technically advanced.

The trend toward stylishness could continue as computers move from functional devices to consumer products, but phones won't become less functional. Most manufacturers plan to build some kind of wireless Internet capability into all of their mobile phones, along with basic computer functions. There is already a wide choice of phones and other devices based on WAP and similar standards, with better services that approach the quality of the wired Web on the way.

If you want the mobile Internet now, your choices depend mainly on where you live. In Europe and America, WAP is becoming ubiquitous. Most analysts agree that it is more of a gimmick than a true wireless Internet service, but it could still be worthwhile. WAP's main problem has been that users needed to dial in to a computer to use it, meaning they are charged for every second spent online and can't make phone calls at the same time. In Japan, the i-mode system overcomes both these problems and has become more successful than anyone predicted. New 2.5G and 3G technologies could enable WAP to do the same.

The most successful wireless data services don't mean accessing the Web at all. Short messaging, originally intended just to test the capability of GSM phones, is hugely popular in both Europe and Japan. Messages are still fairly primitive because they're limited to a few characters, rather like telegrams from many decades ago. Emerging standards will change this, adding multimedia and, more importantly, integration with Internet e-mail.

Globalization

Movies like to show the hero using a cell phone aboard a jumbo jet or underneath the desert in Iraq. Both these scenarios will remain fiction for many years; it's still impossible to get a cell phone that will work everywhere in the continental United States, let alone the world. Only satellite systems achieve true global coverage, and they don't work indoors.

For world travelers, the best choice is probably GSM, but this is actually available in five different varieties. There are two versions of the American Digital AMPS (D-AMPS) system and two of cdmaOne, the Code Division Multiple Access (CDMA) cellular technology first developed by Qualcomm. Many phones support more than one version of a system, or even different systems, but it's important to make sure that the one you choose will work where you want to take it. In particular, American GSM uses different frequencies than does European GSM, and phones supporting both are still quite rare. The companies assume (probably rightly) that most people who buy a cell phone in Europe will never take it to America, and vice-versa.

Despite early hopes of a global standard, the incompatibility is set to continue into 3G. This is due partly to the commercial interests of rival companies, partly to the political machinations of national governments, and partly to genuine practical difficulties in making a new system compatible with older networks. Because 3G networks are initially limited to a few small areas, people want phones that can also be used with existing 2G networks. This affects the design of the 3G networks themselves, as it's easier to make dual-mode phones for systems that have something in common.

There is officially a worldwide standard for 3G, but it's really just a name ("IMT-2000"). It contains so many options that no phone or network will support them all. Three countries built 3G networks in 2001—Japan, Korea, and the Isle of Mann—and all used different systems. Whereas all European countries are building the same system, America will be a microcosm of the world: U.S. cellular operators are planning at least three different types of 3G, which may splinter into even more.

There is greater hope for worldwide standards in shorter range wireless systems, which are already replacing wires as a means of connecting computers together and may form the basis of 4G mobile. Wireless LANs based on the Institute of Electrical and Electronics Engineers (IEEE) standard 802.11 (Wi-Fi) system can be used nearly everywhere, as can the emerging Bluetooth technology. These really will enable a phone or a computer to communicate anywhere in the world.

WEB RESOURCES

www.s3.kth.se/radio/4GW/
The Personal Computing and Communication research group at Sweden's Royal Institute of Technology is trying to develop a 4G mobile system for the year 2010 onward. Its site has lots of interesting papers covering different possible directions that mobile communications could take in the future and a free 100-page report (in PDF format) called **Telecom Scenarios 2010**.

www.bt.com/bttj/
British Telecom publishes the quarterly BT Technology Journal, a combination of in-depth tutorials on 3G technology and futurology covering the wider applications of 4G.

www.wirelessweek.com
The trade magazine **Wireless Week** publishes most of its daily news stories online and has a huge archive of information about the cellular industry.

www.wirelessdevnet.com/
The **Wireless Developer Network** is a news and analysis site that covers every aspect of the wireless industry from the perspective of programmers and Web designers.

www.thefeature.com
The Feature is an online magazine about wireless technology and its applications. The site is run by Nokia, so its analysis is hardly objective, but it can still be interesting.

www.unstrung.com
Unstrung is an online magazine featuring daily news and analysis of wireless technology, applications, and business.

BIBLIOGRAPHY

Gralla, Preston. **How Wireless Works**. Que, 2001.
A picture book illustrating many aspects of wireless communications in full-page spreads and describing them in a very simple, nontechnical way.

Stetz, Penelope. **The Cell Phone Handbook**. Aegis, 1999.
A consumer-oriented guide to cell phones and service plans, teaching people how to avoid getting ripped off by slick salesmen and small print.

Webb, William. **The Future of Wireless Communications**. Artech House, 2001.
An exploration of how wireless communications might develop over the next 20 years, with a look at 4G and beyond. The author is much less optimistic (i.e., more likely to be right) than the companies touting virtual reality and direct brain links.

SUMMARY

- The Web is going wireless. By 2003, more people will access the Internet via mobile phones than through computers.
- Most existing mobile phone systems are 2G. New 3G terminals will support higher-speed data services. Further in the future, 4G may enable true mobile broadband.
- Short-range wireless LANs and longer range cellular systems are fundamentally different, but can be used for similar applications. They are both competing and complementary.

2 Radio Spectrum

In this chapter...

Radio is at the heart of wireless communications. Its basic principles are more than a century old, but it continues to evolve almost as fast as computing. Digital broadcasting has managed to cram more capacity out of old wavebands while new technology opens up new ones. Advances in electronics have made radio circuitry smaller and lighter to the point where transceivers that fit into a single microchip are no longer a fantasy.

Despite the advances, radio spectrum remains a finite resource. Although anyone can lay fiber cables in the ground, not just anyone can start his or her own cell phone network. Licensing remains a controversial issue, with governments, corporations, and people unable to agree on how the spectrum should be divided and who is entitled to use it, and for what.

There are some wireless technologies that don't rely on radio. Infrared is used by common household devices, such as remote controls, as well as for linking computers to each other or to peripherals. Point-to-point links can use all kinds of other signals, including laser beams. But as yet, these are niches, suitable only for limited applications. In the foreseeable future, most wireless applications will remain dependent on radio.

RADIO 101 ....

Radio signals are a type of *electromagnetic* radiation, a category that also includes light, infrared, and many other types of rays. They are usually thought of as waves, which means they have a particular set of mathematical properties. Only scientists and engineers really need to worry about the exact equations, but some of these properties are important to understanding wireless applications. In particular, a radio signal has a *wavelength* and a *frequency.*

Electromagnetic waves are *transverse*: Like waves in the sea, they vibrate at right angles to their direction of travel. This makes it easy to measure the wavelength: It's just the distance between the peaks of sequential waves, as shown in Figure 2.1. (The wavelength is more difficult to measure for *longitudinal* waves, such as sound, which vibrate in the same direction that they travel.) The frequency is the number of wave cycles occurring each second. Cycles per second are usually called *Hertz* (Hz), after Heinrich Hertz, the physicist who discovered radio.

The speed of any wave can be calculated by multiplying the frequency and the wavelength, but all radio waves automatically travel at a constant speed—the speed of light, which in empty space is exactly 299,792,458 meters per second. Passing through any material slows them down slightly, but air and even clouds are so thin that, for wireless communications, the speed can still be thought of as around 300,000 km per second. That's 186,000 miles per second, but nobody working with wireless technology uses miles anymore.

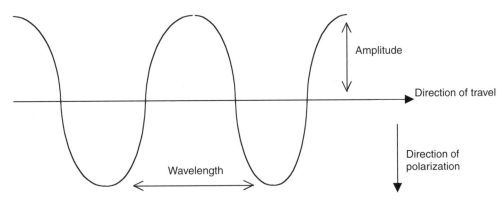

Figure 2.1
A transverse wave.

The constant speed means that, as frequency is increased, wavelength is shortened. It's easy to calculate each from the other (divide the speed of light by the one you know to get the one you don't), so only one is ever specified. Unfortunately, conventions about which should be used have changed through the history of radio. Most scientists now prefer frequency, but older equipment and even the names of different types of radiation use wavelength.

The *amplitude* of a wave is its height, measured from the axis to the peak. This represents the power of the transmission, or how loud it is. Amplitude usually decreases as a wave moves further away from its source and spreads over a wider area, a phenomenon called *divergence*. Such weakening of the signal means that very powerful transmitters are needed to cover a wide area.

Waves moving through anything other than a vacuum also experience *attenuation*, which is a loss of energy to whatever they happen to hit or pass through. The most important type of attenuation for most wireless communications is caused by air, but some technologies are designed to take account of the signal passing through clouds, rain, and even walls.

SCALE

Most electromagnetic waves have frequencies far higher than 1 Hz. To avoid having to write large numbers out in full, radio engineers use several prefixes based on International System (or SI, from the French "Système International d'Unités") metric units:

1 kilohertz (kHz) = 1,000 or 10^3 cycles per second
1 megahertz (MHz) = 1,000,000 or 10^6 cycles per second
1 gigahertz (GHz) =1,000,000,000 or 10^9 cycles per second
1 terahertz (THz) = 1,000,000,000,000 or 10^{12} cycles per second
1 petahertz (PHz) = 1,000,000,000,000,000 or 10^{15} cycles per second
1 exahertz (EHz) = 1,000,000,000,000,000,000 or 10^{18} cycles per second

Conversely, wavelengths are often smaller than 1 meter, particularly for the types of radio used by modern communications systems.

1 millimeter (mm) = .001 or 10^{-3} m
1 micrometer (μm or micron) = 0.000 001 or 10^{-6} m
1 nanometer (nm) = 0.000 000 001 or 10^9 m
1 picometer (pm) = 0.000 000 000 001 or 10^{-12} m
1 femtometer (fm) = 0.000 000 000 000 001 or 10^{-15} m

The only area where SI prefixes aren't used exactly is in computing, because computers use powers of two rather than ten. A **kilobyte** (KB) is actually 1,024 bytes, and a **megabyte** (MB) is 1,048,576 bytes. Communications technologies do use exact thousands and millions, so 1 kbps = 1,000 bps.

This can be important because programs such as Web browsers usually show data rates in KB or MB per second. (The reason for this inconsistency is that different computers originally used bytes of different sizes, but now almost all follow the standard 8 bits to a byte.) As data rates get higher, the difference between the communications and the computing measurements becomes more significant.

1 byte per second = 8.0 bps
1 KB per second = 8.19 kbps
1 MB per second = 8.39 Mbps
1 GB per second = 8.59 Gbps
1 TB per second = 8.80 Gbps
1 PB per second = 9.01 pbps

Radio and Radiation

The complete range of electromagnetic radiation is known as the *spectrum*. Though the full spectrum is thought to be infinite, radio waves lie at one end of the part that is well understood, with a lower frequency and a longer wavelength than most other radiation. The spectrum is a continuum; the boundaries between different types don't exist naturally, but were invented by scientists trying to classify them. Some of these classifications are obvious: For example, the range of radiation that our eyes have evolved to see is known as *light*. Others are not, so there is some overlap, and even disagreement about where exactly the boundaries lie. The complete spectrum is illustrated in Figure 2.2.

Radio is the name given to the types of electromagnetic waves that can be used for communication purposes. Its scope is expanding all the time, thanks to new technology. At the low-frequency end, waves of around 5 kHz have been used to send signals underwater. At the upper limit, the overlap between radio waves and microwaves became particularly valuable in the late twentieth century, because this region can be used for high-capacity communications over a relatively small area. Microwave radio is employed by all cell phone systems and by most satellites.

Some new and experimental technologies use even higher frequencies at the overlap between microwave and infrared (IR). These are known as *T-Rays* (the *T* is for THz, their frequency), or the *near-infrared*. They're sometimes described as optical rather than radio, though true optical networks use higher frequencies (the *far-infrared*) or even visible light.

Electromagnetic waves are generated whenever an electric charge is accelerated. Technically, *acceleration* doesn't just mean getting faster: It can also mean slowing down (deceleration is just acceleration in the opposite direction) or a change in direction for something that is already moving.

A radio transmitter works by vibrating electrons, the charged particles that surround all atoms and are responsible for electricity. The frequency of the wave depends on how fast the electrons are vibrating; the faster they move, the higher the frequency. A receiver uses the same principle in reverse: The waves stir up electrons in the antenna, creating electric currents.

Beyond the radio spectrum, higher frequency waves are produced and absorbed in the same way. A light bulb is essentially just a transmitter that heats electrons so that they vibrate millions of times faster than those in a radio antenna. Likewise, eyes are receivers, tuned to interpret radiation at those high frequencies.

Waves at even higher frequencies than visible light can strike electrons so hard that they are knocked free of their atoms, a process called *ionization*. Ionizing radiation is extremely dangerous to living things, which is why the word *radiation* has become,

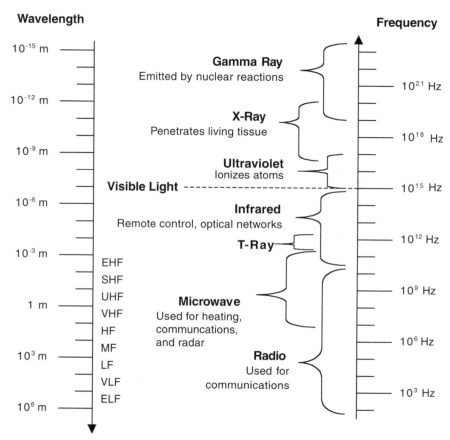

Figure 2.2
The electromagnetic spectrum.

to many people, synonymous with danger and death. Radio waves are way below these ionization frequencies, so they are not harmful in the same way as ultraviolet or nuclear radiation. But this does not mean they are entirely safe; they do cause heat, as anyone who uses a microwave oven knows.

Bands

The radio spectrum is subdivided into a series of regions known as *wavebands*. Table 2.1 shows the names and uses of these, in order of increasing frequency. Although now named after frequencies, the bands were originally defined in terms of wavelengths, hence the convenient powers of ten.

Because frequency is measured on a logarithmic scale, each band contains ten times the spectrum of the one above it in the table. For example, there is a thousand

Table 2.1   Radio Wavebands

Wavelength	Frequency	Common Name	Main Purposes
Above 100 km	Below 3 kHz	Extremely Low Frequency (ELF)	Submarine communications
10–100 km	3–30 kHz	Very Low Frequency (VLF)	Maritime communications
1–10 km	20–300 kHz	Low Frequency (LF) or Long Wave (LW)	AM broadcasting
100–1,000 m	300–3,000 kHz	Medium Frequency (MF) or Medium Wave (MW)	AM broadcasting
10–100 m	3–30 MHz	High Frequency (HF) or Short Wave (SW)	AM broadcasting, amateur radio
1–10 m	30–300 MHz	Very High Frequency (VHF)	FM broadcasting, TV
0.1–1 m	300–3,000 MHz	Ultra High Frequency (UHF)	TV, cell phones
10–100 mm	3–30 GHz	Super High Frequency (SHF)	Fixed wireless, satellites
1–10 mm	30–300 GHz	Extra High Frequency (EHF)	Satellites, radar

times as much spectrum in the UHF band, used for most broadcast TV, than in the MW band, used for most AM radio. This means that the high-frequency bands are most useful for fast data services, whereas the lower ones are suitable only for broadcasting.

Spectral bandwidth is not the only difference between the bands. Signals at high frequencies have a much shorter range than at lower frequencies because the shorter wavelengths suffer greater attenuation. As radiation frequency gets higher, more things are able to block it. That's why high-frequency light can't pass through walls, whereas lower frequency radio can. Ionizing radiation can be blocked entirely by gas, which is fortunate for us—much of the deadliest radiation from the sun is (or used to be) stopped by the ozone layer, a region of oxygen molecules slightly larger than those that we breathe.

This attenuation effect is particularly apparent in broadcast radio. Stations in the LW band are able to cover several European countries with a single transmitter, whereas those in the VHF band typically serve only a single city. The short range is a problem when trying to communicate across a great distance, but it can be a benefit when designing a cellular network because it means that different cells can reuse the same spectrum.

Satellite systems use high frequencies but extend the range by using very powerful transmitters and, in many cases, a parabolic *dish* to focus the radiation.

Many frequencies in the HF band are able to travel right around the world by reflecting off the ionosphere, a layer of electrically charged particles at the top of Earth's atmosphere. Before satellites, this was the only way of communicating across oceans, but it is very unreliable. Because the ionosphere is created by ultraviolet radiation from the sun, it intensifies with sunspot activity and gets thinner at night. Nevertheless, a short-wave radio receiver can be used to hear broadcasts from around the world.

Microwaves

The UHF, SHF, and EHF bands are collectively known as *microwaves* because of their small wavelengths—small compared to other radio waves, not to the electromagnetic spectrum as a whole. Their high bandwidth and short range make them very useful for communications. They do have disadvantages, notably that they are easily blocked by obstacles such as walls and hills, and weakened by rain and cloud.

The microwave spectrum is subdivided into bands, shown in Table 2.2. Most of their names don't actually mean anything: They were originally chosen by the military, based on random letters of the alphabet in an attempt to confuse the enemy. An exception is the very large K-band, which was later subdivided into the higher Ka- ("above") and Ku- ("under") bands.

Table 2.2   Microwave Bands

Wavelength	Frequency (GHz)	Band	Main Communications Use
193–769 mm	0.4–1.5 GHz	L	Broadcasting, 1G cellular
57.7–193 mm	1.5–5.2 GHz	S	2G and 3G cellular, LAN
48.4–76.9 mm	3.9–6.2 GHz	C	Satellite, LAN
27.5–57.7 mm	5.2–10.9 GHz	X	Fixed, satellite
17.1–27.5 mm	10.9–17.5 GHz	Ku	Fixed, older satellite
8.34–17.1 mm	17.5–31 GHz	Ka	Fixed, newer satellite
6.52–8.34 mm	36–46 GHz	Q	Fixed
5.36–6.52 mm	46–56 GHz	V	Future satellite, fixed
3.00–5.36 mm	56–100 GHz	W	Fixed, LAN, 4G cellular

The military codes stem from microwaves' original use in radar systems. However, they have since found a new role in communications. The most important (and most crowded) is currently the S-band, because this has the right combination of capacity and range for cellular systems. Other bands may be opened up as new technologies are invented: Many researchers are working on ways to overcome the high attenuation in the currently little-used W-band.

Noise and Interference

One of the most important properties of waves is that they can't collide: Two waves will pass harmlessly through each other, no matter what the frequency. However, if a receiver happens to pick up two or more signals at the same frequency, it has no way to distinguish one from the other. Unwanted signals are called *noise* and can severely limit the effectiveness of a radio signal through *interference*.

Some interference is much louder than the real signal, effectively drowning it out. This happens to satellites for a few minutes each year when they align with the sun, a much more powerful source of radiation than any communications antenna. Some people also find that their TV or radio reception is hampered by household appliances such as vacuum cleaners, which unintentionally radiate some waves at the same frequencies as the stations they are trying to watch or listen to. More common is for two similar communications signals to meet, either reinforcing each other or canceling each other out.

Wave signals are superimposed on each other, so the effects of two on the same frequency depends on how their cycles are aligned. If both go through peaks and troughs at the same time (the waves are *in phase*), they add together to make a stronger signal, a situation known as *constructive interference*. If one is at a peak while the other is at a trough (the waves are *out of phase*), they will cancel each other out entirely, a process called *destructive interference*. Figure 2.3 illustrates constructive and destructive interference.

To ensure that radio signals remain free of interference, frequencies have to be carefully planned and controlled. However, interference does have some applications. Lasers use the constructive type to increase the energy of their beams. Destructive interference is not yet used with electromagnetic radiation, but it has been applied with great success to sound waves. In an "antinoise" system, a computer plays the precise opposite of an unwanted sound. The listeners hear nothing, or at least they hear what would be a loud sound made very quiet. The advantage of this over wearing earplugs is that other sounds are unaffected. It allows pilots on a flight deck to hear each other but not the roar of the jet engine outside.

The same principle could work with radio, jamming a transmission in such a way that it appears never to have been sent. However, this would require advance

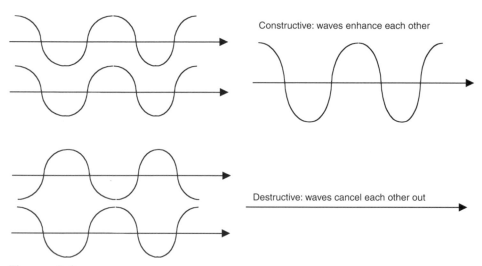

Figure 2.3
Constructive and destructive interference.

knowledge of the transmission: Sound waves move so slowly that a computer has time to intercept them, then to generate the opposite signal before they reach a listener, but radio waves are too fast. It wouldn't work with an inherently unpredictable signal, such as nuclear radiation.

The Multipath Problem

Most types of interference can be overcome by turning up the transmission power or through cooperation among users. A louder transmission can make naturally occurring interference seem less significant, and two radio stations can agree (or be forced by law) not to transmit on the same frequency in the same place. However, *multipath* interference cannot be overcome in either of these ways. It affects every type of wireless communication designed for use indoors or in an urban environment.

As the name suggests, multipath interference is caused by the various different paths that a radio signal can take from one point to another. The best path between two points is a straight line, of course, but radio transmitters rarely target their signals directly toward one receiver. They broadcast in many different directions so that, as shown in Figure 2.4, a user can pick up the same signal reflected off buildings, walls, and other objects. The different versions of the same wave cause destructive interference, making the signal weaker or even unintelligible.

Most TV viewers have experienced multipath interference as the "ghost" images that sometimes appear on a screen. Each ghost represents a different path that the

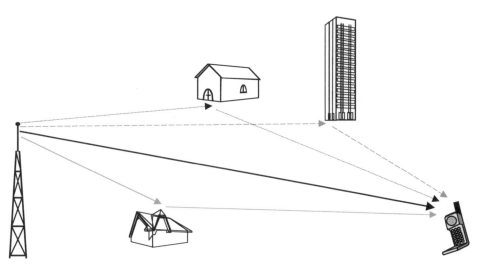

Figure 2.4
Multipath interference.

signal has taken, usually by bouncing off or traveling through walls in the same room as the TV. The only way to solve the problem is to move the TV or use an antenna mounted outside.

Some newer technologies, described in the next chapter, are designed specifically to reduce multipath interference. However, it puts an important constraint on many existing mobile systems by reducing the available capacity and making it harder to use devices deep inside a building.

ANALOG VERSUS DIGITAL ....

Most twentieth-century radio systems were designed to transmit sound, which is an *analog* signal: It varies continuously and is usually represented as a wave. Because electromagnetic radiation is also a wave, this made transmitters and receivers relatively simple. Whether in broadcasting or cellular telephony, a radio terminal is a device for converting sound waves to radio waves and back again. Television uses the same principle, including light, as well as sound.

Wireless networks are increasingly being used for computer data, inherently *digital.* Instead of a continuous wave form, they consist of a series of pulses. Many sound and video applications are also beginning to use digital signals, though new digital services are hampered by the large installed base of analog equipment. Figure 2.5 shows the difference between analog and digital.

Surfing on What?

Waves as we know them have to travel through something; sound waves go through the air, water waves through the sea. But what do electromagnetic waves move through? This question greatly bothered scientists at the end of the nineteenth century. Eventually, they invented a medium called the **luminiferous aether**, which they said filled the Universe.

The trouble was, experiments showed that the aether didn't exist. In 1905, Albert Einstein published a theory that explained electromagnetic radiation as a stream of tiny particles called **photons**. These particles often behave like waves—they still can't collide with each other in the same way as solid objects, for example—and many of their properties are analogous to waves. The frequency depends on the energy of each photon, and the signal strength or amplitude corresponds to the number of photons. Sixteen years later, Einstein was awarded a Nobel Prize for this discovery, rather than for his better known theory of relativity.

So, is radiation made from waves or particles, or from something in between? A century after Einstein's insight, we still don't know. Both explanations work, so scientists are free to choose whichever is most convenient. Most radio engineers prefer to do their calculations using waves, but photons are often used when discussing fiberoptics and some satellite applications.

Encoding analog information as data requires sophisticated electronics, which were not portable or affordable before the 1990s. This means that digital is more likely to be used for newer services, such as mobile telephony. Analog broadcast radio and television reached saturation coverage much earlier, so their move to digital has been much slower.

The first digital radio and TV services were launched in Britain in 1999, but radio, in particular, was hampered by the high cost of reception equipment. TV proved slightly more popular because receivers were subsidized by companies eager to use digital's extra capacity for pay-per-view movies and sports events. The earliest adopters of digital TV have been cable and satellite networks, because new customers for these already had to buy or rent a new receiver.

Advantages of Digital

Voice and video are intrinsically analog, so converting them to data and sending them over a digital link may seem unnecessary. However, digital technologies have several advantages, making the conversion worthwhile. Among these are:

Figure 2.5
Analog and digital wave forms.

- **Noise reduction.** All communication channels suffer from static interference, a particular problem for wireless networks. With an analog wave form, there is no way for the receiver to distinguish between this noise and the actual signal. A digital wave form is different; it can have only two levels, so anything in between can automatically be discarded by receivers or relay stations. Although every piece of interference has an effect on an analog signal, it would have to be very severe to prevent a digital signal from being received intact.

- **Reliability.** Digital signals can be encoded with extra bits called *checksums*. These are the result of a calculation performed on the preceding bits; they allow a receiver to check that it has interpreted the signal accurately. If the checksum is wrong, at least 1 bit has been lost in transmission, so a portion of the signal has to be sent again. For greater reliability, additional error-correction code can be sent along with the signal, which allows some lost bits to be reconstructed if others are intact. This is known as *forward error correction* (FEC) because it anticipates errors in advance of their occurrence. The simplest method is to send each bit and its checksum twice, though most systems use more complex formulae that combine the checksum with extra bits. An example is the Hamming code which calculates a 3-bit checksum for every 4 bits of a signal. A single error in the resultant 7 bits can then be corrected, though 2 bits or more require a resend. The obvious problem with checksums and FEC is that they reduce capacity. The more extra bits being sent, the less room there is for real data. The extra bits are known as *redundancy*; in general, greater redundancy means a more reliable connection. This redundancy forces a trade-off between capacity and reliability, and wireless network planners need to make a choice based on the importance of their information and the time taken to resend it.

- **Spectral efficiency.** Thanks to its greater resilience to errors, a digital system can transfer more information than can an analog system over a given amount of spectrum. The digital version of the Advanced Mobile Phone System (AMPS) used in many parts of the United States carries three conversations in exactly the same frequency bands that the analog version uses for just one. Digital signals also allow compression, which reduces the amount of capacity needed to send data by looking for repeated patterns. Compression is commonly used in all forms of data transmission, particularly for images, where it is built into the file formats used by Internet browsers.

- **Security.** Wireless systems are very open to eavesdroppers. A private conversation can easily be picked up by anyone with a suitable radio, so analog cellular was a boon to the nosy and to muckraking journalists. Simple scanners are readily available in electronics shops and are perfectly legal in many countries. They have been used in a few notorious incidents, most famously when Princess Diana and other royals had their affairs exposed across the world's press. To prevent such scandals, modern digital cellular encrypts all data, using mathematical algorithms. Encryption is possible using analog equipment, but it is often unreliable and easy to crack; hence the surge in illegal descramblers for analog cable and satellite TV. Digital signals can be encrypted to arbitrary degrees, depending only on the processing power of the transmitter and receiver. No matter what strength the encryption, an encrypted digital signal uses no more capacity than an unencrypted one.

- **Timing.** Digital information can easily be stored in computer memory, allowing a communication channel to be shared in sophisticated ways. In a Time Division Multiple Access (TDMA) system, each user of a channel transmits and receives for only part of the time, so the data has to be held in memory until it can be sent. A packet-switched system uses capacity only when required, storing data in the memory of a special computer called a *router* while calculating the most efficient path by which to send it. Packet-switching is the basis of the Internet and of the newest wireless networks.

Voice versus Data

Though voice is often digitized, it still has unique characteristics that set it apart from other types of data. This can mean that voice communications systems are not ideal for data and vice-versa, even though both are now digital.

For most kinds of data transmission, the most important property of a communications link is *reliability*: In a computer program, even a single bit out of place can cause a crash. This forces computer protocols to be relatively slow and methodical: They check that every bit has been received correctly. If it hasn't been received, they resend it until it has. The slight delay that this causes is usually acceptable, even for less critical applications, such as e-mail.

However, accuracy is much less important for a voice link. When people are talking on the phone, they would usually prefer to suffer a slight background noise than long interruptions while a computer tries to send a perfect high-fidelity recording of their last few words. This means that voice protocols frequently ignore accuracy in favor of speed and ensuring that data bits are received in the same order that they are sent.

This fundamental incompatibility between voice and data causes a lot of problems. It's why voice conversations often sound bad when sent over the Internet (intended for data) and why checking e-mail through a 2G cell phone (intended for voice) is such an unpleasant experience. One of the intentions behind 3G cellular was to design a system that could be used equally well for both voice and data.

BITS AND BANDWIDTH

The term **bandwidth** originally referred to radio spectrum and described the frequency range allocated to a particular technology or service. For example, the channel between 824 MHz and 893 MHz, commonly used for cellular services in America, has a bandwidth of 69 MHz (because 893 − 824 = 69). The channel from 92.7 MHz to 92.9 MHz, used for a radio station, has a bandwidth of 200 kHz.

The amount of digitized information that can be sent over a channel is related to its bandwidth through an equation known as **Shannon's Theorem**, or simply the **Bandwidth Theorem**. The two are directly proportional, so that in the example above, the cellular network could carry 345 times as much information as the radio station—hardly surprising, because it has to handle many two-way conversations at the same time, whereas the station has to cope with only a single broadcast.

AT&T mathematician Claude Shannon devised the theorem in 1948, as part of a groundbreaking scientific paper entitled "A Mathematical Theory of Communication." At the same time, he defined the word **bit** (binary digit), which represents the smallest possible unit of information. To a computer, this would be a switch with two positions, usually represented as 1 and 0.

Shannon's Theorem is used so much by engineers that the word **bandwidth** has come to mean the data capacity of a channel, measured in bits per second (bps). However, the data bandwidth is not always the same as the spectral bandwidth. It also depends on the signal-to-noise ratio of a channel: The more noise or interference, the less data that can be sent.

(continued)

BITS AND BANDWIDTH (CONTINUED)

The information content of a message increases exponentially with the number of data bits—1 bit can represent only two possibilities, 2 bits can represent four, 3 would give eight, and so on. This means that for each bit that can't be read because of interference, the information content of the message is halved.

AM AND FM

Whether in analog or digital format, information has to be converted into radio waves before it can be sent. This process is known as *modulation*. It involves altering a radio wave of the desired frequency, called the *carrier wave*, so that a receiver will be able to extract useful information. There are two main types, familiar to all radio listeners: amplitude modulation (AM) and frequency modulation (FM).

Most wireless communications systems now use a combination of both. The intention is nearly always to cram as much data as possible into a given slice of bandwidth, usually called *increasing the spectral efficiency*. Because spectrum is either sold for a lot of money or rationed, it's important to use it as efficiently as possible.

When the information being sent is digital, modulation is also known as *shift keying*. The term comes from music, where *keying* means tuning an instrument to play a specific note. Like the keys of a piano, a digital modulator needs to produce only a finite number of frequencies.

Amplitude Modulation

The simplest way to transmit a signal is to superimpose it over the carrier wave at the transmitter. As illustrated in Figure 2.6, this results in waves with amplitude (height) that varies in proportion to the information signal.

AM is unusual in modern communications systems because it uses spectrum inefficiently, compared with other methods. Many cycles of the carrier wave are needed to transmit a small amount of information. The process of superposition creates extra signals in frequencies on either side of the carrier, known as *sidebands*. A variant of AM, called *single sideband* (SSB), filters out these extra signals from one side, reducing the spectrum requirement by half.

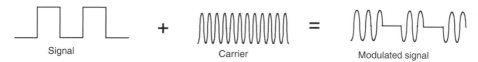

Figure 2.6
Amplitude modulation.

The only popular wireless application that still uses pure AM is broadcast radio. Several blocks of spectrum are dedicated to analog AM broadcasting in the long-wave, medium-wave, and short-wave bands, though the AM tuning dial on most radio receivers covers only medium wave. AM stations usually carry only monophonic (as opposed to stereo) broadcasts because of the limited bandwidth.

Though AM radio is analog, the technique can also be used with a digital signal. At its simplest, this just means switching the carrier wave on and off to transmit short pulses, so it's also known as *pulse modulation*. Its most important application is in fixed telephony: Wired networks also use radio waves, except that they're sent through a piece of copper, instead of through free space. The wire confines the signal, so that most of the waves travel along it, rather than spreading throughout space.

Pulse modulation is also used for some satellite systems and has a revered history as the earliest type of radio. Up until around 1915, capacity was so restricted that all information had to be sent as *Morse*, an early code that used audible beeps. Radio listeners had to learn which series of beeps represented each letter of the alphabet, so that they could transcribe messages manually. By international agreement, amateur radio broadcasters, known as *hams*, still have to pass tests in Morse.

Many digital AM systems use more than two different amplitude levels, as shown in Figure 2.7. For example, instead of switching a signal off and on, a transmitter might switch the signal between off, low, medium, and high. This is known as *quadrature amplitude modulation* (QAM), because the amplitude has four different steps. In engineering jargon, each step is called a *symbol*, and the number of symbols per second is the *symbol rate* or *baud*.

Because early modems used simple modulation schemes, baud is often confused with the data rate. However, this is true only if there are only two symbols (as in pulse modulation). Under QAM, each symbol can represent 2 bits, so the data rate is twice the symbol rate.

It's possible to increase the data rate further by adding more symbols, but the number required increases exponentially with the bit rate: For each extra bit per second, the number of symbols must double. This is rarely worthwhile using AM alone, because interference makes different amplitude levels difficult to measure accurately. Instead, QAM is often combined with another modulation technique.

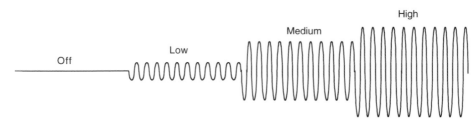

Figure 2.7
Quadrature amplitude modulation.

Figure 2.8
Frequency-modulated carrier wave.

Frequency Modulation

FM keeps the amplitude constant, meaning that a transmitter can operate at full power all the time to maximize its range. Instead, it alters the frequency (and the wavelength) of the carrier wave to represent variations in the signal being sent. Figure 2.8 shows a simple FM wave.

FM is more resistant to noise than is AM. Both weather phenomena and machinery can produce random interference, which is more likely to affect the amplitude of a signal than its frequency. It can also use spectrum more efficiently, though the precise amount it needs depends on how much the signal is modulated. This is usually written mathematically. For example, BBC Radio 4 broadcasts to southern England at 92.8 MHz. It varies the frequency by 100 kHz either side, so its frequency is written as 92.8 ± 0.1 MHz. The total spectrum requirement is 200 kHz, so stations have to be spaced at least this distance apart to avoid interfering with each other. In the United States, the Federal Communications Commission (FCC) only licenses FM stations in even multiples of 200 kHz (for example, 96.2–96.4 MHz), so the last digit of an FM station's frequency is always an odd number (in this case, 96.3 MHz).

Analog FM is most well known through broadcasts in the VHF band, where it carries stereo radio stations. It's also used for TV and for many two-way radio systems, including first-generation cell phones.

Phase-Shift Keying

Digital wireless systems are usually based on *phase modulation* (PM), a special type of FM. Instead of just compressing and expanding waves, it rapidly moves them to different points in their cycles. This is useful for transmitting data, because the different points in a wave's cycle can represent bits.

The type of PM shown in Figure 2.9 interrupts the wave very suddenly, a process known as *phase-shift keying* (PSK). The problem with this is that it requires a very large slice of spectrum because these sudden interruptions produce interference similar to AM sidebands. To minimize this and reduce the necessary spectrum, many systems use a technique called *differential PSK* (D-PSK), which smooths out the interruptions by using phase differences, rather than phase itself. The popular Global System for Mobile Communications (GSM) standard uses yet another variant, Gaussian minimum shift keying (GMSK), a method which smoothes the signal by passing it through various filters.

Phase modulation is particularly useful because it allows flexible bit rates. The two waves in Figure 2.9 interrupt their waves at equal intervals, but the lower one is carrying twice as much information as the other; it moves the wave to one of four different points on the cycle, rather than to just two. As in AM, these points are known as *symbols*.

Many technologies increase the number of bits per symbol when reception is clear, often to a maximum of 64. This provides 6 bits per symbol, effectively multiplying capacity by the same amount. Some also combine 64-symbol PSK with QAM, for a total of 256 modulation symbols, or 8 bps per baud.

Polarization

Transverse waves always vibrate at right angles to the direction of travel, which appears to be a single direction when they are drawn in two dimensions, as in the previous diagrams. But real space has (at least) three dimensions, giving the waves an entire plane in which to vibrate; if a wave was coming straight out of this page, it could be vibrating relative to the top or the sides of the page, or some angle in between. This angle is known as *polarization*, illustrated in Figure 2.10.

Though angles can vary infinitely, it's impossible to measure polarization to within more than two values: horizontal or vertical. These can be used to represent the two states of a bit, providing another way of encoding data into a light beam. Such polarization modulation is not used in present-day communications systems but has

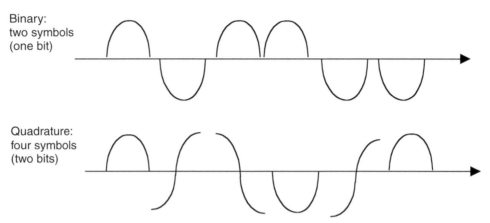

Figure 2.9
Binary and quadrature phase modulation.

been demonstrated in physics labs. It is proposed for various science fiction-like systems, including teleportation.

Some satellites already apply polarization but as a means of increasing capacity, rather than encoding data. Two beams polarized at right angles to each other do not produce interference, allowing the same frequency to be used twice. This effectively doubles bandwidth, but it requires a clear line of sight.

Mobile transmissions reflect off walls and other objects, which has traditionally made polarization difficult to measure. However, in 2001, researchers working for Lucent Technologies demonstrated a system that could use polarization without a line of sight. It requires three separate perpendicular antennas at each base station, but Lucent claims that it allows users to keep their existing cell phones.

SPECTRUM REGULATION ....

Because radio communication depends on a clear channel, free of interference, spectrum has to be strictly rationed. Much of this rationing is handled by national regulators, such as the FCC in the United States, but there is an increasing trend toward international cooperation. This is needed both to handle the long-range frequencies that can spread across international boundaries and to promote compatibility between systems in different countries.

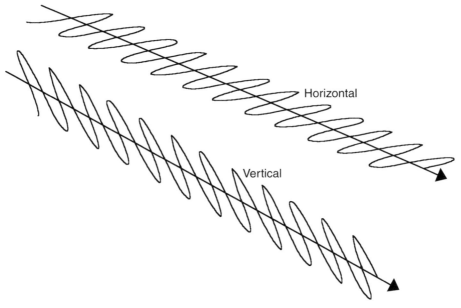

Figure 2.10
Horizontal and vertical polarization.

The International Telecommunications Union

The international body responsible for radio spectrum is the International Telecommunications Union (ITU). Though an agency of the United Nations, it actually predates the "parent" organization by nearly a century. It was founded in 1865 to handle interconnection between the national telegraph networks and has managed radio spectrum since 1906. Its mandate covers all kinds of radio services, from broadcast television to satellite phones.

For spectrum purposes, the ITU divides the world into three regions, shown on the map in Figure 2.11. Though some services, such as communications satellites, do need to use the same spectrum throughout the world, historical and political differences mean that others cannot. For example, the United States allows more AM radio stations in the MW band than does Europe, but none in the LW band.

Very roughly, the regions include Europe, the Middle East, and Africa in the first; America in the second; and Asia in the third. Because they were defined during the Cold War, the entire former Soviet Union is placed in the same region (Europe).

Every two to three years, the ITU holds a World Radiocommunication Conference (WRC), a four-week summit to discuss how radio spectrum is assigned. Though mostly dominated by government and industry, other interest groups, such as scientists and radio hams, are also represented. Its official purpose is to discuss more efficient ways to use the available frequencies, but economic and social factors also come into play.

A current example is the analog television system, which occupies a vast swathe of the UHF band and uses obsolete technology developed in the 1950s and before. Governments and wireless operators would love to use this spectrum for new advanced data services but can't, because they fear a backlash from TV viewers and from the media companies that currently control it. For example, the United Kingdom has committed itself to shutting down all analog TV stations but not until 90% of its population have access to digital TV. During the telecom boom, spectrum-hungry cellular operators considered buying everyone a digital TV set to speed up this process.

The United States has more spectrum allocated to television than do most other countries, so the FCC has pressed ahead with selling some of it off to mobile operators. The first chunk in the 700-MHz band, representing channels 60–69, was supposed to be auctioned in 2000. However, many operators were put off applying, thanks to the requirement that they would not be able to use it until 2007 or until 90% of the U.S. population has a digital TV set, whichever occurs *last*. On their request, the sale was postponed until 2001, so that they would have a chance to develop business plans. It was later postponed indefinitely, after lobbyists for TV broadcasters demanded that some of the auction proceeds go to them, rather than to the government.

At the time of this writing, the most recent WRC was held in 2000. Another is scheduled for 2003. The main topic of discussion at WRC-2000 was the new generation of broadband wireless technologies, collectively known as *International Mobile Telecommunications* (IMT) *2000*. Other issues discussed included:

- Global satellite systems, such as Iridium and Globalstar which require the same frequency allocation all over the world.
- Broadband fixed wireless technologies, such as Local Multipoint Distribution System (LMDS), which can compete with wired local loop services but are held back in many countries by slow licensing procedures.
- Concerns of astronomers and alien-hunters that the boom in wireless communications will drown signals from outer space.

Regional Licenses

European regulators issue licenses for mobile voice and data on a nationwide basis, allowing (and often requiring) every operator to build a network that spans the entire

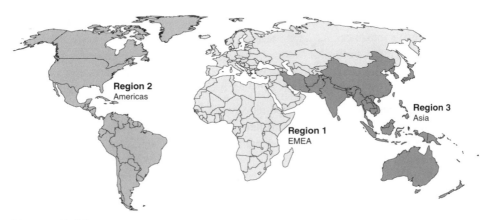

Figure 2.11
ITU regions.

country. The United States and Canada don't, because these countries are so large that a single license is impractical. The FCC instead divides the United States into several regions, which differ depending on the type of service being licensed:

- **MSA** (Metropolitan Service Area) and **RSA** (Rural Service Area) were defined for analog cellular (1G) licenses, at around 800 MHz. There were 305 MSAs and 429 RSAs, with two competing operators allowed in each. This gives a total of 1,468 separate licenses, most of which eventually found their way to the local phone companies. The operators that have this spectrum are now recycling it into 2G and 3G systems.

- **BTA** (Basic Trading Area) replaced the old MSA and RSA in the 1990s, though previously issued licenses continue to follow the old boundaries. There are a total of 493 BTAs, originally based on where residents did their shopping, so they tend to be centered around towns and malls. Four digital cellular (2G) licenses at around 1,900 MHz were issued in each. The same areas continue to be used for licensing almost all new spectrum, including fixed wireless services and some kinds of television. The borders of BTAs do not always correspond to those of the old MSAs and RSAs, leading to overlap and complexity: An operator aiming for a seamless national network cannot easily mix and match licenses issued under the two different systems.

- **MTA** (Major Trading Area) is a group of BTAs. There are only 51 of these, and some span many small states. Another two Personal Communications Services (PCS) licenses were issued in each of these, aimed at operators who wanted a wide coverage area without having to collect lots of smaller licenses separately.

Many cellular operators have criticized the FCC's regional licensing policy, because it makes building a national network very difficult: With the old MSAs and RSAs, each operator had to acquire 734 separate licenses in order to cover the entire country. Not surprisingly, none managed to achieve this, leading to a fragmented network. No single operator manages to cover even the 51 MTAs.

The FCC's defense is that it was trying to encourage small local operators, rather than the huge companies that are inevitably the only buyers of licenses covering a wide area. This policy may have been well intentioned, but it was unsuccessful: Most local operators in the United States have been bought by one of six carriers that aspire to national coverage. Others were simply fronts for the larger corporations, set up to get around rules that favored local companies.

Large operators have also criticized the FCC's *spectrum cap*, a rule that limited the amount of spectrum any one company can own in a given area. (The limits varied, depending on the area, but were roughly equivalent to two licenses.) Like the regional licenses, it was designed to encourage competition: Spectrum is a finite resource, and allowing a single operator to control too much of it could lead to a monopoly. It was also intended to help promote development of new technologies, the theory being that operators would try to use their limited spectrum very efficiently.

Most other countries have much stricter limits on spectrum ownership, so the U.S. spectrum cap shouldn't have been a problem. However, the regional licensing meant that it was. The boundaries of MSAs and RSAs don't correspond to those of BTAs and MTAs, making it difficult for operators to piece together the jigsaw of licenses that they needed to create a national network. Wherever the areas overlapped, the spectrum cap was exceeded. Operators also complained that they could not roll out new spectrum-hungry 3G technologies, because they were already using most of their quota to support existing customers.

In October 2001, the FCC decided to abolish the cap from January 2003. This will make it easier for large operators to build nationwide networks and deploy new services but also risks the emergence of a monopoly. The FCC has not explained why it decided to abolish the spectrum cap entirely, rather than simply raise it to a level that would permit larger operators and still ensure some competition.

The fundamental problem is that, compared with other countries, the United States simply has not made enough spectrum available for cellular services. Although other countries have licensed new spectrum specifically for 3G, U.S. operators must reuse older frequencies. The main reason for this is that the United States has allocated more spectrum for other purposes, in particular, for TV broadcasting and military use.

Service-Specific versus Open Licenses

Below the level of global cooperation aimed at by the WRC, many countries also collaborate in smaller regional groups. The most influential is the European Union (E.U.), which frequently issues legally binding directives ordering its 15 member states to license particular spectrum for certain services. In contrast, the FCC allows U.S. operators freedom to deploy whatever technology they like.

The E.U. usually mandates technologies devised by the European Telecommunications Standards Institute (ETSI), a wider group that includes representatives from major companies doing business in Europe as well as non-E.U. countries such as Norway and Switzerland. Their greatest success so far is GSM, explained fully in Chapter 4, "PCS Standards." It was originally devised in 1982 by the *Conference Européenne des Administrations des Postes et Telecommunications* (CEPT), a government body now largely superseded by ETSI. The standard was expandable enough to be used as the basis for advanced Internet services, yet simple enough to be deployed throughout Europe. It later grew way beyond, to become the world's most popular telecom system; in 1999, GSM networks were growing by a million new subscribers each week.

GSM's critics say that its dominance is due to government interference, not technical superiority: when European governments licensed mobile phone spectrum, they insisted that every operator deploy GSM. American companies accused the E.U. of protectionism because GSM systems tended to be made by European manufacturers, primarily Nokia, Ericsson, Siemens, and Alcatel. In particular, Qualcomm said that its CDMA (Code Division Multiple Access) technology, described in Chapter 3, "Cellular Networks," was being kept out unfairly.

Protectionist or not, Europe's policies gave it a seamless, continent-wide, mobile network, compared with a mess of incompatible systems in the United States. Preventing competition between technologies also helped to reduce costs through economies of scale and by promoting competition between manufacturers and, later, operators—if they're all offering the same kind of equipment and services, it's easier to compare prices.

In the United States, freedom for operators means confusion for customers. Most travelers cannot be sure that the same phone will work in different cities across America, let alone in other countries. Because national networks are built from smaller local operators that have merged or been taken over, this is true even for people who stick with one company. Cingular and AT&T Wireless, for example, both operate three different incompatible systems. They plan to upgrade all three to the same technology—one based on GSM.

Most countries worldwide are now following the European lead, not just in using GSM, but in licensing service-specific frequencies. Many have already earmarked a 155-MHz portion of spectrum in the 2,000-MHz region for 3G mobile data and are making licenses conditional on deploying specific technologies and fulfilling service obligations. As always, the United States is the odd one out: It still has not settled on a frequency for 3G, let alone considered licensing conditions.

Standards Bodies

In addition to the regulators that actually issue spectrum, there are several important groups whose decisions affect how it is used. Some are branches of government and some are alliances of large corporations. However, the most significant are the engineering bodies that actually develop the technology and set the standards:

- **The Institute of Electrical and Electronics Engineers** (IEEE, at www.ieee.org) is a venerable organization with a vast remit, from the voltage of mains power to the data rate of Local Area Networks (LANs). Founded in 1884 and initially dealing only with light bulbs, it has expanded to influence the design of almost every electric device. In principle, anyone can get involve din the standards process by joining one of its many mailing lists or attending its meetings, though final standards are set only after extensive debate and negotiation. Because the IEEE is so large, it's subdivided into several sections. The important one for networking is the IEEE Communications Society and, in particular, its group number 802.

- **The Internet Engineering Task Force** (IETF at www.ietf.org) develops ways for computers to communicate over the Internet. Like the IEEE, it's run by engineers and programmers and claims to be independent of government and corporate interests. Because it officially has no regulatory power, all the standards that it publishes are known as Requests for Comments (RFCs), but the name is deceptively humble. All RFCs go through a process similar to scientific peer review, so they have already been extensively commented on before they are published on the IETF's Web site, though many are given the status of "recommended best practices" rather than official standards. At the time of this writing, there were more than 3,000 RFCs, though not all are actually used. Many are obsolete, and the IETF also has a tradition of publishing satirical (but still technically correct) RFCs every April 1st.

- **The World Wide Web Consortium** (W3C, at www.w3.org) develops the standards used byWeb pages and browsers. It is frequently involved in controversy, thanks to attempts by companies such as Netscape and Microsoft to develop their own proprietary extensions to the Web. In theory, any Web page written using W3C code should display correctly in a W3C-compliant *browser*, but in practice, *no* browser has *ever* implemented W3C standards exactly. Its most recent fight has been over a plan to allow

Web standards to include patented technology, which would allow the patent holder to collect a royalty from everyone who uses it. At present, Web standards have to be open to all to use, royalty free.

- **The Internet Assigned Numbers Authority** (IANA at www.iana.org) is responsible for the internal numbering scheme used to identify computers on the Internet. Unlike the rest of the Internet, it's still highly U.S.-centric, reflecting the network's origins: There is only a finite supply of these numbers (known as *IP addresses*), and most of them have already been allocated to American companies or organizations. IANA is technically also in charge of the more visible *domain names* that people see when they type in an Internet address, but it has delegated their management to the Internet Consortium for Assigned Names and Numbers (ICANN), which, in turn, has contracted the task out to private companies.

- **The American National Standards Institute** (ANSI, at www.ansi.org) is a U.S. counterpart to ETSI, though with a larger scope: It covers everything, not just telecommunications. Because of this, many American cellular standards ignore ANSI and instead go through the Telecommunications Industry Association (TIA). Its standards are technically unofficial, because they haven't been ratified by ANSI, so they are prefixed by the letters *IS* (Interim Standard).

- **Industry Forums** are groups of companies that cooperate to ensure that their products work together. Because the companies involved are usually competitors, there is usually some tension within a forum: No manufacturer wants to share its own research and development work with others, but all want to claim compliance with a standard. There is also a risk that they will cooperate too closely and conspire to keep prices high. Some forums, such as the GSM Association, are concerned mainly with promoting an existing standard already set by someone else. Others, such as the Bluetooth Special Interest Group, actually set standards of their own. In wireless communications, the most influential is the Third-Generation Partnership Project (3GPP), which works with ETSI to develop standards for 3G phones.

LICENSING METHODS.......................................

Although different countries often agree on how spectrum should be used, there is less agreement on *who* should be able to use it. Even within the normally strict E.U., national regulators are free to decide how many companies the spectrum for a given service should be split between, as well as who those companies should be. Worldwide, four approaches have been used so far: beauty contests, lotteries, auctions, and a free-for-all.

Beauty Contest

Also known as *comparative bidding*, beauty contests are the traditional method of licensing. Everyone who wants to use a part of the spectrum must submit a plan to the government or regulator, detailing the kind of services it intends to provide. This works very well for services such as broadcasting, whose specific character can have a great effect on a community. In theory, the government can make intelligent decisions about such issues as programming quality and content, then select the TV or radio stations that will best serve the people's needs.

Some countries also use beauty contests for cellular services. Applicants are judged on criteria such as pricing, quality, technology, and competitiveness, usually with the aim of protecting the public interest and providing the best possible service to customers.

The biggest objection to beauty contests is that the government's judgment is rarely entirely objective. There is potential for both actual and perceived corruption; even if the criteria are announced before bids are submitted, there is still room for argument. When licensing communications services, governments tend to favor large, well-established corporations, and take into account factors such as national pride in a country's native companies. This is particularly relevant when the state actually owns a large shareholding in the largest telecom carrier, as most still do.

Sometimes, not all licenses offered in a beauty contest are actually issued, because the government decides that no bids come up to par. Most countries originally licensed fewer commercial television and radio stations than could fit in the available spectrum, because they feared (correctly) that advertising revenues would be spread too thinly to support quality programming.

Many countries still use beauty contests for television or low-bandwidth private radio, but they are becoming less popular for mobile telecom and data services. A variant on the system is for the regulators to ask various bidders to form consortia until there are enough licenses to go around. This method was used by Finland in 1999, when it initially had 15 bidders for four 3G licenses.

Lottery

Lotteries were used by the FCC during the 1980s, as the costs of the beauty contest system began to escalate. Each new license was attracting so many applicants that lengthy hearings were needed to decide whose proposals best served the public interest. By 1990, applications were requiring an average of three years to accept or reject, imposing enormous expense on both the government and the applicants.

Lotteries enabled licenses to be awarded quickly, with no accusations of bias. But they soon drew criticism for other reasons—they took no account of the public interest and attracted large numbers of speculators. A cellular telephony license was a valuable commodity, which a speculator could obtain at little cost by winning the lottery, then resell to a genuine communications company. Some licenses took nearly 10 years to get from the lottery winners to a company that would be able to provide a service.

Auctions

With companies already selling each other licenses for millions of dollars, economists began to suggest a market mechanism for initial licensing. The theory is that, if licenses are awarded to whoever is willing to pay the most, the winner will be the company that can put it to the most valuable use. Charging a high price for spectrum should also encourage it to be used more efficiently, because operators have an economic incentive to invest in better radio systems.

Spectrum auctions were pioneered by New Zealand in 1989, when it also formalized a system of license trading. Spectrum was not actually sold but leased for 20 years to whoever was willing to pay the most. For those 20 years, licensees were free to use the spectrum for whatever purposes they wanted, either deploying services or selling the lease to another operator. To protect noncommercial users, not all spectrum was auctioned, and some was given away free to the indigenous Maori people.

New Zealand's auctions attracted great interest from other governments, who saw it as both a solution to licensing problems and a way to raise revenue. Australia began to auction radio frequencies in 1989; two years later, the United Kingdom did the same for TV. But the biggest user of auctions became the United States, which in 1993 passed an act enabling the FCC to abandon lotteries and beauty contests and to auction virtually all spectrum.

Most countries have not gone this far. Auctions consider only economics, not other values, and most governments want at least part of their airwaves to be open to nonprofit use. In particular, many people feel that the right to broadcast TV and radio programming should not be sold to the highest bidder. However, auctions are becoming increasingly popular for telecom spectrum. The most profitable use of TV spectrum is cheap programming that is frequently interrupted by commercials, which doesn't serve the public interest. The most profitable use of telecom spectrum is advanced communication, which does.

The licensing authorities have tried several different auction methods. Secret sealed-envelope tenders were originally popular in the United Kingdom but have since been abandoned because they result in every bidder trying to second-guess what others will bid. The original New Zealand system used a "Vickrey" auction, which also requires secret bids but makes the winner pay only the second-highest price. Economists say that this encourages companies to bid their actual estimate of the spectrum's value, not the minimum they think they can get away with, but it's perceived as unfair by taxpayers.

Most modern spectrum auctions use a system devised by Professor Ken Binmore of University College, London. It is designed to make the process completely transparent and to maximize the revenue brought in for the government. Every license for a particular type of service is auctioned simultaneously, with an infinite number of bids; this lets every bidder see what the others are doing at each stage and adjust its strategy accordingly. The results can be very high bids because the companies that don't win want to ensure that their competitors are put at a disadvantage. Some may participate simply to drive up the price for others, inadvertently increasing revenue to governments.

This style of auction has been controversial. Many operators claim that high charges for spectrum extract money from the industry and put wireless local loop technology at a disadvantage, compared with its competitors, such as cable or DSL. But the FCC and other regulators argue that this is exactly what it is designed to do— unlike other local loop technologies, wireless does use scarce radio spectrum and ought to pay accordingly. Even when the cost of a license is included, wireless can still be relatively cheap, because it doesn't require digging up streets and pavements.

There is a danger that operators will overpay for a license, particularly if engaged in a bidding war with a competitor. In 1996, NextWave Telecom successfully bid $4.8 billion for 90 digital cellular licenses. It filed for Chapter 11 bankruptcy two years later, unable to pay this sum. A lengthy legal battle followed, during which the FCC fought to reclaim the spectrum. It eventually held another auction and sold the same spectrum for a total of $16.9 billion, a price increase of more than 350%.

The rise in the spectrum's value angered NextWave and its creditors, who argued that they were entitled to some of the profits. The company petitioned the Washington D.C. Court of Appeals, which agreed. In a June 2001 judgment, it said that spectrum licenses should be treated like any other asset of a bankrupt company and the FCC like any other creditor. At the time of this writing, the case is on its way to the U.S. Supreme Court. The FCC and the successful bidders in the new auction are trying to negotiate a financial settlement, but NextWave now says that it wants to keep the spectrum. It attracted a new investment of venture capital in September 2001 and hopes to emerge from bankruptcy as a genuine wireless operator.

Legal wrangling over the NextWave spectrum has already held back wireless services by five years, because no company will build a network based on licenses that could be revoked. Most regulators now try to prevent bids based on unrealistic future revenue projections by asking for payment in full as soon as an auction is won. This ensures that governments get their money but does not seem to have helped operators make rational investment decisions.

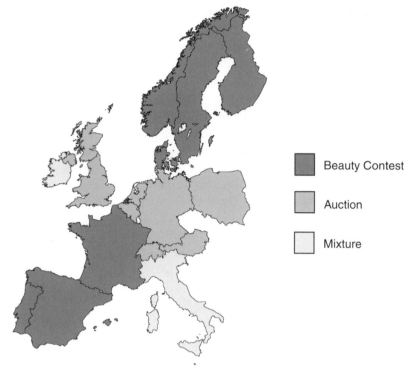

Figure 2.12
3G Licensing in the European Union.

In May 2000, the United Kingdom held an auction for five 3G licenses that shocked the industry. The British government had hoped to raise about $4 billion, but it ended up bringing in $32 billion. Four months later, the German government got nearly $45 billion for similar licenses. The prospect of such huge revenues persuaded many other European countries to do the same. Governments that had previously favored beauty contests began to look at auctions. Italy and Ireland proposed a combined version, holding competitions in two rounds: The winners of a beauty contest went forward to bid in an auction. As shown in Figure 2.12, most European licenses included some auction element.

Most of these governments were too late, as the German auction proved to be the peak of the licensing boom. In October 2000, the Italian 3G auction raised "only" $10.2 billion—many times more than anyone would have predicted only a year before but still less than half of what analysts had hoped for, based on the German and British results. By 2001, licenses were selling for their reserve prices: Belgium's 3G auction attracted only three bidders for four blocks of spectrum, and the United Kingdom's auction of fixed wireless licenses attracted none at all in some regions.

During the British and German auctions, most outside observers assumed that the participants had some kind of business case to justify their high bids. If the companies' statements afterwards are to be believed, this was not the case: The bids were the product of an extreme stock market bubble, not a calculation involving the types of services that customers might pay for. Although the operators making the bids knew that 3G had very little chance of making a profit in the long term, their short-term stock prices were dependent on a reputation as "technology" companies. Maintaining this reputation meant winning a 3G license, no matter what the cost.

When the bubble burst, the winners of the British and German auctions began to criticize the auction process and even their own high bids. However, the auction worked exactly as intended: It brought in revenue for the government and encouraged the deployment of advanced technology. If there is a problem, it's with the short-term nature of the stock market. The operators of 3G networks might never make money, but users will still benefit from the advanced services that 3G enables.

A year after the auctions, operators had largely given up on early attempts to get back some of the money they'd paid for licenses. Instead, some were attempting to shut down competing broadband data services that use wireless LAN technology on freely available spectrum. They have no real legal case for this—a 3G license is simply a permit to operate a particular type of radio system on a particular frequency, not a monopoly concession covering all high-speed data—but they might still attract a hearing. Cellular operators are large and well-established corporations with close ties to government, whereas wireless LAN services are often run by small upstarts who can't afford lobbyists.

Free-For-All

The wireless LAN services that worry many cellular operators all use unlicensed wave bands, which are not auctioned or allocated to specific users. There are several of these bands scattered throughout the spectrum, intended for various uses. At its best, unlicensed transmission can give a voice to people who might not otherwise be heard, while allowing innovative new technologies to be tried out on a small scale.

Some people say that *all* radio spectrum should be unlicensed and claim that any restrictions on spectrum use amount to impairment of free speech. They point to wireless LANs as an example of an innovative technology that would not have been possible if all spectrum were allocated to one specific user. This argument is particularly popular in the United States, though so far the government has not been impressed by it. Some U.S. courts *have*, however, found that certain restrictions on radio transmission violate the constitutional right to free speech.

Unlicensed does not mean unregulated. There are limits on all radio transmissions for safety reasons and to prevent interference. Some bands permit only voice, others only data. The main ways to use spectrum without a license are:

- **The Citizens' Band** (CB Radio) is a set of frequencies at around 27 MHz on which anyone can transmit voice messages. It started in the United States in the 1950s but had spread worldwide by the 1980s. Unlike traditional ham radio, it does not require users to pass tests in Morse, though there are restrictions on the kind of broadcast: You can't advertise over CB, nor can you program your telephone to relay calls across it.

- **The Industrial, Scientific, and Medical** (ISM) spectrum is not intended for communications at all. It was designed by the ITU as a "sink" for waste radiation: Many devices use microwaves for other purposes—usually heating—and these must operate at ISM frequencies to avoid interfering with licensed communications systems. This hasn't stopped communications systems from using the ISM bands, though any that do have to be very resilient to interference. The most important ISM band is at 2,450 MHz, used by most wireless LAN systems and by microwave ovens.

- **The Unlicensed National Information Infrastructure** (U-NII) band has been designated by the FCC for wireless LAN and local loop technologies. It's at about 5 GHz, close to an ISM band, so it is sometimes treated as a "cleaner" extension of that. European countries have a similar band, called *HiperLan,* with more specific requirements about the type of technology that is deployed in it.

- **Digital Enhanced Cordless Telephony** (DECT). European regulators have allocated specific frequencies at just under 2 GHz for DECT, a cordless phone system designed for private use. In the United States, these don't have their own frequencies, instead using either the ISM or PCS bands.

- **Part 15.** The FCC allows anyone to set up a private AM or FM radio station under its Part 15 rules. The catch is that these rules limit the power output to less than 1 W and range to about 30 m (100 feet). There were plans in 2000 to open up the spectrum further, allowing certain nonprofit groups to transmit at a slightly higher power, but these were heavily curtailed after a major lobbying campaign by large broadcasters. However, the plans haven't been abandoned altogether, and even without them, the FCC is more open than most European countries, many of which don't permit private broadcasting at all. Part 15 broadcasting could be an important part of future short-range wireless LAN systems.

- **Pirate Radio.** The name *pirate* originally referred to ship-based radio stations, which avoided national laws by sailing out to international waters. Most pirate radio stations are now land-based and illegal.

Who Owns the Airwaves?

When spectrum is licensed (whether by beauty contest, auction, or lottery) to a specific company, the license usually lasts for only a finite time—often 20 years. For example, the licenses for 3G sold in most of the European Union run only until 2020. At that time, the government and the wireless operators will have several decisions to make. The governments might decide that 3G has failed or that technology has moved on to something better and reallocate the spectrum to 5G or 6G. If they don't do this, each company will have to decide whether it wants to continue operating a 3G network and, if so, how much to bid for the privilege. The economics of running a wireless network will probably change significantly in 20 years, so the bids (if the spectrum is auctioned again) may be substantially higher or lower than in 2000.

This is important, because it means that the wireless carriers don't actually own the radio spectrum. It still belongs to the people and is simply leased by the license holders. In return, the public receives a tax cut or an improved government service, paid for by the licensing fees. Even where an aftermarket in spectrum exists, licenses still follow the leasing principle: New Zealand's license holders are free to sell their licenses, but they're really selling leases, not spectrum itself. Whoever buys the license still has to comply with its terms and must stop using the spectrum when the license ends.

Some companies don't like the idea of leasing spectrum from the public. In particular, TV companies in the United States want to *own* the spectrum that they currently use and have mounted an aggressive lobbying campaign to promote their plan. They hope that the government will grant them a permanent property right to the UHF frequencies, now used for analog broadcasting but due to be switched over to new cell phone systems at some point after 2007. This would enable the broadcasters to decide whether and when the changeover should be made, and allow them to keep any proceeds from selling the spectrum to cell phone companies.

The broadcasters say that they should be entitled to this as compensation for the UHF spectrum. What they don't say is that the UHF spectrum was originally licensed to them for free and that they have already been compensated for its future loss in the form of new spectrum intended for digital television. However, the broadcasters are a powerful force within the U.S. government, so it may meet at least some of their demands.

WEB RESOURCES

http://wireless.fcc.gov/
The Wireless Telecommunications Bureau at the Federal Communications Commission is responsible for all spectrum licensing in the United States. Its site includes detailed charts of spectrum usage, as well as information about auctions and other regulatory matters.

www.etsi.org
The European Telecommunications Standards Institute publishes consultation papers about proposed future standards, as well as details of standards in use.

www.itu.int/ITU-R/
The Radiocommunications Sector of the International Telecommunications Union site publishes its recommendations on the use of spectrum, as well as suggestions for worldwide standards.

www.med.govt.nz/pbt/
The New Zealand government's site about radio regulation explains some of the reasons behind the first spectrum auctions.

www.spectrumauctions.gov.uk
The official site of the United Kingdom's spectrum auctions explains the process devised by Professor Binmore. In 2000, it sold five 3G licenses for $35 billion.

http://prometheusradio.org
Prometheus Magazine has a detailed guide to low-power and free radio, covering both technical and regulatory issues.

http://www.law.nyu.edu/benklery/
Law professor Yochai Benkler has some interesting papers regarding spectrum management for free download.

....

BIBLIOGRAPHY

Gibilisco, Stan. **Handbook of Radio and Wireless Technology.** McGraw-Hill, 1998.
A general reference covering most aspects of wireless communications from a fairly technical point of view.

Kobb, Bennett Z. **Wireless Spectrum Finder.** McGraw-Hill, 2001.
A reference guide listing the complete radio spectrum allocation in the United States.

Shannon, C.E., and W. Weaver. **The Mathematical Theory of Communication, 2/e.** University of Illinois Press, 1968.
The ground-breaking book by the inventor of information theory himself.

SUMMARY ....

- Wireless technology uses radio waves, a type of electromagnetic radiation. Radio signals have a longer wavelength and a lower frequency than do other parts of the spectrum, such as visible light.

- The higher the radio frequency, the shorter the range will be. Mobile phones and wireless data systems use microwaves, which have a higher frequency and, thus, a shorter range than the waves used for broadcast radio and TV stations.

- The range of frequencies used by a radio system is called the *bandwidth*. The greater the bandwidth, the more the information it can carry.

- Most radio systems encode information by modulating the frequency, which provides a high-quality connection. Older technologies modulate the amplitude instead.

- The radio spectrum available within a given area is a finite resource, so its use needs to be regulated to ensure that different systems do not interfere with each other. The type of regulation varies greatly between countries.

3 Cellular Networks

In this chapter...

The American mobile industry is full of hype about Personal Communications Services (PCS) technology, as opposed to cellular. The latter is often used as a pejorative term, representing the older analog phones still popular in many parts of the world, including the United States. But in truth, nearly *all* mobile systems are cellular—they rely on a network of cells, with a powerful radio transceiver at the center of each. The basic design of a cellular network remains the same, whether it is used for second-generation (2G) PCS or even third-generation (3G) multimedia.

There has traditionally been a distinction between cellular and Private Mobile Radio (PMR) networks. Take a look at Figure 3.1 to see the difference. PMR networks either rely on direct handset-to-handset communication (like a walkie-talkie) or use a single base station. Cellular networks use many base stations, allowing them to cover a much wider area. The base stations are usually connected to each other using fiberoptic cables or high point-to-point wireless links, then to external networks, such as the phone system and the Internet.

Cellular networks have proved so successful that this distinction is now blurring. Former users of PMR, such as the emergency services, have started to adopt cellular technology, and private networks have also begun to use hybrid technologies. These do use cells but add features such as direct links between handsets so that they can be used outside of their coverage area.

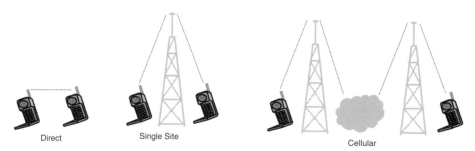

Figure 3.1
Types of mobile radio.

CELLS

A *cell* is the coverage area of a single base station. As a mobile phone moves through a network, it accesses services via the base station of whichever cell it is in. The precise shape of a cell depends on the geography of the region; hills and tall buildings can block signals, and different types of soil or depths of water also have some influence. Ignoring these effects, radio waves form an arc radiating out from a transceiver, as

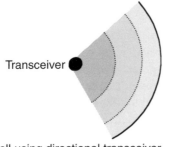
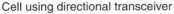
Cell using directional transceiver

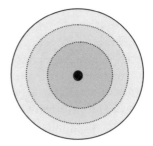
Cell using omnidirectional transceiver

Figure 3.2
Cell and transceiver types.

shown in Figure 3.2. The signal gets weaker as it gets further from the base station, so the cell boundary is the limit where the mobile terminal can no longer send and receive reliably. Unfortunately, the signal doesn't stop conveniently at this limit, resulting in interference for neighboring cells.

The simplest type of transmitter is *omnidirectional*, meaning that it broadcasts equally in all directions. This produces a cell shaped like a slightly distorted circle, the distortions due to geographic features. Circles don't tessellate very well, so mobile network architects usually approximate them to hexagons, as shown in Figure 3.3. This is useful for planning a cellular system, but it isn't strictly accurate—the overlap between cells also has to be taken into account, because in some parts a user may be able to communicate with two or many more base stations.

Overlapping circular cells

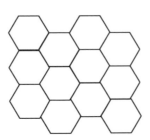
Idealized hexagonal network

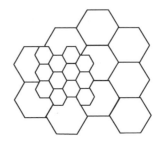
Microcells within a network

Figure 3.3
Arrangement of cells.

Microcells

Urban areas have a far greater density of mobile phone users than do rural areas. To serve these extra users, mobile operators deploy *microcells*, small cells that cover a particular street or even a particular building, such as a conference center. An *overlay* (or *underlay*) network has some areas covered by both large and small cells, usually because the larger cells were built first and the microcells added as demand increased. Current technology limits cell diameters to a minimum of 100 m (330 feet) because the internal circuitry of a transceiver generates so much radiation that it would interfere with very low-power transmissions.

Some mobile vendors also produce private base stations designed for indoor use, which allow a company to set up its own cell within an office or warehouse. This means that employees can use their mobile phones within the office, with internal calls routed via the switchboard. They tend to be most popular in the United States, which has poor cellular coverage and lots of large buildings. These *picocells* can also be installed in crowded public areas, such as airports, railway stations, and even railway carriages.

Cellular operators occasionally use portable microcells to cover large, one-time events, such as major sporting fixtures. These rely on a low-power transceiver, either mounted in a vehicle or set up on a scaffold. The problem here is how to connect the temporary base station to the rest of the network. Such locations usually lack fiberoptic cables and the line of sight required by fixed wireless equipment, meaning that the operator has to rely on satellite links.

Obstacles can sometimes actually help microcells by reducing interference between transceivers in the different cells. A large building may block low-powered signals, allowing streets on either side of it to support different users on the same frequencies.

Handoff

One of the most important features of a mobile network is the ability for a user to move from one cell to another. This movement was originally known as *roaming*. Many operators charged higher rates to users moving outside their home cells, just as fixed-line carriers charge more for long-distance than for local calls. But most operators now tend to bill calls at the same rate everywhere on their networks, and the idea of a phone having a single home cell is quickly disappearing, at least as far as customers are aware. The term *roaming* is usually reserved for using a phone on a network operated by a different company, usually one in another country.

The process of switching a user from one cell to another while a call is in progress is called a *handoff* or *handover*. Handoffs are very complex procedures because the base stations have to calculate exactly when a user is crossing the cell boundary. This can take several seconds, so if users move too fast, their calls will be dropped.

The speed limit for analog systems is usually no more than about 100 kilometers per hour (kph), the same as freeway traffic. Many digital systems can function at speeds above 300 kph, meaning that they can be used on Japanese and European high-speed trains. Some systems can even complete a handoff at the cruising speed of an airliner, though this is illegal and potentially dangerous.

There are three types of handoff systems in use:

- **Soft handoff** ensures that a link is set up to the base station in the new cell before the old one is torn down. Sometimes called *make before break,* this system is very reliable. It should result in dropped calls only if the user is moving extremely fast or actually passes outside the cellular net-work altogether.

  The trouble with soft handoff is that a connection with two different base stations is very difficult to maintain; in most types of network, adjacent base stations need to use different frequencies, while a phone can be tuned to only one at a time. Consequently, few existing systems can achieve a soft handoff. The process is included in most 3G and wireless LAN technologies, which try to maintain connections with multiple base stations or access points to improve reliability.

- **Hard handoff** requires that a phone break its connection with one base station before connecting to another. This is less reliable than soft handoff because a phone is not always able to establish a new connection. The new cell could already be full, or there may not be another cell at all. A base station sometimes decides to make a handoff based on how far away a phone is, without considering whether another one can pick it up. This means that in areas of poor reception, a phone may be repeatedly handed off, only to reconnect with the same cell.

  Hard handoffs cause a noticeable break in conversation, even on fairly advanced digital systems. This can be very annoying to a user moving rapidly between small cells, so networks with microcell overlays sometimes try to detect which users are moving and connect them via the main, larger cell. In such a system, microcells are reserved for stationary users or those walking slowly.

- **No handoff** is very simple and relies on the mobile terminal actually making a new call once it has moved out of the range of one transmitter. It is very rare in traditional cellular networks because many mobile phone systems can take up to 30 seconds to set up a new call, an unacceptable delay. However, it is

used by some newer systems aiming at the PMR market, which has traditionally demanded fast call setups for customers such as the police. The only real
advantage of not having a handoff mechanism is this short setup time: Fast
connections are offered to new calls, as well as to those already in progress.

Effect of Frequency

The frequencies used by cell phones all lie within the UHF microwave band, the same as
used by TV transmissions. They range from 400 MHz to around 2,000 MHz, with the
precise frequency affecting the cell size. Higher frequencies are more easily blocked by
droplets of cloud or mist in the atmosphere, so they have a shorter range. Networks
based on these higher frequencies require smaller cells and more base stations.

Lower frequencies initially seemed preferable because fewer base stations mean
lower costs. Governments licensed bands in the 450-, 800-, or 900-MHz regions,
allowing operators to deploy networks quickly and cheaply. Competitors were later
given frequencies around 1,800 and 1,900 MHz, which disadvantaged them because it
meant higher initial costs. The increased number of cells also led to bad publicity,
both because of perceived health risks and because many people simply think base
stations look ugly.

As mobile phone usage grew, the 1,800-MHz operators found their investment
paying off. The smaller cells meant that they could service a greater density of customers,
whereas their lower frequency competitors had to build microcells. Mobile data typically
requires higher capacity than does voice, so most 3G systems will use even higher
frequencies, around 2,000 MHz.

TWO-WAY COMMUNICATION ....

A single communications channel can be used to transmit information only one way,
as in a broadcast radio or TV station. Simple two-way radios use the same channel for
both but require the radio to stop receiving information when it is transmitting—the
user holds down a button while talking, then releases it to listen for a reply. This is
known as *half-duplex*. True two-way, or *full-duplex,* communication requires two
channels.

Paired Spectrum

Frequency Division Duplex (FDD) uses two separate frequency bands, meaning that
the mobile terminal is transmitting on one frequency while receiving on another. The
frequency at which the base station transmits is called the *downlink*, and the frequency

at which the mobile terminal transmits is called the *uplink*. Satellite systems often have an optional uplink, meaning they can be used for either one-way or two-way communication.

Most cellular systems use FDD, so many governments actually grant licenses in pairs: one set of frequencies for the uplink and another for the downlink. This is known as *paired spectrum*. The pairs are usually equal in size, meaning the communications channel is *symmetric*: The same amount of information can be transmitted to the mobile phone as from it. This is ideal for voice links but not for many Internet applications. Web surfing is inherently *asymmetric*: Users download Web pages and graphics but upload only mouse clicks.

A symmetric connection to the Web often wastes most of its bandwidth, though it can be necessary for other applications, notably, e-mail. People who frequently send file attachments, for example, frequently complain that these take a lot longer to send than to receive. This is a problem with both wireless and wired networks, and is exacerbated by the tendency of marketers selling asymmetric technologies to quote only the higher (downstream) data rate. Customers requiring high upstream bandwidth should very closely read the small print of any service agreement they are asked to sign.

Spectrum pairs always use the higher frequency for the downlink and the lower one for the uplink. This is because high frequencies have a slightly shorter range, thanks to atmospheric interference, and the base station can increase its transmission power to compensate. Mobile terminals can transmit using slightly lower power, which lengthens battery life and reduces the risk of radiation harming the user.

TDD

Time Division Duplex (TDD) uses only one channel but alternates between transmitting and listening—essentially a faster, automated version of the button-to-transmit system. Its great advantage is that bandwidth can be allocated dynamically between the uplink and the downlink, allowing asymmetric data links. The distinction between the two can also be eliminated entirely in a *peer-to-peer* network, where each node transmits directly to another (or to every other) without using a base station.

Most wireless LANs are based on a peer-to-peer architecture, so that users are able to communicate directly. Though they often use access points fixed to walls, these usually serve only to connect the network with a wired one or to extend its range. As shown in Figure 3.4, each user simply broadcasts to all others. This is very flexible, but it means that the available radio time is divided between even more users.

As with asymmetric technologies, the data rates quoted for TDD and peer-to-peer systems can be very misleading. They usually refer to the total bandwidth, which is shared by two (for TDD) or more (for peer-to-peer) network nodes. For example, the real throughput of many wireless LANs is about 6 Mbps. This means that one user

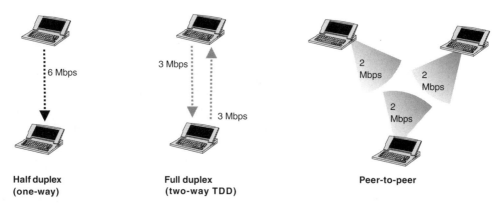

Figure 3.4
Ways to share 6 Mbps through TDD and peer-to-peer networks.

can send data to another at 6 Mbps, but only if the other user never replies. As soon as the link becomes two-way, the bandwidth has to be shared, so each can transmit at only 3 Mbps.

In a TDD system, the total shared bandwidth (6 Mbps, in the above example) is described as *half duplex*, because it's only available to one half of the link at a time. It is usually twice the two-way bandwidth (3 Mbps), which is described as *full duplex*.

MULTIPLEXING ....

Within a cell, mobile operators want as many customers as possible to use the network. They achieve this by using *multiple access* technology, which allows the available spectrum to be shared between several users. Analog systems usually separate conversations by subdividing the spectrum into narrow frequency bands and by using directional transceivers at the base station. Digital systems also divide each frequency into time slots or encode transmissions so that more than one can use the same airwaves at the same time.

Frequency

All radio systems use some kind of frequency division: They transmit in only part of the spectrum. At its most basic, this just means that broadcasters keep to the frequencies which the government or International Telecommunications Union (ITU) has allocated: Cell phones don't interfere with TV transmissions; wireless LANs don't interfere with satellite dishes.

Most systems go further. They partition their available spectrum into sub-bands, each of which can be tuned into by one or more users. A system that gives each communication channel its own specific frequency is described as using Frequency Division Multiple Access (FDMA). Examples include broadcast radio, TV, and analog cellular networks. Digital cellular systems also use FDMA, but they combine it with other multiplexing schemes.

The only analog cellular network still in widespread use is *AMPS* (Advanced, or American, Mobile Phone System). It uses paired spectrum bands of 25 MHz each, divided into 30-kHz channels. This gives a total capacity of 832 channels in each direction, though not all can be used for phone conversations. About 42 are needed for signaling information, and the entire spectrum is usually divided between two competing cellular operators. This would give each operator a maximum capacity of 395 calls.

The whole point of a cellular network is that building more cells can reuse channels, so the 395-call limit applies to an isolated cell, not to an entire network. Unfortunately, interference means that adjacent cells cannot reuse the same frequencies, so no one cell can broadcast (or receive) on all channels. The most efficient pattern can use only one third of the channels in each cell, as shown in Figure 3.5. Because the pattern repeats itself in groups of three cells, it is said to have a *cluster size* of three. In AMPS, this gives each cell 131 channels.

Cluster sizes of three are unusual in real networks because cells are not exactly hexagonal and not all the same size. The interference between cells is still too great, so larger clusters have to be used. The most common systems use cluster sizes of 7 or 12, but others are possible and may be necessary, depending on the particular structure of a network and whether it includes microcells. Figure 3.6 shows the number of channels per cell for various repeat patterns.

The biggest problem with pure FDMA is that nearby frequencies interfere with each other, something with which most radio listeners are familiar. Frequency needs to

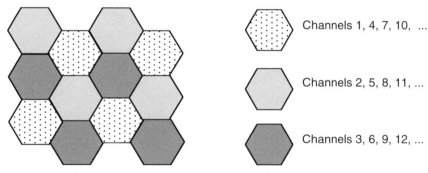

Channels 1, 4, 7, 10, ...

Channels 2, 5, 8, 11, ...

Channels 3, 6, 9, 12, ...

Figure 3.5
Three-cell clusters.

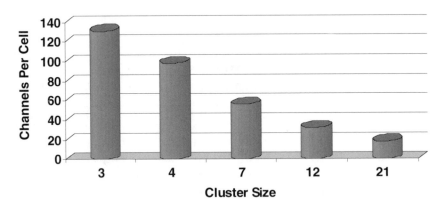

Figure 3.6
Channels per cell for a 395-channel AMPS network.

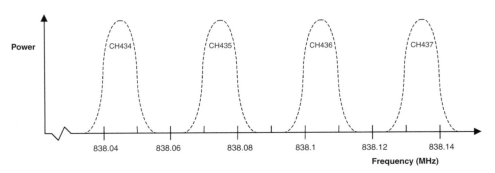

Figure 3.7
FDMA spectrum use.

be separated by a gap, which is very wasteful of spectrum. Table 3.1 lists some analog cellular systems—for all of them, the spectrum actually used by a channel is less than that which needs to be allocated. Figure 3.7 shows how the frequency is used in some AMPS channels. Because of this spectrum waste, most of the systems in the table are now obsolete, in the process of being upgraded to more efficient technologies that use wider bands.

Space

Space Division Multiple Access (SDMA) uses directional transmitters to cover only a part of an arc, rather than an entire circle, as in a cell. It is most valuable in satellite systems, which often need a narrowly focused beam to prevent the signal from spreading

Table 3.1 *Analog Cellular Systems*

System	Frequencies (MHz)		Spectrum per Channel	Channel Size	Max. Data Capacity	Locations Used
	Downlink	**Uplink**				
AMPS (Advanced Mobile Phone System)	869–894	824–849	24 kHz	30 kHz	9.6 kbps	Americas
C-Netz	461–466	451–456	8 kHz	20 kHz	5.3 kbps	Central Europe
J-TACS (Japanese TACS)	925–940	870–885	10 kHz	25 kHz	0.3 kbps	Japan only
NMT (Nordic Mobile Telephony)	463–467.5 935–960	453–457.5 890–915	9.4 kHz	25 kHz	1.2 kbps	Scandinavia, Eastern Europe, Asia
TACS (Total Access Communications System)	935–950 917–933	890–905 872–888	19 kHz	25 kHz	8.0 kbps	Western Europe, Asia

too widely and becoming too weak. A single satellite can reuse the same frequency to cover many different regions of Earth's surface.

In cellular networks, interference means that SDMA usually cannot actually reuse the same frequencies. It can, however, be used to reduce the number of base stations needed to cover a given number of cells. Instead of putting an omnidirectional transceiver at the center of each cell, three directional transceivers can be placed on a single site at the three-way cell boundary. Though the actual radio equipment is more complex, a single site makes it easier for the operator to obtain planning permission, build the fixed infrastructure, and perform maintenance.

Though SDMA is an old technology, new versions of it are currently being developed. *Smart antennas* at base stations continually track where a user is and try to point a signal directly toward him or her, as shown in Figure 3.8. This can help, even when there is not a direct line of sight between the transmitter and receiver, because the antenna monitors and partially corrects for attenuation and multipath interference. Arraycomm has developed a smart antenna system called *IntelliCell*, which it claims *will* enable the same frequencies to be reused within a single cell. Smart antennas also improve a base station's reception, which means that cell phones can transmit at a lower power. Like other power-saving measures, this prolongs the life of the battery and perhaps of the user.

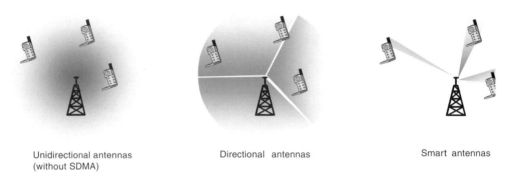

Unidirectional antennas
(without SDMA)
                          Directional antennas   Smart antennas

Figure 3.8
Space Division Multiple Access (SDMA).

Time

Most current digital systems, including the European GSM standard, rely on Time
Division Multiple Access (TDMA). To American consumers, the name *TDMA* has
come to mean the digital version of AMPS, but to engineers, this is just one of many
TDMA systems. The technology is also found in many other systems, including the
Japanese Personal Digital Cellular (PDC), which is the world's second most popular
cell phone standard.

TDMA works by dividing a band into several time slots, each of which corresponds to one communications channel. A cell phone usually transmits and receives
in only one slot, remaining silent until its turn comes around again. The number of
slots, cycle length, and bandwidth depend on the particular technology. Most TDMA
systems are *synchronous*, which means that transmissions are coordinated in advance.
Each transmitter must keep to its own time slot to avoid interference. Similarly, each
receiver needs to listen to the correct time slot to avoid a crossed line.

GSM's wide frequencies give it an advantage of scalability and reduce the wasted
bandwidth shown in Figure 3.7. But the short time slots can cause problems with
synchronization. Radio signals take just over 3.3 µs to travel 1 km, which adds up to a
round-trip delay of around 400 µs for a phone only 60 km from the base station. The
time slot lasts only 577 µs, so such a delay is enough to make the phone miss its slot
entirely, even though it would be unnoticeable to a human listener. In practice, this
means that GSM cells cannot have a radius of more than 35 km (22 miles), no matter
how strong the signal.

In the late 1990s, many in the cell phone industry thought that TDMA systems
provided an easy upgrade path to higher capacities: A mobile phone could simply transmit
or receive on more than one time slot, without having to retune to different frequencies.

This is the basis of High-Speed Circuit-Switched Data (HSCSD) and General Packet Radio Service (GPRS), described in Chapter 4, "PCS Standards." GSM had eight time slots, so an upgrade could theoretically provide eight times the data capacity.

Unfortunately, no upgrades yet come close to this. The companies advertising HSCSD and GPRS forgot that, because of the multiplexing scheme, a regular GSM phone transmits for only one-eighth of the time. It turns its transmitter off during six of the other time slots, saving energy. The transmitter becomes a receiver for the remaining slot, saving on components. Transmitting all of the time would need separate transmitters and receivers and would use eight times as much power—enough to make a phone burst into flames. It would also use eight times as much network capacity, so it would cost the user eight times as much.

SPREAD SPECTRUM AND CDMA...........................

Spread spectrum systems enable many users to transmit on the same frequency, in the same place, and at the same time. It has a remarkable history, dating back to the 1940s, though it didn't reach widespread deployment for more than 50 years. Whereas most technologies come from government or corporate research labs, spread spectrum was first thought of by Austrian actress Hedy Lamarr and American composer and writer George Antheil.

Lamarr had fled the Nazi regime in Germany, where she'd been married to an arms dealer and noticed that most of the torpedoes he sold missed their targets. Spread spectrum was intended as an unjammable radio system that would enable torpedoes to be guided by remote control. The Navy initially dismissed it as too complicated, but the complexity later became manageable, with the arrival of transistors and silicon chips. Spread spectrum is now the basis of most mobile data systems, including Bluetooth, 3G cellular, and wireless Ethernet.

Before spread spectrum, most radio signals were very easy to detect. This caused serious problems for the military: Even though transmissions could be encrypted, this didn't stop enemies from intercepting them and trying to crack the codes or simply jamming the signal with a more powerful one of their own. Spread spectrum was an attempt to make transmissions resemble random noise, so that eavesdroppers would not even know whether a communication was taking place.

The signals were not truly random, of course: They were agreed upon in advance so that the intended recipient would be able to decode the signal, just as in modern encryption systems. Because these random patterns are similar to encryption codes, spread spectrum is also known as Code Division Multiple Access (CDMA). There's no real difference between the two. For no reason in particular, cell phone companies prefer the name *CDMA*, whereas wireless LAN people prefer to call it spread spectrum.

Frequency Hopping

The first spread spectrum systems were based on frequency-hopping spread spectrum (FHSS). It uses narrowband FM signals, just like traditional radio communication, but rapidly switches between each one in a seemingly random pattern known only to the sender and recipient. (It was inspired by the seemingly random notes in some of Antheil's music.) This doesn't stop the enemy from knowing that a communication is in progress but makes it very difficult to listen in to or jam.

In a civilian communications network, intentional jamming by enemy users is not a serious problem. However, nonintentional interference can be. In a congested part of the radio spectrum, such as the Industrial, Scientific, and Medical (ISM) band at 2.4 GHz, the ability to change frequency quickly can be useful in finding one that isn't already in use by someone else.

Frequency hopping is now used mainly by short-range wireless technologies, of which the most well known is Bluetooth, aimed at replacing cables in very small Personal Area Networks (PANs). Others include HomeRF, a system intended for both home LANs and cordless phones, and the original version of the very popular Institute of Electrical and Electronics Engineers (IEEE) standard, 802.11. However, later versions of this standard (often branded as *Wi-Fi*) abandoned frequency-hopping in favor of other technologies that can achieve higher data rates. Older IEEE 802.11 networks based on FHSS are *not* compatible with these.

Direct Sequence

Direct sequence spread spectrum (DSSS) also covers a very wide range of frequencies but transmits on all at once. This means that the bandwidth required is very high, usually measured in MHz rather than kHz. The extra bandwidth is used to send extra copies of the transmitted signal and is known as the *gain*. The higher the gain, the more resistant the signal will be to interference.

This "interference" is often not background noise but another user (or many other users) transmitting in the same band. The transmissions are each encoded slightly differently, so that they can be separated by receivers. The large number of users that can share a channel means that, despite the high bandwidth requirement, DSSS is actually more spectrally efficient than TDMA-based cellular. This is why it was chosen as the basis for most 3G networks: The Europeans plan ultimately to replace GSM with *Wideband CDMA*, a direct sequence system that uses very wide channels to increase either the data rate or the number of voice conversations.

A communications channel in a direct sequence network is often compared with an airport transit lounge, where many people are speaking different languages. Listeners each understand only one language, so they are able to concentrate on their own conversations and to treat the rest as random noise. The analogy isn't exact, because a room full of people all talking at once soon becomes very loud. Everyone ends up trying to shout above the background noise, which just makes the problem worse.

To prevent such runaway growth in background noise, direct sequence codes are not truly random; they are carefully calculated to cancel each other out as far as possible. When expressed as a series of 1s and 0s, the codes are described as *orthogonal*, a mathematical term meaning two quantities that result in zero when multiplied together. When modulated onto a bit stream, the codes should cause destructive interference, as shown in Figure 3.9. This is the same phenomenon that prevents adjacent cells from using the same frequencies in an FDMA network, but here it is turned to the system's advantage.

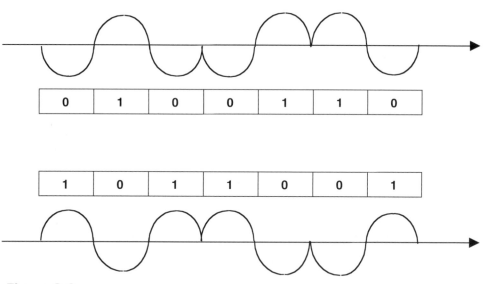

Figure 3.9
Two orthogonal bit streams modulated on to waves.

The transmitters can't actually get together and coordinate their signals, so codes have to be set in advance. They are usually hard-wired into the phone or data terminal, and based on one of several mathematical sequences. Types of codes and their main uses are listed in Table 3.2. Each code has a different length and number of possible values, making it suitable for different kinds of networks. For example, the *Walsh* codes used in most CDMA cell phones have 64 different values, which in theory means that 64 different terminals can use the spectrum at once. The IEEE 802.11 family of wireless LAN standards uses several different codes; the one used is dependent on the data rate. In general, longer and more complex codes allow a higher data rate or more users.

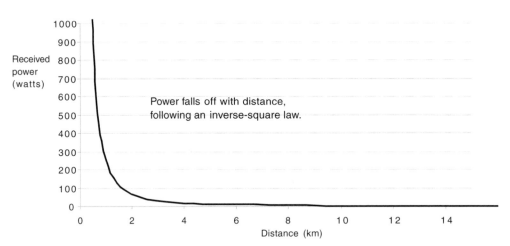

Figure 3.10
The power of a signal decreases rapidly as it spreads out across space.

Orthogonal codes alone could ensure that transmissions cancel each other out only if all transmitters are at exactly the same distance from the receiver. If they're not, one signal will probably be stronger than the other. Signal power falls off very rapidly with distance, thanks to divergence. This follows an *inverse-square law*, which means that received power decreases by a factor of 4 if distance doubles, as shown in Figure 3.10. Attenuation and an increased probability of multipath effects over longer distances can weaken a signal still further.

Wireless LANs are designed for short-range transmission, so they can largely ignore this problem, but CDMA cell phones can't. They have to vary their transmission power continuously, depending on the distance between the phone and the base station. This is known as the *near-far problem* and is solved by sophisticated electronics, which can accurately measure the distance. The availability of such electronics was the main reason that spread spectrum did not become widely used before the late 1990s.

If more than one phone can use the same frequency at the same time, so can more than one base station. This means that every cell can use all the spectrum available, a major saving because each cell in other systems can use at most only one-third of it. Cells are designed to overlap. Instead of a cell boundary, CDMA has a *handoff region*, where the mobile unit is actually connected to two base stations simultaneously. This allows soft handoffs and makes it easier to pinpoint the exact location of each user.

Table 3.2   Spreading Codes Used in DSSS and CDMA

Type of Code	Main Use
Walsh	CDMA (cdmaOne) cell phones
Gold	GPS satellites, W-CDMA (3G) cell phones
Barker	Radar, obsolete wireless LAN (802.11)
Complementary	Current wireless LAN (802.11b)
Convolution	Future wireless LAN (802.11g)

Ultra-Wideband

One of the most heavily promoted new wireless technologies is *Ultra-Wideband* (UWB). Companies claim that it is a revolutionary new way of transmitting signals or even that it abandons radio's traditional reliance on modulated waves at a specific frequency. Such claims are untrue—all radio signals need to use radio waves, and UWB is no exception—but the technology does show promise. Researchers have demonstrated that it can potentially reach speeds far in excess of other techniques, though it does require some sacrifices.

The most ridiculous claims about UWB say that it uses no spectrum. In fact, nearly the opposite is true: A UWB device transmits across an extremely large part of the spectrum at once, hence the name *Ultra-Wideband*. In this respect, it is just like DSSS but with the signals spread out even more. The bandwidth occupied by a UWB signal is at least 2 GHz, far more than the DSSS technologies, as shown in Figu re3.11. It's also more than the bandwidth used by *all* existing cell phones, broadcast media, and wireless LANs put together.

Such high bandwidth requirements mean that UWB has no dedicated part of the spectrum. Fortunately, it doesn't need one. Because the signals are spread out over such a wide bandwidth, the power at any particular frequency is very low. This means that it should cause very little interference, provided that it is used only for short-range transmissions, such as wireless LANs. Wide area networking using UWB would require much higher power, risking more interference with other spectrum.

In the United States, a UWB system is allowed under the FCC's Part 15 regulations, which permit very low-power transmissions on broadcast bands. The theory is that it might degrade some TV, radio, or cell phone signals but only over a few meters, which often would not extend beyond the home or office of the UWB user. Of course, this could cause problems at boundaries if people complain that their neighbors are interfering with their reception.

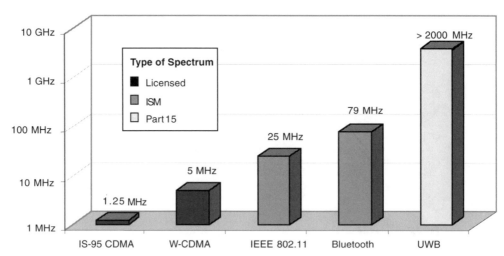

Figure 3.11
Spreading bandwidth of common spread spectrum systems.

UWB is more than just a sneaky way to reuse spectrum. Its other major advantage is that a very wide band signal can be generated using very simple equipment, without the need for the complex spreading codes used by DSSS systems. This reduces cost and power consumption, and means that UWB can use a simple pulse modulation scheme, essentially turning the transmitter on and off very rapidly in the same way as early radios based on Morse code. For this reason, it is sometimes called *time-hopping spread spectrum* (THSS).

At the time of this writing, UWB is still under test. One of its largest promoters is Intel, which estimates that the first commercial products should appear around 2006.

OFDM

Orthogonal Frequency Division Multiplexing (OFDM) is designed to reduce multipath effects, the destructive interference caused by waves that reflect off different surfaces. It is the newest and most complex wireless technology to have reached widespread deployment: Unlike UWB, it's already used for several applications—among them, wireless LANs and digital broadcasting. Many researchers are also investigating it for fourth-generation (4G) cellular systems, scheduled for deployment between 2006 and 2010.

Multipath interference becomes more of a problem as data rates get higher, because each bit must be represented in a shorter time interval. A shorter time interval means that a receiver is more likely to be confused by the short time differences that different path lengths can introduce, as shown in Figure 3.12. If each modulation symbol lasts 20 ns,

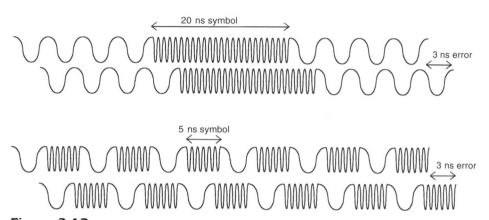

Figure 3.12
Higher data rates are more vulnerable to timing differences between different versions of a signal.

different versions of the signal arriving 3 ns apart will not cause a significant problem. However, if the symbol size is reduced to 5 ns, the different versions could render each modulation symbol indistinguishable from another.

OFDM reduces the bit rate by splitting a high-speed data stream into several lower speed streams and sending each one separately. Figure 3.13 illustrates this, showing a stream split into three separate channels, but real OFDM systems are much more complex: Some wireless LANs split a signal into 104 channels, meaning that each one can be transmitted at under 1% of the total data rate. In this respect, OFDM is the opposite of CDMA and TDMA: They share a frequency between many users, whereas OFDM shares a user between many frequencies.

Splitting solves the multipath problem but reintroduces an older one—the waste of bandwidth shown in Figure 3.7. Regular FDMA systems need a gap between each frequency to make them clearly distinguishable. OFDM eliminates this, moving the frequencies closer together until they overlap. Interference is prevented by using *orthogonal* carrier waves, which means that they (just like the spreading codes in CDMA) are carefully calculated to cancel each other out as far as possible. This requires very precisely tuned antennas and sophisticated processing, which prevented OFDM from becoming available in cheap or portable devices during the twentieth century.

There are many different types of OFDM technology, though some of these are very similar. Vendors or standards groups seem to like inventing new names for their particular OFDM implementations, both to differentiate themselves and to avoid other companies' patents:

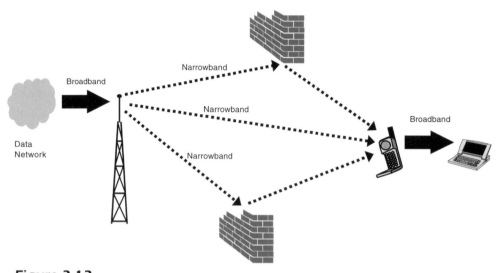

Figure 3.13
OFDM spreads a broadband signal across several narrowband channels that travel via different paths.

- **C-OFDM.** *Coded* OFDM is the standard used for European digital radio and TV broadcasts. The name is slightly meaningless, because all OFDM transmissions are coded in some way. It was chosen for its ability to overcome multipath interference: TV viewers should be able to get perfect reception from a small set-top antenna, without needing to stick anything on the roofs of their houses.

- **BST-OFDM.** *Band-Segmented Transmission* OFDM is a more advanced version of C-OFDM, developed for use in Japanese digital TV networks. It splits a signal up into even more frequencies than other forms of OFDM, which improves reception while mobile, though it is slightly less spectrally efficient. This will ultimately enable people to watch TV on their cell phones without using up scarce transmission capacity on the cellular network.

- **W-OFDM.** *Wideband* OFDM is a system developed by Wi-Lan for both wireless LAN and fixed local loop applications. It is so called because it uses a very wide range of frequencies. Wi-Lan claims that its patents on W-OFDM cover the type of OFDM used by IEEE 802.11a wireless LANs, but some other vendors of 802.11a equipment dispute this, saying that, instead, it is based on C-OFDM. Their differences are likely to be resolved in court.

- **V-OFDM.** *Vectored* OFDM was developed by Clarity Wireless Corporation, a small company later taken over by networking giant Cisco Systems. Intended for fixed wireless only, it aimed to improve path diversity by using more than one antenna. Though it could achieve fairly high data rates. Cisco announced in November 2001 that it was winding down the business. Other companies have licensed the technology, so it may not die entirely. Lucent has demonstrated a similar system called *BLAST* (Bell Labs Layered Space Time), which isn't actually OFDM but is based on the same concept. It uses up to 10 antennas, each transmitting on the *same* frequency but pointed in a slightly different direction, so that signals take a different path.

- **Flash OFDM.** Also known as *frequency-hopping* OFDM, this is the first type of OFDM to be used for wide-area mobile data and, thus, is a potential candidate to become a 4G cellular standard. As the name suggests, it combines OFDM with a frequency-hopping technique similar to that used by Bluetooth and HomeRF. After successful trials in the 700 MHz band—the one currently occupied by TV in the United States but set to be reallocated to cellular—the first systems went into production in early 2002. It was developed by Flarion, a startup company that aims to sell network infrastructure equipment (base stations and mobility management tools) while licensing the technology to cell phone and computer manufacturers who will build end-user terminals.

Is OFDM Really Spread Spectrum?

Many engineers say that OFDM is not spread spectrum. In some ways, it seems the reverse: Instead of spreading a signal across a very wide bandwidth, it splits a signal up across many different narrowband frequencies. But in 2001, some companies convinced the FCC that it is spread spectrum, despite the differences.

The arguments were more than academic. Most people in the wireless LAN industry believe that OFDM is a more advanced technology than spread spectrum, thanks to its resistance to multipath interference. However, FCC rules say that communications technologies transmitting in the popular 2.4 GHz ISM band must use some form of spread spectrum. As a result, the main OFDM-based wireless LAN standards (IEEE 802.11a and HiperLan2) need to use different bands at higher frequencies (usually 5 GHz).

(continued)

IS *OFDM* REALLY *SPREAD* SPECTRUM? (CONTINUED)

These higher frequencies do have some advantages—the main one is the lack of interference from microwave ovens and cordless phones—but they make it hard for equipment to interoperate with existing IEEE 802.11b networks. (For more on these, see Chapter 9, "Short Range Wireless Networks.") To get around this, several companies led by Intersil proposed IEEE 802.11g, an OFDM-based standard at 2.4 GHz.

The FCC was initially skeptical but finally decided that OFDM could be considered to be spread spectrum if it used a wide enough range of frequencies. OFDM does actually share some characteristics with traditional spread spectrum systems: Both make use of orthogonal frequencies calculated to cancel each other out, and splitting a broadband signal into lots of smaller components can be thought of as spreading it across the spectrum.

LOCATION TRACKING...

Some of the most promising (and threatening) new cellular services depend on location technology. Unlike wireless Web surfing, this is new and unique to the mobile world. If the precise location of a user is known, carriers can offer precise traffic and weather forecasts, a phone that guides police to a thief whenever it is stolen, and even the ability to keep a record of a person's movements both on- and offline.

Europe's carriers began experimenting with location technology in 1999, and the first commercial services were deployed in Japan in 2001. (These are discussed further in Chapter 7, "M-Commerce.") They don't always require high bandwidth—people can get directions over a text-only link or by talking to a real person—but they do require new technology, either in the cellular network or in the phone itself.

Triangulation

Most location technologies rely on some variant of *triangulation*, which means calculating the position of a phone by measuring its distance from two or more known points. In the simplest systems, known as *time of arrival* (TOA), these points are the base stations that sit at the center of every cell. This allows all the processing to be done by the network and doesn't require new phones.

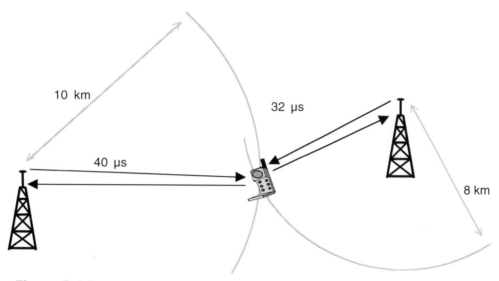

Figure 3.14
Triangulation using time-of-arrival measurements from two base stations.

Distances are generally measured using a primitive form of radar: Each base station sends out a radio pulse, timing how long the response takes. In Figure 3.14, base station A has calculated that the phone lies somewhere on an arc 5 km from point A. Base station B does the same, calculating that it is on another arc, 8 km from B. Therefore, the phone must be at the point where the two arcs intersect.

Some systems also try to infer distance from signal degradation: The further away the phone, the weaker its signal. Neither of these is particularly accurate, because radio waves don't always travel directly between two points. They're reflected off walls, trees, and hills, which can make a phone appear to be further from a base station than it really is.

For increased precision, most systems try to triangulate using at least three sites. This reduces errors, and is vital when omnidirectional antennas are used, because two full circles always intersect at two points. The problem with this is that not all areas are within range of three or more different base stations, because networks are usually designed to minimize the overlap between cells. Many remote areas are served by only one, which makes any kind of triangulation impossible. A single measurement can usually ascertain how far away a user is from the tower but not in which direction.

Some base stations now incorporate smart antennas, which try to point directly at a user. These *can* get a rough idea of the direction and, in principle, calculate the location using only one station. This system is known as *angle of arrival* (AOA). It is still quite rare but might become more popular as smart antennas become more widespread. Where possible, it is combined with triangulation measurements, because alone it isn't extremely accurate: It can reduce the size of an arc to a few degrees but not eliminate the uncertainty entirely.

GPS Phones

The most precise way to determine location is through the Global Positioning System (GPS), a constellation of 24 satellites (called *Navstars*) run by the U.S. Air Force. Its weaknesses used to be that terminals cost thousands of dollars and that the military introduced a random error to frustrate civilian or enemy users. Both of those have gone: The error was switched off in 2000, and GPS receivers are now small and cheap enough to put inside a cell phone.

GPS works in the same way as ground-based systems that measure time differences, though it's complicated by two factors. First, the satellites are moving, so they continuously transmit their own position, rather than sending a simple radio pulse. Second, there's no return path from the receiver back to the satellite. The satellites overcome this by transmitting the precise time, measured by an onboard atomic clock.

A receiver can calculate its distance from each satellite by comparing the received time with its own clock, then triangulating. The receiver needs to lock on to four satellites simultaneously: three to triangulate (because the system is three-dimensional, measuring altitude as well as map coordinates) and one extra to keep its clock synchronized with the network. This results in a location pinpointed to within 5 m (16 feet) and time measurements more accurate than Earth's rotation.

The satellites all transmit at the same frequency, shared using DSSS (CDMA). The spreading codes are actually the same as those used in the European and Japanese 3G standard, so some of the hardware inside a 3G phone ought to be reusable for GPS. This should make GPS phones relatively cheap to manufacture.

Qualcomm was the first company to produce a GPS phone, sold in Japan in 2001, but all the other major manufacturers plan to produce them. They claim that because the receivers need only pick up the satellite signals, not transmit back, they can be the same size as regular cell phones—not the bricks usually associated with satellite telephony. Most phones may eventually be equipped with GPS, whether customers want it or not.

No matter what the marketing literature from manufacturers says, a phone that includes a GPS receiver is *not* a "satellite phone." This term refers to a phone that actually transmits voice and/or data via satellite, rather than a base station on the ground, meaning that it can be used where terrestrial cellular networks are unavailable. (There's a lot more about satellite phones in Chapter 12, "Internet in Space.") The Navstar satellites are designed only to transmit positioning data, not to listen for a reply. This means that stranded backpackers with GPS receivers are often able to determine their own position but not to call and tell anyone where they are.

Some conspiracy theorists believe that the GPS satellites *can* receive data in some way, a capability that the U.S. government is keeping secret. That seems unlikely: Though some of the Navstars may double as spy satellites, this is just because satellites are expensive, and any spy functions would be unrelated to their positioning use. It is impossible for the satellites to know who (if anyone) is picking up the positioning data that they broadcast, so users don't have to worry about being tracked by the U.S. military.

Assisted GPS

An ordinary GPS receiver can take several minutes to find four satellites when first switched on, which isn't acceptable for location-based services. (A cell phone's battery would be drained too quickly if it kept the GPS receiver on all the time.) Instead, most use a system called *Assisted GPS*, which also keeps an active GPS receiver at every base station. This broadcasts the precise time, eliminating the need for a fourth satellite, and tells the phone where to look for the other three.

Assisted GPS is particularly useful in CDMA networks, because all their base stations already include GPS receivers for timekeeping purposes. (The GPS time signal provides the accuracy of an atomic clock at a much lower cost.) It also has two other advantages over regular GPS: The base stations can fall back to regular TOA or AOA when satellites aren't visible, as often happens inside buildings, and it has the potential to be even more accurate.

In the 1990s, enthusiasts invented a system called *Differential GPS*. This uses a stationary GPS receiver to calibrate the system and correct errors, providing a simple workaround for the military's security. (That's why the deliberate error was eventually removed.) A cellular system with Assisted GPS could easily be converted into a large-scale Differential GPS network, though no carriers have yet announced plans for this. With the military scrambling now gone, Differential GPS could correct for natural errors due to atmospheric interference and multipath effects, potentially pushing the resolution to within a few centimeters.

Unlike Differential GPS, Assisted GPS also offloads all the positioning calculations to a computer somewhere on the cellular network. No matter what mobile operators claim, this is not to reduce the weight or power consumption of the handsets: The math involved in calculating a position is trivial to that required in the modulation and multiplexing devices that phones already include. Manufacturers even say that they could build the triangulation capability into a phone but aren't going to. The reason is that operators don't want customers determining location without help. They want it to be a premium service for which they can bill.

AUDIO CODING ....

Whether based on CDMA or TDMA, all digital systems need to encode the analog wave forms of speech into a bit stream. The program used for this is called a *codec* (coder/decoder), often embedded within a special chip called a *DSP* (digital signal processor). Many different codecs are used in cell phones, and new ones are developed each year. The aim is to produce the lowest possible bit rate while maintaining acceptable sound quality. Because computing power is increasing continuously, newer phones and networks are capable of using more advanced compression technology. Some popular codecs are listed in Table 3.3, together with their main uses.

The standard by which voice codecs are judged is the *G.711* system, used in the Public Switched Telephone Network (PSTN). Though most actual fixed phone lines are still analog, the fiberoptic networks at the carrier's core transport use this codec, as does Integrated Services Digital Network (ISDN), the digital phone standard. A system that sounds as good as G.711 is described as *toll quality*.

Though toll quality is the holy grail for speech codec designers, anyone who has ever used a telephone knows that it's far from perfect. Many operators are interested in streaming music or video over their networks, which require much higher data rates. The unofficial standard for digital music on the Internet is *MP3* (Motion Picture Experts Group Audio Layer 3), which supports a variety of bit rates. At its lowest, it sounds like a badly tuned radio; at its highest, it is indistinguishable from a CD.

Table 3.3   *Popular Codecs*

Codec	Bit Rate	Main Use
Compact Disc	1,411 kbps	Stereo music
MP3, WMA, Ogg Vorbis	16–256 kbps	Music
MP2	usually 192 kbps	Digital broadcast radio
RealAudio	5–352 kbps	Streaming audio
PSTN (G.711)	64 kbps	Fixed telephony
GSM 06.10	13 kbps	GSM phones
Adaptive Multirate (AMR)	4.75–12.2 kbps	3G phones
G.729	8 kbps	Satellite communications
IS-54	8 kbps	D-AMPS phones
G.723.1	5.3 kbps	Voice over Internet
Department of Defense	2.4 kbps	Military applications

DATA CODING

All the codecs here can be used to reduce the bandwidth requirements for voice but not for data. This is because they all use lossy compression, meaning that it is impossible to recover the original sound wave. The human ear doesn't mind this because many sounds are inaudible to human listeners. Some lossy algorithms, such as MP3, employ a system called **psychoacoustic** coding, which tries to calculate which bits can safely be discarded, based on models of human perception.

This doesn't work with data because computers notice everything; even a single bit out of place in a program could prevent it from running. Data requires **lossless** compression, which uses mathematical algorithms to search for repeated patterns. Web surfers might be familiar with the two types, thanks to the file formats commonly used on the Internet. GIF files use lossless compression and are ideal for line drawings or pictures containing text. JPG files use lossy compression and are more suited to photographs.

But even without compression, the data rate that can be sent over a cellular system is often slightly more than that of the system's codec; for example, while the GSM codec needs 13 kbps, 14.4 kbps can be made available for data. The reason is that data is more tolerant than voice of **jitter**, the variation in the time (**latency**) that different packets of a message take to arrive at their destination.

Wave Form Sampling

The simplest way to digitize a sound signal is to sample the wave form at regular intervals. This is called *PCM* (pulse code modulation) and is used by the CD and PSTN codecs. As shown in Figure 3.15, a shorter interval will result in more accurate sampling but a higher bit rate. The problem is that low bit rates require long intervals, which represent the wave form inaccurately and eventually make it unrecognizable.

Adaptive differential PCM (ADPCM) codecs attempt to predict the value of the next sample from the previous samples. This increases the accuracy for a given bit rate and can compress a voice call down to about 16 kbps while maintaining acceptable quality. This alone is still too high for mobile systems, but prediction is used together with other techniques in most cell phone codecs.

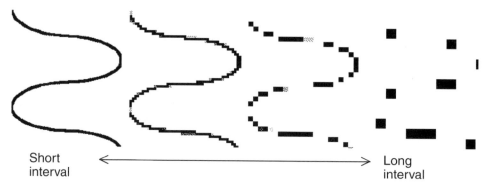

Short   ◄────────────────────────────► Long
interval   interval

Figure 3.15
Pulse code modulation.

Vocoding

Although sound waves look random, the sounds produced in speech actually share many common characteristics, thanks to their common source: the human speech organs. *Vocoders* take advantage of this by trying to represent the human anatomy with simple mechanical devices, as in Figure 3.16.

When a person says something, sound is modulated by the vocal tract to produce the speaker's characteristic voice; it is then shaped by the nose, tongue, and lips to make individual words. This sound is either white noise, direct from the lungs, or a wave form produced by the vocal chords. Sounds made by the vocal chords are described as *voiced* and include all vowels, as well as soft consonants, such as *d* and *b*. The hard consonants, such as *t* and *p*, are *unvoiced*.

Instead of sending an actual signal, a vocoder calculates how speech was produced and sends only the relevant pitch and tone information, as well as a description of the sender's mouth movements and vocal tract. A decoder then synthesizes a voice, using computerized equivalents of the sender's organs. This results in a very low data rate but also poor quality—the precise characteristics of a vocal tract are very difficult to simulate, so the voice sounds synthesized.

Vocoders are typically used only in very low data rate situations, for example, military and space communications. They can reach data rates as low as 1 kbps, at which it is hard to tell who is actually speaking. Another problem is that they fail to transmit any sounds other than the human voice, though this can be an advantage if the speaker is surrounded by undesirable background noise.

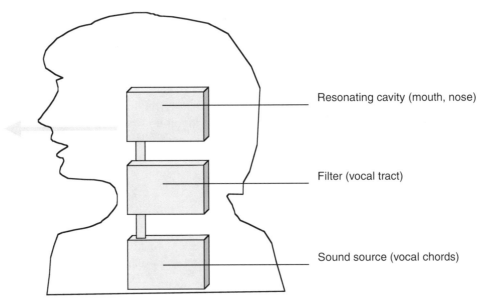

Figure 3.16
Model of human speech.

Hybrid Codecs

Most codecs use a mixture of wave form and vocoding, usually based on synthesized speech with some PCM information. They also use characteristics of the human ear to strip out inaudible sounds, for example, a quiet musical instrument in the background of a louder one.

The precise bit rate depends on the quality of the sound and on the type of hardware available. For a mobile phone, the limiting factor is usually the need to compress and decompress in real time, with one end of the link a pocket-sized, battery-operated device. This limit becomes less significant all the time as advances in technology pack more computation capability into smaller and lower power chips. (This is Moore's Law, described in Chapter 1, "The Wireless World.") Because the GSM standard is about 20 years old, more advanced processing is possible now than when it was first devised: Most modern GSM phones include a *half-rate* codec, which sounds (almost) as good as the original but uses only half the bandwidth.

One-way broadcasts sometimes use asymmetric codecs, which are a lot easier to decompress than to compress. For example, a digital TV or radio station can put a powerful computer at the transmitter's end of the link but must rely on a relatively primitive receiver at the other. The MP3 format is also asymmetric, because most users encode files only once but play them lots of times. When it first appeared, an average desktop PC could take hours to encode a single five-minute track in MP3 format, whereas it could play the same track in real time and still have processing cycles to spare for other tasks. Most computers are now powerful enough to encode MP3 as fast as they can read from a CD.

Some newer speech codecs also include Digital Speech Interpolation (DSI), which can vary the bit rate, depending on the complexity of the speech. Almost no information at all is sent during periods of silence, enabling the channel to be used for something else, usually data. Because channels are allocated by the base station, this works more effectively on the downlink than the uplink.

Music and Streaming

Many cell phones now incorporate MP3 players, so that users can listen to digital music and automatically be interrupted if a call comes through. The MP3 format is popular because it allows the music files stored on a CD to be compressed to a fraction of their original size, with nearly no loss in quality. This has led some cell phone operators to consider offering music in MP3 or another format.

Though users like MP3, several groups have criticized it. The music industry complains that MP3 files can be freely copied, most famously over file-sharing systems such as Napster and later Morpheus. Programmers who develop free software dislike it for the opposite reason: Though there are no technical limitations on copying files, parts of the format itself are patented by the companies that make up MPEG. This means that anyone who writes an MP3 encoding or decoding program and even everyone who distributes music in the MP3 format may have to pay royalties to the patent holders.

The music industry has repeatedly tried to replace MP3 with its own technologies that include ways to restrict how music is played. All of these failed, for the obvious reason that people would prefer to have an open standard than one that restricts how they use their data. The latest is Microsoft's Windows Media Audio (WMA) format, which might be more successful among PC users simply because it is built into Windows. The intention is that users with broadband connections will buy music over the Internet and that this will then be locked to their particular computer. It's unlikely to succeed on cell phones, which don't run Windows and have limited bandwidth.

On the other side, the free software community has developed a system called *Ogg Vorbis*, which is entirely free and open: It can be included in any hardware or software without royalty payments. Both Vorbis and Microsoft claim that their newer systems are more efficient than MP3, producing better quality sound at any given bit rate. However, these claims are hard to judge. Aside from the subjective nature of sound quality, different encoding programs can produce very variable results. Quality depends as much on the particular encoder used as on the file format.

Most MP3 and similar files are stored on a user's computer or portable device. When they are transferred over a network or copied to a player, the user waits until the entire file has been transferred before playing it. This works only if the user has a high-speed connection or is willing to wait a long time for a file to download. It's also unsuitable for applications such as live radio: People want to listen to the news as it happens, not download a large file and play it later.

Online radio stations instead use a technology called *streaming*, which means playing an audio file that is stored on a remote computer or encoded live. In most cases, the file is not stored on the user's computer. Like the speech sent through a cellular network, it's deleted as soon as it has been played. Cellular operators hope to stream music and even video to mobile phones, though this will require a lot more bandwidth than is currently available.

For quality similar to broadcast FM radio, MP3 requires at least 96 kbps, a data rate that 3G systems should be able to achieve. However, they won't have enough capacity to give every user access at this speed. If customers have to pay based on how much time they spend online or on how much data they download, music downloads could become impractical. The first 3G service was launched by NTT DoCoMo in 2001 and charged about 5 cents per KB of data. A single track encoded in MP3 format has a file size of at least 2,000 KB, which means it would cost $100 to download.

Until genuine mobile broadband is available, most streaming audio will be limited to lower data rate codecs, probably very like existing Internet radio stations. Rather than MP3 or one of its direct competitors in stored music, most of these use the *RealAudio* format. This is a proprietary system just like WMA, so it would seem to have the same disadvantages without the advantage of being distributed with Windows. However, it does allow very low bit rates—as small as 5 kbps, which (as Table 3.3 shows) is lower than that of many cell phones. This won't seriously threaten the music industry, but it is good enough for speech radio.

The BBC World Service is a mostly speech station that, as the name suggests, broadcasts all over the world. It started streaming over the Internet in 1996, and within a few years found that this was how most of its North American audience was listening. As a result, it shut down regular AM transmissions to most U.S. cities in 2001. This decision was probably premature, because accessing the Internet is still a lot more difficult and expensive than turning on a radio, but that will change.

WEB RESOURCES

www.totaltele.com
This site publishes telecom-related news and features from several magazines, as well as newswires. Though it covers all kinds of telecom services, mobile and cellular make up a large proportion of its content. There's also a satellite site called **Roam** that specializes in wireless, but the main site is usually more interesting.

www.wsdmag.com
The magazine **Wireless System Design** is more technical, full of detailed information about the various cellular technologies. The print version is free to subscribers in the right (high-spending) demographic, and all the content is also available online.

www.ofdm-forum.com
The OFDM Forum tries to promote OFDM for all wireless applications, including LANs, fixed networks, and 4G. Its site has plenty of technical and promotional material.

www.uwb.org
The Ultra-Wideband Working Group tries to develop UWB-based applications and has some information about this new technology and its potential.

BIBLIOGRAPHY

Smith, Clint. **Wireless Telecommunications FAQs**. McGraw-Hill, 2000.
A guide to cellular systems, based on one radio engineer's real-life experience of questions often asked by his nontechnical colleagues.

SUMMARY

- A cell is the coverage area of a single base station. Wireless operators cover a wide area by using lots of overlapping cells.
- The cell size depends on the frequency and the number of customers within the cell. Higher frequencies require smaller cells.
- All cellular networks use separate frequencies for the uplink to the base station and the downlink to the mobile subscriber.

- Simple analog networks use FDMA, which gives each conversation its own frequency band.
- Digital networks use TDMA or CDMA, which share a frequency band by assigning each communication channel a time slot or code.
- On digital networks, speech has to be converted to bits using software called a *codec*. In any codec, there is a trade-off between bandwidth and speech quality. Cellular networks typically use codecs between 5 and 13 kbps.

4 PCS Standards

In this chapter...

$\mathbf{T}$he mobile technologies invented in the late 1990s are collectively known as *Personal Communications Services* (PCS). This term was originally used by the Federal Communications Commission (FCC) to describe a particular group of frequencies in the 1,900-MHz band but has been hijacked by marketers to include any digital system that provides high-quality voice and narrowband data. In the greater scheme of things, it is the second generation of wireless technology, between analog cell phones and broadband mobile multimedia.

There are three main categories of PCS in use today, all providing different features to the end user, as shown in Table 4.1. Digital cell phones are by far the most popular, offering intelligible voice and limited data, usually text-only. Other services still use a cellular network but concentrate on data only, either to make the terminal smaller and cheaper or to provide simple graphics. Noncellular technologies are relatively little known but important for many emergency services and some large businesses. They can work without a base station and support automatic conference calls between predefined groups.

Also classified as PCS are the 2.5G systems, which offer higher data rates through relatively simple upgrades to twentieth-century networks. The difference between one of these and a genuine 3G network is open to some debate and really just depends on the speed; a 2.5G system ought to provide performance similar to that of a fast dial-up modem, whereas 3Gs should be significantly higher. The first deployments, however, have failed to live up to these aspirations.

Table 4.1   PCS Categories and Features

Technology		Voice	Max. Data Speed	Base Station Required
Digital Cellular	GSM	Yes	14.4 kbps	Yes
	HSCSD	Yes	57.6 kbps	Yes
	GPRS	Yes	115.2 kbps	Yes
	D-AMPS	Yes	9.6 kbps	Yes
	PDC	Yes	14.4 kbps	Yes
	cdmaOne	Yes	64 kbps	Yes
	Airfone	Yes	9.6 kbps	Yes

Table 4.1   PCS Categories and Features (Continued)

Technology		Voice	Max. Data Speed	Base Station Required
Data Only	CDPD	No	19.2 kbps	Yes
	DataTAC	No	19.2 kbps	Yes
	Mobitex	No	8.0 kbps	Yes
	MCDN	No	128 kbps	Yes
Noncellular	TETRA	Multiparty	28.8 kbps	No
	iDEN	Multiparty	64 kbps	No

CELLULAR VOICE AND DATA ....

By far the largest category of PCS system is the group of standards used for digital cell phone networks. Although these were all designed primarily for voice, they can also support data transmission at varying rates. The data rates shown in Table 4.1 are those that use the voice circuit, usually by connecting a phone to a laptop computer, though increasingly in a "microbrowser" on the phone itself. Many also include far slower data services that can operate at the same time as the user is talking, usually used to send short text messages of just a few words.

Most PCS systems are based on Time Division Multiple Access (TDMA). Frequency Division Multiple Access (FDMA) is too wasteful of bandwidth, and Code Division Multiple Access (CDMA) had not yet been invented at the time they were standardized. The exception is cdmaOne, which most scientists agree is technologically the most advanced system. However, this doesn't mean it is necessarily superior to the others; for example, GSM offers the best coverage, and D-AMPS is compatible with older networks still in use across North America. And 3G systems, now coming on line, are even more advanced.

The arguments between proponents of different systems are often heated, even referred to as "religious wars," because many participants seem to rely on faith rather than actual evidence. Most of the debate centers around *spectral efficiency*, which means how much capacity a system can squeeze out of its allocated frequencies. Because operators each have a relatively small band of spectrum, it is in their interest to use this efficiently. It is also in the public interest because the total spectrum is finite, and use that is more efficient should keep costs down. Up to a limit, any system can be made more efficient by installing more lower power base stations, which was part of the rationale behind spectrum auctions—if operators have to pay for spectrum, they are more likely to invest in equipment to use it more efficiently.

Unfortunately, spectral efficiency depends on so many variables that it is not easy to calculate accurately. Table 4.2 tries to do this for the main systems, with the important results in the final column. Note that these are very approximate, though they do show that GSM is generally less efficient than the others. This is in part because it provides better quality and a more reliable connection than the other TDMA systems, though cdmaOne offers similar benefits without the extra spectrum requirements. This is because it was standardized more than a decade after GSM, by which time technology had moved on.

Table 4.2   Spectral Efficiency of PCS Technologies

System	Channel Bandwidth	Calls per Channel	Cells per Channel	kHz per Call	kbps per Call	Hz per bps
GSM	200 kHz	8	about 4	100	14.4	7
D-AMPS	30 kHz	3	about 7	70	9.6	7
PDC	25 kHz	3	about 7	58	9.6	6
cdmaOne	1250 kHz	about 15	1	83	16	5
Airfone	6 kHz	1	10	60	4.8	13

HOW IS SPECTRAL EFFICIENCY CALCULATED?

Every system divides its frequencies into relatively wide FDMA channels, which are shared between a number of calls. The amount of spectrum used by each call should, therefore, be:

$$\text{Spectrum per call} = \frac{\text{Channel Bandwidth}}{\text{Calls per Channel}}$$

This is true for a single transmitter, but most real cellular systems don't allow every frequency to be used in every cell. Except in CDMA, neighboring cells cannot use the same frequencies, so the equation becomes:

$$\text{Spectrum per call} = \frac{\text{Channel Bandwidth}}{\text{Calls per Channel}} \times \text{Cells per Channel}$$

(continued)

HOW IS SPECTRAL EFFICIENCY CALCULATED? (CONTINUED)

This is the traditional measure of spectral efficiency, shown in Table 4.2 as kHz per Call. It applies only to voice calls and does not take into account the type of codec used. GSM and cdmaOne use higher bit-rate codecs than do the other systems, resulting in higher quality speech, which in part explains why they require more kHz.

In the age of mobile data, it may be more appropriate to divide by the capacity available if the voice calls are replaced by data. This measures the numbers of wave cycles needed to transmit each bit:

$$\text{Hz per bps} = \frac{\text{Channel Bandwidth} \times \text{Cells per Channel}}{\text{Calls per Channel} \times \text{Data Rate}}$$

The results of this calculation are in the final column of Table 4.2. Again, this is not the full story. GSM and cdmaOne both include built-in error correction not found in D-AMPS and PDC. Some people also like to express spectral efficiency as a function of the area covered by a cell, to measure the **information density** of a technology. However, this depends very much on how many base stations are used and how large each cell is made.

GSM

Now known as the *Global System for Mobile Communications*, GSM originally stood for *Groupe Spéciale Mobile*, the name of the committee that designed it. The technology is used by about two-thirds of all mobile phones and by 2001 had reached more than 10% of the Earth's population. Its popularity is due partly to relatively high-quality voice but mostly to early standardization by European governments. Another advantage is that it is easily upgradeable to higher data rates, a deliberate decision on the part of its inventors but not something appreciated by its early adopters.

The system now operates on five different frequency bands, shown in Table 4.3. It was originally designed for frequencies around 900 MHz, to reuse the spectrum intended for Europe's analog Total Access Communications System (TACS) networks. It was later adapted to bands around 1,800 MHz, licensed in Europe specifically for GSM, and then to the 1,900 MHz band used in America for several different digital networks. These higher frequency variants are sometimes called *DCN* (Digital Communications Network), but they're really just GSM. The latest variants use the lower 450-MHz and 800-MHz frequencies, so that they can replace aging analog networks based on Scandinavian NMT and the North American AMPS.

Table 4.3   *GSM Frequency Allocations*

GSM Type	Uplink Frequency	Downlink Frequency	Cell Size
GSM 450	450.4–457.6 MHz or 478–486 MHz	460.4–467.6 MHz or 488.8–496 MHz	Biggest
GSM 800	824–849 MHz	869–894 MHz	Big
GSM 900	880–915 MHz	925–960 MHz	Big
DCN 1800	1,710–1,785 MHz	1,805–1,880 MHz	Small
PCS 1900	1,850–1,910 MHz	1,930–1,990 MHz	Smallest

Like other digital cellular technologies, GSM encodes data into waves using a form of phase modulation, a system that uses the different parts of a wave form to represent information. The precise type is known as *GMSK* (Gaussian minimum shift keying), which achieves a symbol rate and data rate of 270.8 kbps in each of its 200-kHz channels. This transmission is only one-way, so GSM uses separate paired channels to send and receive.

As anyone who has tried to send data over GSM knows, the achievable rate is a tiny fraction of the maximum 270.8 kbps. The main reason is that, like other TDMA systems, GSM divides the channels into a number of time slots, in this case, eight. Each phone transmits and receives for only one-eighth of the time, reducing the data rate by the same factor, to about 33.9 kbps.

Some of this capacity is effectively wasted. It's left empty to counteract *propagation delay*, the time taken for a signal to travel from a base station to a mobile phone. At the speed of light, radio signals take just over 3.3 μs to travel 1 km, which adds up to delay of around 100 μs for a phone just 30 km (20 miles) from the base station. Each of the time slots lasts only 577 μs, so this delay is enough to make around 27% of the slot unusable.

Each 577-μs slot has room for exactly 156.25 bits, arranged in the structure illustrated at the bottom of Figure 4.1. Each bit can be allocated to four different uses, whose proportions are shown in Table 4.4.

Table 4.4   *Use of Bits in GSM Slot*

Data Type	Bits in Slot	Equivalent Data Rate	Proportion of Total
Head and Tail	14.25	3.1 kbps	9.1%
Training	26	5.6 kbps	16.6%
Stealing	2	0.5 kbps	1.3%
Traffic	114	24.7 kbps	73%

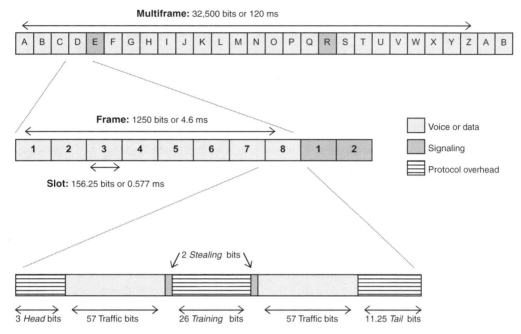

Figure 4.1
GSM slot, frame, and multiframe structure.

- The *header* and *footer* are empty spaces at the beginning and end of the slot. They serve to separate a slot from its neighbors, negating propagation delay at any distance up to 35 km from the base station. Beyond this limit, GSM phones cannot be used, even if a clear signal is available.

- The *training sequence* is a fixed pattern in the middle of the slot. It is used to help a receiver lock on to the slot but does not carry any useful information. It also acts as a header and footer if the slot is further divided, as happens when a half-rate voice codec is used.

- The two *stealing* bits identify whether the slot is used to carry actual data or control information. The name comes from the perception that the slot is being "stolen" from a call for use by the GSM system itself.

- The *traffic* bits are available for other uses, which include control information and error correction, as well as actual speech and data. In a typical GSM system, this payload is 24.7 kbps.

A complete cycle of eight time slots is known as a *frame*, illustrated in the center of Figure 4.1. Not all frames are open to the user; for every 24 that carry voice or data, one needs to be "stolen" for signaling and another reserved for other types of traffic, such as short text messages or *Caller Line Identification* (CLI, the service that displays a caller's number on the phone's screen). This means that another unit of structure is needed, known as a *multiframe*. Each contains 26 frames, labeled *A* to *Z* in Figure 4.1. The two "stolen" frames are *E* and *R* in the diagram, but each of these move on by one every multiframe to help with timing.

Signaling reduces the total capacity per user to 22.4 kbps, but even that is more than the user will ever see. Forward error correction (FEC) and encryption reduce the data rate by at least another third, though the precise amount depends on how the phone and network encode voice and data. GSM originally used a voice codec which required 13 kbps, producing what was then (1982) considered high-quality voice. Advances in microelectronics allowed phones to be developed with a half-rate voice codec. This halves the bandwidth required per call, thus doubling the capacity, with a slight decrease in quality. Data cannot take advantage of half-rate codecs, which is one reason why some operators charge more for data than for voice calls.

There is also an *enhanced full-rate* codec, which uses the same bit rate as the regular full-rate but provides better quality. Most phones and networks now support all three codecs, though because of the lower quality of half-rate, they usually don't advertise it. Some operators use the enhanced codec as a standard but drop down to half-rate if the network becomes busy. Others offer the enhanced rate to specific customers, usually those paying higher tariffs, while giving a discount to people who will accept the slightly lower quality of half-rate.

The earliest schemes for sending data over GSM actually had to route it through the full-rate codec, at a rate of only 9.6 kbps. An enhancement, not supported by all phones or networks, bypasses the codec entirely and pushes it to 14.4 kbps. This rate is higher than the output of the voice codec because data can miss some of the error correction; it's actually more tolerant of errors than highly compressed voice because it doesn't matter in which order packets arrive. The full range of codes is shown in Tabl e4.5.

FEC anticipates that errors will occur and tries to preempt them by sending extra correction code. Most data protocols, including those of the Internet, take a different approach: They wait to see whether errors actually happen, then ask for garbled information to be sent again. Users of these protocols can omit FEC entirely, for a raw data rate of 21.4 kbps. Salespeople sometimes quote this as a realistic capacity, which is misleading—some errors will still creep in, requiring retransmission that pushes down the effective speed.

Table 4.5   How Capacity Is Used by GSM Codecs

	Voice			Data		
	Full-Rate	Half-Rate	Enhanced	Regular	Enhanced	Raw
Codec	13 kbps	6.5 kbps	13 kbps	9.6 kbps	14.4 kbps	21.4 kbps
FEC	8 kbps	4.0 kbps	8 kbps	11.1 kbps	6.6 kbps	0 kbps
Encryption	1.4 kbps	0.7 kbps	1.4 kbps	1.4 kbps	1.4 kbps	1.4 kbps

HSCSD

High-Speed Circuit Switched Data (HSCSD) is a very simple upgrade to GSM that gives each user more than one time slot in the multiplex. Standardized by the European Telecommunications Standards Institute (ETSI) in 1997 and first released commercially in 2000, it is the equivalent of tying two or more phone lines together and aggregating their capacity.

All HSCSD-capable networks or terminals use the enhanced data codec, so that each channel allows rates of 14.4 kbps. The standard allows up to four of these to be tied together, for a maximum of 57.6 kbps. Intermediate steps of 28.8 kbps and 43.2 kbps are also possible and actually more common. It's also possible to have asymmetric data rates; for example, three slots from the base station to the mobile and only two the other way.

The limit of four channels was not just picked at random. It would be possible to aggregate all eight channels in a time slot together, but this would have made handsets more difficult to design, and HSCSD was supposed to be a simple upgrade. With four channels, a phone never has to both transmit and receive at once; each time slot in a GSM uplink frame is paired with one "opposite" it in the corresponding downlink, as shown in Figure 4.2. Other problems with using additional channels include power consumption (by the end-user terminal) and overall capacity (of the cellular network).

Many GSM networks are already near the limit of their capacity, struggling to build new base stations to keep up with their growth in customers. Full-rate HSCSD means that each customer requires four times as much bandwidth as for a regular call, and eight times as much as a call using the half-rate codec. Most people are unwilling to pay four or eight times the cost of a regular call, particularly with the perception that data should be free or cheap. For this reason, many GSM operators have decided not to deploy the system at all, instead waiting for other technologies that use bandwidth more efficiently.

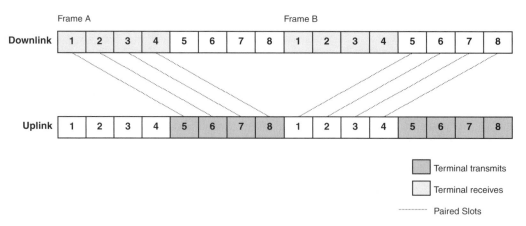

Figure 4.2
Four-slot HSCSD.

HSCSD terminal design also proved difficult. Four time slots need to transmit for four times as long as a regular GSM phone, with corresponding increases in battery drain and radiation. Aside from possible health risks, there is a more immediate problem: Early full-rate terminals are reported to have burst into flames.

Because of the overheating problem, most HSCSD devices are asymmetric, allowing greater download than upload speeds. Happily, Web browsing is a highly asymmetric application, with most data traveling from the network to the user. Unhappily, the paired spectrum system means that there is no way to reallocate the unused upstream bandwidth to downstream, meaning that some slots have to be left empty.

The only symmetric application touted so far is two-way video, long a dream of science fiction, but not popular in the real world. The British operator Orange has even developed a videophone with a built-in camera and a 28.8-kbps HSCSD terminal. It was supposed to be launched in early 2000 but was postponed for at least two years when the company was successively taken over by Mannesmann AG, Vodafone Airtouch PLC, and France Telecom SA. It is unclear whether this will ever be released commercially.

GPRS

Of all the wireless Internet schemes, General Packet Radio Service (GPRS) is the one most popular among operators. Designed for data, it promises to give every user a permanent and high-capacity connection to the Internet.

This promise may be fulfilled, but not yet and not for everyone. GPRS was envisaged as an upgrade to any TDMA-based system but, in fact, works only with GSM. The first generation of terminals supports data rates less than that of the more primitive HSCSD technology, rather than the 115.2 kbps seen in promotional literature. And it arrived late, with products announced early in 1999 that did not finally ship until late 2001.

Nevertheless, GPRS represents a major step forward in mobile networks. Its key improvement is packet switching, which for most data applications is more efficient than circuit switching. Under GSM or HSCSD, each user has to keep open a full circuit of 9.6 kbps or more for the duration of their time online, even though surfers spend more time reading Web pages than actually transferring information. This is wasteful for both the customer and the operator—one is paying call charges for an idle connection, while the other is committing spectrum that could perhaps be more profitably deployed elsewhere.

Packet switching uses bandwidth only when needed, freeing up gaps in the data stream for other users. Under GPRS, a single 14.4-kbps time slot can be shared by hundreds of people, provided that they don't all try to use it at the same time. Users have a continuous connection at a very low data rate of 0.1 kbps or less, which bursts to higher speeds when they receive e-mail or click on a hyperlink.

Because of this greater efficiency, the full specification calls for terminals capable of using all eight time slots at once. This would effectively eliminate the rigid TDMA structure, allowing each user up to 115.2 kbps. However, such speeds have so far proved elusive—GPRS suffers from the same overheating problems as HSCSD, and until they are overcome, it will have the same speed limit.

Like HSCSD, most GPRS systems are asymmetric. This is partly because of terminal design issues and user demand but also because of the way packet switching is implemented. A base station can monitor all downlink traffic and arrange it in the most efficient way possible, but a phone cannot do the same for the uplink because it does not have access to other transmissions. The result is that there is actually more capacity available downstream than upstream.

The plan is that GPRS networks will eventually carry voice over packets, using a variable-rate codec so that data can be transmitted during gaps in conversation. In the meantime, GPRS has to coexist with GSM and perhaps HSCSD, meaning that phones have to include both packet and circuit switching. Three different *grades* of GPRS handsets have been defined, corresponding to how these are supported:

- **Grade C** terminals can operate in either packet-switched or circuit-switched modes but not both at once. When a voice call is made, the otherwise permanent data connection has to be dropped.
- **Grade B** terminals can maintain a packet-switched connection while a circuit-switched call is in progress but cannot send any data over it. A customer can be notified of, for example, incoming e-mail while a call is in progress but has to hang up in order to receive it.

- **Grade A** terminals are capable of simultaneous circuit-switched and packet-switched connections. A customer can chat on the phone and surf the Web at the same time.

To make GPRS even more complicated, terminals are also divided into 29 *classes*, depending on their particular combination of slots. A full list is given in Table 4.6, which shows the maximum number of slots and their corresponding data rates. The *slot gap* is the time that the terminal takes to find a channel and frame in which it can transmit; a shorter gap will mean a lower latency.

Not all classes are capable of *full duplex* operation, which means utilizing both their full uplink and downlink capacities at once. For example, a Class 3 terminal can use up to two slots in each direction but cannot exceed a total of three. This means that if it transmits using two, it can only receive using one, and vice-versa.

The most ambitious classes are numbers 15 through 18, because these require a terminal that can transmit and receive on two time slots simultaneously. One of these would essentially need to include two radios, one for transmission and another for reception. Only a Class 18 terminal would fulfill GPRS's promised data rate of 115 kbps in both directions.

In addition to new terminals, GPRS requires extensive new investment by operators; they need to build an entirely new backbone network, replacing the existing telephone system with one more similar to the Internet. However, this can be reused for 3G technologies, most of which are based entirely on packet switching.

Table 4.6   Data Capacities of GPRS Terminal Classes

Slot Class	Maximum Time Slots			Slot Gap	Capacity (kbps)		Full Duplex	Networks
	Up	Down	Total		Up	Down		
1	1	1	2	3	14.4	14.4	Yes	GSM, GPRS
2	2	1	3	3	28.8	14.4	Yes	HSCSD, GPRS
3	2	2	3	3	28.8	28.8	No	HSCSD, GPRS
4	3	1	4	3	43.2	14.4	Yes	HSCSD, GPRS
5	2	2	4	3	28.8	28.8	Yes	HSCSD, GPRS
6	3	2	4	3	43.2	28.8	No	HSCSD, GPRS
7	3	3	4	3	43.2	43.2	No	HSCSD, GPRS
8	4	1	5	3	57.6	14.4	Yes	HSCSD, GPRS

Table 4.6 Data Capacities of GPRS Terminal Classes (Continued)

Slot Class	Maximum Time Slots			Slot Gap	Capacity (kbps)		Full Duplex	Networks
	Up	Down	Total		Up	Down		
9	3	2	5	3	43.2	28.8	Yes	HSCSD, GPRS
10	4	2	5	3	57.6	28.8	No	HSCSD, GPRS
11	4	3	5	3	57.6	43.2	No	HSCSD, GPRS
12	4	4	5	2	57.6	57.6	No	HSCSD, GPRS
13	3	3	6	1	43.2	43.2	Yes	HSCSD, GPRS
14	4	4	8	1	57.6	57.6	Yes	HSCSD, GPRS
15	5	5	10	1	72	72	Yes	GPRS
16	6	6	12	1	86.4	86.4	Yes	GPRS
17	7	7	14	1	100.8	100.8	Yes	GPRS
18	8	8	16	0	115.2	115.2	Yes	GPRS
19	6	2	8	3	86.4	28.8	Yes	GPRS
20	6	3	8	3	86.4	43.2	No	GPRS
21	6	4	8	3	86.4	57.6	No	GPRS
22	6	4	8	2	86.4	57.6	No	GPRS
23	6	6	8	2	86.4	86.4	No	GPRS
24	8	2	8	3	115.2	28.8	No	GPRS
25	8	3	8	3	115.2	43.2	No	GPRS
26	8	4	8	3	115.2	57.6	No	GPRS
27	8	4	8	2	115.2	57.6	No	GPRS
28	8	6	8	2	115.2	86.4	No	GPRS
29	8	8	8	2	115.2	115.2	No	GPRS

GPRS OR HSCSD?

There's a lot of misinformation about GPRS and HSCSD, and not all is due to misleading sales pitches from vendors. Many press reports have focused on the idea of a conflict between the two systems, implying that they are incompatible or even that vendors and users will have to choose one or the other.

In reality, the systems are very similar and entirely compatible with each other. All GSM operators plan at some point to upgrade to GPRS, and the only choice they have to make is whether to bother with HSCSD in the meantime. HSCSD is very easy to deploy, so this is really just a question of whether they have enough capacity to give every user several dedicated time slots.

GSM, GPRS, and HSCSD can all coexist in a single network, and the terminal will also be backward-compatible for roaming purposes. For example, if Class 18 (eight-slot) GPRS terminals are ever produced, users will be able to drop down to four-slot operation when roaming on HSCSD and one slot while on GSM networks.

Some GPRS operators that claim not to support HSCSD may, in fact, do so for roamers but not for their own subscribers. This is because operators usually subsidize the cost of handsets to their subscribers, so have some control over what technology they use. Similar policies are already in force covering half-rate codecs in regular GSM; operators have put their own customers on the more efficient system but still allow connections at full-rate when necessary.

D-AMPS

As the name implies, Digital AMPS is designed to be compatible with the older analog AMPS technology, which is widely deployed in the United States. It uses the same 30-MHz frequency channels as AMPS but divides each one up into three TDMA slots, so is often known simply as *TDMA*. Some people also refer to the same system as *ADC* (American Digital Cellular), *NADC* (North American Digital Cellular), *USDC* (U.S. Digital Cellular), or by the name of one of the standards that govern it, *IS-54* and *ANSI-136*.

D-AMPS uses the same paired spectrum and structure as regular AMPS, described fully in Chapter 3, "Cellular Networks" (see Table 3.1). The difference is that, instead of sending a single FM radio transmission over a 30-MHz channel, it allows each one to be used by three simultaneous conversions. Operators of AMPS networks can selectively allocate channels to either digital or analog, allowing the two systems to coexist.

The modulation scheme is called *DQPSK* (differential quadrature phase shift keying) and is even more complicated than GSM's. It also requires more power than GMSK, resulting in shorter battery life and higher radiation, but is about 20% more spectrally efficient. The resultant raw data rate is 48.6 kbps, shared between three users. Each occupies the channel for one-third of the time, giving each one 16.2 kbps.

Time slots last 6.67 μs, more than 10 times longer than GSM's. These bigger slots have room for signaling information, allowing the original IS-54 specification to mandate no separate signaling frames. However, the later ANSI-136 standard added a hyperframe structure similar to GSM's, allowing advanced services such as text messages to be transmitted in one or more frames.

The complete D-AMPS hyperframe, frame, and slot structure is illustrated in Figure 4.3. It looks more complicated than GSM, because the uplink and downlink slots have a slightly different internal arrangement of bits. However, the data rates in each are the same. As Table 4.7 shows, more than 80% of each slot can be used for traffic, which compares well to GSM's 73%. The greater efficiency is achieved by using longer slots, which waste proportionately fewer bits on training and tail sequences.

Table 4.7   Use of Bits in D-AMPS Slot

Data Type	Bits in Slot	Equivalent Data Rate	Proportion of Total
Tail	12	0.6 kbps	3.7%
Training	28	1.4 kbps	8.7%
Control	24	1.2 kbps	7.4%
Traffic	260	13 kbps	80.2%

The uplink slot may seem unnecessarily complicated, with traffic carried in three separate sequences. The reason for this is that when the half-rate codec is used, extra bits are needed for signaling. Under the half-rate scheme, the small 16-bit sequence is used instead for control data, while the larger 122-bit sequences each go to a user. To allow for the extra signaling, the half-rate codec actually codes at *less* than half the full rate.

D-AMPS's transmission speeds are listed in Table 4.8. As with some versions of GSM, data has access to higher capacity than the output of the voice codec because it requires less error correction. However, the total capacity is less than GSM, meaning that voice has noticeably poorer quality.

Table 4.8   D-AMPS Codecs

	Full-Rate Voice	Half-Rate Voice	Data
Codec	7.95 kbps	3.73 kbps	9.6 kbps
FEC	5.05 kbps	2.37 kbps	3.4 kbps

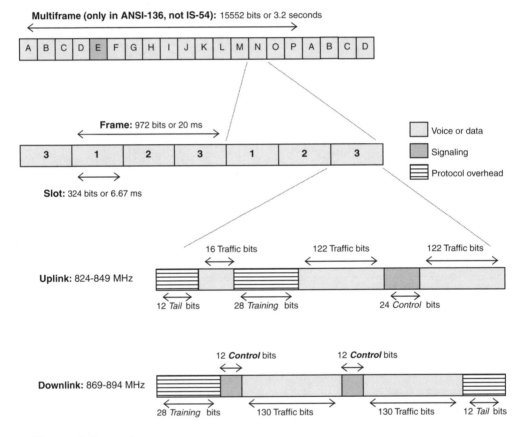

Figure 4.3
D-AMPS (ANSI-136) slot, frame, and multiframe structure.

PDC/JDC

Japan uses a system based on D-AMPS but designed for backward compatibility with its own J-TACS analog system. This is known as *PDC* (Personal Digital Cellular), or sometimes *JDC* (Japanese Digital Cellular). Despite being limited to just one country, it is the world's second most popular mobile standard (behind GSM), thanks in part to the wireless Internet service *i-mode*.

J-TACS used channels of only 25 MHz, which means that some changes were needed to the D-AMPS system designed for 30 MHz. The same size time slots and modulation are used, resulting in a lower overall bit rate. However, the D-AMPS voice codecs and data rate of 9.6 kbps can still be achieved, by omitting some of the error correction and protocol overhead. This makes the system less reliable, a problem overcome by keeping cells small so that every user has a relatively clear link to the base station. Table 4.9 shows how PDC differs from D-AMPS and GSM.

Japan is much more crowded than the United States, so small cells are not a problem—operators want to make cells as small as possible to provide the highest density coverage. However, interference and handover problems put a minimum practical limit on the cell size of any system, which meant that PDC had already run out of capacity by 2000. To counter this, operators introduced packet switching to use the existing capacity more efficiently.

PDC's early packet-switching enabled Japanese operator NTT DoCoMo to deploy i-mode, the first wireless Web service on a cell phone. Using the regular 9.6 kbps or slower data connection, it provides access to thousands of Web sites specially adapted to fit onto the phone's small screen.

Not coincidentally, the only other wireless Web services to become really successful so far are also Japanese and based on packet-switched PDC. By the end of 2001, J-Phone's J-Sky and KDD's EZweb each had about 8 million subscribers—far less than i-mode's 30 million, but still the kind of number that non-Japanese operators only see in projections from the most bullish analysts.

Table 4.9   PDC Compared with Other TDMA Technologies

System	Channel	Slots	Slot Length	Bits/ Slot	Modulation	Raw Bit Rate	Data Capacity
GSM	200 MHz	8	0.577 ms	156.25	GMSK	33.9 kbps	14.4 kbps
D-AMPS	30 MHz	3	6.67 ms	324	DQPSK	16.2 kbps	9.6 kbps
PDC	25 MHz	3	6.67 ms	290	DQPSK	14 kbps	9.6 kbps

D-AMPS+

GPRS's designers hoped that it could be applied to *every* TDMA-based system, including D-AMPS and PDC. The principle is simple: Use more slots in the multiplex, increasing capacity until a single user has the entire channel all of the time.

GSM has eight time slots, so it theoretically allows data capacity to be multiplied by a factor of eight. Unfortunately, D-AMPS has only three, and each of these already offers a data rate of only 9.6 kbps, compared with GSM's 14.4 kbps. The result is that the maximum capacity, even if all slots are used, is only 28.8 kbps (3 x 9.6), a long way from the 115.2 kbps hyped by GPRS enthusiasts.

Yet another problem is that, to achieve even this rate, terminals need to be able to transmit and receive at the same time. A standard D-AMPS phone transmits for one-third of the time, receives for another third (on a different frequency), and is idle for the remaining third. Without simultaneous transmit and receive, there is only one spare time slot (compared with six in GSM), limiting speeds to only 19.2 kbps in one direction and 9.6 kbps in the other.

Nevertheless, a scaled-down version of GPRS was marketed by some vendors in the United States under the name *D-AMPS+*. Japanese operators immediately chose not to apply it to PDC because they already have so many users that there is no spare capacity. Instead, Japan has accelerated its plans to deploy third-generation (3G) systems based on the European version of CDMA. After trials, U.S. operators decided not to apply it, either. Instead, they're ripping out their D-AMPS networks and replacing them with GSM or real GPRS.

cdmaOne

The only twentieth-century system to use CDMA is *cdmaOne*, developed by Qualcomm but now supervised by an independent organization called the *CDMA Development Group* (CDG). It has been standardized by the Telecommunications Industry Association (TIA) as *IS-95a*.

CDMA systems seem superficially simpler than those based on TDMA. They involve no slot or frame structure; every phone just transmits and receives all the time, sending many duplicates of the same information to ensure that at least one gets through.

As explained in Chapter 3, "Cellular Networks," the number of duplicates is known as the *gain* and depends on both the channel bandwidth and the length of the code used. cdmaOne uses the *Walsh* codes, a set of 64 numbers, each 64-bits long, that have been calculated to cancel each other out. Each user has a different Walsh code, by which every bit of data is multiplied before it is sent. Thus, every bit is effectively sent 64 times: The raw speed per user on the downlink is 19.2 kbps, but the phone is listening to 1,228.8 kbps (64 x 19.2).

The very high transmission rate is achieved by using two different phase modulation techniques, QPSK on the downlink and offset quadrature phase shift keying (OQPSK) on the uplink. The second type requires more FEC, necessary because individual phones cannot coordinate their transmissions in the same way that base stations can. The extra correction means that the raw uplink data rate per user is higher, 28.8 kbps.

The uses of the 19.2 kbps are shown in Table 4.10. The codec is similar to GSM's, producing the same high-quality (for a cell phone) voice. Note that, although the system may appear to be asymmetric in favor of the uplink, it isn't; all of this extra capacity is needed for error correction.

Table 4.10   cdmaOne Codecs

	Voice	Data
Codec	13 kbps	14.4 kbps
FEC (Uplink)	15.8 kbps	14.4 kbps
FEC (Downlink)	6.2 kbps	4.8 kbps

Sending every bit 64 times may seem incredibly wasteful. However, the same channel can be used by several different phones and by every base station. This means that adjacent cells can use the same frequencies, unlike FDMA and TDMA systems. This alone makes CDMA very efficient in terms of spectrum, as an operator's entire allocation can be used by each cell.

Because there are 64 codes, up to 64 users could theoretically share each channel. Unfortunately, this doesn't yet work in practice, and real cdmaOne systems typically fit between 10 and 20 users on a channel. Even this is slightly more efficient than other systems, and the prospect of increased efficiency in the future is real.

One big disadvantage of CDMA systems is their power consumption. By transmitting everything 64 times, a cdmaOne phone would seem to drain its battery 64 times faster than necessary—and bathe its user with 64 times as much microwave radiation. It gets around this problem by carefully controlling the transmission power. Every phone has to be as quiet as possible, with the allowed power increasing steadily for phones moving further away from the base station. The aim is to ensure that the signal strength at the base station is the same for every user, assuring that all can be heard equally.

Base stations also have to synchronize their transmissions accurately to prevent too much interference—unlike TDMA, every cell is using every frequency. They do this using signals from Global Positioning System (GPS) satellites, which can pinpoint any location on Earth to within 5 m and measure time more accurately than the Earth's own rotation. Receivers for the GPS signal are built into every base station, and the distance of each phone is calculated by measuring the time it takes for a radio signal to travel there and back from the base station. This is a less sophisticated version of the systems used by location technology.

There are technically two different versions of the cdmaOne standard, listed in Table 4.11. The only difference is the frequency that they are designed for and, thus, how large the cells can be. The two different versions are needed because of the precise timing requirements, which make CDMA very sensitive to differences in cell size.

Table 4.11   cdmaOne Versions

Version Name	Uplink Frequency	Downlink Frequency	Cell Size	Competition
TIA/EIA/IS-95A	824–849 MHz	869–894 MHz	Bigger	(D-)AMPS
ANSI J-STD-008	1,850–1,910 MHz	1,930–1,990 MHz	Smaller	GSM

cdmaTwo

Phones based on cdmaOne already transmit and receive simultaneously and at very high data rates. Most of this data is redundant, but it doesn't have to be. A phone could use more than one of the available Walsh codes, multiplying its 16-kbps capacity by any factor up to the number of calls per channel. The theoretical maximum is 64, pushing speeds up to more than 1 Mbps. This may not be possible in reality, but the practical maximum of about 15 codes still gives a respectable data rate of 240 kbps.

Unfortunately, a lack of operator capacity and problems with electronics in phones have so far made these high rates unattainable, but cdmaOne does have another upgrade that provides speeds similar to those of GPRS and HSCSD. Known as *IS-95b*, or occasionally cdmaTwo, it uses four Walsh codes to produce a total bit rate of 64kbps. Operators can deploy it with a simple software upgrade, though their customers have to buy new phones.

IS-95b doesn't mark the end of cdmaOne evolution. The prospect of 15 or more codes is tantalizing, and vendors have touted several rival schemes to achieve megabit speeds. Many operators are even going straight to these, skipping IS-95b. They are discussed further in Chapter 5, "Third-Generation Standards," along with upgrades that add CDMA technology to GSM.

GTE Airfone

Most airliners now include a pay phone in every row of seats, usually part of GTE's *Airfone* system. As well as voice communication, these usually allow data transfer at up to 9.6 kbps, usually promoted as a way to check for urgent e-mail. Frequent fliers can even have their cell phone numbers temporarily rerouted to the in-flight phone, but this option isn't yet popular, due to the high charges. Making or receiving a voice call often costs several dollars per minute, with slightly lower costs for data.

Over most of the world, these phones work by relaying signals via satellite, usually Inmarsat or Globalstar. However, North America is such a large market for air travel that Goeken (now GTE) has built a dedicated digital cellular network to serve aircraft. While flying over the continental United States, traffic is instead routed via the ground. This is slightly faster than satellite transmission, as well as cheaper.

The Airfone network uses cells with a radius of about 300 km (200 miles), each of which covers at least a hundred times the area of even the largest GSM cell. It can get away with such big cells because its users are very spread out, and because there is no signal blocking or multipath interference: A jet flying in the stratosphere is in view of almost every point on the ground. The antennas mounted on the outside of planes can also transmit at a higher power than those on a regular cell phone because they aren't battery powered or hand held. The large cells allow the Airfone network to cover the 48 contiguous U.S. states, all of Mexico and much of Canada, using only 135 base stations, compared with the many thousands needed by other systems.

Many people would prefer to use their own cell phones on planes, but airlines and regulators are very much against this. Current Federal Aviation Administration (FAA) rules let passengers make calls only while their plane is docked at a terminal gate. They must switch off once the doors are closed. Similar regulations apply abroad and in international airspace, though no cell phone will work over the oceans, anyway.

Some airlines *do* allow receive-only radios, such as pagers and GPS devices. (These work only in a window seat because the GPS signal is able to pass through glass but not metal.) Others ban electronic gadgets entirely in the name of security. This is probably going too far, but cell phones and other devices certainly need to be X-rayed. Many U.S. airports started this only after the hijackings of September 2001, even though police in the United Kingdom had intercepted guns disguised as cell phones more than a year earlier.

Contrary to popular belief, in-flight cell phone use was not originally banned because it interferes with navigation systems (though it may do this). It was banned because a phone at high altitudes will be in view of many base stations and try to connect with all at once, as shown in Figure 4.4. (The cells used in the Airfone network are so large that the plane is usually in view of only one.) On older cellular standards, including GSM, this risks overloading the network and preventing other users from getting through. Newer

CDMA-based systems are designed to maintain multiple simultaneous connections, so this reasoning no longer applies, but airlines will still cite safety fears—partly out of legitimate concern and partly because they like the revenue from the pay phones.

Legal systems tend to agree with the airlines about safety fears, and have been willing to find in-flight cellular users guilty of endangering an aircraft. In 1999, a British court punished a man with a year in jail simply for trying to send a text message from his cell phone during landing. In 2001, a Saudi court sentenced another man to 70 lashes for the same offense during takeoff.

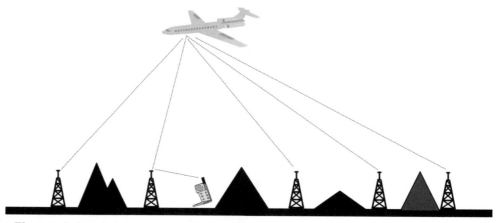

Figure 4.4
More base stations are visible from high altitudes than on the ground.

PACKET DATA SYSTEMS......................................

Although Internet access via a mobile phone is hyped, there are already several data-only cellular systems. Though none offer the capacity needed for full-scale Web surfing, they are used for simple messaging and telemetry applications.

The best known data systems are *pagers*, which have traditionally carried information in only one direction. The first were known as *numeric* because they handled only the digits 0 through 9. They were intended to be used for phone numbers, the idea being that someone who was paged could find a pay phone and call the number. Modern pagers are nearly all *alphanumeric*, meaning that, in addition to numbers, they can display letters of the alphabet, and some include many different character sets.

Pagers are beginning to incorporate a return link, enabling them to be used for real interactive applications. These two-way systems are known collectively as *narrowband PCS* because they require less spectrum than the voice networks. For data, their great advantage is that they are always on, meaning that users are not billed for time spent connected. Customers either pay a flat monthly rate or are billed per KB.

With the exception of Ricochet, none of these systems, summarized in Table 4.12, are able to provide dedicated capacity to a single user. The data capacity is shared between all users in a cell, which can be very large, because they tend to operate at lower frequencies.

Table 4.12   *Paging and Narrowband PCS Systems*

System	Downstream	Upstream	Round-Trip Latency
POCSAG	2.4 kbps per cell	0	N/A
ERMES	6.4 kbps per cell	0	N/A
Flex	6.4 kbps per cell	0	N/A
ReFlex	9.6 kbps per cell	6.4 kbps per cell	5 seconds
CDPD	19.2 kbps per cell	9.6 kbps per cell	2 seconds
Mobitex	8.0 kbps per cell	8.0 kbps per cell	4 seconds
DataTAC	19.2 kbps per cell	19.2 kbps per cell	6 seconds
Ricochet (MCDN)	128 kbps per user	128 kbps per user	5 seconds

Paging

With the growth of mobile phones and wireless data, paging often seems an endangered industry. The European Public Paging Association says that around 3% of all Europeans carry a pager, compared with more than 10 times that number who have a cell phone.

Nonetheless, pager subscriber numbers are still growing in most countries, and the technology does have some advantages. Most important, pagers are cheap, both to buy and to own. Callers make a short call to a premium rate number, resulting in no cost to the person being paged. Pagers themselves are usually smaller and lighter than voice telephones. Coverage is also better, because paging systems tend to use lower frequencies, which allow a much larger cell size, and because the networks are well established.

In America, paging has been given a new lease on life, thanks to two-way systems. These allow it to compete with the more advanced packet-switched systems, targeting both businesses and consumers with devices like the Blackberry. Two-way systems are less developed or absent entirely in other parts of the world, thanks to regulatory issues. They need paired spectrum, which the FCC was relatively quick to license. European countries were not, and many still have no band allocated to the pager uplink.

Many different paging systems have been developed. Among the most common:

- **POCSAG** is named after the Post Office Code Standardization Advisory Group, a British project set up to design a paging standard in 1982. It was later adopted by ETSI, then by operators throughout the world, but it has been replaced in many areas with more advanced systems.
- **ERMES** (European Radio Message System) was defined by ETSI in 1992. Though developed for use in Europe, it was intended to be installed internationally and has partly succeeded. The ITU has adopted it as the recommended paging standard, and it has been deployed in parts of Asia. To promote international use, it allows paging in up to 32 different character sets. Its other innovation is multicast paging: A single message can be sent to everyone in a predefined group.
- **Flex** was invented by Motorola and is the most popular paging system in America. It later extended the system to **ReFlex**, a two-way system designed for short text messages. Motorola itself stopped producing equipment for ReFlex (and Flex) in 2001, but other companies have licensed the technology.

CDPD

Cellular Digital Packet Data (CDPD) is a simple packet-switched overlay to AMPS and D-AMPS cellular networks. It uses a single channel in each cell for data, with a maximum capacity of 19.2 kbps down and 9.6 kbps up, the same as the ill-fated D-AMPS+. It's used in the United States, China, and some parts of South America.

Though seemingly faster than regular D-AMPS, the fact that this capacity is shared between all users in a cell makes the throughput available to an individual user much lower. Some operators have begun to address this problem by allocating more channels, so that the total capacity per cell is higher. However, each user can still access only one channel at a time, so the maximum data rates remain the same.

Because CDPD is packet-switched, it's usually cheaper than circuit-switched D-AMPS, though can still result in high bills when charged on a per-packet basis. But as 2.5G and 3G technologies appear, operators have lowered the cost of unlimited CDPD access to the point where it is viable for many messaging applications. In a span of only five months during 2001, one company reduced its flat rate plan from $200 to $40.

CDPD can be used in virtually all major cities in the United States and Canada and is the only way of sending data through an analog AMPS network. Terminals are usually inside PC cards designed for laptop computer users, but sometimes they are also built into AMPS or D-AMPS phones, which use the system for sending brief text messages.

Mobitex

This system was developed by Ericsson and intended for telemetry applications, such as monitoring the location of delivery trucks or remote meter reading. Its data rate of 8 kbps is fairly slow, and the time taken to process data creates a long round-trip delay. However, it does offer very good coverage, both in the United States and abroad.

Most Mobitex networks worldwide are operated by Cingular Wireless (formerly Bell South) or by its subsidiary, RAM Mobile Data. Cingular also runs a nationwide cellular network in the United States, based on a combination of D-AMPS and GSM. This is often confused with Mobitex, but the two are entirely separate.

Mobitex operators traditionally sold telemetry services directly to businesses, mostly for telemetry applications. In 1988, Palm Computing realized that it would make an ideal low-speed Internet access technology. (Palm chose Mobitex over CDPD because of its wider coverage.) It began selling the Palm VII, a Palm device with an integrated Mobitex terminal, which proved very successful, despite low speeds and high charges. Many Palm devices still include Mobitex, but these work only in the United States because every country's version of Mobitex uses different spectrum. International versions are based on GPRS.

Like CDPD, Mobitex has become cheaper as other technologies promise higher data rates. Where customers previously had to pay per byte, flat rate plans are now available for under $40.

DataTAC

Better known under the brand name *Ardis*, DataTAC was originally developed by Motorola and IBM. It differs from the other systems in that it is connection-oriented, meaning that the network contacts the pager and waits for a reply before sending any data. This should make it more reliable but also increases latency. Two versions exist and have been deploye din many countries worldwide:

- **MDC4800** (Mobile Data Communication) was the original standard, running at 4.8 kbps
- **RD-LAP** (Radio Data Link Access Protocol) is backward-compatible with MDC4800 but increases the speed to 19.2 kbps

The largest DataTAC operator is Motient, which covers most of the United States. Its network was used by the original version of the Blackberry, a two-way pager that includes a tiny keyboard so users can actually type messages. Later, versions were produced for Mobitex and GPRS.

Ricochet

The *Microcellular Data Network* (MCDN) was invented by the U.S. company Metricom, which operated it under the brand name *Ricochet*. It offered far higher speeds than any other data-only technology, because it was designed specifically for Internet access. Unfortunately, the network cost so much to construct and the company was so poorly managed that Metricom declared bankruptcy less than a year after it entered service.

This doesn't mean that the system is dead. Though it couldn't make money for Metricom, the Ricochet network was still a great technical achievement, actually providing substantially *higher* speeds than the dial-up modems still used by most Web surfers. It gave customers an average throughput of about 100 kbps—not much by the standards of 3G hype but a lot more than anything else actually available around 2000, especially in the backward United States. It even worked while moving at up to 100 kilometers per hour (70 miles per hour) on a train or in a car, though usually at a reduced throughput.

MCDN's high capacity was achieved by using tiny cells of radius no more than 500 m. It needed hundreds of small base stations in every town, known as *poletops* because they were often mounted on top of lampposts. Building these proved to be more expensive than the company had calculated: As well as the cost of building and installing each one, Metricom needed to negotiate with the municipal authority that controlled the street lights in every town, and sometimes many different private land-lords too. These negotiations often resulted in Metricom paying more rent for the right to build its network than it received in revenue from customers.

Pricing was the system's other great weakness. Because it was so innovative and cost so much to build, Metricom positioned Ricochet as a very high-end business service. Every customer had to pay between $70 and $80 a month, for which each got unlimited Internet access. This was actually a lot cheaper than many of the per-packet technologies, such as CDPD, but it was still too much for most users to commit themselves to. Businesses ordered it for only their highest level executives, not everyone who needed to access the Web outside of the office.

Near the end, Metricom did announce a lower cost version of the service, aimed at home users. For about half the cost, they were given a maximum throughput of "only" 64 kbps and were limited to just one city. This did prove more successful, but it didn't attract the huge number of customers needed to save the company. It collapsed in August 2001, leaving behind debts of more than $1 billion and cutting off just 40,000 customers (less than NTT DoCoMo's i-mode service signs up in a day).

Shortly after the system was switched off, the City of New York temporarily reactivated part of it. Ricochet's distributed architecture had proved more resistant to the September 2001 terrorist attack than did most other communications networks, allowing rescue workers and cleanup workers at the World Trade Center site to communicate. A few months later, parts of the system were bought by Aerie Networks, a fiberoptics company that planned to reactivate it.

Because the new owners paid a lot less for the system than Metricom paid to build it, Aerie may be able to operate it profitably. However, there are still difficulties. Aerie did not buy most of poletops themselves, because ownership reverted to the landlords or local governments on whose property they were installed.

Most other countries are smaller and more densely populated than the United States, so Metricom once had great plans to expand Ricochet into Europe and Asia. Those plans have now been put on hold, along with plans for additional U.S. coverage. There are also problems with spectrum availability: The present system uses a mixture of licensed and unlicensed bands, which are not all available outside of North America. In particular, it needs frequencies in the 900-MHz region, which are unlicensed in the United States but used in Europe and many other parts of the world for GSM. A Ricochet system in Europe would need to be adapted for different unlicensed frequencies.

PRIVATE MOBILE RADIO ....

Private Mobile Radio (PMR) systems were once separate from the public network, used only to communicate between closed groups of people. They existed before mobile phones became widespread and were used by people for whom radio communication is absolutely critical. The main users included emergency services, public utilities, and taxi companies.

With the arrival of cell phones, private mobile radio has become less private. Although groups such as the police still operate their own networks, third-party providers have begun to offer services that interconnect to the public network and compete directly with cellular. Marketed at all kinds of businesses and even consumers, these publicly available PMR systems are sometimes known as *PAM* (Private Access Mobile Radio) or *SMR* (Specialized Mobile Radio).

There are two main types of digital PMR, both of which are used in public and private systems worldwide. Called TETRA and iDEN, they have many similarities with each other and with GSM, on which they are loosely based. Both use TDMA technology and paired spectrum, and both have all the usual cell phone features, such as voice and short data messages. They add the ability to provide extra services, most importantly:

- Group calling, which sets up conference calls to predefined groups at the press of a button
- Phone-to-phone mode, where two phones communicate without a base station
- Instant call setup for voice and data, similar to ISDN on the fixed network
- Prioritization, so that certain calls are dropped in favor of others if the network becomes overcrowded

PMR systems also tend to have greater spectral efficiency, though at the cost of reduced quality. This is because call quality is generally considered less important to groups such as the military than to most business and personal customers. Table 4.13 shows how TETRA and iDEN differ.

Table 4.13   TETRA and iDEN Compared

System	TETRA	iDEN
Designer	ETSI	Motorola
Channel bandwidth	25 kHz	25 kHz
TDMA slot length	14.17 ms	15.0 ms
Calls (TDMA slots) per channel	4	6
Maximum data rate per channel	36 kbps	64 kbps
Modulation	D-QPSK	QAM
Switching	Circuit	Packet and Circuit

TETRA

Originally *Trans-European Trunked Radio*, TETRA was designed by ETSI in close cooperation with Europe's police forces. As with its other standards, ETSI hoped that TETRA would eventually be deployed beyond Europe and renamed it to *Terrestrial Trunked Radio*.

Aside from the PMR services described above, TETRA's main feature is its extreme security. Although most protocols provide some way for the cellular network to authenticate the mobile phone, TETRA also requires that the network prove its identity to the phone. This was designed so that criminals would not be able to fool the police by setting up a fake network, though critics of the system say it verges on the paranoid.

Paranoia may be justified. Although other mobile systems allow operators to track a user's location, only TETRA also offers a feature called *ambient listening*. This literally turns the phone into a bug—the operator can listen into and record anything that the user is saying, even when the phone is apparently switched off. It was designed by police for hostage situations and as an antitheft measure but is understandably not widely advertised by commercial operators.

For users not interested in security or other PMR services, TETRA does have one more advantage: It uses very low frequencies, around 400 MHz, enabling large cells of up to about 100 km in radius. This means that a network can be rolled out very quickly. The largest public operator, Dolphin Telecommunications, managed to build a network across six European countries (Britain, France, Belgium, Germany, Spain, and Portugal) in little more than a year. However, TETRA's incompatibility with GSM networks made it unpopular, and the company filed for bankruptcy protection in August2001.

iDEN

The *integrated Digital Enhanced Network* is a proprietary system but a popular one. It was developed by Motorola and is operated by several companies, the best known being Nextel in the United States. (Don't confuse this with NextWave, the bankrupt operator whose spectrum others are trying to buy.) Unlike most other 2G systems, iDEN already offers packet-switching with no upgrade necessary.

The real throughput of an iDEN packet network is about 20 kbps. That isn't much compared with the claims made for GPRS, but it is about the same as the first GPRS phones. As a result, Nextel claims that it has the first nationwide 2.5G network in the United States. So far, the only way to use this with a computer is to connect a PC to a cell phone: The system has been around since 1998, but Motorola had still not produced a data card by the end of 2001.

Though it might have been the first to 2.5G, iDEN has no upgrade path to 3G. This means that Nextel and other operators will have to replace their existing networks entirely with new 3G systems if they want to get higher data rates. Their hope is that these systems will embrace most of the extra PMR features, such as fast call setup, that are not yet available with cellular.

The one PMR feature that 3G does *not* yet include is direct phone-to-phone communication. This is a useful capability, because it means that a phone can still work even if disaster strikes the cellular network. However, modern networks are fairly reliable, so it isn't used much. It may also be added to 3G networks in the future.

WEB RESOURCES

www.gsmworld.com
The GSM Association site also covers GPRS and HSCSD.

www.gsmdata.com and **www.pcsdata.com**
Designed to aid anyone who wants to send data over digital cellular networks, these two sites contain many articles on existing and future wireless systems. The sites are run by Intel, which has an obvious interest in promoting data apps but is not tied to any particular phone technology or vendor.

www.ece.wpi.edu/courses/ee535/hwk11cd95/tara/tara.html
This site from Worcester Polytechnic Institute in Massachusetts contains a detailed description of D-AMPS. It's part of a wider online resource aimed at engineering students, covering all kinds of mostly nonwireless telecom topics.

www.cdg.org
The CDMA Development Group promotes all types of CDMA technology, including cdmaOne and future 3G systems. It also provides detailed technical and mathematical information about spread spectrum technology.

www.electricrates.com/trforum/
This is a Web forum set up to discuss all forms of PMR, including TETRA, iDEN, and APOC25.

www.tetramou.org and **www.tetraforum.org**
These sites are offered by the TETRA Memorandum of Understanding, which oversees the TETRA standard and its U.S. subsidiary, the NATF (North American TETRA Forum).

....

BIBLIOGRAPHY

Hart, Lawrence, and Roman Kirta. **CDMA IS-95 for Cellular and PCS.** Mc-Graw Hill, 1999.

An in-depth technical guide to the cdmaOne system aimed at people working in the industry.

Seybold, Andrew M. **Using Wireless Communications in Business.** Van Nostrand Reinhold, 1994.

A nontechnical guide to the data systems used in the United States, written when they were still relatively new. It's interesting to see how little things have changed over a decade.

Webb, William. **The Complete Wireless Communications Professional: A Guide for Engineers and Managers.** Artech House, 1999.

A mildly technical book that provides a good explanation of digital cellular and PMR systems, especially those used in Europe.

SUMMARY ....

- Most 2G systems, including GSM, are based on TDMA.
- CDMA is a more advanced technology but does not have the installed base of GSM. It is used as the basis for 3G systems.
- TDMA usually allows each user to transmit or receive only part of the time. The capacity available to each user can be increased by allocating more time slots.
- One-way paging systems are evolving into two-way data networks.
- Metricom's Ricochet system provided high-speed wireless Internet access but only in U.S. cities.
- PMR has moved from a niche application to a viable alternative to digital cellular. It offers faster call setup and other features, such as conference calling, though many owners of PMR terminals use them as regular cell phones.

5 Third-Generation Standards

In this chapter...

Third-generation (3G) systems are critical to the wireless Internet services often touted as the future of mobile communications. Eventually, they will offer permanent access to the Web, interactive video, and voice quality that sounds more like a CD player than a cell phone. Many of their future applications are as yet unknown, with optimistic pundits often saying that we will discover them as we go along. Pessimists say that there are *no* more applications.

The term *3G* has become rather vague, but it was originally quite specifically defined as any standard that provided mobile users with the performance of ISDN or better—at least 144 kbps. Some of the earlier 2.5G standards, such as General Packet Radio Service (GPRS) and IS-95b, might be able to do this but only under optimal conditions. Third-generation systems need to provide ISDN speeds for everyone, not just for people who are equipped with the most expensive terminals and standing next to a base station.

Technologically, the increased capacity is found in part by using extra spectrum and in part by new modulation techniques that squeeze higher data rates from a given waveband. At the very lowest level, this new modulation works by abandoning computing's traditional binary system and replacing it with a system such as *octal*, which allows every symbol to have eight values instead of only two. They also tend to be based on Code Division Multiple Access (CDMA), rather than Time Division Multiple Access (TDMA) because of its increased spectral efficiency and smoother handoff mechanism.

The arguments over 3G are a continuation of the earlier battles regarding Personal Communications Systems (PCS). Vendors, operators, and regulators all accept that the move toward higher data rates and better services will be evolutionary, as illustrated in Figure 5.1. Standards have to be backward-compatible with their predecessors so that phones can maintain a connection while moving between cells based on the old and the new.

Europe has defined a type of CDMA that will work with the Global System for Mobile Communications (GSM), which should eventually be compatible with a system already operational in Japan. Elsewhere, cdmaOne supporters are split between several upgrades known collectively as *CDMA2000*, none of which will work with the Japanese or European standard. In America, D-AMPS and GSM operators want to stick with TDMA. The result is a "federal standard," more accurately described as a fudge.

Global roaming will be possible only with special multimode phones. As shown in Table 5.1, the United States is set to have three different, incompatible 3G systems operating within its borders. These are in addition to its multiple 2G standards.

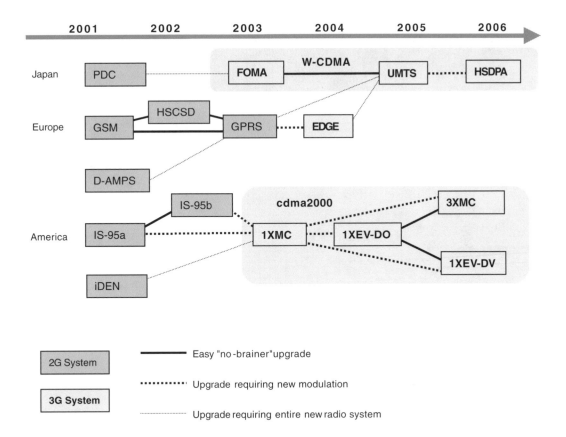

Figure 5.1
Upgrade paths to 3G.

Table 5.1   3G Plans of U.S. Service Providers

Company	Licensed Areas (Population)	Customers (at year end 2001)	2G	2.5G	3G
Verizon Wireless	90%	28 million	IS-95a (CDMA)	1×MC	1×EV
Cingular Wireless	70%	22 million	GSM and D-AMPS	GPRS	EDGE or UMTS
AT&T Wireless	98%	18 million	D-AMPS	GPRS	EDGE or UMTS

Table 5.1   3G Plans of U.S. Service Providers (Continued)

Company	Licensed Areas (Population)	Customers (at year end 2001)	2G	2.5G	3G
Sprint PCS	83%	13 million	IS-95a (CDMA)	1×MC	1×EV
Nextel Communications	77%	8 million	iDEN	iDEN	1×MC / 1×EV
Voicestream	97%	6 million	GSM	GPRS	EDGE or UMTS

IMT-2000 . . . .

Third-generation systems were first planned in 1992, when the International Tele-communications Union (ITU) realized that mobile communication was playing an increasingly important role. An international study group predicted that mobile phones would rival fixed lines within 10 years, a prediction that came true somewhat earlier in many countries. It began work on a project called *FPLMTS* (Future Public Land Mobile Telecommunications System), aiming to unite the world under a single standard.

The acronym was awkward, even compared with other telecom jargon, so the ITU soon adopted the (slightly) friendlier name *IMT-2000*. *IMT* stands for *International Mobile Telecommunications*, and the number 2000 had three meanings. It was supposed to represent:

• The year 2000, when the ITU hoped the system would become available
• Data rates of 2,000 kbps
• Frequencies in the 2,000-MHz region, which the ITU wanted to make globally available for the new technology

None of these aspirations were fulfilled entirely, but the name has stuck. Though prototypes were built in 1999, the "phones" were the size of a truck, and very limited commercial service did not start until late in 2001. The target data rate *is* achievable but only under optimal conditions.

Perhaps most important, not every country handed over the ITU's requested frequencies. Europe and many Asian countries did, but the United States has made no spectrum at all available for IMT-2000. The technology is still relevant to American operators, who will deploy it in place of their existing networks, but the lack of new bandwidth may entrench the backward position of the United States in mobile communications.

MORE THAN MOBILE?

With the more general moniker came a more general set of requirements. Whereas FPLMTS dealt only with mobile phones and mobile data, IMT-2000 was supposed to encompass everything in the wireless universe:

- IMT-2000 wireless Local Area Networks (LANs) would give users even higher data rates when they were inside their own offices or homes.

- IMT-2000 satellites would allow people to access basic voice and low-rate data services from literally anywhere on Earth, even when they moved outside an area covered by the cellular network. These are sometimes called **Mobile Satellite Service** (MSS) or **Global Mobile Personal Communications Service** (GMPCS).

- IMT-2000 fixed wireless networks would bring telecommunications to poorer countries for the first time, providing a cheaper and faster alternative to laying landlines.

The theory was that, by basing all types of wireless services on a single radio system, many people would need to carry only one device—they could use their home cordless phone as a mobile or even to make calls via satellite from the middle of the ocean. The industry would also save money, because components developed for one type of technology could easily be used for another.

Most of this vision had been abandoned by 1999, when vendors built the first prototype IMT-2000 equipment. Fixed wireless systems work best at much higher frequencies than do mobiles, while satellite phones are more expensive and much bulkier than most people are prepared to carry around. Wireless LANs are still mandated in some official standards, but they, too, seem unlikely to be implemented, because other types of wireless LAN can already reach more than 50 times IMT-2000's target data rate. The grand plan has effectively reverted to FPLMTS's original aim—a cellular network for high-speed data.

3G Defined

The ITU's original definition of IMT-2000 concerned only the data rate. Three different rates were suggested, each corresponding to a different type of ISDN, then the standard for carriers' core voice networks.

- **144 kbps** was the absolute minimum acceptable capacity. It is the same speed as a B-rate ISDN line, the type that can be deployed over ordinary telephone wires. B-rate ISDN makes up a large proportion of regular phone lines in some European countries, especially Germany. It is also marketed as a high-speed fixed Internet access technology in areas where DSL and fiber have yet to arrive.

- **384 kbps** was the ideal capacity, which the system should aim for. It corresponds to an H-rate ISDN channel, often used for videoconferencing. Though video is possible at much slower speeds, this was considered the minimum necessary for picture quality approaching that of television.

- **2 Mbps** was the capacity that should be achievable inside a building. It corresponds to a European P-rate ISDN line, which is usually a fiberoptic cable carrying up to 30 separate phone lines into an office switchboard. The idea was that small picocells could be set up in public areas, such as on trains or in airport departure lounges, giving people access to very high data rates.

These recommendations, shown in Figure 5.2, were made back in 1992, when the Internet was still not widely known outside of academic and technical circles. Politicians talked vaguely of an "information superhighway," but no one knew what form it would take. IMT-2000 was supposed to form the mobile part of this highway, complementing the interactive TV that it was assumed would reach people through cables in the ground.

As the Internet hit the public and commercial consciousness, the ITU realized that Web surfing would become one of IMT-2000's most important uses. This entailed an additional requirement: that it support the Internet protocols and be based on a packet-switched network backbone. The previously set data rates remained, but circuit-switched ISDN itself was abandoned.

Service Requirements

Just as none of 3G's 1992 founders foresaw mobile Web access, many of its ultimate applications may still not have been discovered. The great fear, unvoiced by many operators, is that it may not have any applications. However, the industry is clear

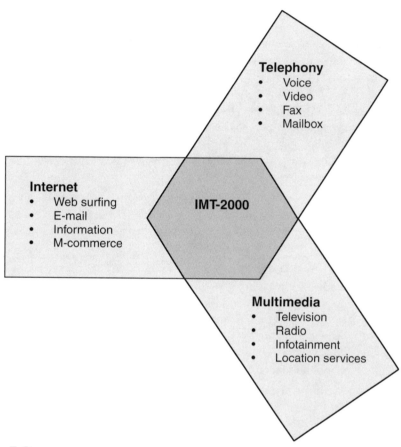

Figure 5.2
Convergence of services in IMT-2000.

about the direction in which it wants to move. The buzzword is *convergence:* Third generation aims to combine the Internet, telephones, and broadcast media into a single device.

To achieve this, IMT-2000 systems have been designed with six broad classes of service in mind. None of them are yet set in hardware; operators will be able to offer whatever data rates they can achieve, and customers will be free to buy whatever they can afford. But they are useful for regulators planning coverage and capacity, and perhaps for people buying terminals when they finally become available. It's likely that 3G devices will be rated according to the types of service they can access, from a simple phone to a powerful computer.

Three of the service classes are already present to some extent on 2G networks, and three more are new, involving mobile multimedia. In order of increasing data rate:

- **Voice.** Even in the age of high-speed data, this is still regarded as the "killer app" for the mobile market. 3G will offer call quality at least as good as the fixed telephone network, possibly with higher quality available at extra cost. Voice mail will also be standard and eventually integrated fully with e-mail through computerized voice recognition and synthesis. This category also includes enhanced (or "rich") voice services, such as conference calling, which are presently available only through Private Mobile Radio (PMR) systems.

- **Messaging.** This is an extension of paging, combined with Internet e-mail. Unlike the text-only messaging services built into some 2G systems, 3G will allow e-mail attachments. It can also be used for payment and electronic ticketing.

- **Switched Data.** This includes faxing and dial-up access to corporate networks or the Internet. With always-on connections available, dial-up access ought to be obsolete, so this is mainly included to support legacy equipment. In 3G terms, *legacy* means anything that doesn't support a fully packet-switched network. This includes many 2.5G products that are still not available. Video is also a switched application, though whether this will be a significant market is in doubt.

- **Medium Multimedia.** This is likely to be the most popular 3G service. Its downstream data rate is ideal for Web surfing, assuming that the Web has not changed beyond recognition by the time that relatively inexpensive mobile data finally becomes available. Other applications include collaborative working, games, and location-based maps.

- **High Multimedia.** This can be used for very high-speed Internet access, as well as for high-definition video and CD-quality audio on demand. Another possible application is online shopping for "intangible" products that can be delivered over the air; for example, a music single or a program for a mobile computer. As 3G's limitations have become clear, operators have warned that these types of services may have to be postponed until 4G.

- **Interactive High Multimedia.** This can be used for fairly high-quality videoconferencing or videophones, and for *telepresence*, a combination of videoconference and collaborative working. This, too, is very unlikely to be achieved under 3G alone.

The data rates of these services are shown in Table 5.2, together with their levels of asymmetry and switching types. Although three of them require circuit switching, this will eventually be accomplished via *virtual circuits,* rather than real ones. Everything is packetized, including voice, fax, and video, but packets in a virtual circuit are given priority over others. This guarantees capacity to a customer who has paid for it and frees it up for others when not in use.

Table 5.2   Service Types Available over IMT-2000

Service Classification	Upstream Data Rate	Downstream Data Rate	Asymmetry Factor	Example	Switch
Interactive multimedia	256 kbps	256 kbps	Symmetric	Videoconference	Circuit
High multimedia	20 kbps	2 Mbps	100	Television	Packet
Medium multimedia	19.2 kbps	768 kbps	40	Web Surfing	Packet
Switched data	43.2 kbps	43.2 kbps	Symmetric	Fax	Circuit
Simple messaging	28.8 kbps	28.8 kbps	Symmetric	E-mail	Packet
Speech	28.8 kbps	28.8 kbps	Symmetric	Telephony	Circuit

The classic example to show how virtual circuits are more efficient than real ones is a system that sends data during the gaps in conversation, but there are others. Most videoconference and videophone protocols send only the parts of a picture that have changed, rather than a complete new image for each frame, allowing significant bandwidth savings. A video feed of someone sitting in an unchanging room can be transmitted using very little data, though the rate rockets up as soon as the person starts moving.

At present, voice accounts for the lion's share of traffic across mobile networks, with messaging and data services small but growing fast. The Universal Mobile Telecommunications System (UMTS) Forum has carried out detailed research into customer demand and predicted that these types of traffic are likely to keep growing until around 2005. It believes that, by then, nearly everyone within the IMT-2000 service area will have a mobile phone of some kind. There will still be growth after that, but it will be accounted for mainly by multimedia. This continued growth, according to the Forum, will put serious pressure on even 3G systems. Figure 5.3 shows how new services will require additional spectrum.

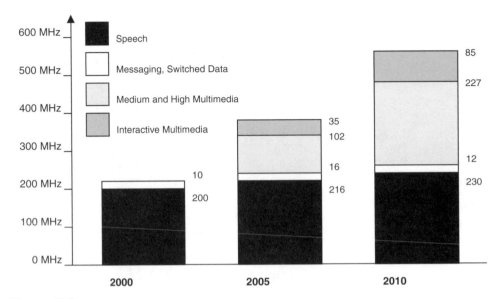

Figure 5.3
Use of spectrum by different mobile communications services.

Spectrum Requirements

In 1992, the ITU recommended that the entire world allocate the same frequencies to 3G services. This would enable easy global roaming, particularly if everyone was using the same IMT-2000 standard. No matter the location, the user could be sure that his or her mobile phone or data device would work.

Unfortunately, the only large country that actually followed the ITU's recommendation exactly was China. As shown in Figure 5.4, the Europeans and Japanese were already using part of the spectrum for cordless phones and GSM, and America had already used *all* of it for PCS or fixed wireless. The result is that U.S. carriers will need 3G networks that can be deployed gradually in place of their existing infrastructure, using spectrum originally intended for 1G or 2G.

The only part of the 3G spectrum available worldwide is that dedicated to satellite services, which, of course, has to be the same everywhere. The problem is that, although cellular 3G is only a year or two behind its original schedule, many analysts doubt that satellites capable of mobile 144-kbps operation will ever get off the ground. Broadband satellites tend to need much higher frequencies, leading many in the industry to suggest that the band now allocated to MSS be released for cellular IMT-2000. However, the Federal Communications Commission (FCC) officially licensed six 3G satellite providers in 2001. It is unlikely that all of these will actually be launched.

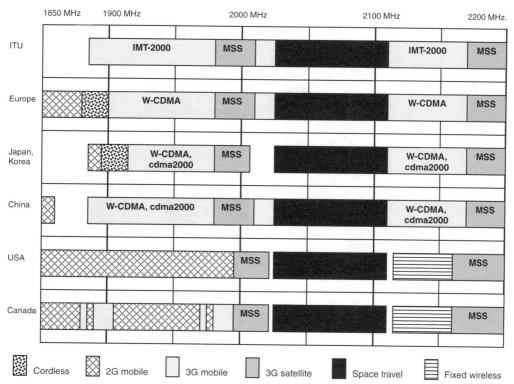

Figure 5.4
Spectrum allocation for 3G cellular and MSS in major world economies.

If analysts' predictions of mobile growth are accurate, there will certainly be a need for extra spectrum. Accepting the UMTS Forum's forecasts of traffic growth, the ITU in 2000 calculated the extra spectrum needed to accommodate it in each of the three global regions. Its results are shown in Figure 5.5, together with the spectrum already used by 1G or 2G services and that allocated to 3G.

Even assuming that existing 2G networks will eventually be upgraded to 3G, the ITU believes that at least 160 MHz more will be needed in each region before 2010. Where this spectrum will come from is not yet clear, though the ITU and various industry groups are considering several proposals. The obvious bands—around the spectrum already allocated—are not an option. They're already widely used by the likes of NASA to keep in touch with astronauts and space probes. The latter can still transmit useful information for many decades after they have been launched, so adjusting them to use different frequencies is impossible.

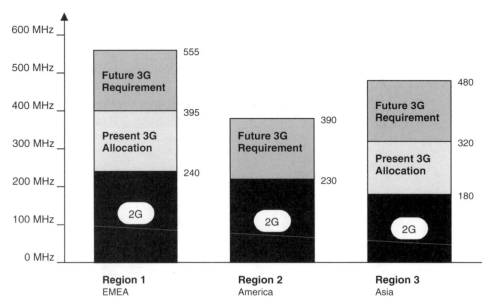

Figure 5.5
Spectrum required by cellular systems in different ITU regions.

The suggested extension bands are:

- **420–806 MHz.** Better known as *UHF*, these frequencies are used for analog TV broadcasting in most countries. They may be turned over to mobile phones when digital TV becomes ubiquitous, though this is unlikely to happen everywhere before 2010.

- **1,429–1,501 MHz.** This band is used for several different purposes worldwide, including cordless phones, fixed wireless, and broadcasting. Parts of it are unused on Earth, kept free so that scientists can listen for possible signals sent by an alien civilization.

- **1,710–1,885 MHz.** Some parts of this band are already used for mobile services in Europe and Asia, but it may provide additional capacity in America (ITU Region 2). Other parts are used worldwide for air traffic control.

- **2,290–2,300 MHz.** This very small slice of spectrum is used for fixed wireless and by radio astronomers conducting deep space research.

- **2,300–2,400 MHz.** This band is used for fixed wireless and some telemetry applications. It is fairly close to the spectrum already allocated to IMT-2000, so it is favored by many operators and regulators.

- **2,520–2,670 MHz.** Different countries use this band for different applications, usually broadcasting and fixed wireless. Some parts are also used by satellites communicating with Earth. This is the extension band favored by the UMTS Forum, and also the one selected by the FCC as the most likely candidate for 3G services in the United States. In many areas within the U.S., the spectrum has already been licensed to companies including Sprint and AT&T Wireless for fixed services, so they can simply build 3G networks instead. This pleased them, but angered rival companies and customers of the fixed services. In January 2002, AT&T Wireless shut down its fixed service to make way for 3G.

- **2,700–3,400 MHz.** Frequencies above 2.7 GHz are used mainly for radar, though some have other applications, such as satellite communications. In particular, the bands 3,260–3,267 MHz, 3,332–3,339 MHz, and 3,345.8–3,352.5 are needed by radio astronomers because they correspond to important radiation emitted by stars.

Compatibility

The ITU originally wanted a single global standard, but this has not been achieved. Instead, there are two main types of CDMA and a third based on TDMA. The main reason for the dispute is compatibility with existing systems, which can be defined in three ways:

- **Direct Upgrades.** Network operators without a license for new spectrum need to deploy a system that is essentially just an improvement of what they already have, so that new phones will work with the older base stations and vice versa. Upgrades typically add packet-switching and better modulation but keep existing cell sizes and channel structure. This limits their operators' options substantially; in particular, most 2G systems are based on TDMA, so direct upgrades need to retain the TDMA structure. Because of these limitations, direct upgrades are usually considered 2.5G.

- **Roaming.** In principle, a mobile terminal can be made to support any number of different systems, enabling it to be used worldwide. This is how the ITU can get away with calling IMT-2000 a standard: It involves multiple modes of operation, each representing a different 3G system. Some phones may well support all the IMT-2000 systems, but the first are based on only one, and the cheapest will continue to be so. From the network operator's point of view, the different sub-standards within IMT-2000 are mutually exclusive.

- **Handover.** Roaming is inconvenient for most users, because phones have to be reset to use a different network. To make it easier, a 3G system can be built so that it actually hands over users to a 2G network as they move outside its coverage area. The user should notice no difference, unless he or she is accessing a 3G service, such as multimedia, that is not available under 2G. This places some constraints on the design of the 3G system and means that phones have to able to operate in both 2G and 3G modes simultaneously.

The fundamental problem for IMT-2000 is that no single standard could both upgrade cdmaOne and hand over to GSM. This means that two very similar CDMA-based IMT-2000 standards are set for deployment, and which one is used depends entirely on the local 2G system.

W-CDMA ....

Wideband CDMA (W-CDMA) is the system favored by most operators able to obtain new spectrum. It has been designed to allow handovers to GSM, but is otherwise unlike it. GSM networks cannot be upgraded to W-CDMA, though some components, such as the GPRS backbone, can be reused.

The *wideband* designation refers to the channel bandwidth of 5 MHz. This is four times that of cdmaOne, and 25 times that of GSM. A wider bandwidth was chosen to allow higher data rates, though only in uncrowded areas with very clear reception. Unlike cdmaOne, which automatically sends every bit of information 64 times, W-CDMA adjusts the gain depending on the signal strength. Every bit is sent between 4 and 128 times, so greater bandwidth is available in areas with a stronger signal.

The other major difference between W-CDMA and cdmaOne is the need for time synchronization. W-CDMA was designed to operate without the Global Positioning System (GPS) timing signals required by cdmaOne base-stations, in part because its designers envisaged indoor microcells that would not always be able to receive transmissions from a satellite. International politics were also a factor in its decision: GPS is controlled by the U.S. Defense Department, on whose goodwill many European and Japanese companies are reluctant to rely. Instead of GPS, it uses a simpler power-control mechanism based on negative feedback: Every phone increases its transmission power until a base station tells it that it is too loud.

This power control system requires a slightly different coding technique, called *Gold codes*, which ironically are also used by GPS itself. Combined with the same differential quadrature phase shift keying (QPSK) modulation as cdmaOne, these give a maximum raw data rate of around 4 Mbps per channel per cell, theoretically beating the IMT-2000 requirements. Each channel is reused by every cell, boosting spectral efficiency, compared with TDMA systems, and enabling soft handovers. However, handovers to GSM are still hard (one connection has to be set up before another is torn down) because GSM doesn't support soft handover.

Realistically, no W-CDMA system using QPSK can achieve 4 Mbps. To do so would require only one user per cell, and a channel entirely free of interference. Most vendors say that the maximum data rate is 2 Mbps using indoor microcells, or 384kbps while outside. Even that is very optimistic.

TD-CDMA

Time Division W-CDMA (TD-CDMA) sounds like a contradiction and is often referred to as a hybrid between TDMA and CDMA. This is somewhat misleading; the multiplex technique is still CDMA, but time division *duplexing* is used to share a channel between uplink and downlink. This makes the most efficient use of spectrum, because it means that spare bandwidth not used for the uplink can be used for the downlink (or vice versa).

TD-CDMA requires a lot of management traffic that eats up bandwidth, so most W-CDMA operators use it for only one channel, pairing the others off in the same way as regular cellular systems. For example, Canadian company Telesystem International bought spectrum in the United Kingdom totaling 35 MHz at a cost of around $8 billion. It is using this to give a core capacity of 15 MHz each way (three pairs of channels), plus an extra 5 MHz (one TDD channel) that can be reallocated in real time to either.

This is not as flexible as it sounds. Telesystem's decision, like that of every operator, was already made by regulators and equipment manufacturers. To keep cost and complexity down, W-CDMA terminals and carrier-side infrastructure are hard-wired with specific access methods in mind for every frequency. Each channel is licensed with a requirement specifying whether it is to be used for uplink, downlink, or TDD. Europe's precise layout is illustrated in Figure 5.6. Shared between all operators, there are 12 paired and 7 unpaired channels.

The UMTS Forum has calculated that, to offer multimedia, each operator will need at least three pairs, as Telesystem has. However, several governments are issuing spectrum in smaller amounts than this; the United Kingdom gave operators British Telecom, Orange, and One2One only two pairs each, and the German government considered giving some only a single pair. They say that this is necessary to encourage competition and that the Forum is biased because it consists mainly of existing operators. User groups point out that if governments actually had allocated all the spectrum that the ITU originally told them to, there would be enough for both competition and bandwidth-hungry services.

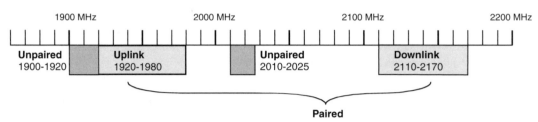

Figure 5.6
Initial frequency use by W-CDMA/UMTS.

UMTS AND FOMA

Since 1996, the planned European W-CDMA standard has been known as the *Universal Mobile Telecommunications System* (UMTS). Its development was spearheaded by the 3GPP (Third-Generation Partnership Project), an industry and government group charged with developing a successor to GSM. Its plan was that the new standard would be as successful as GSM, quickly spreading to the rest of the world. It is heavily promoted by the UMTS Forum, a subsidiary of the 3GPP.

The 3GPP has published several draft proposals for a W-CDMA system that is compatible with GSM. It originally planned to publish one each year, with a final version by 2000. However, it underestimated both the worldwide demand for mobile communications and the time that a standard would take to develop. The different iterations, shown in Table 5.3, were at first named after the year in which they were published. Later, they were known by simple version numbers, because the 3GPP realized that it would not be able to publish a new version each year. In particular, it failed to publish a version in 2000, the year that the standard was supposed to be ready.

Japan's NTT DoCoMo needed to start building its 3G network in 2000, because it was running out of 2G capacity, thanks to the success of both voice and data services. Rather than wait for the full UMTS standard, as Europe's carriers planned, it took the third draft, published in 1999. This was enough to build a complete cellular network, but it lacked some important features. In particular, the 1999 version of UMTS didn't include a messaging system or content-based billing, both of which are vital parts of DoCoMo's i-mode services. To add these and some other compatibility features, DoCoMo had to extend the standard. Its version is called *Freedom of Mobile Multimedia Access* (FOMA).

The FOMA network officially began service on May 30, 2001, but only for a few thousand specially selected test customers. Commercial services did not begin until October, and then only in central parts of three cities (Tokyo, Yokohoma, and

Kawasaki). However, DoCoMo has an aggressive building schedule. It estimates that its 3G network will be able to serve 97% of the Japanese population by the beginning of 2004.

DoCoMo has defined three applications that it ultimately wants to support, which are slightly more ambitious than the ITU's. As well as voice and video over 8 kbps and 64 kbps, respectively, it wants a two-way 348-kbps connection for cars that can be connected to "Intelligent Transportation Systems," a central traffic computer that will be able to drive them by remote control. The current system allows uploads at up to 64 kbps and downloads at up to 384 kbps, but typical speeds are lower.

Europe's first working 3G system was installed on the Isle of Mann, an island in the Irish Sea of only 75,000 inhabitants. It has just one mobile operator, Manx Telecom (a subsidiary of British Telecom), which can cover the entire island using 30 base stations. It began service in December 2001 and is based on the full UMTS v4 specification. This means that it is not compatible with FOMA, though few people are likely to need to use a 3G phone in both the Isle of Mann and the three cities covered by DoCoMo.

Both DoCoMo and Manx Telecom plan to upgrade their networks to UMTS v5, the same version that most other operators in Europe (and many elsewhere) will use for their 3G networks. This means that UMTS is likely to become even more widespread than GSM. Because most UMTS operators are using the ITU's recommended frequencies, the same cell phones will work across almost all networks—unlike GSM, which even in Europe uses three separate bands. The exception is the United States, where (if UMTS is deployed at all) it will need to use a different portion of spectrum, requiring modified phones.

Table 5.3   *Different Versions of the UMTS Standard*

Iteration	Published	Deployed by	Main New Features
UMTS v99	late 1999	NTT DoCoMo	First working version
UMTS v4	early 2001	Manx Telecom	Content-based billing, IP support, GSM roaming
UMTS v5	mid-2002	European carriers	Packetized voice, data prioritization, messaging, HSDMA
UMTS v6	early 2004 (expected)	Most carriers worldwide	Further 3.5G enhancements

Upgrading to 3.5G

Though initial services have been relatively disappointing, many in the industry believe that real UMTS systems will eventually be able to meet—and even exceed—the ITU's original aims for 3G. The standard is continuously evolving and will continue to do so, even after networks are built across Europe and worldwide.

Versions 6 and later of the UMTS specification will include several enhancements, designed to push the technology beyond its original specification. These are collectively known as *3.5G*, because they will allow mobile operators to increase data rates or improve spectral efficiency without building an entire new network.

Most 3.5G enhancements are so far in the future that they are still experimental. However, one has made it into version 5 of the specification, so may be deployed in Europe and Japan almost as soon as UMTS itself. Known as *High-Speed Downlink Packet Access* (HSDPA), this uses improved modulation to boost the total downstream data rate of a channel to about 10 Mbps. (The upstream capacity is still only 2 Mbps.) It is envisaged that each network will have only one HSDPA channel, shared between all users and dedicated to data. Because it increases speed only for downloads, it is ideal for Web surfing.

Like many systems that try to use more advanced modulation, HSDPA is more vulnerable to interference: Its 64-symbol quadrature amplitude modulation (64-QAM) requires a receiver to distinguish between 64 differently shaped waves (representing 6 bits), whereas the QPSK modulation of regular UMTS requires the receiver to distinguish between only four (representing 2 bits). The usual way to get around this problem is to use a less complex modulation scheme when reception is poor: If a receiver can't pick up the 64-QAM signal reliably, HSDPA can drop down to 32-QAM, then to 16-QAM, and so on. Unfortunately, this negates many of the gains made by using HSDPA and means that the maximum data rate is only achievable when there is no interference.

As an alternative to varying its modulation to suit a poor connection, HSDPA can simply give *all* its available bandwidth to users who have good reception. This is sometimes called "maximum unfairness," because it doesn't even attempt to share capacity out among all users, instead aiming for the best possible spectral efficiency. The theory behind it is that reception quality changes very frequently, and so each user is likely to be cut off for only a few seconds at a time.

CDMA2000 ....

Of the 2G systems, only cdmaOne is already based on CDMA. This gives it a head start in the race to 3G, because operators are able to upgrade their existing networks with new software or modulation, rather than by building a whole new radio system. These upgrades are collectively known as *CDMA2000*, and all are backward-compatible with existing IS-95 systems.

Until mid-2000, the upgrade path for cdmaOne seemed clear. The end result was supposed to be a system named *CDMA2000 3×MC,* so called because it combines three channels together, resulting in a wider band. Unfortunately, this system was not compatible with the form of W-CDMA favored by Europe and Japan, though its specifications are almost identical. The difference is the *chip rate*, the frequency at which the transceiver resonates. CDMA2000's chip rate needs to be a multiple of cdmaOne's, whereas W-CDMA's has to fit the GSM framing structure.

In 2000, Motorola and Nokia together launched a system called *1Xtreme*, which they claim can reach speeds similar to that of 3×MC but using only one channel and, thus, a third of the spectrum. Their claims are as yet unproven, and some analysts say they are simply trying to avoid many of rival Qualcomm's CDMA patents. However, if their assertions are justified, 1Xtreme does present cdmaOne operators with a chance to increase their capacity beyond that of any rival system.

The competing CDMA upgrades are listed in Table 5.4, along with IS-95b and W-CDMA. The real capacities are only manufacturers' estimates and should not be fully trusted until actual systems have been tested.

Table 5.4   *CDMA Systems Compared*

CDMA System	Channel Bandwidth	Chip Rate	Max Capacity	Real Capacity
cdmaOne IS-95b	1.25 MHz	1.2288 MHz	115.2 kbps	20 kbps
CDMA2000 1×MC	1.25 MHz	1.2288 MHz	384 kbps	64 kbps
CDMA2000 1×EV-DO	1.25 MHz	1.2288 MHz	2.4 Mbps	384 kbps
CDMA2000 1×EV-DV	1.25 MHz	1.2288 MHz	5.2 Mbps	Unknown
CDMA2000 3×MC	3.75 MHz	3.6864 MHz	4 Mbps	Unknown
UMTS (W-CDMA)	5 MHz	4.096 MHz	4 Mbps	384 kbps

1×MC/1×RTT

For all cdmaOne operators, the next step up from IS-95b is a system called *1×MC* (the *MC* is for *Multi Carrier*), also known as *1×RTT* (the *RTT* is for *Radio Transmission Technology*) or *IS-856*. It requires new hardware in base station controllers but no new radio interface and claims to double capacity by using each of IS-95's Walsh codes twice.

The first 1×MC network was switched on in early 2001 by Korean operator LG Infocomm. The technology is also being used in China and Israel, and is being considered by operators in other countries. The one place it seems unlikely to reach is Europe, where regulators insist on W-CDMA.

In the United States, three major carriers have chosen 1×MC: Verizon, Sprint PCS, and Nextel. The first two already have networks based on cdmaOne, so it was an obvious upgrade for them. Nextel's choice is more interesting: Its current iDEN network has no upgrade path, so it had to choose a complete new system for 3G. It decided on 1×MC because of its relatively low spectrum requirement: only 1.25 GHz per channel, compared with W-CDMA's 5 GHz. Nextel says that if more spectrum were available, it might have picked W-CDMA instead.

Because 1×MC cannot meet the ITU's official 3G requirements, even in theory, it should really be regarded as a 2.5G technology. However, initial deployments have shown it to reach typical data rates of between 40 and 60 kbps, which is better than GPRS. There are two main reasons for this:

- It uses spectrum more efficiently than the technology it upgrades (IS-95b), whereas GPRS just adds packet-switching to GSM. This means that, all other things being equal, it can offer double the data rate. More importantly, it gives operators an economic incentive to upgrade, because it means that they can carry twice as much lucrative voice traffic.

- There is no extra limitation on data rate built into the user terminal itself. Whereas each class of GPRS phones can use only a certain hard-wired number of radio channels—hence the need for the 29 different classes, shown in Table 4.6—all CDMA-based systems automatically transmit on all available channels at once. 1×C is able to take full advantage of this, so the available data rate is limited only by interference from other users on the network.

1× Enhanced Version

Beyond 1×MC, most cdmaOne carriers are planning a further upgrade called *1×EV* (Enhanced Version). It uses the same 1.25-MHz spectrum channels as 1×MC but adds improved modulation to increase the data rates. Cell phone operators, equipment vendors, and governments are divided over how great this increase is, but the details of the modulation scheme give some clues.

Like any enhanced modulation system, 1×EV increases the number of shapes that the radio waves can take. The older 1×MC uses QPSK, which shapes waves into four different symbols, representing 2 bits. 1×EV instead uses 8-PSK (8-symbol phase shift keying) or, when reception is clear, 16-QAM. The *8* and *16* refer to the number of symbols that the waves are shaped into, representing 3 or 4 bits, respectively. This means that the data rate (and the spectral efficiency) is increased by either 50% or 100%, depending on the quality of the radio link. If reception is very poor, 1×EV will drop down to ordinary QPSK, offering no improvement over 1×EV.

The extra capacity of 1×EV can, in theory, be used for either voice or data. However, carriers are so far committed only to using it for data, because it is easier to implement on the downlink than on the uplink, rather like HSDPA in UMTS. This has led 1×EV to splinter into two standards:

- **1×EV-DO** (Data Only) was originally known simply as *High Data Rate* (HDR). It is intended to be applied to only a single 1.25-MHz channel, leaving the rest of the network as 1×MC. The maximum data rate is 2.4 Mbps on the downlink and 307.2 kbps on the uplink, which has to be shared between all users in a cell and can only be used by a maximum of 29 at once. The number 29 is not picked at random; there are 32 Walsh codes available for the uplink, of which three are needed for signaling. The downlink is more flexible, using TDMA as well as CDMA to divide a channel into 240 time slots, each of which can be allocated to a different user. However, the limit still applies because the system is designed for two-way communications. Users can only be sent data that they have actively requested.

- **1×EV-DV** (Data/Voice) has still not been fully standardized. It uses the same modulation techniques as 1×EV-DO but applies them to an entire network, rather than a single channel. This is a lot more complex than 1×EV-DO because it must ensure quality of service and symmetric data rates. There are several competing proposals, of which, the most likely to be accepted is 1Xtreme, described earlier. Some vendors have also proposed even more advanced modulation schemes, such as 256-QAM, which would double the data rate. However, others say that these would require such a clear and interference-free link that they would be useless in a real network.

3×MC/3×RTT

3×MC is the CDMA2000 proposal accepted by the ITU as part of IMT-2000. Its claimed performance is almost identical to that of W-CDMA, but it uses slightly less spectrum and inherits some of cdmaOne's features, notably, the chip rate and the need for GPS timing. The ITU hopes that phones will be produced with a variable chip so that they can easily be used for both W-CDMA and 3×MC.

So far, no operators have actually announced plans for 3×MC. The reason is simple: The various 1× technologies all promise similar capacity but require only one-third as much spectrum. It is particularly unlikely to reach the United States, where operators simply don't have the spectrum to spare. A future version of the system may eventually be deployed in some countries for compatibility with HSDPA, the W-CDMA-based 3.5G technology.

EDGE ....

Not all 3G systems are based on CDMA. The TDMA camp is promoting a technology called *EDGE*, which originally meant *Enhanced Data Rates for GSM Evolution*. As the name indicates, it was planned as an upgrade for GSM networks, one more step for operators who had already deployed the 2.5G HSCSD and GPRS.

EDGE was never intended to be a competitor to CDMA-based 3G technologies. The plan was that GSM operators would deploy it in their existing networks while building UMTS to take advantage of the newly licensed IMT-2000 spectrum. Because UMTS can hand over calls to GSM, the two would even be compatible; many handsets sold in Europe would support both.

This changed when EDGE was adopted by the Universal Wireless Communications Consortium (UWCC), a group representing the American TDMA industry. Working with the GSM Association, they developed a way to migrate D-AMPS to EDGE via GSM and GPRS. The rationale for doing so was that traditional D-AMPS had run its course, so operators needing 3G would have to build new networks.

Both CDMA2000 and W-CDMA were considered for these new networks, but their wide channel sizes were a problem. Any radio system needs at least one channel to work; for an operator without a new license, this channel represents spectrum that can't be used for D-AMPS services. The aim is to move spectrum from the old to the new network in blocks as small as possible.

EDGE's channel size is only 200 kHz, the same as GSM's. Even allowing for the inability of adjacent cells in a TDMA network to reuse channels, an EDGE system can be set up in only 600 kHz. This is less than half of that needed by even narrowband CDMA, making it very attractive to D-AMPS operators. In 2000, the ITU accepted EDGE as a mode of IMT-2000 and standardized it as *UWC-136*.

To make EDGE sound less GSM-centric, the UWCC changed the *G* in the name to *Global*. Meanwhile, the GSM industry itself has almost ignored EDGE in favor of W-CDMA. This has more to do with politics than any technical limitation: Most European GSM operators won UMTS licenses, which require them to construct W-CDMA networks by certain deadlines. Though they may eventually turn to EDGE, they're currently more focused on W-CDMA.

Enhanced GPRS

EDGE inherits almost all its main features from GSM and GPRS, including the eight-user TDMA structure and even the slot length of 577 μs. The *only* difference is in the modulation scheme. Instead of the binary GMSK, it uses 8-PSK, the same as HDR. This immediately triples the capacity, compared with GSM.

Keeping the same GSM slot layout shown in Figure 4.1 (but with every "bit" having eight states instead of two), the raw data rate per slot is increased from 21.4 kbps to 64.2 kbps. As in GSM, a large portion of this—usually at least half—needs to be used for signaling and error correction, rather than actual data.

EDGE *could* be applied to a regular GSM system, giving every user a landline-quality voice or data connection, but it is such a major upgrade that every operator installing it will also use GPRS and perhaps HSCSD. For this reason, the services deployed over EDGE are sometimes referred to as *EGPRS* and *EHSCSD*. For customers who don't have an EDGE-equipped phone, it is fully compatible with regular GSM, HSCSD, and GPRS.

Because 8-PSK is more susceptible to errors than GMSK, EDGE has nine different MCSs (Modulation and Coding Schemes), each designed for a different quality of connection. They differ in how much forward error correction (FEC) is needed and in whether 8-PSK can be used at all—for noisy connections, it automatically drops down to GMSK. The type of modulation and amount of FEC necessary for each is shown in Table 5.5, along with the data capacity available from a single slot and from the entire channel. As in GPRS, most terminals will be able to support only a few slots, not all eight in an entire channel, so the full capacity is unlikely to be achieved.

EDGE is very attractive to GSM operators that don't have a UMTS license because it actually increases capacity, for voice as well as data. If reception is good and everyone uses the half-rate codec, up to six voice conversations can share one slot. If the voice is packetized and sent as data, the system can be made even more efficient.

Table 5.5   The Nine MCSs of EDGE

MCS	Slot Capacity	FEC	Modulation	Channel Capacity
MCS-1	8.8 kbps	143%	GMSK	70.4 kbps
MCS-2	11.2 kbps	91%	GMSK	89.6 kbps
MCS-3	14.8 kbps	45%	GMSK	118.4 kbps
MCS-4	17.6 kbps	22%	GMSK	140.8 kbps
MCS-5	22.4 kbps	187%	8PSK	179.2 kbps
MCS-6	29.6 kbps	117%	8PSK	236.8 kbps
MCS-7	44.8 kbps	43%	8PSK	358.4 kbps
MCS-8	54.4 kbps	18%	8PSK	435.2 kbps
MCS-9	59.2 kbps	8%	8PSK	473.6 kbps

EDGE Compact

To make EDGE deployment easier for D-AMPS operators, the UWCC has defined a simplified standard called *EDGE Compact*. This can only be used for data, not voice, so it omits many of the control channels found in the full-scale system, which, in the context of EDGE Compact, is referred to as *ETSI EDGE* or *EDGE Classic*.

EDGE Compact is regarded as an intermediary step, not a complete system. The plan is for customers to continue to use D-AMPS for voice, with EDGE Compact as an overlay data service, rather like HDR on 1×MC or HSDPA on UMTS. As customers buy new phones, EDGE Classic will be deployed, and customers will gradually migrate over to the full system.

REALITY CHECK ....

All these technologies sound impressive, but the first networks based on them have been very disappointing. None have provided anything like their promised speeds. The only one that came close was Metricom's Ricochet, a service that has been discontinued. The difference between hype and reality is often so great that they can't be compared properly on a chart. If some of the bars showing the real data rates in Figure 5.7 were drawn to their full height, they would extend right off the page.

These poor data rates have encouraged operators to turn toward a very old technology: compression. Some claim that even though the real speed may be only 20kbps, the "apparent" speed for users will be four or five times this, allowing the technology to live up to the hype. Such claims ignore the fact that most dial-up connections already include compression, so people are already used to apparent speeds greater than the actual data rate. For example, a v.90 modem usually receives compressed data at about 40 kbps, which is still twice the speed of compressed data at 20 kbps.

A few operators, such as Sprint in the United States, use extra compression for images. This really does increase speed, but it's based on lossy compression, the same type used for cellular voice, meaning that the image quality is reduced. The operator's computers can intercept high-resolution images before they are transmitted to mobile users, converting them into chunky block graphics that require less bandwidth.

Whether lossy or not, no type of compression works with encrypted traffic. This makes it useless for applications that require encryption, including corporate network access and secure e-commerce sites.

WEB RESOURCES

www.itu.int/imt2000/
The IMT-2000 site, set up by the ITU, charges for the detailed technical standards needed actually to build a system but also has plenty of free background information for nonengineers.

www.3gpp.org and www.3gpp2.org
There are two parallel standards organizations developing CDMA-based 3G systems. The Third Generation Partnership Project (3GPP) is focused on W-CDMA, and the Third Generation Partnership Project 2 (3GPP2) is focused on CDMA2000. Both are composed of vendors and regulators, and both publish detailed technical information on their Web sites.

www.umts-forum.org
The UMTS forum is really the marketing arm of the 3GPP, but its site does contain a large archive of nontechnical information about 3G applications.

www.uwcc.org
The Universal Wireless Communications Consortium promotes TDMA as a 3G access technology and, in particular, the EDGE standard.

www.3gnewsroom.com
This site collects 3G-related news from many sources around the Web, as well as press releases from vendors and reports from analysts. It doesn't provide much analysis, but it's very focused on 3G.

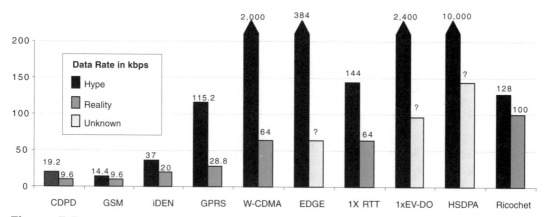

Figure 5.7
Hyped and real data rates of mobile systems.

BIBLIOGRAPHY

Bates, Regis J. **Wireless Broadband Handbook.** McGraw-Hill, 2001.
A nontechnical guide to many high-speed wireless technologies with a particular emphasis on 3G mobile.

Holma, Harri and Antii Toskala. **W-CDMA for UMTS: Radio Access for Third-Generation Mobile Communications.** Artech House, 2000.
A very technical and detailed reference work aimed at engineers designing and setting up 3G networks.

SUMMARY

- There are three main 3G systems: W-CDMA, CDMA2000, and EDGE. They are collectively known as *IMT-2000* and will offer packet-switched data at rates exceeding 384 kbps.

  - *W-CDMA* is designed to be backward-compatible with GSM and requires new spectrum. It is also known as UMTS and can be extended to 3.5G data rates.

  - *CDMA2000* is a straightforward upgrade to cdmaOne but consists of several competing proposals.

- *EDGE* is a straightforward upgrade to GSM and GPRS and requires far less spectrum than other systems.
- The first 3G systems entered service in 2001. The most advanced is Japan's, which uses a variant of W-CDMA called *FOMA*. Other pioneers were the Isle of Mann, using UMTS, and South Korea, using CDMA2000.

6 Mobile Data Services

In this chapter...

The most extravagant claims for wireless technology surround mobile data. If the cell phone vendors are to be believed, we will soon be able to watch high-definition TV streamed live to a pocket-sized panel, while surfing the Web and participating in a videoconference. Nokia and Ericsson have both committed themselves to making every new cell phone "Internet-enabled".

This mobile Internet is a long way from the cyberspace that surfers know and love. Data rates are still painfully slow, and the first wireless Web technologies are aimed at reducing the features of sites rather than increasing the data rate. Amidst the hype, it's worth remembering that most mobile data traffic still takes the form of messaging services—text transmissions, which seem horribly primitive to anyone who has used e-mail.

But mobile data is still exciting, its potential perhaps greater than any other consumer technology. The mobile phone companies say that messaging services were really designed just to test out the technology, not as a serious application. Yet *texting* became an incredibly popular means of communication, especially among children. Ironically, these "test" services are more popular than many of the much-hyped ways to access the Web from a cell phone.

MESSAGING ....

Every digital phone system already incorporates some form of *messaging*. This allows subscribers to receive and sometimes send short text messages—essentially the same as paging, but with the data appearing on a mobile phone instead of a separate pager.

In theory, messaging services should allow people to receive e-mail through their mobile phones and to dispense with pagers altogether. But in practice, neither of these objectives has yet been achieved, even in markets such as Europe—where every phone can receive messages and more than 90% can send them. The reasons are partly technical, thanks to length limits imposed by the very low data capacity, but mostly commercial.

In Europe and America, most operators charge for Short Message Service (SMS), using the same model as for phone calls themselves—whoever sends the message pays for it. This allows customers to control their own costs; no matter how many messages they are sent, they won't be charged unless they decide to reply. Some operators have begun to offer e-mail to SMS gateways, where a customer can be sent a message through e-mail or a form at a Web site, but there is no way to charge for this using the sender-pays model. Japanese operators do charge to receive messages but have faced many customer complaints over this. NTT DoCoMo was forced to reduce its charges after people began switching their phones off to avoid unwanted advertising messages. During 2001, it also admitted that two-thirds of its customers had changed their e-mail addresses at least once to avoid marketers.

The other barrier to replacing paging is that mobile phone operators are not geared up to deal with the type of services offered by paging companies. Most of the messages sent to a pager originate on the regular telephone network—to page someone, the user calls a human operator, who transcribes the message and transmits it. Setting up call centers that employ actual people is very expensive, and voice recognition technology is still too primitive to automate the process. Many operators also have interests in paging businesses, which they are reluctant to cannibalize. They *could* switch their call centers from paging to messaging, but this would increase the load on their cellular networks while leaving the paging networks empty.

The cell phone companies have made slightly more progress in interconnecting their own messaging networks so that customers of one operator can send messages to those of another. They were originally more keen to form international alliances than to cooperate with their direct competitors at home. This meant that, up until 2001, it was easier to send a message from Paris to London than to send a message within the same city. Customers found this very annoying, so most carriers in Europe have now interlinked their networks, though (as with phone calls themselves) it is usually more expensive to send a message to someone who is connecting via a different cell phone company.

Digital cell phones currently use five types of messaging services, though only one is truly universal. These are summarized in Table 6.1 and described in the following pages.

Table 6.1   *Messaging Services*

Service Name	Message Length	Phone System	Direction
SMS (Short Message Service)	140–260 bytes	Most 2G and 2.5G systems.	Two-way and one-way
CBS (Cell Broadcast Service)	1,395 bytes	GSM only	One-way only
USSD (Unstructured Supplementary Services Data)	182 bytes	GSM and UMTS	Two-way only
EMS (Enhanced Messaging Service)/ Smart Messaging	140-260 bytes	Most 2.5G and some 2G systems.	Two-way and one-way
MMS (Multimedia Messaging Service)	No limit	All 3G and some 2.5G systems.	Two-way and one-way

Short Messages

The only messaging standard to have achieved widespread acceptance is the *Short Message Service* (SMS). It began as part of the original Global System for Mobile Communications (GSM) specification but has since spread to all the other digital systems, some of which have improved on it. Limited versions have also been standardized for Advanced Mobile Phone System (AMPS) and Nordic Mobile Telephony (NMT) analog networks, though few operators have implemented these, because they would prefer that customers upgrade to digital.

SMS's greatest limitation is hinted at in its name: Messages have to be short. GSM imposes a limit of only 160 bytes, or characters—the length of this paragraph.

The length limit is caused by the way that SMS is transmitted. It usually rides on the control channels, the same frequencies or time slots used for call setup information. This means that users can send or receive SMS messages while they are making a phone call, though they need a hands-free kit to read the screen or type on the keypad. Different systems use different types of control channels, so the precise limit depends on the system. Table 6.2 shows a full list. The exception is the analog NMT, which uses the same channels as phone calls themselves. This means that message size is limited only by the handset's memory, but also that simultaneous talking and texting cannot be accomplished.

A byte usually corresponds to a single alphanumeric character, but it doesn't have to. The AMPS system can use its 14 bytes to represent numbers instead, allowing up to 33 digits. This is useful for sending someone a long phone number or credit card details. At the other end of the scale, many Asian countries need more complicated character sets, such as the Japanese or Chinese alphabet. GSM, cdmaOne, and Personal Digital Cellular (PDC) can all support these but allow only around 70 characters because each one requires 2 bytes.

SMS is known as a *store-and-forward* service because messages may be held in a computer's memory for a few seconds (or occasionally longer) before being transmitted. In this respect, it is like e-mail or the regular postal service—a sender has no guarantee that the message will be received within a certain time limit and no automatic acknowledgement when it does. This makes SMS unsuitable for interactive services.

Some implementations of SMS only allow messages to be sent from the network to the mobile phone and are known as *Terminate Only*. Others allow two-way messaging, called *Terminate and Originate*. SMS support also needs to be built in to the phone. Every GSM phone can terminate SMS, and most manufactured since 1996 can also originate it, but for other standards, many low-end phones can only terminate, or they lack SMS altogether.

Because SMS is so popular, some fixed-line phone companies have tried to extend it beyond cellular networks. The idea is that people will be able to receive messages via their regular phone or perhaps on a cordless phone in a public place. In 2001, European Telecommunications Standards Institute (ETSI) published a standard that covered fixed SMS, but this doesn't use the signaling channels in the same way that most mobile implementations do. Users will not be able to send SMS while speaking on the phone.

Table 6.2   *Mobile Phone Systems Supporting SMS*

Technology		Message Length	Simultaneous Speech	Direction
Digital	GSM/GPRS	160 bytes	Yes	Terminate and Originate
	D-AMPS	160 bytes	Yes	Terminate Only
	cdmaOne	256 bytes	Yes	Terminate and Originate
	PDC	160 bytes	Yes	Terminate and Originate
	TETRA	260 bytes	Yes	Terminate and Originate
	iDEN	140 bytes	Yes	Terminate and Originate
Analog	NMT	No limit	No	Terminate and Originate
	AMPS	14 bytes	Yes	Terminate Only

Cell Broadcast

If the same information needs to be sent to many different users, broadcasting is more efficient than routing a separate transmission to each one. This is the theory behind the *Cell Broadcast Service* (CBS), a variant of SMS used only in GSM. Each message is known as a *page* and can be only 93 bytes long, but up to 15 pages can be concatenated for a total message length of 1,395 bytes—enough for several paragraphs of text or a short program.

Despite these clear technical advantages, CBS is not widely used. The main reason is that it offers operators no way to charge for the services; by definition, a broadcast message can be picked up by anyone within a cell. In theory, there should be a way to overcome this using GSM's encryption facilities, but no operator has managed it yet. A message has to be intended for just one user (in which case it is sent via SMS) or for everybody.

Unstructured Services

GSM networks have access to a third messaging technology, *Unstructured Supplementary Services Data* (USSD). Like SMS, it uses the control channel and can operate while a phone is in use. Messages are slightly longer, with a maximum of 182 bytes, compared with the 160 bytes of SMS under GSM.

The main advantage of USSD is that it is *connection-oriented*. This means that the network establishes a connection with the phone before sending any data, rather like a phone conversation. The sender knows when a message has been received, and if necessary, a response can be sent very rapidly over the same connection. This makes it ideal for interactive applications such as the Web at a (very) low data rate or wireless access to remote databases.

USSD is designed to be accessed by programs running within a phone, rather than directly from a menu-driven user interface. However, people willing to enter long strings of code numbers can sometimes use it to access network features otherwise unavailable from their particular phone. To distinguish them from ordinary phone numbers, these strings usually begin with the * and # keys.

Though GSM is the only existing system that supports USSD, it has also been written into the specification for the Universal Mobile Telecommunications System (UMTS), the European third-generation standard. SMS has not, so the GSM Association expects its use to start declining from about 2005.

Enhanced and Smart Messaging

As SMS became more popular, the mobile industry looked for a way to overcome its basic limitations—the tiny message size and inability to send anything except basic text. Unfortunately, the two largest phone manufacturers could not agree on a common specification. Ericsson wanted to wait for a standard approved by the Third-Generation Partnership Project (3GPP) and usable by other companies, whereas Nokia pressed ahead with its own proprietary system.

Nokia's system is called *Smart Messaging* and has been built into many of its phones since 1997. The official 3GPP standard is called *Enhanced Message Service* (EMS). Developed by Ericsson, it was formally standardized in 2001, when it was adopted by Alcatel, Motorola, and Siemens. This left Nokia almost isolated, so it opened up the formerly proprietary Smart Messaging, allowing other manufacturers to use it royalty free.

The result is two different, incompatible ways to do almost the same thing. EMS clearly has a better long-term future, because it is included in the official 3G standards, but Nokia has a lot of market power as well a large installed base of Smart Messaging users, thanks to its four-year head start. It's possible to build a phone that supports both, but this requires extra memory and processing, and would also mean one or more of the large manufacturers accepting defeat in the standards war.

Though not interoperable with each other, both Smart Messaging and EMS are fully backward-compatible with SMS, so users of one are still able to send simple text messages to users of the other. Both embed special codes into an SMS message, representing graphics, text formatting, or sound. As far as the mobile network is concerned, Smart and EMS messages are just SMS, so operators don't need to upgrade any of their own infrastructure. The codes are added in and stripped out by the phones themselves.

The extra features that EMS adds are:

- **Text positioning.** Text can be set to be appear to the left, center, or right of the screen. Because screens are so small, this feature is likely not to be popular.

- **Text formatting.** In addition to plain text, four options are available: **bold**, *italic*, <u>underlined</u>, and ~~strikethrough~~.

- **Graphics.** These are simple monochrome bitmaps, measuring either 16×16 or 32×32 pixels. Users can edit these on screen, and combine up to six together for a maximum size of 96×62. Some phones also have predefined icons such as the smiley face, which don't need to be sent again each time they are used.

- **Animations.** Several graphics can be made to appear in sequence, producing simple animations. These require a lot of capacity, so some are built in to the handset, though users with a lot spare time can also produce their own.

- **Sounds.** Ten are predefined (built into every phone), and users can also compose their own through a system called *i-melody*, which is also used for keying in new ring tones.

- **Message concatenation.** Several messages can be joined together and sent in sequence, producing the illusion of messages longer than the 160-byte limit. This is important, because all of the new embedded control codes use up bytes, meaning that fewer of the 160 are available for actual text. Each note in an i-melody, for example, requires the equivalent of three text characters.

Multimedia Messaging

Although EMS and Smart Messaging extend SMS, they are still limited by its very low data rate. It uses spare bandwidth in the signaling time slots, which in GSM have an absolute maximum capacity of only 15.2 kbps per channel. That sounds like a lot by cell phone standards, but after error correction, it's less than 10 kbps, which has to be shared between up to 16 users (there are eight time slots, and a half-rate codec enables two voice conversations on each). This has to carry vital information regarding everything from phone numbers to handoff, with SMS using whatever is left over.

There is no danger of regular SMS users actually overloading a network, because of the relatively long time that it takes to compose each message on a phone's keypad. However, the network could be stretched if many users at once tried to send long EMS messages, each of which is composed of several concatenated SMS messages. This would annoy users by slowing down data transfer, and directly threaten the operator's balance sheet. SMS is immensely profitable: Operators usually charge about the same to send one text message (160 bytes) as to make a one-minute voice call, even though the minute of voice costs the operator at least *three hundred* times as much network capacity.

To increase the capacity for messaging, the 3GPP has standardized the *MMS* (Multimedia Message Service). Unlike all the other messaging systems, this uses the same communications channel as other traffic, meaning that it has access to the same bandwidth. On a four-slot General Packet Radio Service (GPRS) terminal, for example, MMS messages could be received at up to 57.6 kbps, with no limit in length.

This effectively turns messaging into e-mail, but the 3GPP says it is actually *more* advanced than that. MMS phones have built-in support for all the added features of EMS, as well as the ability to display color graphics and play short video clips. The industry hopes that people will use videophones to make short home movies, then transmit them to friends using the messaging system.

The disadvantage of these extra features is that they require a new messaging infrastructure within the cellular network, not just new phones. They will also require a new charging structure, especially if they are to interface with the (unmetered or free) e-mail systems used on the Internet.

Applications of Messaging

Though messaging is not really e-mail or paging, it is starting to find applications of its own. The most popular are:

- **Voice Mail Notification.** Almost all mobile operators provide their customers with a voice mail facility, which is used while the phone is switched off or is out of range. Once a customer reestablishes a connection with the network, she receives an SMS telling her about the voice mail. Most phones intercept these messages and illuminate an icon so that the customer does not have to read and delete "You have voice mail" several times a day.

- **Reprogramming.** Many phones can have some of their software updated remotely, using SMS or CBS messaging. Customers can also download new ring tones, for which a surprising number are even willing to pay.

- **Advertising.** Though operators rarely tolerate blatant spam from outsiders, some like to use CBS to tell their customers about new features or special offers. They tend not to do this too frequently, however, as it can become very annoying. Most also send SMS reminders to people whose bills are overdue.

- **Broadcast Information Services.** Many operators are beginning to offer simple information services using CBS. These are free to the customer and give basic news headlines as they happen. Unfortunately, there is usually no way to choose between types of headlines—everything is broadcast to everyone. If customers want news, they have to take the whole package of finance, sports, and weather with it.

- **Specialized Information Services.** SMS can be used to notify people of particular events, such as stock prices reaching a certain level or airline flights being delayed. Operators usually charge extra for these types of services, but customers are often prepared to pay.

- **Person-to-Person Messaging.** This is the fastest growing area of messaging and requires a phone with SMS Originate capability. It is particularly popular among primary-school children, who usually don't have much money and know that sending text costs less than making a long voice call. They also have the time to type in messages on a phone's awkward keypad, often while in class. Nokia says that SMS has replaced passing notes around class in Finnish schools and estimates that teenagers send an average of more than 100 messages each month. Because of input difficulties and space limits, most are written in a code that resembles early telegrams, for example, "c u 2nite."

Instant Messaging

This is a special case of person-to-person messaging, which ties SMS to one of the Internet's messaging systems. It usually requires a gateway between the mobile operator and the instant messaging provider, because the different instant messaging services are not interoperable (rather like SMS a few years ago). This means that each mobile operator has partnered with one particular instant messaging service, making it very awkward for customers whose phone company hasn't struck a deal with the instant messaging provider that all their friends use.

In the United States, Verizon has linked up with Yahoo! and Nextel with Microsoft, while both Sprint PCS and Voicestream have connected their networks to AOL Instant Messenger (AIM), the largest service. Despite its popularity, AIM is not yet linked to any SMS network outside the United States. Most GSM operators worldwide are instead connected to ICQ ("I seek you"), which was both the first instant messenger and the first to offer SMS capability.

Instant messages delivered via SMS do not include all the features that desktop users are accustomed to. They are still text-only and subject to the 160-character limit, which means that they offer no file transfer, audio, or video capabilities. Some do, however, implement a version of the "buddy list" feature, which tells users when a friend is online. Some also use EMS or Smart Messaging to reproduce embedded "emoticons," though not with the same color or graphic quality as on a desktop computer.

The other difference between PC- and phone-based instant messaging is cost. Whereas the services offered by AOL, ICQ, and Yahoo! are all free, mobile operators usually charge for each message sent. (Incoming messages are usually free, subsidized by the replies that they generate.) This can mean an unpleasant shock to heavy users of instant messaging. To avoid complaints, some operators charge a flat monthly fee for instant messaging service. However, the flat fee usually only covers SMS sent to an instant messaging system, not SMS sent to other mobile phone users.

The SIM Toolkit

At the heart of every GSM phone is a *Subscriber Identity Module* (SIM), a tiny smart card that stores each customer's identity and other information, such as a phone book. The theory was that cards could be swapped around between phones operating on different frequencies, and that phones themselves could be upgraded by replacing the SIM, rather than the whole phone. The former worked, though was rendered unnecessary by the arrival of dual-band and triple-band phones. The latter didn't, because improvements in battery and electronic technology usually render the rest of the phone obsolete long before the card.

Some people like to keep two or more SIM cards so that they can use their phones to access different networks without paying roaming charges. A few phones are even specially designed to hold two or more cards for this purpose, with information such as the user's personal directory stored on the phone itself.

The *SIM Application Toolkit* is a standard that gives the SIM access to the full range of phone features, including messaging services. The operator can send messages to the SIM to reprogram it, adding specific features or even applications. These might range from a simple program allowing the user to switch between business and personal lines to a more complicated one offering mobile banking. When the program runs, it can then send messages as the user enters or requests data. A mobile banking application might request the user's balance using USSD, then send an instruction to transfer money via SMS.

The big disadvantage of the SIM Toolkit is that many phones and operators do not support it. Though first introduced early in 1998, it has suffered from a much slower take-up than most wireless technologies. It is perceived as too complex and has been overshadowed by technologies that promise—but usually fail to deliver—mobile Internet access.

THE WIRELESS WEB ....

Of all the new mobile data applications, none is more hyped than wireless Web browsing. The Web proved to be the "killer app" for fixed data networking, persuading millions of people to buy their first computers and prompting the largest stock market bubble in economic history. The wireless industry hopes to repeat this, and has devised several schemes for presenting Web content on mobile phones or personal digital assistants (PDAs).

Transferring the Web to cell phones presents several challenges, including variable latency and input device design. But the two that have preoccupied the mobile industry most are:

- **Low Capacity.** Most existing cell phone systems allow data speeds of only 9.6 or 14.4 kbps, the same as modems circa 1995. Even relatively advanced 2.5G technologies, such as GPRS and 1×MC, will push the speed up to only that of today's 56-kbps modems. By comparison, Web surfers using a corporate network or a home DSL line are used to speeds limited only by the congestion on the Internet itself.

- **Small Screens.** Many cell phones can display only a few lines of monochrome text, severely limiting the "multimedia" experience of the Web. PDAs have larger displays, often in color, but even these have their limits— it simply isn't possible to squeeze a desktop-sized screen into the palm of a user's hand. Most sites are designed for a minimum resolution of 640×480 pixels, and some require better; Web designers work with multiple, wide, high-resolution screens and sometimes forget that most surfers have to rely on less sophisticated equipment.

Table 6.3 shows the resolutions supported by mobile computers, together with the approximate LCD (liquid crystal display) sizes that they typically use. The *aspect ratio* refers to the shape of the screen and is the proportionate size of the width and height. The most common is 4:3, which was originally a compromise between the limitations of television technology and the human field of vision. Television tubes work best with a circular display, whereas we prefer a wider screen because we have two eyes separated horizontally.

The VGA (Video Graphics Array), SVGA (Super VGA), and XGA (Extended Graphics Adapter) standards were originally designed by IBM for television-style CRT (cathode ray tube) monitors but have become common in laptop PCs. VGA is also used by some machines that run Windows CE, but these are too large to be considered true PDAs. Known as *Jupiter-class*, they are becoming quite rare, because most people prefer a full-featured PC, despite its added weight, cost, and power consumption. PDAs with a *clamshell* design have a screen that folds down over a small keypad, as opposed to the hand-sized Palm and Pocket PC, which lack keyboards altogether.

Table 6.3   Laptop and PDA Display Technology

Display	Resolution (pixels)	Aspect Ratio	LCD Diagonal*
XGA	1024 x 768	4:3 (landscape)	35 cm (14")
SVGA	800 x 600	4:3 (landscape)	30 cm (12")
VGA	640 x 480	4:3 (landscape)	27 cm (11")
Clamshell PDA (Psion or WinCE)	640 x 320*	2:1 (landscape)	14 cm (6")
Symbian Quartz or MS Pocket PC	240 x 320	3:4 (portrait)	10 cm (4")
Palm	160 x 160	1:1 (square)	10 cm (4")
Mobile Phone	96 x 64*	3:2 (landscape)	3 cm (1")

Typical size. Exact value depends on manufacturer.

The theory behind many mobile data services is that the problems of low capacity and small screens will solve each other—if a device can only display text and simple graphics, it doesn't need a high-speed connection. This is true, but it fails to take into account the expectations of customers, who may be used to a multimedia Internet, rich with animation and video. This is why people are often disappointed when they buy a phone on the basis of spurious claims that it will enable Web surfing on the move.

HTML

Web pages were originally written in a code called *HTML (*Hypertext Markup Language*),* devised in 1990 by Tim Berners-Lee and other scientists at CERN, a giant particle accelerator beneath Geneva. It was intended to be a flexible way for the thousands of physicists who worked at the accelerator to share information and quite deliberately lacked any descriptions of how that information would appear. Whereas a document produced by a word processor or desktop publishing (DTP) program contains formatting instructions such as **bold**, *italic,* and different-sized text, HTML documents were intended to describe what the information actually means.

For example, instead of printing all definitions in italic, HTML would contain a code to say that they were definitions. The precise formatting was left up to software on the reader's computer, called a *browser*, which would read the code and display it however the user wanted. In theory, readers could choose to highlight definitions in capitals, in pink, or not at all, or (even more usefully) program their browsers to scan through a document and display all definitions in a separate glossary file.

This Web that its founders envisaged was ideal for access via a multitude of different devices, including cell phones. There would be no problem if a phone were unable to display fancy fonts or colors, because the user could choose to highlight information in different ways. The small screen size could also be overcome with properly structured information and a browser able to display different levels of headings. Instead of scrolling through long screens of text, people could select only the headings and subheadings that interested them.

Unfortunately for the mobile Internet, the Web soon evolved away from this model. With the introduction of graphics and the realization of the Net's commercial potential, presentation became more important than meaning, and often even than content. Many sites require either the Microsoft or Netscape browsers, neither of which are available in their full form for non-PC devices. Users of computers, let alone other devices, find it difficult to change the way that different codes are rendered on-screen. Even the heading display feature, which has found its way into word processors, is absent from browsers.

Consequently, several different open standards and proprietary systems have appeared in an attempt to "mobilize" the Web. As shown in Table 6.4, they share some common features. All use a *microbrowser*, which lacks many of HTML's more complex functions and restricts the length of files to sizes not seen in the computer world since the pre-PC era. They are also mutually incompatible—most browsers for Wireless Application Protocol (WAP) will not read sites designed for Web Clipping, and vice versa. All are independent of the underlying air link technology, just as HTML is independent of how the user connects to the Internet.

Table 6.4 Wireless Web Technologies

System	Style Sheets	Tables	Fonts, Frames	Bitmap Graphics	Security	CTI	Cookies	Applets	Scripting Language
HTML 4.0/ XHTML	Yes	Yes	Yes	GIF, JPG	Full	No	Yes	Yes	Several supported
C-HTML	No	No	No	GIF	Full	No	Yes	No	No
Web Clipping	No	No	No	No	None	No	No	No	No
HDML	No	No	No	WBMP	None	No	No	No	No
MeXE	No	No	No	WBMP	Partial	Yes	No	Yes	WMLScript
WAP 1.2	No	No	No	WBMP	Partial	Yes	No	No	WMLScript
XHTML Basic/ WAP 2.0	Yes	Limited	No	GIF, WBMP	Full	Yes	Yes	No	WMLScript

Compact HTML

As the Web became more focused on powerful computers with high-bandwidth connections, the W3C (Word Wide Web Consortium), the nonprofit group that oversees Web standards, decided to create a special version of HTML for devices with limited computing power. Known as *C-HTML* (Compact HTML) and published in 1998, it is literally a simplified version of HTML. Gone are additions to HTML, such as fonts, frames, tables, and style sheets, leaving behind the core textual display language that its founders wanted. Graphics are still supported, but more advanced extras, such as animations and Java applications, are not.

The great advantage of C-HTML is that it displays perfectly normally on any regular Internet browser. Indeed, the specification is quite similar to the recommendations of many Web design gurus, who caution against fancy effects that waste bandwidth and distract from content. A site coded in C-HTML should be accessible by almost anyone, including users of the Lynx and Mosaic browsers. It's usually implemented along with other standard Internet technologies, including those used for encryption and security. Among other applications, this allows customers to spend without fear of their credit card or other details being compromised.

The disadvantage is that such a lowest-common-denominator approach means missing out on features optimized for different types of devices. In particular, most popular Web sites rely very heavily on tables and cascading style sheets, which are missing from C-HTML. These are important for laying text and graphics out across the large area of a desktop screen, to maximize the amount of content and the number of advertisements seen by a user without having to scroll.

Although C-HTML is virtually unknown in America and Europe, it was actually the first mobile data standard to become widely adopted. By the end of 2001, it had more than 30 million users in Japan, all customers of the *i-mode* service from NTT DoCoMo. Thousands of Japanese sites were supplying content for it, nearly all of whom decided to design separate pages, rather than remove the non-Compact features from their regular sites.

The i-mode service has been an unprecedented success, becoming so popular that DoCoMo has tried to expand it to NTT's fixed-line phones, through a service called *l-mode*. Its success isn't just because of C-HTML: DoCoMo was also the first mobile operator to introduce packet-switching into its network, enabling phones to remain connected to data services at all times.

Web Clipping

Many Palm organizers use a proprietary system called *Web Clipping*, which is designed to download miniaturized versions of entire sites. Developed in 1998 by

Palm Computing's parent company, the networking giant 3COM, it was intended for the very low data rates of Cingular's Mobitex network.

Sites designed for Web Clipping are similar to those for C-HTML, in that they use a subset of standard HTML and do not support features such as frames and tables. But it is more limited: Most Palm organizers made before 2002 cannot interpret HTML directly. Instead, they require a special program called a *PQA* (Palm Query Application), which tells the Palm which parts of which pages on the site it should download. A separate PQA is needed for each site and has to be installed before the site is accessed.

The need for these PQAs severely limits a Palm user's surfing options, but it does have some benefits. The PQA can span multiple pages, so it is able to grab an entire site at once. Users can then read the site offline, saving money on connection charges. Perhaps most importantly, latency is reduced to zero, because many pages are already cached on the Palm device. Of course, this doesn't allow up-to-date content or interactive applications.

The first organizer to use Web Clipping was the Palm VII, which had a built-in Mobitex terminal and was sold only in the United States. Cingular's subsidiaries do operate Mobitex networks in several European and South American countries, but these use different spectrum, so they don't work with the Palm VII's internal radio modems. Web Clipping was later added to most other Palm organizers, which could access the Internet by connecting to a cell phone, allowing them to be used on many different networks all around the world.

Palm's latest Mobitex organizer, the i705, is based on a new version of Web Clipping that doesn't require a PQA. This makes the system much closer to C-HTML, though it still isn't exactly the same.

HDML

The *Handheld Device Markup Language* (HDML) is a more radical departure from HTML than either the compact version or Web Clipping. It was first developed in 1996 by Unwired Planet, then a small startup company but now one of the giants of the mobile Internet, thanks largely to the language's success.

As with C-HTML and Web Clipping, HDML requires that a site avoid the use of tables, frames, flashing lights, and other complicated features. But it replaces the familiar concept of Web pages with two new text layout metaphors: *cards* and *decks*. A *card* is defined as "a single user interaction," which in HTML would equate to a page but for such a small screen is more likely to be a menu. A single HDML file can include many cards, so it is called a *deck*. This differs from HTML, where each file represents a single page.

The advantages of the deck and card model are similar to those of the Palm VII's querying an entire site at once. Users can select items from a menu and see them instantaneously, without having to wait several seconds while their request travels across the wireless operator's network and then to the Internet. This is more important on the mobile than the fixed Web because of the small screen size; users can read a phone's screen full of text in less than a second, meaning they'd spend most of their time waiting if each one had to be downloaded separately.

The analogy between cards and pages is not exact. A Web page may include many different interactions with a user, known as a *form*: First it asks for a name, then an address, and so on. A card can contain only one of the following kinds:

- **Display** cards present data to the user. Here, the interaction is simply the ability to move on to the next card.
- **Entry** cards let the user type in a string, such as a password or a phone number.
- **Choice** cards are menus, the equivalent of Web hyperlinks. They allow the user to navigate between cards by selecting different items, similar to hyperlinks.

HDML was quickly adopted by AT&T, which launched a service called Pocket-Net in 1996. It ran over Cellular Digital Packet Data (CDPD) and initially could access 22 sites. Sprint followed with its PCS Wireless Web, which ran over cdmaOne. The leading mobile phone companies also became interested, and HDML eventually formed the foundation of the WAP standard.

XML

The W3C thinks that HTML's problem is a lack of flexibility. Whether the language is based on meaning or appearance—and at present it includes elements of both—Web page authors are limited to the descriptions built in to the language. They can specify that text should appear bold, but not upside down. They can specify that a piece of information is an address, but not a phone number. Each new version adds new descriptions, known as *tags*, but these just make it harder to learn and increase the size of browser software.

The solution is *XML* (Extensible Markup Language), a code that lets Web authors define their own tags and other elements. This means that it can be used for every type of device: computers, mobile phones, TVs, or anything else that becomes Internet-enabled. It can also replace the proprietary file formats used by application software such as word processors and spreadsheets, a direction in which several companies, including Microsoft, claim to be moving. Most of the hype is around *Web*

Services, which aim to link different computer systems together using machine-readable Web pages.

The W3C has defined special subsets, or *schemas*, of the language to use for such purposes as solving equations and in 2000 rewrote the HTML standard to make it a subset of XML, now known as *XHTML*. For once, the wireless Internet was actually ahead of its tethered counterpart. In May 1998, Unwired Planet and its phone vendor partners announced *WML* (Wireless Markup Language), a type of XML based on HDML.

WAP AND I-MODE ....

In 1997, the U.S. operator Omnipoint decided to roll out a mobile Web service. It had no idea how to go about this or which technology to deploy, so it opened the process to competitive tender. Anyone who could come up with a wireless data proposal was free to submit it to Omnipoint and to explain how it would serve the company's customers and increase revenue.

Four companies eventually took up this challenge. The cell phone manufacturers Nokia, Ericsson, and Motorola all suggested their own variants on messaging, while Unwired Planet submitted HDML. All had their advantages but the big disadvantage of being proprietary: Omnipoint's customers would be locked into buying phones and software from a particular supplier, similar to the way that most PC users are locked into Microsoft.

Omnipoint told the bidders that it would not accept a single-vendor solution—they had to get together and thrash out a standard. The result was the formation of the WAP Forum, which originally consisted of these four companies, though not Omnipoint itself. A year later, they threw the Forum open to new members and announced the first version of WAP.

WAP isn't the only standardized solution. In fact, it isn't really a standard at all, as many companies claim that they have patents on parts of the system. C-HTML is open to all and endorsed by the W3C. However, WAP differs from other wireless Web systems, in that it isn't just a markup language—it's a complete new *stack* of *protocols* designed to overcome some of a wireless network's specific problems, such as high latency and jitter. This makes it more complicated than C-HTML but also more suited to mobile devices.

Unfortunately, WAP's new protocols aren't compatible with the rest of the Internet. NTT DoCoMo, which uses C-HTML, compares WAP with Esperanto: It's ideal in theory but not much use for communicating in a world where people speak English or Japanese. For this reason, version 2.0 of WAP includes support for the existing Internet protocols as well as its own. The first phones based on WAP 2.0 were produced in early 2002.

WAP Protocols

In networking, a protocol is a set of rules for communication between similar devices. They can cover anything, but in general, protocols regulate such conditions as whose turn it is to transmit, how errors are detected or fixed, and how to distinguish data from signals sent alongside it.

Protocols were originally designed separately by dominant companies such as IBM and Novell. This meant that it was very difficult to get different vendors' devices to communicate with each other. It was as though they were not only speaking different languages, but also using different vocal chords to produce them. To get around this, the International Standards Organization developed a standard called *OSI* (Open System Interconnection), which defined a *stack* containing seven different layers of protocols. Each layer was responsible for a different function and independent of the layers above and below. The standard itself failed, because the specifications for the protocol were very expensive, but the concept of the stack lives on.

For example, the most popular protocol today is *IP*, the *Internet Protocol*. IP devices have to conform to strict rules, but they don't care about what the IP traffic is actually used for or what it travels over. Below IP lies the physical network infrastructure: a LAN, a telephone line, a fiberoptic cable, or a radio link. Above it are the applications that run on the Internet, such as Web browsers and e-mail.

Few real protocols follow the OSI model exactly, but networking professionals frequently refer to the different layers of the stack, so they are worth knowing about. The seven layers, along with an added security layer, are:

1. **Physical Layer.** This layer covers the actual transmission medium, such as radio waves. It also governs the type of modulation used (amplitude, frequency, or phase) and the design of interface plugs.

2. **Data Link Layer.** In a fixed network, this layer corresponds to the type of LAN architecture, usually Ethernet, or the phone system. In a wireless network, it covers the Time Division Multiple Access (TDMA) or Code Division Multiple Access (CDMA) multiplexing schemes of standards such as GSM and UMTS.

3. **Network Layer.** This layer is responsible for actually transferring data between different machines. The most common is IP, which routes small packets, or *datagrams,* based on an address (actually a number) encoded into them. Others include IBM's *NetBui* and Novell's *IPX* (Internet Packet Exchange), but these are becoming very rare.

4. a. **Transport Layer.** This layer covers error control and traffic prioritization. On the Internet, the original Layer 4 Protocol is *TCP* (Transport Control Protocol), which is connection-oriented like USSD; it waits until

an acknowledgement that one batch of datagrams has been received before sending another.

TCP is still used for fixed Web surfing and e-mail, but an alternative, called *UDP* (User Datagram Protocol), is becoming more popular for wireless access and streaming audio or video. This is connectionless like SMS, just sending datagrams off into the ether without checking that they arrive. This makes it less accurate but faster.

Version 1.x of WAP can use UPD/IP but as an alternative also contains its own protocol, called *WDP* (Wireless Datagram Protocol). This covers both Layers 3 and 4, resulting in more efficient transmission. Version 2.0 of WAP includes support for true TCP/IP, which is needed by many Internet applications but not really suited for wireless networks. It tries to get around this by using a slightly adapted version called *WP-TCP* (Wireless Profiled TCP), which alters some variables to make it more tolerant of jitter, the variation in the time that packets take to arrive at their destination.

4. b. **Security Layer.** This layer is not part of the OSI spec, but both the regular Internet and WAP include optional encryption standards that sit just above the Transport layer. The wired Internet's standard is officially called *TLS* (Transport Layer Security), but many programmers refer to it as *SSL* (Secure Sockets Layer), an older protocol on which it is based. Surfers sometimes call it *https*, because this appears at the beginning of Web addresses that encrypt the content. It's used when connecting to Web sites that ask for sensitive information, such as credit card details. Many browsers use a key symbol at the bottom of the screen to show when it is in use.

WTLS (Wireless Transport Layer Security) was not standardized until 1.2 of WAP, published at the end of 1999. This meant that the first generation of WAP phones lacked any security features except GSM's own encryption, which is why the acronym is sometimes pronounced *witless*. Even when WTLS did finally appear, it wasn't perfect: Converting between TLS and WTLS requires that data be decrypted, then re-encrypted, rendering it vulnerable to eavesdroppers. For this reason, version 2.0 of WAP also supports regular TLS.

5. **Session Layer.** According to the OSI standard, this is supposed to control who can send or receive information. However, on the wired Internet, it is largely irrelevant. SSL sits where the Session layer should be.

As if to make up for this, the original version 1.x of WAP requires two protocols at this layer. The lower one, *WTP* (Wireless Transaction Protocol), is designed to ensure that data has actually been sent correctly;

it checks for error messages from the recipient, then resends the data if necessary. The wired Web doesn't need this, because it incorporates error control into TCP at the Transport layer.

Above WTP is *WSP* (Wireless Session Protocol), sometimes pronounced *whisper.* It does nothing itself but enables traffic to bypass WTP or WTLS if error control or encryption are not needed.

Because WAP 2.0 attempts to include more Internet standards, it can eliminate both of these protocols in favor of *HTTP* (Hypertext Transfer Protocol), the protocol used to transfer Web traffic, which spans Layers 5 to 7.

6. **Presentation Layer.** This was supposed to control how data is presented to applications, but few real networks bother with it. The closest that they have is XML, which may emerge as a Layer 6 protocol.

7. **Application Layer.** This is the one most familiar to users and can often be seen in Internet addresses; the first few letters tell the browser which protocol to use. The most common on the Web is the aforementioned HTTP, but *FTP* (File Transfer Protocol) is also popular. E-mail has its own protocols, *SMTP* (Simple Mail Transfer Protocol) and *POP* (Post Office Protocol), as do individual applications, such as the distributed music system Napster.

In WAP's own protocols, the Application layer is known as the *WAE* (Wireless Application Environment). It supports four different applications:

- **WML**, the XML-based variant of Unwired Planet's HDML. This was the only way to code pages in WAP 1.x, so it was the basis of all WAP sites from 1999 to 2002.

- **XHTML Basic**, also known as *WML2*. This is a new language introduced for WAP 2.0, designed to be backward-compatible with both WML and C-HTML. It is a subset of XHTML, the W3C's recommended language for the regular Web. This means that WAP pages written for the new standard will display correctly in a regular browser.

- **WMLScript** (or Wscript), a programming language based on Java-Script.

- **WTA** (Wireless Telephony Application), an interface that allows WAP to access the phone's features, such as the address book, and even to make calls. Like WTLS, this was not added to the standard until version 1.2, so it was not implemented properly in the first batch of WAP phones, which appeared in early 2000.

Bearers

WAP is designed to be *bearer-independent*, meaning that it can run over any wireless technology. It is really designed for digital cellular systems but also works over shorter range radios. For example, Finnish telecommunications company Sonera has actually demonstrated how WAP and the single-chip Bluetooth radio can operate together, by bypassing the cell phone network when two devices are close together. It is testing Coke machines equipped with a WAP server and a Bluetooth transceiver, enabling any users nearby to access a menu of drinks. If they too have Bluetooth chips, the menu appears in their WAP microbrowsers, and the costs of any drinks they buy are added to their phone bills.

Most of the first real WAP services ran over GSM, usually requiring the user to dial a special phone number, as they would when calling an ISP (Internet Service Provider) from a fixed phone. This is inefficient for two reasons. It means both that users' phone lines are tied up and that they are charged for every second that they remain online. For most of this time, the connection is being wasted—the phone transmits or receives for only a fraction of the time.

"Bursty" traffic is ideal for packet-switching, which does not require a phone line to be kept open. Some operators have experimented with running WAP over SMS or USSD, allowing the user to make phone calls and surf the Web simultaneously, but the limits on message length usually make these services too slow. Many analysts think that WAP will really take off when it is integrated with GPRS, the upgrade to GSM that adds packet-switching and higher data rates. It also works well, though not as fast, with existing packet-switched services, such as CDPD and Mobitex.

Figure 6.1 shows the complete WAP protocol stack, along with some of the lower level bearers over which it can travel.

Architecture

Although WAP has its own protocols, these are designed for limited compatibility with the Internet. Pages written in WML can travel across the Internet using regular HTTP over TCP/IP, then be converted to WAP at a *gateway* between the Internet and the wireless network.

This protocol conversion leads to a security weakness, because the two protocol stacks use different encryption systems. Data is encrypted over the Internet using SSL; it's also encrypted over the wireless link using WTLS. But in between, it is vulnerable. Under WAP 1.x, operators of sites where security is important must either act as an ISP or fully trust whomever their customers are dialing through. In most cases, this is the mobile operator, though it could be anyone. WAP 2.0 tries to solve this problem by implementing the Internet's own HTTP and TCP protocols.

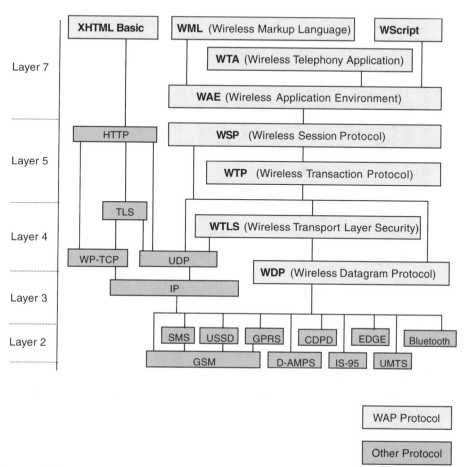

Figure 6.1
WAP 2.0 protocol stack.

WAP is often described as a *network-centric* protocol, meaning that most intelligence is located at a remote server on the network, rather than embedded within the comparatively "dumb" phone. This can cause compatibility problems, particularly where WMLScript is concerned. Although regular Internet browsers can contain an interpreter for their scripting language, most mobile phones can't. Instead, the script has to be compiled by the gateway, a process that depends on the type of processor chip inside the phone. To ensure that WAP actually works, gateways have to be tested with every processor, then upgraded whenever a phone based on a new processor is released. This problem is exacerbated by the lack of standards for phone processors; while the Intel x86 family acts as a de facto standard for PCs, there is as yet nothing comparable in the cell phone world.

WAP phones often don't look any different than their non-Internet-enabled counterparts. They may have a slightly larger screen or a wheel to navigate around it, but even these are no guarantee. Many phones have begun to include screens to play simple games or display SMS messages.

To make WAP devices easier to identify, most are marked *WWW:MMM*, which stands for *World Wide Web: Mobile Media Mode*. The phone companies hope that this will become a cross-industry brand, eventually lasting beyond the lifetime of WAP.

i-mode Security

Whereas the WAP Forum built a standard around several proprietary systems, DoCoMo took the opposite approach: It took Internet standards and used them in its own service, adapting them as necessary. This meant using C-HTML, which made sites easier to build, and several of the Web's other protocols.

Because regular TCP/IP doesn't work very well over a wireless link, the original i-mode service used DoCoMo's own (proprietary) midlayer protocols, instead. However, it retained regular HTTP for Layer 5 and above, as shown in Figure 6.2. This meant that it can also use TLS, the same security protocol used by Web sites. Data can be encrypted all the way from a phone to a Web server, without DoCoMo being able to peek inside in the way that WAP operators can.

These proprietary protocols are still used by the i-mode service that runs over DoCoMo's 2G Personal Handyphone System (PHS) network, but they've been abandoned for 3G. The i-mode service that runs over FOMA is based on Internet standards all the way, using the same WP-TCP as WAP 2.0. This doesn't affect the functioning of i-mode sites themselves but should mean that users see more reliable connections.

Java and BREW

The *Mobile Execution Environment* (MExE) sounds like a reference to the possible health effects of mobile phones, but it's actually another wireless standard from ETSI and the 3GPP. It aims to provide a thorough specification for running programs on a mobile phone, enabling sophisticated services to be provided by operators or downloaded by users. As well as a WAP browser, this requires a Java interpreter built in to the phone, which will enable it to run applications written in Java in the same way as PC-based Web browsers do.

The problem with MExE is that, so far, cell phones lack the processor power needed to interpret and compile programs. A typical PC is capable of calculating more than 1,000 MIPS (millions of instructions per second), whereas most phones can handle only 10 MIPS or less. This will change as technology advances, so MExE speci-

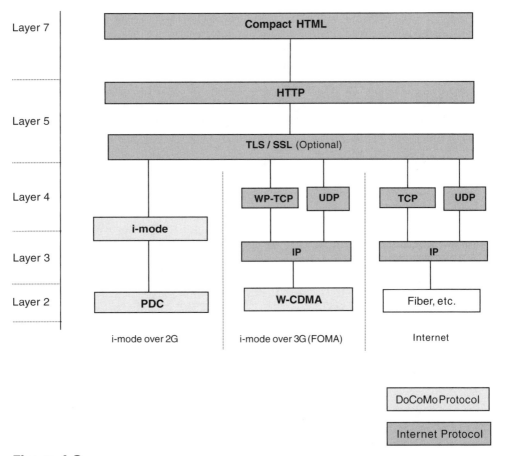

Figure 6.2
Protocols for i-mode are the same as the Web above Layer 4.

fies three different levels of support. Each allows more complex programs to run but requires a more advanced device. Level 1 simply means WAP, and Level 3 means full support for Java.

To help phone companies fit Java into devices with limited computing power, Sun has produced a cut-down version of the language, called *J2ME* (Java 2 Platform, Micro Edition). Plenty of vendors and operators plan to support this, including the giants Nokia, Ericsson, and NTT DoCoMo. As ever, DoCoMo is ahead of the others: In 2001, it launched a service called *i-appli*, which combined Java with i-mode (not WAP) to offer mobile access to corporate data centers.

Some programs that use .Net, Microsoft's rival to Java, will also be able to run on cell phones. Like Java, .Net requires an interpreter built into the device, known as the .Net *Compact Framework Common Language Runtime* (Compact CLR). This is currently available only on PDAs running Microsoft operating systems, but with several phones now incorporating PDAs, this will not prevent wireless Web surfers from downloading and running .Net software from their cell phones.

Because Java and .Net require relatively complex processing, Qualcomm has developed a simpler system called *BREW* (Binary Runtime Environment for Wireless). This supports precompiled machine code, which means that, all other things being equal, it should run faster than Java. However, the benefits of Java—that the same program can run on many different devices—are lost. BREW is so far limited to phones based on Qualcomm's own chips.

Qualcomm's chips are used in nearly all narrowband CDMA phones, so the potential market for BREW is still very large—about 100 million by the end of 2001. Of America's two large cdmaOne operators, Verizon is basing its services on BREW, whereas Sprint has instead chosen Java. Korea's LG Infocomm is working on combining both, because there's no technical reason why a phone can't support BREW and Java. Programs written in Java can even call routines written in BREW, and vice versa.

As computer power improves, the speed benefits of BREW will become less important and phones will be able to support more complex applications requiring J2ME or Compact CLR.

SITE DESIGN ....

If you want your site to be accessible over the wireless Internet, the choice is between WAP and C-HTML. But first, you need to understand how content is affected by users' access methods. If your site is full of long articles, forget about a WAP version—no one is going to read an online book through a device that can display only a few words at a time and has to load each paragraph separately.

The same applies to pictures. Pornography, one of the few markets in which dot-com companies consistently make money, is so far absent from the wireless Web because the image quality it depends on won't fit into a phone. Likewise, businesses that depend on banner ads will lose (more) money if they go wireless, because there's no room for them.

C-HTML Pages

If you know HTML or XHTML, "compacting" your site isn't difficult. There's no new language to learn and nothing new to add to your Web pages. You just have to strip away the unsupported tags, while rearranging the site so that it still makes sense without using frames or tables. Users of visual Web design software may find the process more difficult; these programs are very heavily oriented toward the features that C-HTML doesn't provide and can even need nonstandard extensions to HTML itself.

Every Web document is supposed to begin with a document identifier, which lists the version of HTML used. In practice, many sites just leave this out because browsers don't care, but if you want to follow the rules, the first line of a C-HTML document should be:

```
<!DOCTYPE HTML PUBLIC "-//W3C//DTD HTML 3.2//EN">
```

Headers in C-HTML are much more limited than in the full version of the language. Most *meta*tags, which HTML uses to add information such as the author's name and keywords for search engines, are not supported. The header should contain only the title of the document and, if necessary, a metafield describing how often the browser needs to refresh it. *Refreshing* means loading a new version from the Web server, rather than relying on a local copy stored in cache memory.

```
<HTML>
   <HEAD>
   <TITLE>A Wireless Web Site</title>
   <META NAME="refresh" CONTENT="xx">
</HEAD>
```

Other than the content of tags, the main restriction on the body of a C-HTML document is its length. The standard itself imposes no limits, but because phones have such limited computing power, it is normally recommended that the entire page does not exceed 4 KB. This is shorter than most existing Web pages but does allow for a complete text article or a form asking the user several questions.

```
<BODY>
   <P>A simple Compact HTML Page
   <P>Add other code here, up to maximum 4KB.
   </BODY>
</HTML>
```

The tags that are valid in a C-HTML document include most of those used for:

- Paragraphs and line breaks
- Horizontal lines
- Hyperlinks and their anchors

- Images in the JPG and GIF formats
- Forms asking for user input

Features not supported include:

- Frames
- Tables
- Clickable image maps
- Programming (applets and scripts)
- Font styles and sizes
- Emphasis (bold, italic, etc.)
- Meaning descriptions (address, acronym, etc.)

WAP Decks

A WAP site is more difficult to set up than one based on C-HTML. It requires a new language, new protocols, and probably new content.

Consider whether you need to develop an entirely separate site, potentially doubling the amount of time (for an individual) or the number of people (for a large corporation) that you devote to your Web presence. An alternative is to look at one of the many software translators available. Plenty of companies say they have programs that convert HTML to WML, but don't believe their claims—the languages are so different that, for many sites, the results aren't something you'd want to post on the Net.

Companies intent on serious m-commerce will probably use more sophisticated software that plugs straight into their backend database systems and generates WML on the fly. Many are already doing this with HTML, and adapting the process for WAP—or the other wireless Web systems—is comparatively trivial. Web design software is also beginning to incorporate WML capabilities, though often tailored for one specific brand of phone.

Assuming that you're doing it yourself, the header of a WML document should specify that it is a variant of XML and provide an Internet address where the full specifications can be found. In this case, the version of WAP is 1.2.

```
<?xml version="1.0">
    <!DOCTYPE wml PUBLIC "-//WAPFORUM//DTD WML1.2//EN"
"http://www.wapforum.org/DTD/wml_1.2.xml">
```

WML arranges files into smaller chunks called *cards*, each of which should represent about one screenful of information. Each card has its own title, which is displayed on screen, and an identifier, which usually is not. The identifier is used by hyperlinks, similar to the A HREF tag in HTML.

```
<wml>
   <card id="card1" title="Intro">
   <P>A WAP Site</P>
</card>
```

Mobile phone screens are so small that a single card could easily take longer to download than read, so several can be grouped together into a single file, or deck. The number of cards in a deck is unlimited, though some phones won't work very well if the total file size is more than about 1 KB. This makes the concept of decks and cards a lot less useful than it could be, because 1 KB is rarely enough for more than a few cards. Without any formatting or codes, this paragraph alone occupies exactly 0.5 KB.

Many WML tags are the same as those used in HTML. However, like all XML variants, it is much stricter. All text, for example, must be enclosed within a pair of tags. HTML authors usually omit the </P> tag at the end of paragraphs, but WML pages *must* include it or risk an error message.

```
<card id="card2" title="WAP Prototype">
   <P>Add other code here, up to a maximum 1 KB.</P>
   </card>
</wml>
```

Once a WML file is complete, it can be uploaded to a Web server. The server may then need to be programmed to know what WML files are, as most don't yet recognize them by default. This is usually as simple as adding one line to the server's *MIME* (Multipurpose Internet Mail Extensions) database and ought to become unnecessary as WAP grows more popular. But if you don't run the server yourself, it's important to check with whoever does as to whether WML files will actually be recognized.

The final step is to decide on a Uniform Resource Identifier (URI) for the site. Users will find it very inconvenient to type in a full filename on a phone's keyboard, so the Internet standard is *wap.domain.com*. This usually requires either a separate IP address or a special script that will automatically direct surfers to the right type of file, depending on whether they are using WAP or HTML. If you are registering a new domain, the number of key presses needed to enter the characters in its name could also be worth considering. For example, most phones require three key presses to type *C* or *F* but only one to type *A* or *D*. The word *WAP* was deliberately chosen because all of its three letters can be typed with a single key press each.

WEB RESOURCES

www.wapforum.org
This is the official site of the WAP Forum, where the official specifications for WAP can be downloaded for free.

www.gelon.net
If you'd like to see what WAP looks like but don't have a compatible phone, you can download a Java program that simulates a microbrowser here. It works on Netscape or Internet Explorer and has plenty of links to WAP sites.

www.palmos.com/dev/tech/webclipping/
Palm's official Web Clipping site offers details of the technology. If you have a Palm, you can download PQAs for many sites here. If you're feeling adventurous, you can also download Windows and Macintosh software for writing your own PQAs.

www.mobileussd.com and www.mobileems.com
These sites have a lot of information on the less well known messaging systems. They're both run by consultancy Mobile Lifestreams, which also has several other sites in the same vein, covering other types of messaging.

www.appelsiini.net/keitai-l/
This site has the archives of an English-language mailing list about i-mode and related Japanese mobile systems.

www.w3.org/TR/
The Technical Reports section of the W3C's site has details of C-HTML and XHTML Basic, as well as more general suggestions for sites to make themselves more accessible to browsers with limited capability.

http://www.x-9.com/mimic/beta.asp
This site contains i-mimic, an i-mode emulator that enables people outside of Japan to see what we're missing.

BIBLIOGRAPHY

Andersson, Christoffer. *GPRS and 3G Wireless Applications*. Wiley, 2001.
Despite the title, this book is more about WAP and its successors than the high-speed systems themselves. It's aimed at programmers, but it is also an interesting guide for the rest of us.

Bennett, Chris. **Practical WAP: Developing Applications for the Wireless Web**. Cambridge University Press, 2001.
A nontechnical and readable introduction to WAP, aimed at managers and site designers, rather than programmers.

Bulbrook, Dale. **WAP: A Beginner's Guide**. McGraw-Hill, 2001.
A comprehensive to designing both simple sites and more complex applications for WAP.

Vacca, John R. **i-mode Crash Course**. McGraw-Hill, 2001.
A look at NTT DoCoMo's i-mode system, covering both business issues and the technical details of C-HTML and PDC.

SUMMARY

- The most popular wireless data applications are *messaging* services. These originated in GSM but have spread to other technologies. They provide a very limited form of e-mail, though not one that is compatible with the Internet.

- The wireless "Web" lags far behind the fixed Internet in terms of both the data rates achievable and the power of devices used to access it.

- All existing techniques for presenting data on mobile devices miss out on some of the Web's most popular features, such as multimedia and even color.

- There are two competing standards for wireless sites: C-HTML and WAP. C-HTML was developed by Web designers, WAP by mobile phone manufacturers. XHTML Basic hopes to merge the two.

- NTT DoCoMo's very popular i-mode service uses C-HTML and other protocols compatible with Internet standards.

- WAP is a complete stack of protocols, not just a markup language. But it has a significant and perhaps deliberate security flaw, which gives mobile ISPs the ability to see encrypted information.

7 M-Commerce

In this chapter...

The hype around mobile data and the wireless Web is ultimately driven by one thing: the hope of a vast new market for products and services. In Germany, which auctioned its airwaves at the height of the 2000 telecom boom, cellular operators chose to pay a total of nearly $45 billion for third-generation (3G)-spectrum licenses. This works out at more than $600 for each potential customer, simply for the privilege of using a set of radio frequencies.

Operators all around Europe faced similar costs, even after the bubble burst. In Italy, where auction bids were lower than the government had hoped and the companies had feared, each potential customer cost the winners "only" $250.

The billions spent on spectrum are only the beginning. Operators then have to build their 3G networks and probably subsidize the phones themselves to encourage more subscribers. They also need to run high-tech research departments and mass-market advertising campaigns, all the while making payments on high-interest debt. All of this means that people will need to increase their spending on cellular services by an order of magnitude if the operators are to avoid bankruptcy, let alone make a profit.

Not surprisingly, many people doubt that 3G networks can be run profitably. The stock prices of companies involved in the wireless market have fallen with the rest of the telecom and Internet sector: By summer 2000, Vodafone had overtaken the venerable British Telecom to become the largest communications company in its native United Kingdom, then the largest company of any kind by market value. It was big enough to swallow both the American Airtouch and the mighty German conglomerate Mannesmann and to bully the British government over tax and planning laws. A year later, its market capitalization had fallen by half. Even companies that hadn't spent on spectrum were badly hit: Operating system maker Psion, the company that Bill Gates once described as the greatest threat to Microsoft, lost more than 90% of its value over the same time.

Mobile services probably won't produce the extravagant profits that operators once hoped for, but they're still an important and growing part of the economy. Nokia and Ericsson are still among Europe's largest companies, NTT DoCoMo was one of the few Japanese corporations to prosper during Japan's 1990s depression, and new startups are emerging to replace the companies that fail. Even if the operators themselves never make a profit, a high-bandwidth communications link that works anytime and anywhere will mean opportunities for others.

Some of the operators' planned profits will come from familiar telecommunications services: phone calls and Internet access. Although prices in this area are continuously moving down, the overall amount spent on them is going up, thanks largely to the popularity of mobile phones and the Internet. Wireless operators hope that they will be able to grow their own business faster than the industry as a whole, by taking customers from fixed-line telecommunications carriers. But this alone will not produce anything like the revenue these companies need to stay in business.

Much of the money is thought to be in mobile electronic commerce, or *m-commerce*. Most analysts predict that the cell phone will overtake the PC as the dominant Internet access method by 2005, with a corresponding increase in the amount of business transacted through it. Skeptics point out that the experience of using a Wireless Application Protocol (WAP) phone or similar technologies compares poorly with surfing the familiar Web, let alone with the offline world. Given that life is filled with so many other opportunities to conduct commerce, why should people choose to use a mobile phone?

The answer says more about operators than customers themselves. Most people keep their phones with them at all times, even when they're away from a shop, an Internet-connected PC, or anything else that can be used to sell them something. M-commerce gives marketers the ability to contact potential customers at any time and to track their movements both in cyberspace and in the real world.

M-BUSINESS PLANS...

Many people associate e-commerce with selling things over the Internet. This is understandable, given the high-profile Internet retailers that burned through venture capital, but many successful Internet companies have no relation to electronic mail-order catalogs. They are based on communication: helping people to stay in touch with friends, family, and business associates, or enabling companies to link their central network to remote employees and customers.

Back when analysts still thought that e-commerce would take over the economy, wireless carriers saw m-commerce as their chance to join the bubble, connecting buyers and sellers in return for a small cut of every transaction. In fact, m-commerce is even less focused on retail than e-commerce. Most people use cell phones as a means of communication, not to buy things. This is likely to remain the case once mobile data capability becomes widespread, though the type of communication may change: Basic voice service will be supplemented by e-mail (with attachments), database access and perhaps video or multimedia.

As companies have realized this, mobile business plans have been rewritten. People are not suddenly going to start doing their shopping over a cell phone. However, mobile services could play an important role in people's personal and professional lives. The most detailed studies of these potential services were carried out by the UMTS Forum, which categorized them into the taxonomy illustrated in Figure 7.1. Most of the service names are self-explanatory, with the exception of "rich voice." This means any voice-style service except basic telephony, and might eventually include videophones or voice recognition.

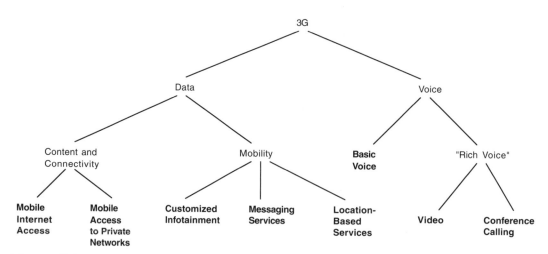

Figure 7.1

Types of service that 3G operators expect to offer.

The Forum has also predicted the likely worldwide market for each type of service, shown in Figure 7.2. As an organization promoting the industry, it's obviously biased, so the absolute dollar figures are probably overestimated. However, their relative sizes are more interesting. The Forum predicts that, even in 2010, the single largest money maker for cellular operators will be basic voice, just as it is today.

The other aspect of the Forum's figures that many people find surprising is the relatively small proportion of operators' revenue predicted to come from mobile Internet access, both in 2005 and later. This is because it believes that people will buy a specific mobile application, not raw Internet bandwidth. Most of what we now think of as the wireless Web is what the Forum calls "customized infotainment"—services such as DoCoMo's i-mode that provide content tailored for a particular user.

There will undoubtedly be more types of wireless service, which neither the UMTS Forum nor anyone else who tries to predict the future has yet thought of. The business plans that make use of such services are still forming within the minds of future entrepreneurs. If any are successful, they will probably not be carried over from the fixed Internet or even from traditional business. They will use a cell phone's unique advantages, namely, mobility and ubiquity, while relying less than the Web on high data capacity and on having the customer's full attention. However, a few ways to make money from the mobile Internet are more apparent and have already attracted heavy interest.

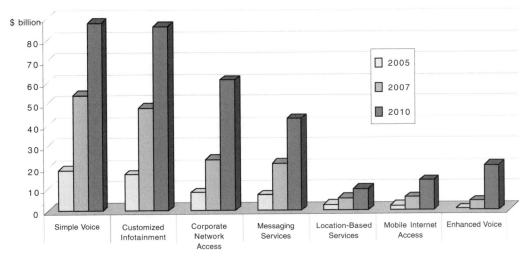

Figure 7.2
Projected worldwide revenues from 3G services.

Comparison Shopping

Though a cell phone is not an ideal channel for mail order, many Internet retailers have still created WAP sites. The reason is simple: The costs are relatively low for a company that already has a database set up to handle purchases made over the Web. It also makes them appear to be at the forefront of technology, even if it results in few actual sales.

Successful online retail businesses (and despite bankruptcies, these do exist) will not necessarily translate well to the wireless Web, because a cell phone is more suited to some types of purchases than to others. The immediacy makes it useful for time-critical transactions, but the small display makes people reluctant to browse extensively; an auction or last-minute bargain site is likely to be more successful than one selling books or computer hardware.

The beauty of Internet commerce, from a buyer's point of view, is that it enables us to shop around without having to move physically between shops. We can just click on a series of hyperlinks or run a program that automatically queries the likes of Amazon, Borders, and Barnes & Noble for the price of a book. This has made the Web a brutally competitive environment for companies involved in b2c (business-to-consumer) e-commerce and has even led to lawsuits in which sellers try to block automated shopping tools from checking their prices. But it may provide opportunities in the wireless area.

A mobile Internet terminal means that customers can access this ability to shop around wherever they happen to be. If a customer sees something she likes in a shop, she can instantly see how that shop's price compares with e-commerce sites all over the Internet. Some phone companies have even proposed data terminals with built-in barcode readers for exactly this purpose. Customers won't even have to fiddle with menus or look at the sites—they will simply scan in the barcode and let an automated shopping agent search the Web for the cheapest price.

There are obstacles to such a system, the most obvious of which is that real shops will disappear if people use them just to look for products, then spend their money online. Another is that shopping malls are notoriously difficult places in which to get a mobile signal. They are often buried next to subway stations or underneath car parks and filled with electromagnetic interference from every store's security systems. The owners of shops can improve reception by installing microcells, but they are unlikely to do this if it means being undercut on their own premises.

Successful comparison shopping will also depend on the ability of Internet retailers to undercut conventional shops, something that has yet to be proven. The early days of e-commerce offered many bargains but usually only by selling things at a loss. Delivery charges often negate any savings that come from not having a physical storefront. In the United States, many e-tailers survive only because of a tax loophole that (unfairly) exempts Internet and other mail-order purchases from the sales tax levied on customers who buy things in person.

Banking

The vision is of a phone linked permanently to a customer's bank account. With the ability to make transactions in real-time, this "bank in your pocket" could replace both cash and credit cards—in the offline world, as well as in cyberspace. At the push of a button, people would beam money to vending machines and electronic tills in shops, or even pay their kids an electronic allowance.

The reality is much more primitive but expected to advance quickly. Several companies claimed to offer "mobile phone banking" by 1999, though this often amounted to little more than sending the customer an SMS message containing her account balance. Some offered more interactive services, using custom-designed applications that run under the SIM toolkit. These usually do allow customers to transfer money, though only between accounts of their own; people can move their savings into their checking accounts, but usually they can't pay their electricity bills, let alone make impulse purchases.

Banks were initially excited by WAP and were among its first adopters in the spring of 2000. At the same time, analyst firm Datamonitor predicted that, by 2004, mobile phone banking will be used by 16 million Europeans, with another 5 million accessing similar services through their TVs. However, these potential customers seem less keen on the idea than do the banks and analysts. In an effort to kickstart their WAP and other Internet services, some British banks have taken to deliberately creating long queues in branches, intending to discourage customers from actually visiting them in person. In their defense, they say that cutting costs by closing branches is the only way to compete with new Internet-only banks.

WAP and similar technologies offer the potential for many more services than simple balance notification, of which share dealing is the one that gets venture capitalists most excited. Their publicity says that people will be able to view real-time quotes and execute transactions while away from their desks, a necessity in a world where many companies are listed on more than one index and exchanges are extending their opening hours. But potential night traders need to keep in mind that around-the-clock service is rarely guaranteed, and the nature of the stock market means that systems are likely to be overloaded just when they are needed most. Many Web brokerages and even telephone brokerages have failed to cope with the demand to sell during even modest crashes, leaving helpless investors with error messages as their assets deflate. Whether fixed or mobile, any connection is only as good as the systems at the other end.

The same applies to more commonplace banking facilities—most importantly, transferring money between accounts. Banks balance their books only once each day; if we deposit money today, we usually can't get at it until tomorrow. Worse, transferring funds between accounts in different names, let alone at different banks or across international borders, can take days or even weeks. This is due to a process called *clearing*, left over from the era when checks had to be physically taken to a bank's head office by horse and carriage. The only way to move money instantaneously around the world is to "wire" it through a company such as Western Union, which of course takes out its own cut.

For mobile phone banking to work, the banks will need a real-time clearing system, something that will take many years to set up. Meanwhile, many companies are trying to promote their own proprietary systems of digital cash—uncopyable files that delete themselves if moved to another computer. Units of digital cash could be downloaded using a mobile phone, then used to make purchases over the Internet or anywhere else. Unfortunately, no form of digital cash has reached anywhere approaching universal acceptance. The restrictions on where it can be spent make it feel more like a digital gift voucher.

The other problem with digital cash is its traceability: In principle, every transaction made electronically can be logged and stored indefinitely. Many people are opposed to this on principle out of a (probably justified) suspicion that their personal information will be abused by marketers or government agencies. Among the largest users of cash are criminals, who will never switch to any system that can be traced by the police.

Advertising

Advertising is a controversial issue among both users and Internet companies. Most users hate it, because they are still connecting to the Internet via slow connections and don't want to waste time downloading large graphics or animations. Advertisers themselves doubt its effectiveness, because the number of people who click on these "banners" has been falling ever since they were invented. By the end of 2001, the rate was about 0.1%, and many of these could be mistakes—people who click on what they think is a blank area of a still-loading Web page in an attempt to bring its window to the foreground, or those new to computers who haven't yet learned to use the mouse.

As a result, the cost of advertising banners on the Web has fallen so low that many media companies doubt whether Web-based advertising is a viable business model. Some general interest sites that rely on advertising cannot even make enough to pay for their servers and bandwidth, let alone produce original content. However, some very specialized sites that target a high-spending demographic can make money through advertising. Some analysts also believe that Web advertising for a more general audience will return, pointing out that it's unrealistic to expect people to click on a banner and purchase a product immediately. Few people buy a product immediately after seeing a TV or newspaper advertisement, yet these are not always considered failures by the companies that place them.

Web advertising probably will be back but not while the Internet remains in its current form. Once broadband wireless networks and Web pads are ubiquitous, people might begin to treat it in the same way as magazines, in which advertising is accepted. People are also willing to pay money or supply personal information (which increases the value of advertising) in exchange for a magazine subscription, but they are not willing to do the same for access to a Web site. Publishers sometimes say that this is because people have been "spoiled" by free content on the Web, but a more likely explanation is that the experience of sitting in front of a cathode ray tube on a desk simply isn't worth paying for. Mobile computing and wireless networks will change this.

In the meantime, banner advertisements are particularly ineffective over today's narrowband WAP and i-mode networks, because the screens are too small. However, mobile operators still see advertising as a key way to make money. They are privy to all kinds of information about their customers, most importantly, where they go and who they telephone. This information has obvious value to advertisers and will become more valuable as more data services become available. An operator that gives its customers wireless Web access gets to see which sites they visit, and one with a mobile phone banking system can see how they spend their money.

Mobile operators can already log every customer's approximate location, provided that the phone is switched on and within range. By cross-referencing this data with a map, it should be possible to learn when customers are at home, how they spend their leisure time, or which shops they visit and for how long. One customer's location log could even be checked against another's to learn about friendships and shared interests, though the operator may already know this from phone call records.

This type of analysis is technically possible but rarely carried out by real operators. At least, not yet. It raises obvious privacy concerns, risks a customer backlash and relies on data-mining technology, which is still fairly expensive. Plenty of Web sites have tried to track every mouse click, a much simpler process than location logging, only to find themselves drowning in data and unsure how to process it. For many a would-be Big Brother, the cost of the hard disks and administration personnel needed to store the huge database exceeds its commercial value.

Nonetheless, mobile operators believe that advertising will be an important market in the future. They know that people will simply switch their phones off if spammed by commercial messages, so they are instead proposing "pull" services. A customer might request the location of the nearest pizza restaurant, for example, and be presented with advertising for one that isn't necessarily the closest but will give them a special offer. This is the "yellow pages" model: Every business is listed, but those willing to pay the most receive a more prominent position. The difference is that the operator can make money from both sides of the transaction—through advertising and by charging customers to look at it.

Content

Like advertising, pay-per-view content has not been a success on the regular Internet. This is partly explained by the poor quality of the Web-surfing experience, compared with other types of media, and may change as technology advances. Tablet PCs and broadband wireless networks will eventually enable the Web to combine multimedia with the portability of a book or magazine, to create something that people will pay for.

In the meantime, DoCoMo has demonstrated that people are willing to pay for content delivered to a wireless device. As shown in Figure 7.3, nearly a quarter of all the data transferred over the i-mode network represents material from subscription sites. Content providers can charge whatever they like per month (forewarning users in advance, of course), with DoCoMo collecting the money for them and taking a 9% commission. This is higher in percentage terms than the cut taken by credit card companies, but there's no minimum charge. And it's much lower than the traditional publishing industry, in which authors are very lucky if they get to *keep* 9%.

The one type of content that does consistently make money on the regular Web is pornography. The small screens and slow data rates of cell phones are not really sufficient for porn, but many companies are trying to provide it, anyway. For example, Playboy and Penthouse both claim that their WAP sites are successful. In the long

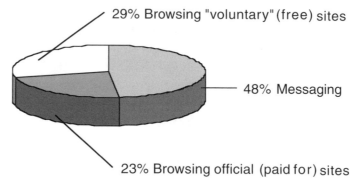

29% Browsing "voluntary" (free) sites

48% Messaging

23% Browsing official (paid for) sites

Figure 7.3
Data traffic on the i-mode network, circa September 2001.

term, porn will probably *not* be as popular on the mobile as the fixed Internet, even when display technology and data speeds improve. Both decency laws and fear of embarrassment will prevent people from consuming it while on a bus or in an airport.

Location-Specific Services

Although people may object to corporations or government agencies knowing where they are, the ability to pinpoint their own location can be very useful. Many operators are planning more advanced versions of existing location-based services, both because their accuracy is increasing and because higher data rates will enable more useful information to be sent in response to a user's request.

The most obvious example is mapping. Instead of having to carry around street plans, subscribers could simply press a button on their mobile devices and see zoomable maps complete with "you are here" arrows. This has actually been possible since the early 1990s, though it required a GPS receiver linked to a laptop computer with all the relevant maps stored in its memory. With a broadband network that can determine location accurately, maps can be downloaded as needed instead of stored on a device. This keeps them up-to-date and means that travelers can access maps while abroad— assuming that their phones are compatible with the local network, of course.

Other location-specific services can be envisaged, such as precise weather forecasts. Though predicting the weather is an inexact science at best, the error is comparatively small for short time periods. People often aren't interested in the weather a week in the future and want answers only to questions such as, "When is it going to stop raining?" or "Will there be lightning in the next two hours?" These can actually be answered to a very high degree of accuracy, but getting the information to the customer has traditionally been more difficult. Television and radio broadcasts cover a very wide area, which means they can't tell every viewer or listener what time their home will be hit by a thunderstorm. A mobile phone can.

Some operators view location-based services as a Trojan horse for location-based advertising. They know that customers will object to their exact positions being logged by marketers, but hope that the services' usefulness will outweigh privacy fears.

Streaming Media

Cell phone vendors often use stereo radio and even high-definition video as examples of applications that will be possible with 3G. The envisaged video-on-demand would enable mobile operators to take a slice of the pay-per-view TV market and let customers watch their favorite programs wherever they are in the world. The same applies to audio—people could listen to radio stations from anywhere and have them automatically interrupted for incoming calls.

Mobile phones already exist with integrated MP3 players, typically able to store up to an hour's worth of music. The problem is actually getting it in there; one hour of music at even sub-CD quality requires at least 32 MB, which would take more than 7 hours to download using a GSM or cdmaOne phone, circa 2000. Real-time music of this quality would require at least 64 kbps, which equates to five GPRS slots. This is a large and expensive commitment of bandwidth, particularly for an application already available over old-fashioned radio.

Far from taking the place of broadcast radio and TV, mobile operators could lose out to them in the market for lucrative data services. Most FM radio stations offer the *Radio Data System* (RDS), a way of broadcasting short chunks of data along with the analog audio signal. Its initial application was simply telling listeners the name of the station they were listening to, and originally it was fitted just to car radios. The idea was that, as someone drives between transmitter areas, the radio could retune automatically.

As RDS finds its way into home stereo systems and even Walkman-style devices, broadcasters are adding more information, such as the name of the artist and track being played on a music station. The in-car system is also being improved with an ETSI standard produced by and named after the *Transport Protocol Experts Group* (TPEG). This will automatically suggest alternative routes for drivers approaching traffic jams or even advise them to use public transport instead and send a list of suitable bus and train timetables.

RDS is limited to a data rate of around 1 kbps, but its successor is far more frightening to the mobile industry. *Digital Audio Broadcasting* (DAB) offers a capacity of 2.4 Mbps per channel, though in most countries, government regulations require that most of this be used for streaming audio. Even so, there is still enough left over to transmit photographs or detailed vector drawings. Several European countries had already begun commercial DAB services by 2000, and the BBC had even used the system to transmit Web pages. The digital version of Teletext, a popular European system that encodes data within TV channels, might also be used for high-speed Web access.

The common weakness of DAB, RDS, and Teletext is that they lack a return channel, so people cannot request information. However, some location-based services, such as travel and weather reports, are so popular that they could simply be broadcast to everyone. A receiver including a GPS system could automatically tailor the information to the user's precise position.

Games

Simple games have been available on mobile phones and handheld organizers for some time, but packet-based communication opens up the possibility of competing against other players. A small portable device is not the ideal games platform—gamers are the main market for the newest, fastest, most expensive desktop PCs—but their portability gives them an advantage. People who might not usually spend their time or money on games still appreciate the distraction they provide while standing in line or waiting for a bus.

Combined with online banking, multiplayer games provide the possibility of betting. This is illegal in many U.S. states, but some are warming to it: California, for example, allows telephone and Internet bets on horse races. Elsewhere, mobile phone gambling is not only legal but actively promoted by governments. The British National Lottery has plans to allow people to play via mobile phone, a prospect that has caused alarm among antigambling support groups. They fear that the phone will act as a pocket-sized slot machine, with a direct link to people's bank accounts.

Voice Portals

As an alternative to mobile data, some companies are now pushing *voice portals*, which they claim will enable Web surfing through a voice interface. Such claims are very misleading, as is the name "portal", which, in the Internet industry, suggests a Web site. Voice portals are essentially no different from interactive voice response (IVR) systems, which almost every phone user tries to avoid.

In 2001, almost every wireless operator in the United States began to offer some kind of voice-based "Web" service, but most of these simply allow callers to access data such as news headlines and stock quotes. Though such services may be useful, they're not the Web, and they're not new: Automated information lines have been around almost as long as touch-tone phones, predating both cellular networks and mainstream Internet use.

Their resurgence is down to four factors:

- **VoiceXML.** This is a schema of XML designed for voice-based applications, in the same way that WML is designed for cell-phones and XHMTL for computers. It provides a simple interface between IVR systems and other applications, but it has the same limitations as WML. A server can't decide by itself which words in a text-filled Web page are important enough to be displayed on a cell phone screen, let alone read out over an audio interface.

- **Voice Recognition.** This is continuously improving, but it's still relatively primitive. An ordinary PC with the right software can now act as an electronic secretary, producing text from a user's dictation. However, the computer still makes mistakes, and it relies on a high-quality microphone and an environment free of background noise. Cell phones produce a relatively low audio quality and are often used in noisy environments. As a result, voice portals are still able only to distinguish between a few words, making them suitable for only simple menu-driven applications. This will change as technology improves, but for now, the keys on a phone are almost always a better way to select items from a menu.

- **WAP can't be used while driving a car.** Many parts of the world ban drivers from talking on hand-held cell phones, requiring them to use hands-free kits. Unfortunately, although there's plenty of proof that cell phone use while driving causes accidents, there's no evidence that hands-free kits actually make it any safer. (See Chapter 13, "Do Wireless Devices Fry Your Brain?" for more on this.) Navigating a voice portal can be even more distracting than holding a phone conversation, thanks to the need to remember computer commands and repeat phrases that the machine hasn't understood.

- **WAP has failed.** Most new phones sold in 2001 included WAP, yet few subscribers actually used it. This led some operators to conclude that WAP had failed and to try another way to access the Internet on the move. However, WAP's problems were due to the circuit-switched connections that it ran over, not the system itself, and packet-switched networks such as GPRS do make it practical. It certainly failed to live up to the hype from companies who promoted it as a way to access the Web through a cell phone, but voice portals will prove even more disappointing.

BILLING...

Before mobile operators can become banks or recoup the billions invested in 3G networks, they need to sort out how they are going to charge their customers. On the customer end, consumers and businesses need to choose whether to pay for their airtime in advance or receive a monthly bill. But behind the scenes, an even more fundamental battle is taking place: Just *who* should pay?

Interconnection

Whether fixed or mobile, most phone companies can issue bills only to their own customers. If a Deutsche Telekom customer in Frankfurt calls a Bell Atlantic customer in New York, only Deutsche Telekom can send the customer a bill. Yet the call has actually passed through Bell Atlantic's network too, as well as that of a long-distance or international carrier. To ensure that all carriers are compensated for carrying each others' traffic, the phone companies have a complex set of regulations known as *interconnect agreements*.

Most countries originally had only one phone company, owned by the government (except in the United States) and known as the *Post, Telegraph, and Telephone Authority* (PTT). These companies had a monopoly at home, so interconnect agreements were needed only for international calls. As shown in Figure 7.4, the telcos in both the country where a call originated and the country where it was received got a share of the profits, with the customer who dialed the call ultimately footing the cost.

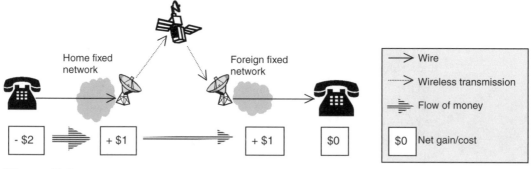

Figure 7.4
International accounting rate system.

The Accounting Rate System

Rather than have every carrier negotiate a separate agreement with every other, the ITU devised the *international accounting rate system*. This allowed each operator to charge as much it wanted to foreign companies terminating calls on its network. Not surprisingly, most wanted to charge a lot.

Though some international calls were once genuinely expensive to set up, using scarce capacity on subsea cables, the charges set by the accounting rate system owed more to politics than recouping costs. Interconnect rates have no impact on a company's own customers or a government's own voters, so there was no incentive to reduce them. Indeed, many poorer countries began to rely on interconnect fees as a major source of hard currency.

The international accounting rate system began to crumble in the 1990s, when alternative carriers first appeared. Each country then had to set up its own national interconnect scheme, so that customers of competing operators would be able to call each other. The rates were usually regulated by governments to encourage competition.

Though new operators usually complained that they had to pay too much, these national interconnect rates were many times lower than those set by the international system. Any entity could set up an international gateway of its own, undercutting the accounting rate system and connecting to the PTT via the national regime. With telcos competing for incoming international calls, prices fell. At least, that was what should have happened.

In Europe, international call prices are still very high. It usually costs more to telephone across a border than across the Atlantic. In part, this is explained by competition—there are more carriers in the United States than in most European countries, fighting more aggressively for traffic. But the popularity of mobile phones is also a factor. Cellular operators keep international call prices high, even for people who don't use a mobile or make calls to one.

Mobility

Although it is actually cheaper to build a wireless network than a fixed one—erecting a single transmitter costs less than digging hundreds of holes and laying cable to every customer—wireless operators have discovered that they can charge more than their fixed-line counterparts. Their excuse is that they need to invest in building new infrastructure and introducing new technologies, one that has some justification, especially where spectrum is auctioned for huge sums.

This *mobility premium* varies widely, according to the customer's contract, the time of day, and the type of call, but is often several hundred percent. The basic philosophy of mobility says that prices shouldn't be distance-dependent, so the premium is highest for local calls and lowest for international. The good news for mobile customers is that the premium is falling as mobile operators attack the fixed-line market. In 1999, one United Kingdom operator charged as much as 70 times the fixed-line rate for a local call made from a mobile; a year later, this was down to "only" five times the cost. For many types of calls—notably, long distance within the United States and international from Europe—it can cost less to use a mobile than a fixed phone.

More controversial is how the mobile operators charge for calls made to their customers. There are two main approaches, both of which are confusingly known by the same acronym, *CPP*:

- **Calling Party Pays.** Used in Europe, this system is shown in Figure 7.5. It adds the mobility premium to the interconnect fee, so that the caller pays the full cost. Mobile phones have special area codes, similar to 900 numbers in the United States, so that people know they will be charged more than for a regular phone call.

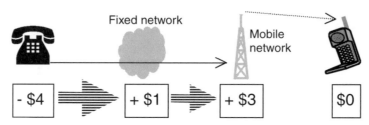

Figure 7.5
Calling party pays.

- **Called Party Pays.** Used in the United States, this system is shown in Figure 7.6. The mobility premium is paid by the mobile customer, so the caller has to dial only a regular number, usually one within the same area code as her home or office. It was needed because Americans are used to local calls being free, whereas in most of the world they are billed per minute.

The mobile mania in Europe is often attributed to the Calling Party Pays approach, because it means that customers are in control of their own costs. Europeans tell every-one their mobile numbers freely, knowing that the high costs of calling a mobile will put off most telemarketers. Because they don't have to pay to receive calls, they also leave

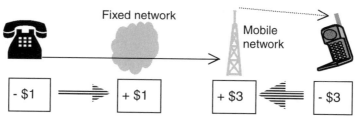

Figure 7.6
Called party pays.

their phones switched on at all times. American customers often turn their phones off, and many don't even know their own number because they never give it out.

Arguments over which method is best sometimes reach the ferocity of the "religious wars" between advocates of different cellular standards. This time, the differences are purely cultural. There's no technical or even legal reason why the Europeans and the Americans couldn't adopt the other's system, and indeed some have tried. Several British operators offer numbers that appear to be fixed lines in London but are actually routed over a mobile network, charging the mobile user as in the United States.

Opponents of Calling Party Pays in the U.S. often claim that "notification" is a problem: People making a call would have to be told that it was to a cell phone and, thus, that it would cost them more than one to a fixed line. However, European operators have a simple solution, giving mobile phones their own area codes. As with premium-rate or free numbers, people know that they will be charged differently from normal calls. For example, all U.K. mobile codes begin with "7," whereas geographic area codes begin with "1" or "2."

But Calling Party Pays has its dark side. Most mobile operators market themselves based on the cost of calls made from a mobile, where there is fierce competition. There is far less competition over the interconnect fees, because few customers bother to check how much it will cost others to call them. This makes the charges for calling a mobile very high, on a par with international rates. In Western Europe, it is usually more expensive to call a mobile phone than to call America. In July 2001, police actually raided the offices of several British and German operators, suspecting them of a criminal conspiracy to keep prices high.

Within a country, charges are passed on to the person making the call, but the accounting rate system allows no way to do the same internationally. A call from France to Britain usually costs the customer the same whether the destination phone is fixed or mobile, yet the interconnect fee charged by the mobile operator is often higher than the international rate charged to the caller. As shown in Figure 7.7, this could mean that the French carrier actually takes a loss.

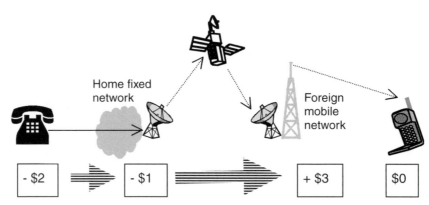

Figure 7.7
International call to a mobile phone.

In an attempt to stem these losses, companies keep their international call rates high, effectively subsidizing calls made to mobiles from those made to fixed lines. There are only two possible solutions: Either charge more for international calls made to mobiles or persuade the operators to end the mobility premium. Neither seems likely, because the former would confuse customers and the latter would give the mobile operator no way to recoup the costs of their licenses and infrastructure.

Roaming

Mobile users suffer the highest charges when roaming internationally, thanks to both the home network and the mobile network wanting to take a cut, as shown in Figure 7.8. The costs are so great in Europe that, in 2000, the European Commission began an investigation into an alleged cartel. It accuses operators of engaging in anticompetitive behavior by charging more to people roaming on their networks than to their own customers.

The problem is particularly severe in countries with large populations close to an international frontier, because radio frequencies don't respect borders and can "leak" between them. The Swiss city of Geneva, for example, is surrounded on three sides by France. Swiss users sometimes find that their GSM phones accidentally connect to a French network, forcing them to pay roaming and international charges. Most modern phones have a facility to display the network they are using, but not all users understand these messages.

Calling Party Pays does not apply when roaming because people making a call to a mobile can't know whether it is roaming or not. As shown in Figure 7.9, the caller pays the usual cost of calling a mobile phone, then the customer pays the extra roaming

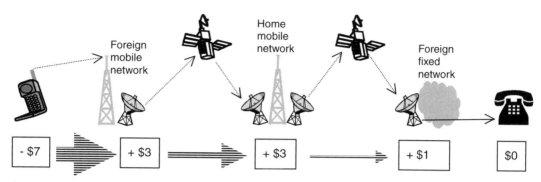

Figure 7.8
Call by a roaming mobile customer.

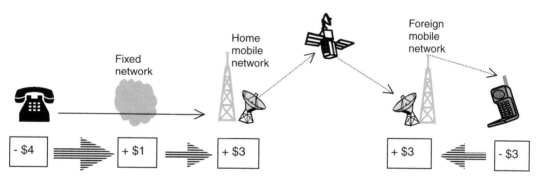

Figure 7.9
Roaming customer pays to receive calls.

fee. The exceptions are some satellite phones, which often connect via a regular cellular network if there's one available. These have their own special country codes and the highest international rates of all.

Present Pricing Strategies

The other big question facing mobile operators is just *what* they will charge for. At present, there are two models, one from the Internet and one from the phone system:

- **Minutes.** Traditional phone operators charge per minute (or other time unit). This is well suited to the circuit-switched world because a circuit has to be kept open, whether or not it is actually being used. It is still the predominant method of charging in both fixed and mobile phone networks, but it is not popular among Internet surfers. Per-minute charges are widely believed to have been responsible for WAP's lukewarm reception when it first arrived in Europe.

- **Bits.** On the Internet, large backbone providers charge each other for the amount of data sent across their networks. This model is sometimes known as *postalized* pricing, because it's based on "snail mail", for which payment is traditionally made by the sender. Most mobile operators use a similar system for SMS text: customers pay per message sent, not received.

On the Web, it may make more sense to charge the recipient, because few people running sites are going to pay mobile operators for people to look at them. This is how DoCoMo charges for access to "free" i-mode sites—those that people do not pay a subscription fee to reach. Data downloads cost about 2 cents per KB, which is also the length of a typical Compact HTML (C-HTML) page. This makes the system very expensive for people who need to transfer large files, but cheap enough for casual surfing.

Future Pricing Strategies

Pricing per bit is growing in the short term, but many companies and analysts believe that neither of these pricing models is sustainable in the long term. In both the fixed and mobile industries, telecommunications visionaries believe that capacity will eventually become "too cheap to meter." By this, they don't mean that data transmission will be worthless, but that the cost of measuring each bit or minute will be far greater than the cost of actually providing the service.

Instead of paying for every file that they download or for every second that they're online, users might instead be billed for:

- **Access.** Most businesses and individuals already pay a fixed fee for Internet access, dependent only on the type of connection they have. The same is true for local phone calls in North America, though the actual cost of connecting a phone call is the same, whether it is local or intercontinental. In the future, people may pay a flat rate for all their voice and data communications, perhaps with a small premium for mobility.

- **Content.** Because all mobile operators already have a billing system, they are easily able to charge customers *micropayments*—fees of only a few cents for looking at specific information. Concerns about fraud have prevented them from implementing a "click here and be charged a penny to view the next page" system on a wide scale, but DoCoMo does use its billing system to charge customers monthly subscriptions for many sites.

It also charges smaller fees on a one-time basis for individual premium services, such as stock quotes. Each customer spends an average of $25 per month through the system, which adds up to huge profits for a network with millions of users.

The closest analogy is to cable TV, where customers pay a set monthly subscription for a limited number of channels, but are also able to access pay-per-view programming.

Payment Plans

Until 1998, mobile phones were given away or sold at a large discount to their true cost. Customers had to sign a contract tying them in to one operator for a minimum period, usually a year. Monthly line rental charges over that year would recoup the cost of the phone, with calls and line rental after that being pure profit. This annoyed customers, who found that the initial "free" phone often locked them into uncompetitive contracts.

Free mobile phones still exist, but in Europe most users don't choose them, nor do they choose to receive a bill. They pay for both their phones and airtime in advance. According to consultants at the Strategis Group, by 1999, this *prepay* system accounted for two-thirds of all new mobile phone subscriptions in Europe and a full 90% in Portugal, where it was invented. Customers "recharge" their phones with money as they run low, usually by keying in special code numbers found on vouchers or by inserting the phone into a special slot within some cash machines.

Prepay's popularity may seem odd in the United States, where it has only about 10% of the market and is restricted to older phones, sometimes even those based on obsolete analog technology. But Europeans aren't as used to buying on credit, and prepay was originally marketed as an alternative to pay phones, rather than to fixed lines or other mobile plans. They generally allow more minutes per euro (the new monetary unit adopted by most countries of the European Union in 2002) than calling cards and, of course, are far more convenient.

From a customer's point of view, the advantage of prepay is that it allows her to buy a phone right away, without a credit check or a contract to sign. It also allows phones to be given as presents or entrusted to teenagers, the most enthusiastic users of all. In Britain, phones regularly top the list of children's most requested "toys" at Christmas.

From an operator's point of view, prepay was originally a great way to grow the market, but it has become something of a threat to their original customer base. Price wars have forced operators to subsidize the cost of prepay phones, so that they can often be bought complete with some airtime for $50 or less. This lets people buy phones and use them only to receive calls, leaving the operator out-of-pocket.

The highest subsidies of all are in the United Kingdom, where phone "smuggling" has become popular. Syndicates buy cheap phones in Britain, then resell them in countries where the market is not so competitive and phones are unsubsidized. This annoys operators but is not actually illegal.

Operators responded to what they saw as abuses of prepay by watering down the concept. Many block incoming calls unless the customer buys a new voucher every few months, and some even tried to charge a fee just for having the phone switched on. Most importantly, call charges are usually far higher for customers on prepay plans. As for many other services, people unable to get credit have to pay more.

The rise of mobile data and banking services gives prepay operators another opportunity—to *become* banks, rather than just partnering with one. Charging phones with prepay vouchers can be thought of as putting money into a deposit account. This money doesn't have to be used to purchase airtime; customers could also use it for m-commerce purchases, with the operator taking a cut, of course. The same applies to traditional billing, though under this system, the operator acts like a credit card company and so has to wait longer for its money. Many traditional banks feel understandably threatened by this and are rushing to develop services of their own.

CELLULAR SECURITY

Keeping data private is a big issue for any wireless network. In the days of voice-only communications, the greatest worry was that an eavesdropper could listen in to a private conversation, as several members of the British royal family discovered when details of their affairs were splashed across tabloid newspapers. But mobile commerce makes security even more critical—if people are going to entrust their bank accounts and personal details to a network, they need to be sure that it cannot be intercepted.

Encryption

Digital mobile systems all provide security through some kind of *encryption* system. Data can be encrypted in many ways, but algorithms used for secure data transfer fall into one of two broad categories: *symmetric* and *asymmetric*. Both rely on performing mathematical operations, using a secret number known as a *key*.

Symmetric algorithms depend on both parties knowing the key. They use mathematical operations that are easily reversible; for example, the sender could multiply the data by a number, then the recipient would divide it by the same number. Breaking the code means finding the key, so the strength of the encryption is measured as how long an eavesdropper would take to guess the key, using trial and error. Larger keys mean more possible permutations and, thus, better encryption. In theory, adding an extra bit to a key means that the code takes twice as long to crack.

The difficulty of cracking a code also depends on the particular algorithm and how it is implemented: A weak implementation often gives eavesdroppers and intruders clues about the key, allowing them to make educated guesses and avoid the lengthy process of trying out each key in turn. The implementation used by many wireless LANs is particularly insecure, as discussed further in Chapter 9, "Short-Range Wireless Networks."

The most widely used algorithm is the *Data Encryption Standard* (DES), invented by IBM in 1977. It uses a 56-bit key, which seemed unbreakable at the time, but not anymore. In 1997, a group of Internet users managed to read a DES-coded message, taking a little over four months using the spare processor cycles of more than 10,000 PCs. By 1999, the same thing could be achieved by a similar project in under a day. Most banks now use triple-DES, which is something of a misnomer. The encryption is performed three times, but the effective key length is only twice that of DES: 112 bits. Nevertheless, to crack triple-DES by trial and error would still take more computing power than is currently available anywhere. The distributed computing projects that can find keys for regular DES in hours would take nearly 200 trillion years to do the same for triple-DES.

GSM encrypts all data between the phone and the base-station, using a code called *A5* (the *A* is for *algorithm*). Its precise specification was originally kept secret to make it harder to crack, but details have leaked out over the years and have even been posted on Web sites and e-mail lists. It is thought to have a key length of 56 bits, the same as DES. This is reduced to 40 bits when shipped outside NATO and its allies, in a futile attempt to prevent strong encryption being used by terrorists. Any terrorist wanting strong encryption already has it, because more modern algorithms than A5 can be downloaded freely from the Internet.

Newer standards have stronger encryption, the algorithms for which are open to all. Unlike the designers of A5, most experts now believe that open algorithms are a better way to ensure security. The theory, which has been borne out by practice, is that a lot of people can test the algorithm for weaknesses. Any weaknesses that are found can be fixed quickly, and users can be sure that their data is secure (if they understand the math involved in cryptography, of course). Some of these are listed in Table 7.1, together with the length and the time that they take to crack by trial and error, using the same distributed computing projects that cracked DES.

The United States used to place far stricter limits on encryption export than GSM's European inventors, so versions of Windows sent to countries outside of the U.S. before the year 2000 all use only 40 bits. This means that, for most users worldwide, the GSM network is thousands of times harder to listen in on than are "secure"

Web transactions. The Web itself is more than a trillion times safer than the fixed phone system, which includes no encryption at all, yet people who don't think twice about giving out their credit card details over the phone still fear doing the same on the Web.

Some people worry that the CIA, MI6, or some other shady government agency is easily able to crack the encryption codes used by cellular phones. The truth is that they don't have to: All cell phone calls are eventually decrypted at the mobile operator's switching center (the equivalent of a telephone exchange). It is far more convenient to place a wiretap there than to scan for radio transmissions all around a country, and all mobile operators are willing to cooperate.

Table 7.1   *Encryption Algorithms Used in Wireless Systems*

System	Algorithm	Key Length	Time to Crack
802.11 LAN	RC4	40 bits	0.7 seconds
GSM	A5	56 bits (NATO)	12 hours
		40 bits (friendly countries)	0.7 seconds
		0 bits (world)	None
cdmaOne	Oryx	96 bits (U.S.)	1.5 billion years
		32 bits (world)	2.6 milliseconds
UMTS	Kasumi	128 bits	6.5 million trillion years

Authentication

The difficulty with symmetric algorithms is that both parties need to have a copy of the key. To transmit the key freely over the air would render the whole exercise pointless, so designers of cryptographic schemes often turn to asymmetric algorithms, instead. These use two separate keys for encryption and decryption. Usually, the encryption key can be publicly distributed, whereas the decryption key is held securely by the recipient.

Several different asymmetric schemes are available, each using a different type of "one-way" mathematical function. The most widespread is *RSA* (named after Rivest, Shamir and Adleman, its inventors), which relies on the fact that factorization is more difficult than multiplication. Multiplying two prime numbers together is easy for a computer, but recovering those two numbers from the product is not.

Unfortunately, the complicated math and large keys involved in asymmetric algorithms means that they use a lot of processing power and memory, so they are not yet found in cell phones. Instead, most mobile networks randomly generate a new *session key* for each voice conversation or data transmission, then send it to the phone in encrypted form. The über-key used to encrypt the session keys is known as the *authentication code* and has to be shared in advance. It's usually hard-wired into the SIM card within every phone and copied to the mobile operator's secure database at the time the SIM is manufactured. The concept of permanent authentication codes and temporary session keys is taken from *Kerberos*, a protocol used for security in many Internet systems.

It would be possible to dispense with session keys entirely and simply encrypt everything using the authentication code. (Some wireless LANs use this approach.) This would make the system simpler, but also more vulnerable: The more encrypted data that eavesdroppers can pick up, the greater the chances are that they will be able to guess the key. It's more secure to send data using disposable session keys, conserving the precious authentication code for the transmissions that really need it.

As its name suggests, the authentication code is also used to *authenticate* users and prevent fraud. Whenever a phone tries to connect to a mobile network, the network sends it a random number, called a *challenge*. The phone encrypts this number with the authentication code, transmitting the result back as a *response*. Because the network also knows the authentication code, it is able to verify the user's (or at least the SIM card's) identity.

The weakness in this *challenge-response* system is that an attacker can impersonate a mobile network, repeatedly sending challenges to a phone. By comparing a large number of challenges with the responses they illicit, the attacker could determine the authentication code, which could then be used to listen into a user's transmissions or even impersonate the user. To increase security, UMTS and Terrestrial Trunked Radio (TETRA) systems can also authenticate the mobile network. This works in the same way, using a second authentication code: The phone responds to a challenge with another challenge and checks the network's response before sending its own.

Wireless Portals

The problem with most wireless encryption systems is that they don't cover an entire connection. Whereas the Internet's SSL encrypts data all the way from a user's browser to the Web server, A5 covers only the air link, and WAP 1.x covers only the mobile part of the network. As shown in Figure 7.10, this leaves a weak link. Data is encrypted over the Internet using Secure Sockets Layer (SSL) or Transport Layer Security (TLS) and over the wireless link using Wireless Transport Layer Security (WTLS), but it is vulnerable at the gateway itself.

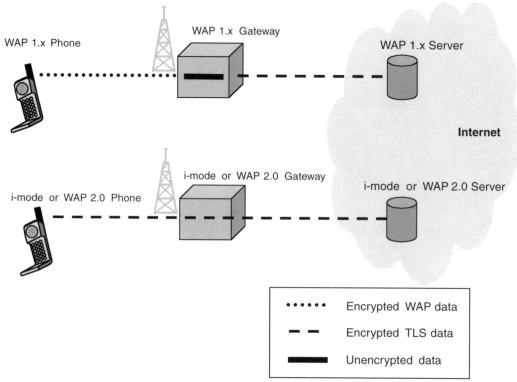

WAP 1.x Phone

WAP 1.x Gateway

WAP 1.x Server

Internet

i-mode or WAP 2.0 Phone

i-mode or WAP 2.0 Gateway

i-mode or WAP 2.0 Server

• • • • • • Encrypted WAP data

— — Encrypted TLS data

████████ Unencrypted data

Figure 7.10
Security vulnerability in a WAP 1.x network.

WAP 2.0 and i-mode both allow end-to-end security, but most cell phones outside of Japan are still based on WAP 1.x. The only way to ensure complete security for these is to own the gateway. Several banks have tried this, not wanting to share their customers with a wireless operator. To control their accounts, customers have to dial in to the bank's own WAP gateway, where they will also be able to access the Internet and pay-per-view content. The banks hope that customers will stay at their sites and return, spending money on services other than banking.

The problem for the banks, at least in Europe, is that they said the same thing about the Internet. In an effort to become fixed Internet Service Providers (ISPs), many offered "PC banking" only over their own dial-up connections, citing security concerns as a reason not to allow true Internet banking. The security vulnerability in WAP 1.x is more real, but customers seem to see it as another excuse.

As an alternative to the banks or the cellular operators, some companies are trying to set themselves up as secure repositories of a customers' banking and other details, automatically passing these to merchants whenever an online purchase is made. The advantages here are convenience—people don't have to type in their details separately for every transaction—and, in theory, better security. However, the security is highly dubious: The company that has made most progress toward offering this service is Microsoft, which has a reputation for very poor security.

Viruses and Malware

Ever since the mobile Internet was first suggested, antivirus companies have warned that viruses could attack cell phones and PDAs. In June 2000, their predictions seemed to have come true, with the media excitedly reporting that a virus known as Timofonica had struck cell phones.

In truth, Timofonica was an ordinary computer virus, programmed to send abusive SMS messages to random users of the Spanish TelefÛnica mobile system. It infected PCs, not mobile phones. The worst a mobile phone user would see was an annoying spam message, something familiar to everyone who uses Internet e-mail.

Unfortunately, spam sent to cell phones can do more than simply annoy. Many of the latest phones include computer-telephony features, which allow programs to initiate calls. In early 2001, fraudsters discovered that they could run programs on some i-mode phones simply by sending a text message. The result was an epidemic of messages that made calls to premium-rate lines, often unknown to the phone's owners until they received their bills. Even more seriously, one spammer sent out programs that made hoax calls to the emergency services.

The spam messages sent to i-mode phones were technically *Trojans* or *mail bombs,* rather than viruses, because they didn't actually spread from phone to phone. (A genuine virus reprograms a device to send out copies of itself.) However, the difference is mostly academic to the users who were attacked, and there's no real reason why viruses won't eventually infect cell phones and other mobile devices.

In theory, viruses are a threat on any computing platform. They didn't strike twentieth-century cell phones, but only because the processing and memory capacity of these phones was so limited. As phones become more powerful, they will gain abilities akin to those of computers. Wireless networks will prove an ideal medium to transmit viruses, and the sheer number of cell phones—they already outnumber PCs—will make them an irresistible target for virus writers.

Nearly all modern PC viruses take advantage of specific weaknesses within Windows operating systems, so it's possible that cell phones won't be quite as vulnerable. Most phone manufacturers plan to use other systems, such as Palm or Symbian, which are more secure. (For more on these, see Chapter 10, "Phones or Computers?") However, they're not immune. Both have already been attacked by malware, even though at the time they could run only on PDAs with no cellular capabilities. People downloaded the malware, using a PC, then copied it to the PDA, believing it to be something else.

The Symbian "viruses" have so far all been jokes. The most alarming is called, appropriately, *Fake*. It displays an animated dialog box together with the message "Formatting disk," which loses its impact somewhat when users remember that PDAs don't actually use disks. Others just flash obscenities on the screen or the even less subtle "You have a virus." Though these frighten some users, they do no damage and can easily be deleted.

Palm viruses are more worrying. The first was a program called *Phage*, which deleted data from a device's memory and could theoretically spread itself through infrared ports when people beamed each other electronic business cards. This sounds bad and was widely reported in the media, but no actual users contracted it. Like most viruses, its writers sent it directly to antivirus companies, and it never reached the outside world. Antivirus company Sophos estimates that only 0.3% of all viruses for any type of computer are ever found "in the wild."

On the basis that prevention is better than cure, many antivirus companies are already developing software that will detect viruses for Palm, Symbian, and Windows CE, the three most popular PDA operating systems. As Table 7.2 shows, most of this requires a desktop PC running desktop Windows. It aims to intercept viruses that are downloaded from the Internet using the PC, before they are transferred to the PDA. To protect against viruses downloaded directly to the device, the antivirus software needs to be run natively on the device.

A WAP or i-mode phone is not powerful enough to run antivirus software, but as spammers and hoaxers have proved, it is powerful enough to run malicious code. Fortunately, the WAP or i-mode gateway provides a natural point where antivirus software can be installed, as shown in Figure 7.11. A special antivirus server between the gateway and the Internet can prevent a virus ever reaching the phone.

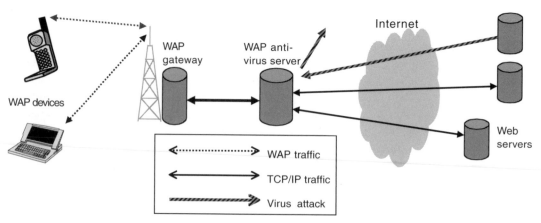

Figure 7.11
WAP antivirus software acts at the gateway, not on the phone.

WHAT IS A VIRUS?

Like "cloning", the name "virus" comes from biology. It refers specifically to a piece of self-replicating code that is attached to another file, in the same way that real viruses attach themselves to cells. Viruses originally targeted programs, but Microsoft's scripting languages have enabled them to hit Office documents and even e-mail messages.

Viruses are not the only type of malicious program, or **malware**. Among the most common threats:

Worms are stand-alone programs that replicate, usually by copying themselves to another computer on a network. Continuing the medical metaphor, they are sometimes known as **bacteria**, because they rely on no other programs. The definition of a modern "program" is fairly nebulous, so the difference between a virus and worm is subject to endless (and futile) debate.

Logic Bombs don't replicate but can be very damaging. They are simply programs designed to damage a system or perform another malicious function, such as deleting all a user's files or calling a certain cell phone number.

Backdoors are programs that lie dormant until they are activated by a cracker, who uses them either to spy on a computer system or to seize control of it. The most famous is a program called **Back Orifice**, which targets Windows servers. Software sometimes contains hidden built-in backdoors, allowing the programmer to bypass any password protection. The most infamous example of this was Microsoft's Internet Information Server, which in 2000 allowed anyone to access it by entering a derogatory comment about rival software company Netscape.

Trojan Horses are viruses, worms, logic bombs, or backdoors that disguise themselves as something else, tricking a user into downloading or running them. Nearly every e-mail virus now incorporates some kind of this social engineering, pretending to be anything from a Christmas card to pornography. The very first malicious program for the Palm PDA was advertised as a Nintendo Game Boy emulator but, in fact, erased all of a user's data when run.

Table 7.2   *Ant-virus Products for Mobile OSs*

Company	Web Site	Palm OS	Win CE	Symbian	WAP
F-Secure	www.f-secure.com	Native, Windows	-	Native	At gateway
Sophos	www.sophos.com	Windows	-	-	At gateway
McAfee	www.mcafee.com	Native, Windows	Windows	Windows	-
Symantec	www.sarc.com	Native, Windows	-	-	-
Trend Micro	www.trend.com	-	-	-	At gateway
Panda Software	www.pandasoftware.com	Windows	Windows	Windows	-

Cloning

Cloning is a serious problem for analog networks. It means copying a cell phone so that calls can be made from a customer's account without her consent. Because it doesn't necessarily rely on a phone being physically stolen, a user often won't know that her phone has been cloned until the bill arrives.

Cellular phones need to keep in constant touch with their networks so that calls are able to get through. They identify themselves by sending out a unique signal, which anyone can pick up, using a special scanner. Cloners record the signal and program it into a new phone, or several phones. These are then sold to other criminals or rented out to unsuspecting members of the public.

To combat cloning, cellular operators analyze usage to check for unusual call patterns. Most obviously, they know that a genuine phone can't be in two places at once. If it's making more than one call at a time, it has definitely been cloned. Large numbers of international or premium-rate calls can also arouse suspicion, though this sometimes irritates genuine users. There have been cases of people traveling abroad who suddenly found themselves cut off because the operator suspected that the phone had been cloned or stolen.

Digital phones are much harder to clone because they use encryption to authenticate each user. A GSM phone could be cloned in theory but only by opening it up and copying the SIM card. This is a difficult process that, even in purely financial terms (not counting the work involved and the risk of criminal charges) is likely to cost far more than the potential gains.

Theft

As wireless devices become smaller and more powerful, they also become more attractive to thieves. Their popularity has led to a large increase in street crime in London, purely as a result of mobile phone theft. Ironically, parents who give cell phones to their children are often motivated by safety concerns, though carrying a phone often makes them more likely to be mugged or robbed.

Technology could help prevent device theft, or at least make it less worthwhile for the perpetrators. Location technology should make stolen phones easier to track down, and a device could also be tailored to its owner using *biometric* technology. This identifies people through unique biological characteristics, such as a retina scan or DNA sequence, which are almost impossible for a thief to crack. The downside is that if someone does manage to fake them, they can't be replaced: It's easy to change a key or a code, but not to change your genetic structure.

The most likely biometrics to be used in handheld devices are fingerprints and *voiceprints* (specific frequency patterns within a person's voice, produced by the unique shape of the vocal tract). Both of these technologies exist today, and cheap fingerprint recognition systems are available commercially from mainstream computer manufacturers. But they are rarely used as antitheft features, even for laptop computers that cost thousands of dollars and often contain invaluable data.

This may be deliberate, according to the Design Against Crime initiative, a British project sponsored in part by the government and the London School of Economics. It claims that manufacturers actually *want* their products to be stolen, so that customers will replace them more frequently.

WEB RESOURCES

www.thecomicreader.com/html/icst/icst-5/icst-5.html
This is a great online introduction to micropayments in the form of a comic strip.

www.bbc.co.uk/digitalradio/
This site provides information on digital radio from the BBC, the first operator to begin broadcasts.

www.rds.org.uk
This site offers an independent forum promoting and explaining the RDS.

http://www.hut.fi/~jrautpal/gprs/
Helsinki University of technology has some interesting white papers about GPRS security.

(continued)

WEB RESOURCES (CONTINUED)

www.redherring.com
Red Herring is (at the time of writing) the only "New Economy" magazine to survive the dot-com bust. Most of its material is available for free online, covering the financial side of the technology industry, including m-commerce and the prospects for investors in wireless business.

www.mbusinessdaily.com
The online version of the (now defunct) M-Business magazine is a useful source of information about all aspects of the wireless business, including the clash between fixed and mobile.

BIBLIOGRAPHY

Aspatare Books Staff. **Inside the Minds: The Wireless Industry.** Aspatare Books, 2001.
A guide to the business strategies of several companies in the wireless business, written by high-level executives from those companies (or their ghost writers). There's obviously a lot of marketing spin and platitudes, but it's interesting to see what the major decision makers in the industry are thinking.

Burnett, Steve and Stephen Paine. **RSA Security's Official Guide to Cryptography.** McGraw-Hill, 2001.
A useful introduction to all the encryption systems mentioned here, and many more.

Grimes, Roger. **Malicious Mobile Code: Virus Protection for Windows.** O'Reilly, 2001.
A very readable account of computer viruses and other malware. It's focused mainly on Windows, because that's what most viruses attack, but it also covers mobile platforms.

May, Paul. **Mobile Commerce.** Cambridge University Press, 2001.
A well-written and readable guide to most of the ways that wireless operators and others are trying to make money from wireless services.

Steinbock, Dan. **The Nokia Revolution: The Story of an Extraordinary Company That Transformed an Industry.** Amacom, 2001.
A history of Nokia, arguably the most successful company in the wireless industry, from the nineteenth to the twenty-first century.

SUMMARY ....

- The wireless Web opens up many new business opportunities, the most important of which use location-based technology.

- A successful fixed-Web concept will not necessarily translate to the mobile environment. It will be used only for time-critical purchases, not those that require extensive information.

- Voice interfaces are usually not suitable for Web content.

- Advertising banners cannot work on mobile phones. The only kind of advertising that will not alienate customers is opt-in messaging sent with the recipient's consent.

- Mobile phones are more expensive to run than landlines and will remain so.

- Europeans generally pay for their airtime in advance and expect people who call them to pay the mobility premium Americans are usually billed later and pay to receive calls. It is unlikely that either continent will change to the ways of the other.

- Analog mobile networks are inherently insecure. Digital mobile networks are much more secure than any other commonly used form of communication.

8 Inside a Mobile Network

In this chapter...

Most mobile phone users come into contact with only a small part of the cellular system: their own handset and, perhaps, the increasingly visible base stations. Network managers may be aware of the other end: The Web servers that store pages formatted for wireless access. But these are only a small part of the mobile network. The base stations need to be connected to each other and to the outside world, and each operator needs its own back-end links and switches. Because of the need to keep track of a user's location and manage spectrum efficiently, the whole setup is often more complex than a traditional telephone network.

The infrastructure is further complicated by the growth of mobile data, which to operate efficiently requires an entirely new network based on high-capacity packet switching. New third-generation systems are designed for data from the ground up, but twentieth-century digital cellular systems are not. A data overlay must be added while maintaining the original voice network, on which users of older phones will continue to rely.

Most operators of 2G systems, such as GSM and cdmaOne, hope that the packet-switched data networks they build for upgrades can be reused in 3G networks. However, this depends on the operators winning a 3G license, which is not always guaranteed. Some governments are keen to license new entrants, rather than existing operators, to improve competition.

Figure 8.1 illustrates the path taken by mobile voice or data through a network, either between a cell phone and a fixed phone or between a WAP terminal and a Web server. The system shown is GSM with a GPRS upgrade, but similar devices are needed by other systems.

THE AIR LINK ....

The *air link* is the mobile equivalent of what telcos call the *last mile* or *local loop*—the final connection between the customer and the network. The name is somewhat misleading because it doesn't refer to every section of the network carried over air. Most operators have some base stations that are connected to the main network via high-bandwidth fixed wireless beams, and these aren't considered part of the air link.

For an air link to function, it requires two radios, one carried around by a user and one connected permanently to the operator's network. These are known to technicians as the *MSU* and *BTS* (discussed next), though most people think of them as the mobile phone and the base station.

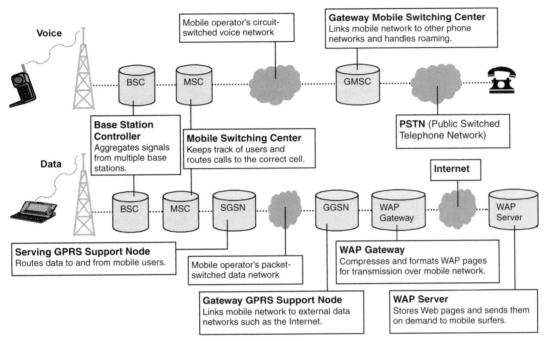

Figure 8.1
Paths taken by voice and WAP data over a GPRS network.

Subscriber Units

The *Mobile Subscriber Unit* (MSU), or *Mobile Station* (MS), is the name given by engineers to the terminal carried by users. For 1G and 2G systems, this is usually a mobile phone, but other cellular devices exist and are expected to become more common. Most non-phone MSs in the twentieth century offered data only, from simple pagers to relatively advanced Web and e-mail devices, such as the Palm VII and Blackberry pager. But 3G prototypes from companies such as Symbian promise true integrated voice and data, featuring two-way video and advanced computing functions. The future of phones and handheld organizers is explained in more detail in Chapter 10, "Phones or Computers?"

Base Stations

Usually called the *base station* or *cell site*, the *Base Transceiver Station* (BTS) is the large radio at the center of every cell. Most BTSs consist of several antennas, usually placed inside white rectangular boxes measuring about 1 × 3 m. They are normally placed high off the ground to prevent signals being blocked by buildings or trees. As well as the transceiver itself, a base station also needs to contain some kind of uplink to the mobile operator's network, which is usually a fiberoptic cable running through the ground or a fixed wireless transceiver. These are fully explained in Chapter 11, "Fixed Wireless Technology." Most also require a cooling system and heat sink, because the microwaves that transmitters generate can overheat their sensitive electronics.

BTSs have become an increasingly common feature of the skyline in many towns, sprouting on rooftops, lampposts, and even church steeples. This has led to a backlash, with local residents worried both about aesthetic and health effects. As a result, mobile operators have begun to camouflage them by placing them inside everything from statues to flagpoles. One of the most popular disguises is the artificial tree, sold complete with refrigeration unit and redundant power supply.

The problem with concealing base stations in this way is that it makes them harder to avoid. Though there is still debate over the safety of cell phones themselves, BTSs are much stronger microwave sources, and there is no doubt that they can be dangerous. Legends abound of military microwave installations in Alaska and Siberia, which gave away their positions by their tendency to boil snow over a wide area. Worse, cold warriors who tried to keep warm by standing in front of the transmitters reported a variety of health problems, including cancer and heart disease.

Both U.S. federal and European Union regulations specify maximum exposure levels for microwave radiation and mandate exclusion zones around BTSs, which depend on their power. For example, a typical base station will require people to be about 10 m away. This doesn't cause a problem for a station on top of a large pole or a tree, but it might be for one mounted on the roof of an apartment block. Such a setup requires extra shielding, though this isn't always enough to reassure the people living below.

If you are worried about cell sites, many phone companies or local planning departments will provide their locations. Failing that, some hobbyists like to drive or cycle around a city, using the signal strength indicator on their phones to determine when they are close to a site. On older phones, this can be made easier by removing the antenna from the handset, meaning that a signal will be detected only when very close to a base station.

VOICE INFRASTRUCTURE ....

A traditional cellular network is based on the fixed *PSTN* (Public Switched Telephone Network) but with some extra databases to deal with mobility. The equipment is analogous to switches, the devices at traditional telephone exchanges, which establish circuits whenever a call is made.

Mobile networks are relatively new, compared with the fixed system—they date from around 1980, rather than 1900—so the switches they use tend to be more advanced. Behind the scenes, all switching is digital, even on 1G systems, which use an analog air link. All mobile phones use tone dialing, which represents digits by musical notes. None use pulse dialing, the older system that sends a series of clicks instead. This is now rare on fixed lines in the United States but is still found in many countries. The name *dialing* refers to the rotary dial that was originally used to generate these clicks.

Though packet data is the hot new technology in the wireless world, the old voice infrastructure is not going away. Even when data networks are complete, many voice calls will still be sent over the existing circuit-switched infrastructure, as will new applications, such as video. Until the upgrades are complete, circuit switching will be the only option for data. This is the rationale behind HSCSD, the upgrade to GSM that increases throughput by binding circuits together.

Station Controllers

The first step in a digital cell phone network is the link from the BTS to the Base Station Controller (BSC). This simply converts signals from a base station to a more landline-friendly format. Analog networks need to place the BSC at the BTS itself so that analog radio waves can be converted to digital signals as soon as they are received. Digital networks prefer to locate it a few km away, which keeps costs down because it allows several base stations to share the BSC. It also means the complex and expensive electronics of the BSC can be kept in a safe and secure environment, rather than in the open air.

The cells linked to a single BSC will often correspond to the clusters, groups of between 3 and 21 cells that together occupy all the operator's available radio spectrum, described in Chapter 3, "Cellular Networks." A BSC can sometimes distribute spectrum among its BTSs dynamically, allowing more of it in a cell that contains more users. The BTS, the BSC, and the links between them are sometimes referred to collectively as the *Base Station Subsystem* (BSS).

Switching Centers

The most complex component in a mobile voice network is the *Mobile Switching Center* (MSC). Analogous to a telephone exchange, the MSC is responsible for keeping track of users and sending them calls when necessary. A network usually contains many MSCs, each of which is responsible for several clusters of cells.

Though they don't know it, all customers of a mobile network are registered with one particular MSC, described as their *home MSC*. This is occasionally used for billing purposes, defining calls within that MSC's area as local, but it is usually irrelevant to the end user. It *is* important to the network itself, because the home MSC is always contacted when trying to connect a call to the user.

Each MSC is linked to several databases, which are used to keep track of users' locations and billing information. These can be stored on a computer at the MSC itself, though they don't have to be—because all MSCs are linked together by a fixed network, they can be located anywhere. Some MSCs use both a local database and a backup copy.

The databases are shown in Figure 8.2, and include:

- **The Home Location Register** (HLR) contains the location of every handset registered to the MSC. Precise geographical information is stored for only users who remain within its own coverage area. If the user has moved outside, it instead stores a number identifying the MSC to which they have moved. This new MSC can be within the operator's own network or that of another operator into whose network the user is roaming.

- **The Visitors' Location Register** (VLR) stores the geographical location of all handsets temporarily within an MSCs coverage area. When a call is made to one of these customers, that user's home HLR contacts the new cell's VLR, enabling the user to be located. The weakness of this system is that all calls have to be routed via a user's home HLR, which can be expensive when roaming internationally—a local call within Paris made by a customer of a British network will be routed via the United Kingdom and charged as two international calls. Many networks are now implementing a newer system called *MAP* (Mobile Application Part), which looks up the HLR and VLR only once, then routes calls locally if possible. This reduces costs to operators, though most don't pass these costs on to customers: Roaming calls are frequently still charged as though they are routed via another country.

- **The Equipment Identity Register** (EIR) lists unique numbers that are used to identify each handset, associating them with phone numbers. This allows calls to be billed correctly. It also stores the details of all phones reported stolen, so that they cannot be used.

- **The Authentication Center** (AuC) exists only in digital networks. It stores the secret authentication codes for each phone on its network, a copy of which is also kept on the phone (usually in a SIM card). For faster processing, the authentication codes are sometimes copied to the HLR and VLR but they are never transmitted over the air. As described in the previous

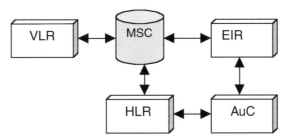

Figure 8.2
MSC database subsystems.

chapter, 2G cellular systems authenticate only the phone, whereas 3G and Private Mobile Radio (PMR) can also authenticate the network, to prevent criminals from setting up a fake mobile system.

- **The Messaging Center** handles SMS text messages, routing them to and from phones. It is included as standard in GSM systems but has to be added separately to networks based on other standards. The new Enhanced Messaging Service (EMS) and Smart Messaging systems can use exactly the same Messaging Center as SMS, but the even newer Multimedia Messaging Service (MMS) system requires a new one. This new MMS-capable Messaging Center is included as in all 3G systems based on the UMTS standard.

Trunking

In early cellular networks, all MSCs were *meshed*—each was connected to each other. This quickly grew uncontrollable, so Trunking Switching Centers (TSCs) became common. These simply aggregate connections from several MSCs, combining them in very high-capacity cables. Not all operators use TSCs; some simply have each MSC cover a very wide area. Where TSCs are used, a network will usually contain very few of them, or sometimes even just one.

Gateways

The *Gateway Mobile Switching Center* (GMSC) sits at the top of the switching hierarchy, as shown in Figure 8.3. It connects a mobile network to the fixed telephone network (the PSTN) and to other operators with which it has roaming agreements. One of its most important roles is to translate the cellular system's own signaling protocols to *Signaling System 7* (SS7), the protocol which regular telephone lines use to carry information such as phone numbers.

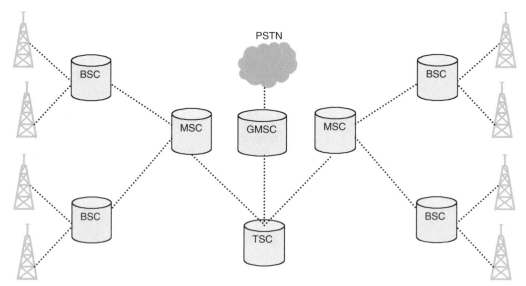

Figure 8.3
Mobile switching hierarchy.

Networks that utilize MAP, the roaming system that enables calls to be connected without being routed via their home network, require the GMSC to have its own HLR. This allows the network to locate all customers, without having to query their home MSCs.

DATA INFRASTRUCTURE ....

Mobile data uses much of the same infrastructure as voice, with a structure similar to BTSs and BSCs. Instead of telephone-style switches, it needs Internet-style routers, which send data in small packets, rather than through a continuous circuit. Most voice operators are now upgrading their systems to handle packet data, with the most common upgrade being GPRS. As explained in Chapter 4, "PCS Standards," this was designed for GSM and can easily be adapted for all TDMA networks. Because CDMA networks are newer, many of these already have some packet facilities built in, which are similar to those of GPRS.

GSM operators are rushing to deploy GPRS because it will enable them to use their capacity more efficiently; data effectively rides free during gaps in voice conversation and when the network is not busy, though congestion will occur at peak times. It is also relatively cheap, because it uses open standards that prevent the manufacturers from monopolizing a market. According to wireless system vendor Nokia, a very basic GPRS upgrade can cost only $1 million, compared with the $8 billion that Vodafone paid for a 3G license in the U.K. Such a basic upgrade would provide limited services, but the cost for a more comprehensive network is still measured only in tens of millions.

Packet Control

The most expensive part of a GPRS network is the *Packet Control Unit* (PCU), needed to adapt the base station for packet data. Each brand of BTS is slightly different, so operators need to purchase PCUs from the same company that supplied their original base stations. Newer networks are *GPRS-ready*, meaning that PCUs are already included or can be activated with a simple software upgrade.

The precise location of a PCU within a network depends on which company supplies it and the base stations. Some require a PCU at every base station, whereas others allow a single PCU to be placed at a BSC or even at an MSC. The PCU is the point where data departs from a voice network, so its position can have an important effect on issues such as latency and capacity. A PCU at every base station will bypass much of the existing infrastructure but is much more expensive to deploy.

Many D-AMPS networks already have some packet data capacity used by the existing CDPD services. Unfortunately, this is usually not sufficient for GPRS, so an upgrade is needed.

Serving Support

The *Serving GPRS Support Node* (SGSN) is the data equivalent of the MSC. Like the MSC, it is connected to various databases, which locate and authenticate traffic. Unlike the MSC, it does not need to be directly linked to each of the cells that it serves. In an ideal network, the SGSN would have a dedicated link to each PCU in its area, but traffic can also be backhauled over the voice network. This is slower and less efficient but allows operators to get a GPRS system up and running quickly.

An operator could theoretically claim (truthfully) to have full GPRS coverage with a single SGSN, though most traffic would be carried to it via the voice network. This is why operators' claims have to be taken with a heavy dose of skepticism. What matters is the *density* of coverage—how many SGSNs the operator has for a given area. In real networks, most operators will start with a few SGSNs and add more as the network becomes crowded.

Unlike PCUs, there are clearly defined standards for connecting SGSNs to cellular networks, so operators can mix and match their suppliers. This is important, because not all SGSNs deliver the same performance; there are plenty of options, such as queue management and quality of service (QoS). The type of SGSN deployed will depend on what kind of customers the operator is targeting.

For example, the German operator T-Mobil has a GSM network based on Nokia BTSs. When it upgraded to GPRS, it had to use Nokia PCUs but opted for Ericsson SGSNs because they were a closer match to the needs of its customers.

The GPRS Backbone

The various SGSNs in a mobile network are connected together with a mixture of fiberoptic cables and point-to-point wireless links. Most operators plan to put SGSNs throughout their coverage areas, gradually building a large data network. This is known as the *GPRS Backbone*.

The main difference between the GPRS backbone and the existing connections between MSCs is that the GPRS backbone employs packet-switching, making it more suitable for data. It uses a protocol called *GTP* (GPRS Tunneling Protocol), which is similar to IP, the protocol used by the Internet.

The GPRS Backbone coexists with the circuit-switched MSC network: It is used only for data, with voice calls continuing to be transferred across the older network. UMTS networks will eventually use packet-switching for voice, too. The packets will be carried across an upgraded version of the GPRS Backbone called the *Universal Terrestrial Radio Access Network* (UTRAN).

The Gateway Node

GPRS is designed to allow access to outside data networks, so it needs another device for this function. The *Gateway GPRS Support Node* (GGSN) can convert GTP data packets to and from TCP/IP, enabling an interface to the Internet. A network requires only one GGSN, though two or more can be used for redundancy.

The GGSN hides the complexity of GPRS from the Internet. Machines based on IP see the entire GPRS system as a single network, like any other on the Internet, and don't know that its users are mobile. This means that popular Internet applications, such as the Web, should function over GPRS, capacity and latency permitting.

The GPRS specification also calls for GGSNs to support *X.25*, a packet protocol popular before the Internet became widespread. Many operators are ignoring this, though some might decide to implement it, because some corporate networks still use X.25 to connect remote sites. It is particularly dominant in banking, used by shops for credit card authorization and by banks themselves for ATMs (Automated Teller Machines).

In communications technology, *ATM* usually stands for "Asynchronous Transfer Mode," a type of packet-switching sometimes used at the core of very large networks. GPRS does *not* support connection to this, though UMTS does.

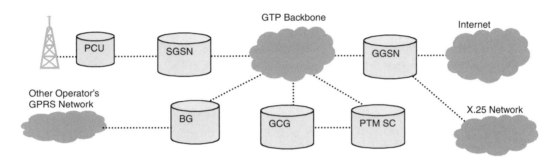

Figure 8.4
GPRS network.

Optional GPRS Infrastructure

The GPRS standard is still evolving, and many other infrastructure devices are appearing from manufacturers or being requested by operators. Some of these are shown in Figure 8.4 and include:

- **The Point-to-Multipoint Service Center** (PTM SC), a server that handles QoS issues. It prioritizes traffic for certain customers, usually those who have paid the most, and ensures that their data jumps to the front of the queue when the network is busy. Traffic can also be prioritized by type; for example, during a videoconference, most users consider the sound to be more important than the picture.

- **The Border Gateway** (BG), which deals with roaming. It is usually connected to a firewall, a device that blocks unwanted traffic by filtering out certain Internet addresses or applications.

- **The GPRS Charging Gateway** (GCG) is needed for specialized billing options. For example, operators might want to charge customers per byte of data sent or to change the pricing based on network congestion.

- **The Lawful Interception Gateway** (LIG) allows authorities to intercept mobile data traffic on a GPRS network. Operators in many countries are forced to provide this, though it's not something they advertise to their customers. Depending on the country, police may need a court order to spy on a particular user, or systems such as Echelon and Carnivore may automate the process and search for "suspicious" types of traffic. Unlike a normal wiretap, the LIG can actually archive all packets going to and from the user who is under surveillance. It can't (yet) archive everything that passes through the network, because this would require a vast data storage capacity.

GPRS Roaming

Though mobile Internet access is often hyped as an application for GPRS and UMTS, wireless operators predict that most of their future revenues will come from more specialized services, such as corporate network access and personalized infotainment. These rely on dedicated links from the mobile network to a corporate network, content provider, or online store, which means they can be used only by subscribers on that particular network—not by just anyone on the Internet.

This causes a problem for GPRS subscribers who are roaming on to a different operator's GPRS network: They are still be able to access the Internet, but not the extra value-added services on which they might depend. The i-mode service, for example, is available only to NTT DoCoMo's customers in Japan. They cannot use it while roaming in another country.

To enable roamers access to these specialized services, mobile operators need to implement a special type of GPRS roaming, as shown in Figure 8.5. There are currently two ways to do this:

- **Internet Roaming** simply passes traffic for the specialized services through the Internet. This is a cheap and simple solution, because every GPRS network is linked to the Internet, anyway. The disadvantage is that it can be slow, because the Internet subjects packets to unpredictable delays, and specialized services might use applications that have been designed for the more reliable direct connections. It also poses a security risk, meaning that packets have to be encrypted.

- **GRX Roaming** uses a new type of service provider called a *GPRS Roaming Exchange* (GRX). This carries GTP traffic directly between several different GPRS networks, bypassing the Internet's congestion and security problems. Because GPRS networks are located all over the world, GRXs need to have their own dedicated international data links, making them more expensive than simple Internet roaming.

Several GPRS operators have already signed up to GRXs, including Voicestream in the United States, the United Kingdom's Orange and Sweden's Telia. Analysts predict that many more will follow. However, the higher costs of GRXs may make some operators rely on the Internet for less profitable consumer traffic, reserving the GRX capacity for the most profitable business customers.

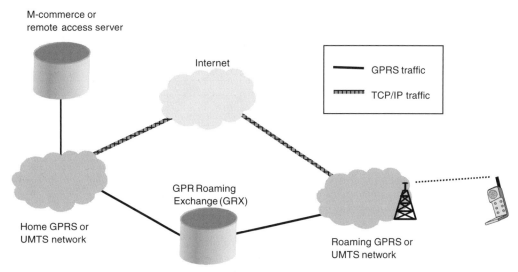

Figure 8.5
GPRS and UMTS roaming via the Internet or a GRX.

Wired Access Points

The MCDN system used by Ricochet is based on a somewhat different architecture from traditional cellular networks. Because its cells are so small—each covers a radius of only about 300 m—fixed networks are impractical for base station links. Instead, each of its small base stations acts as a relay (hence the name *Ricochet*), sending signals on to a larger BTS with a cell size of about 5 km.

Confusingly, these larger BTSs are known as *WAPs* (wired access points). Despite the unfortunate acronym, they are entirely unrelated to the better known WAP (Wireless Application Protocol). Indeed, one of Metricom's greatest boasts was that Ricochet offers the high bandwidths needed for true Web surfing, rather than WAP's scaled-down version.

Figure 8.6 shows how MCDN fits together. The microcell base stations are about the size of a shoebox and are usually placed on top of lampposts so they can use an existing mount and power supply. The WAP is usually much higher up, more closely resembling a traditional BTS. They have to be high up because the technology used to connect the BTS and WAP at high data rates requires a *near line of sight*; their transceivers don't need to be targeted exactly at each other, but they do need to be relatively free of obstructions.

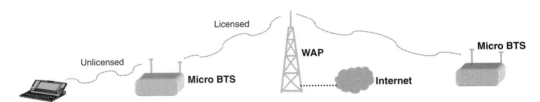

Figure 8.6
MCDN (Metricom Ricochet) data network.

As described in Chapter 4, "PCS Standards," the Ricochet system lost so much money that it drove Metricom into bankruptcy, and its future is uncertain. However, the MCDN architecture is similar to that of many proposed fourth-generation systems, all of which will need to use very small cells. Unless fiberoptic networks have become ubiquitous by the time that 4G networks are built—something that seems very unlikely, considering the high costs of digging holes in the ground for cables—the 4G base-stations will also need to use wired access points.

SERVER-SIDE EQUIPMENT...

Although the majority of users will find the details of the cell network itself irrelevant, many might be interested in what happens at the other end. Some high-bandwidth technologies enable access to the regular Web, but many devices are designed for lower capacities or smaller screens. Anyone running a Web site needs to decide whether and how to support these alternative access technologies.

Unfortunately, setting up a site using WAP or one of the other wireless Web standards is not just a matter of recoding your Web pages. Many cellular operators are keen to restrict customers to their own sites, making it very difficult for users to surf the wider Web. Some even block access to the Internet altogether, just like the old proprietary online services. An operator that does this is said to be *closed*.

The reasoning behind closed services isn't hard to grasp—the mobile operators want a cut of every online transaction, and if they can get away with it, they'd rather charge for information than allow access to other sites, where it may be free. The losers aren't just consumers; companies wanting to develop a WAP site or a wireless intranet may also have to negotiate agreements with carriers.

Many analysts believe that closed services will eventually disappear, thanks to competition between operators. They have already been ruled illegal in France, and other countries' regulators are monitoring the situation closely. Just as AOL and CompuServe were eventually forced to become ISPs (Internet Service Providers), operators will seek to differentiate themselves by offering *open* WAP access, which allows users to surf all over the Internet. This is already happening in some European countries, notably Germany, which has the continent's highest Internet penetration, thanks to the early deployment of ISDN phone lines.

WAP Gateways and Servers

As an alternative to waiting for open networks, webmasters can set up their own WAP gateway, a device that acts as a remote access server for WAP. Instead of connecting to the operator's own WAP service, users dial up the WAP gateway and access it directly. The problem with this, apart from the complexity, is the cost of calls. Dialing into a WAP gateway is billed per second or minute in the same way as a voice call, whereas mobile operators' own WAP services tend to be cheaper.

WAP gateways should not be confused with *WAP servers*, a generic term covering all types of WAP equipment. At its simplest, a WAP server is simply wherever WAP data are served from, usually a computer with an Internet address of the form *wap.company.com*. But some include other features, such as a WAP gateway and the ability to translate pages between different markup languages or to generate them on the fly from a database or an XML document.

Most WAP gateways are sold as hardware boxes, though they're based on standard components, usually Intel-compatible processors running some variant of the UNIX operating system. This means that, in theory, Web site operators can save tens of thousands of dollars by building their own, though they'd need WAP gateway software and some expertise in computing to set it up.

Unbundling and Virtual Networks

In Europe, some lawmakers want to help open WAP services with unbundling, regulation that forces operators to open up their networks to competitors at cost. This would allow ISPs to set themselves up as *mobile virtual network operators* (MVNOs), which use another's base stations and spectrum.

Unbundling is a concept familiar to experts in fixed telecom, but its application to mobile is untried. In the United States, unbundling allowed CLECs (Competitive Local Exchange Carriers) to run high-speed data services over the copper telephone wires owned by RBOCs (Regional Bell Operating Companies). For a time, this seemed to be a good means of promoting broadband Internet access to the home, though many CLECs went bankrupt during 2001. Some of them simply had unsustainable business models, similar to Ricochet and the dot-coms. Others were driven out of business by RBOCs, who calculated that it was cheaper to disobey the unbundling regulations and pay fines for doing so than to risk having to face competition.

Variants of the same principle are now being applied worldwide to end the old telecom monopolies. The Netherlands has devised what many believe to be the most sensible scheme, announcing that it will force unbundling and regulate prices only temporarily. This allows CLECs to win customers quickly but also gives them an incentive to put fiber of their own into the ground, overcoming the major objection that U.S.-style unbundling stifles innovation.

In the wireless world, unbundling has provoked an angry debate. Its supporters argue that there is actually a greater justification for opening up the airwaves, because these are a scarce natural resource—any number of companies can put wires in the ground, but only four or five can run mobile networks. Opponents say that it will slow investment in new wireless systems because, without the prospect of profits, operators will have no incentive to invest. In contrast, the copper wires already exist and, in most countries, were originally built by the government.

Even if unbundling is not eventually forced by regulators, there are already some MVNOs around. The best known is Virgin Mobile in the United Kingdom, which resells capacity on the GSM network owned by One2One and has plans to do the same in the United States, using Sprint PCS's cdmaOne network. By choosing to sell capacity to Virgin, One2One is effectively helping a competitor. However, it has a lot of spare capacity (as does Sprint PCS), so it has calculated that it can make more money by selling it in bulk to Virgin than by trying to sign up customers itself.

Virgin has been quite successful in the United Kingdom, thanks to its reputation: People generally distrust phone companies, but they like Virgin (or at least, they dislike it less). This suggests that any company with a popular brand can become an MVNO for the mass consumer market, without necessarily adding any real value.

Businesses and more savvy consumers are likely to reject MVNOs that simply act as a sales channel. MVNOs targeting this market need to add something extra, such as integration with fixed-line networks or better coverage. No U.S. operator covers the entire country, so an MVNO could buy capacity from several different operators that use the same technology and knit them together to form a nationwide network that doesn't require roaming. Existing operators might initially feel threatened by such a system and refuse to sell capacity to it, but they could change their positions if it helped to drive adoption and usage of mobile phones.

Mobile E-Mail Gateways

E-mail is the most important data application for most people. It's also relatively easy to reproduce on a mobile system, even a narrowband one such as Mobitex, CDPD, or even SMS. Unless they contain attachments, most e-mail messages are short, meaning they are relatively easy to send to a mobile device and to display on a text-only screen. Typing out a reply is harder, but some two-way pagers include tiny keyboards for just this purpose.

Many paging and SMS networks incorporate e-mail gateways, which give each an e-mail address. Unfortunately, this is usually something like *phonenumber@carrier.com*, which isn't very convenient. People may eventually use a mobile device as their primary means of data communication, but most current buyers of data-equipped cell phones and pagers already have an address (or several addresses) on their company's internal e-mail system or from an ISP. What they really want is mobile access to this.

Some wireless service providers will check e-mail accounts for customers, automatically forwarding messages. However, this works well only if the e-mail is stored on a server that supports the *Internet Message Access Protocol* (IMAP), a standard that allows parts of individual messages to be read while still on the server. For example, users could choose to read only the text from each message on her pager, leaving attachments on the server until she gets back to her computer

Most ISPs don't support IMAP, instead using the more primitive *Post Office Protocol* (POP). This forces users to download every message on a server whenever they check their e-mail. To prevent the same message being downloaded over and over again, mail is usually deleted after it has been read. This means that attachments and other content not supported on a mobile device could be lost.

Internal company e-mail systems usually don't support remote access via the POP or IMAP standards, both because they are based on proprietary software and because they are hidden behind a firewall to protect the corporate network from cyber-criminals. The best way to provide mobile access to these is through a dedicated gateway server, which interfaces with the proprietary system and the mobile network. These gateways usually leave all messages on the server, copying only the text that can be transmitted to a wireless device. As well as stripping out formatting used by the proprietary systems and some HTML-based software, they can filter e-mail messages according to predefined criteria. For example, a user might want the gateway to reject all messages from senders that he doesn't know, or only accept messages from a select group of colleagues and family members.

Figure 8.7 shows a gateway that sends corporate e-mail to Blackberry two-way pagers, which are very popular in America. It can interface with the two main proprietary e-mail systems, Microsoft's Exchange/Outlook and Lotus's Domino/Notes. Similar gateways are available for many other wireless devices, such as WAP or i-mode phones. They can also be used by ISPs that want to offer mobile access, as AOL is doing. It sells a device called the *Mobile Communicator*, a rebadged Blackberry that allows U.S. users to send and receive e-mail and instant messages over Cingular's Mobitex network.

Gateway software doesn't have to run on a dedicated server. It can also run on an individual PC, as shown in Figure 8.8. The advantage of this is that it can be made to work with almost any e-mail system, using either an ISP or a corporate server. The disadvantage is that the PC needs to be switched on and connected to the Internet at all

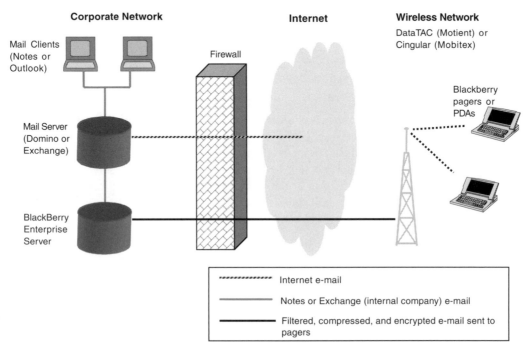

Figure 8.7
Mobile access to internal company e-mail via pager and gateway server.

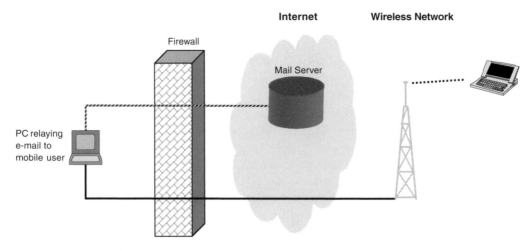

Figure 8.8
Mobile e-mail access via pager and software installed on a client PC.

times—very inconvenient if the user has a dial-up link and impossible if the PC is a laptop that she wants to take along. Some systems, such as Palm's mobile e-mail, support access via either type of gateway. A company may run PC-based gateways for a few employees, then switch to a dedicated server as it mobilizes more of its work force.

THE INTERNET ....

The wireless Web is less hyped than it used to be, but the Internet is an integral part of next-generation wireless services. Vendors and operators alike use slogans such as "Internet anywhere" and "Internet in your pocket," promising to cut the Internet free from its PC-based roots. Trouble is, no matter how advanced the systems sending data over the air, the Internet itself may not be up to the job.

The Internet was founded as an experiment, linking together a few computers involved in academic and defense research. It was never intended to become a communications system for the masses, much less the basis of the world economy. Exponential growth in fixed access has already pushed the network to its limits, and connecting every mobile phone and PDA might be just enough to knock it over the edge.

The problem lies in the addressing scheme that the Internet uses to identify computers and to ensure that each one gets the correct data. Although fiberoptic cables and more powerful computer chips mean that the amount of data passing through the Internet can grow without limit, the number of computers linked to it and the complexity of the network cannot.

Internet Protocol Version 4

Each computer, or node, connected to the Internet is identified by a unique number, known as the *IP address*. This must be encoded into every packet of data that crosses the network, where it is read by *routers*, machines that forward data packets via the most efficient path. The present version of IP represents this address with a 32-bit number, usually written as four 8-bit bytes. For this reason, it is known as *IPv4* (there were no versions 1 to 3).

In theory, there are 2^{32} or 4,294,967,296 possible addresses, but no router can learn the path to every one of them. Instead, routers at the Internet core forward packets based on only the initial bits of the address, known as the *network prefix*. Because all addresses have 32 bits, a shorter prefix means a larger network, and vice versa. The number of machines on each network needs to be a power of 2, which, on average, would waste a quarter of all addresses if every network took the smallest allocation mathematically possible. For example, a network with 100 nodes would need 128 (or 2^7) addresses, whereas one with 300 would need 512 (or 2^9).

Unfortunately, there are further practical limitations. First, most routers at the Internet core do not recognize networks smaller than 4,096 (or 2^{12}) machines, because these require long prefixes, and each extra bit in the prefix doubles a router's memory requirement. Second, the original IPv4specification allowed only three different sizes of networks. They were known as *classes* A, B, or C and used 8-bit, 16-bit, or 32-bit network prefixes, respectively. Routers were programmed to determine the class by looking at the first 4 bits of the address, as shown inTable 8.1; for example, the largest networks were class A, whose addresses always began with a 0. There were also two extra classes, D and E, used for broadcast traffic and for testing.

The class scheme meant that users requiring only a few hundred addresses had to request thousands or even millions. Early adopters were duly handed out class A and B networks, which most still hold on to. In 1996, the Internet Assigned Numbers Authority (IANA) issued an appeal to return unused address space, which has largely been ignored. More than five years later, only one complete class A has actually been returned: network 36, which until May 2000 belonged to Stanford University, one of the Internet's founders. The cybersquatters still holding onto other class As include some of America's largest corporations and most renowned academic institutions.

Table 8.1   *IPv4 Address Classes*

Class	Address Range	Initial Bits	Prefix Size	Nodes per Network	Number of Networks	Proportion of Internet
A	0.0.0.0– 127.255.255.255	0xxx	/8	1,677,7216	128	50%
B	128.0.0.0– 191.255.255.255	10xx	/16	65,536	16,384	25%
C	192.0.0.0– 223.255.255.255	110x	/24	256	2,097,152	12.5%
D	224.0.0.0– 239.255.255.255	1110	/4	268,435,456	1	6.25%
E	240.0.0.0– 255.255.255.255	1111	/4	268,435,456	1	6.25%

The IP Address Shortage

In the twentieth century, many offices and almost all home surfers only connected to the Internet for short periods of time. This meant that they could share IP addresses with many others, requesting a temporary address when connecting, then returning it when disconnecting. An ISP needed only as many addresses as it had modems, not as many as it had users.

This is quickly changing. Many U.S. consumers have already seen the benefits of fast, always-on connections via DSL, the fixed-access technology that achieves high data speeds over ordinary telephone lines. But what really threatens the IP address pool is GPRS, the always-on technology added to GSM phones. Though GPRS's capacity is far lower than that of DSL, each GPRS phone still requires it own unique IP address.

In March 2000, the GSM Association requested two class As, nearly 1% of the entire IPv4 address space. This may not sound like much, but it's just the beginning. The problem is particularly severe in Europe and Asia, where mobile phones are very popular but IP address allocations have traditionally been low, thanks to the Internet's American origins. RIPE (Rèseaux IP Europèens), the regional registry that handles Europe, has control over a space covering only 10 million addresses, whereas U.S. users have been allocated around 2 billion. RIPE simply can't afford to give away its address space to European mobile operators.

Worldwide, wireless manufacturers boast that mobile phones are giving many people the opportunity to make their first-ever phone calls. Mobile networks are easier than fixed to set up in remote areas, and falling costs mean that telecom will soon be within reach of some of the world's poorest people. But with a global population of more than 6 billion and all new phones Internet-equipped, there won't be enough addresses to go around.

Mobile IP

Because of the hierarchical nature of the Internet, users can't just take their computers and IP address wherever they go. IP addresses are specific to whatever network the prefix defines and won't work outside of it. Otherwise, the giant routers at the Internet core would need to remember all 4 billion addresses and their associated routes.

To get around this, the *Mobile IP* standard was published in 1996. It was designed for world travelers using laptops over fixed networks, but has been adopted by the wireless world. It uses a system called *tunneling*, which requires users to adopt a second, temporary IP address whenever they connect to networks other than the one to which their own IP address belongs. The home network then routes packets intended for the user to this temporary address, rather like having mail forwarded from your home while on a long vacation.

The problem with Mobile IP is that it routes all incoming packets via the user's home network, causing the same inefficiencies as roaming between cell phone networks. This isn't as noticeable to the user because Internet usage isn't billed by distance, but it does waste bandwidth and add latency. It also wastes IP addresses, because the user is temporarily given two.

Outgoing data packets should not have to be routed via the user's home network, just as most vacationers would not send a post card via their home address. But security considerations mean that they sometimes are sent this way, a process called *reverse tunneling*, which further reduces performance. Every packet has to contain the sender's IP address, which for a mobile user will not match the network they are actually in. Many firewalls reject such traffic because it is often a sign that the address has been forged, a common trick among attackers who want to conceal their identities.

Internet Protocol Version 6

As a permanent solution to the address shortage, network visionaries since the mid-1990s have been pushing a new IP standard, which uses 128-bit addresses. These split into 16 bytes, so the new standard is known as *IPv6*. Computer engineers often say 6 when they mean 16; Intel did the same with its x86 processor series, where the "6" meant that the processor could handle 16 bits at a time.

IPv6 allows a total of more than 342,000 decillion (or 2^{128}) addresses, which is enough to give every living cell on Earth its own Internet connection. The new standard also includes advanced QoS extensions and allows new ways of dealing with mobility.

In 4G and advanced 3G networks, users will be able to move between networks without tunneling. Each cell phone will be assigned at least *two* addresses: a permanent "home" IP address, along with a "care-of" address that changes as it moves and represents its actual location. When a computer somewhere on the Internet wants to communicate with the cell phone, it will first contact the home address, where a router or server. A directory server or router on the home network will then tell the remote computer where the cell phone user is, so that future packets can be sent directly.

The large number of addresses available under IPv6 will also enable networks themselves to move around, by assigning each one a home and a care-of network prefix. This would be useful for a very short-range PAN linking together all the devices used by a single person, or for a LAN installed inside a vehicle.

By applying different length prefixes, it's even possible to have several different levels of mobility. For example, a passenger on a moving train could carry around an ad-hoc PAN composed of a cell phone, laptop and headset, switching between LAN access points as they walk between carriages. These access points could in turn be linked to the outside world using a cellularWAN, connecting via different base stations throughout the train's journey.

Unfortunately, IPv6 is still in the future. All network architects agree that it is great in theory but don't want to use it in practice. According to the American Registry for Internet Numbers (ARIN), which issues IP addresses in North America, nearly 2,000 new networks requested blocks of IPv4 space in 1999, compared with only two requests for IPv6.

This will slowly change. Equipment vendors now incorporate IPv6 in most large routers, even though it isn't in heavy demand right now. Governments may even step in and try to legislate for IPv6 deployment: the European Commission believes that it is vital to the success of 3G and is consulting with national regulators to find ways to speed up its deployment. The Japanese government has said that it wants all networks to be using IPv6 by 2006.

Voice Over IP

Most cellular operators eventually want to integrate voice and data, which will mean splitting voice into packets and sending it via IP, just like any other kind of data. This should make the network more efficient—partly because packets are transmitted only when someone is actually saying something, saving bandwidth for others, but mostly because it means that the same components and technologies are used everywhere. Instead of maintaining separate voice and data infrastructures, operators will need only one integrated network.

Many of these efficiency gains are negated by the complicated structure of IP packets. All packet-switched protocols require a *header*, a few bytes that are transmitted before the actual data. The header contains routing information, such as the IP addresses of the sender and receiver, and sometimes extra information used to detect errors or apply QoS. Packet switching is often compared to the postal service, with the header represented by the envelope and the stamp.

Most IPv4 packets have a header length of about 20 bytes, which usually isn't considered too wasteful. Packets themselves can be up to 65,535 bytes in length, so the header may occupy only 0.03% of the total bandwidth. The problem is that voice and video produce much shorter packets. Toll-quality speech requires that a packet be sent once every two milliseconds, with a codec at about 8 kbps. This produces packets that each contain only 20 bytes, meaning that half the capacity is wasted by the header, as shown in Figure 8.9.

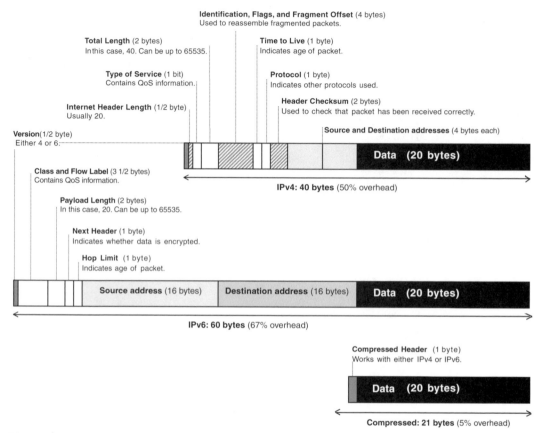

Figure 8.9
Header structure of IPv4 and IPv6.

The longer addresses in IPv6 mean that it is even more wasteful. Though it eliminates some little-used error correction found in IPv4, its headers are still twice as long, 40 bytes. This means that, with packets containing only 20 bytes, two-thirds of the capacity is wasted. Additional protocols at higher layers will waste even more.

The solution is to compress the headers, using a standard called *Robust Header Compression* (ROHC). Built into the UMTS specification, this takes advantage of the fact that most sequential packets have an identical header: Instead of sending a complete header many times over, a 3G phone can simply send the header once, then replace it with a short message telling the UTRAN to reuse the previous header. This results in very high compression ratios, squeezing both IPv4 and IPv6 headers down to only 1 byte. This wastes only 5% of the capacity in a 20-byte packet, which is more acceptable.

Efficiency isn't the only reason to use voice over IP. Many analysts and carriers predict that fixed-line telecom will eventually migrate to IP, too. Basing mobile networks on the same standard will result in greater compatibility.

WEB RESOURCES

www.rfc-editor.org
This site is the master repository for RFCs (Requests for Comment), documents that cover either official standards or suggested "best practices" for Internet communication. They can all be downloaded and copied free of charge, so many other Web sites mirror them, and some "authors" even print them out and bind them into books. There are a total of more than 3,000, of which, the most relevant to this wireless communication are listed in Table 8.2.

www.protocols.com
This site, run by Israeli equipment manufacturer RAD, details all common protocols, from IP down to the bit level.

www.ipv6forum.org.uk
The IPv6 Forum is a consortium of equipment manufacturers and network operators set up to promote the next-generation Internet protocol. It doesn't actually develop standards but has several useful white papers on its site.

www.base-earth.com
The magazine Base Station Earth Station covers the equipment needed to build a mobile network and the issues faced by cellular engineers.

www.ist-brain.org and **www.ist-mind.org**
Two projects set up by the European Commission's IST (Information Society Technologies) program have tried to look at how Internet routing will need to change to cope with mobility. The Broadband Radio Access over IP Networks (BRAIN) group developed a theoretical framework and its successor, the Mobile IP based Network Developments (MIND) group is trying to put this into practice.

Several Web sites cover general Internet news, though these are rapidly disappearing due to financial difficulties. Among the survivors:

www.news.com is run by CNet, the largest online technology publisher, which also operates other popular sites, such as download.com. It covers the computing and Internet industries, with breaking news several times a day.

(continued)

···

WEB RESOURCES (CONTINUED)

www.theregister.co.uk publishes both daily news and analysis, and has scooped many of the bigger sites on important stories. It doesn't pretend to be objective and isn't afraid to take a stand on important issues.

http://slashdot.org links to and allows users to comment on the most interesting Internet-related news stories from other Web sites.

www.techweb.com and www.commweb.com are run by CMP, the largest print publisher of technology magazines (and employer of this author!). Because much of their content comes from the print magazines, they're more focused on in-depth analysis than breaking news. Techweb is based on computing and Commweb on telecom, but there's a wide overlap.

Table 8.2   Major RFCs Affecting the Wireless Internet

No.	Name	Why It's Important
768	User Datagram Protocol	Defines UDP, the protocol used to ensure that information has been delivered in WAP 1.x
791	Internet Protocol	Defines IPv4, the fundamental protocol used for switching packets on the Internet
793	Transmission Control Protocol	Defines TCP, the protocol used to ensure that information has been delivered in many Internet applications and in WAP 2.0
1510	Kerberos Network Authentication Service	Describes Kerberos, an authentication protocol used by many wireless LANs and Web sites
1518	IP Address Allocation with CIDR	Defines Classless Interdomain Routing, a flexible way to assign IPv4 addresses
1889	RTP: A Transport Protocol for Real-Time Applications	Defines the Real Time Protocol, used for carrying voice and video over IP
2002	IP Mobility Support	Defines Mobile IP, the way that the Internet keeps track of users who move between networks
2194	Review of Roaming Implementations	Explores ways that Internet users can move between networks while remaining connected

Table 8.2 *Major RFCs Affecting the Wireless Internet (Continued)*

2246	TLS Protocol Version 1.0.	Defines Transport Layer Security, the encryption protocol built intoWAP 2.0
2414	Increasing TCP's Initial Window	Explores ways that the TCP protocol can be made more suitable for wireless networking
2460	Internet Protocol Version 6	Defines IPv6, the next-generation routing protocol that will be used by 3G networks
2501	Mobile Ad-Hoc Networking	Explains how Internet protocols could be used in short-range wireless networks such as Bluetooth
2636	Wireless Device Configuration	Explains how data terminals can be authenticated and added to a cdmaOne network
2728	Transmission of IP over a Television Signal	Describes a way to send Internet traffic alongside ordinary analog TV broadcasts
2760	Enhancing TCP over Satellite Channels	Describes TCPS at, a way of optimizing the TCP protocol to work with the long delays imposed by satellite networks
2916	E.164 Number and DNS	Describes ENUM, an attempt to integrate the Internet's addressing scheme with phone numbers
2994	Description of the MISTY1 Encryption Algorithm	Kasumi, the algorithm used for security and privacy in UMTS 3G networks, is based on MISTY1
3012	Mobile IPv4 Challenge/ Response Extensions	Defines an authentication system for Mobile IP
3024	Reverse Tunneling for Mobile IP	Describes how Mobile IP networks can use tunneling in both directions, avoiding the need to fake a return address
3077	Unidirectional Link Routing	Defines UDLR, a system that can create a full duplex link by combining two one-way channels (e.g., satellite downstream and analog modem upstream)
3095	Robust Header Compression	Defines ROHC, a compression scheme used in UMTS, especially for carrying voice over IP
3141	CDMA2000 Wireless Data Requirements for AAA.	An authentication scheme for mobile Internet users roaming across CDMA2000 3G networks.

....

BIBLIOGRAPHY

Perkins, Charles E. **Mobile IP Design Principles and Practices.** Prentice Hall, 1998.

A comprehensive technical guide to Mobile IP, the protocol that enables devices to stay connected to the Internet while moving between different networks.

Lin, Ye-Bing, and Imrich Chlamtac. **Wireless and Mobile Network Architectures.** Wiley, 2000.

A look at the infrastructure in a mobile network, focusing on what happens between the base station and the PSTN or Internet. There's also detailed technical information about SS7 and how this interfaces with wireless networks.

Naughton, John. **A Brief History of the Future.** Overlook Press, 2001.

A very readable and even exciting book about the history of the Internet and the pioneers in telecommunications who made it possible.

Solomon, James D. **Mobile IP: The Internet Unplugged.** Prentice Hall, 1998.

A less technical guide to Mobile IP and how it is used in wireless and other networks.

Steinke, Steve. **Network Tutorial, 3/e.** CMP, 2001.

A compendium of tutorials from **Network Magazine**, covering all aspects of networking. They're also available online at **www.data.com**.

SUMMARY ....

- Mobile networks require a complex fixed infrastructure, mirroring that of the telephone network and the Internet.
- Voice networks are formed from MSCs, the equivalent of telephone exchanges. GPRS networks are formed from SGSNs, equivalent to Internet routers.
- A WAP gateway enables users to dial into a network from their mobile phones. A WAP server is equivalent to a Web server.
- Open WAP networks allow access to any site. Closed WAP networks allow access only to those of the operator and its partners.
- Internet phones require IP addresses, which are in very short supply.

- For 3G to reach its full potential, the Internet will have to migrate from IPv4 to IPv6 routers.
- 3G networks will ultimately use the same infrastructure for voice as for data, running voice over Internet protocols.

9 Short-Range Wireless Networks

In this chapter...

Although cellular networks grew at a faster rate than any analysts predicted, shorter-range mobile systems were initially less successful. Wireless LANs (Local Area Networks) have never been as fast or as reliable as their wired equivalents and still suffer from competing standards. Cordless phones have proven more popular, but attempts to extend their scope and introduce roaming have mostly failed. And although infrared ports are built into almost every laptop and personal digital assistant (PDA), most go through their entire lives without being used.

This began to change in 2000, as wireless LANs finally reached acceptable data rates and affordable price-points. The Institute of Electrical and Electronics Engineers (IEEE) says that more than 15 million people used systems based on its 802.11b standard by the end of 2001. That isn't much compared to either cell phones or wired Ethernet, but the growth shows no sign of slowing. Newer systems are increasing data rates to the point where wireless LANs can seriously challenge their copper and fiber equivalents.

Rather than be put off by infrared's failure, the industry has tried to learn from it. The Bluetooth initiative promises to surround us all with personal wireless networks, linking every device that we carry. Though this has taken longer to arrive than expected, thousands of companies are still working on the system.

Most ambitious of all, public access wireless LANs could provide a shortcut to fourth-generation (4G) mobile systems, which will allow data rates in the multimegabit range. By incorporating several access methods into a device, people could roam seamlessly from LAN to 3G cellular to Bluetooth, noticing no difference except a faster or slower data rate.

UNLICENSED SPECTRUM.....................................

Most private wireless systems cannot be licensed in the same way as cellular and other networks. Nobody would use a cordless phone if they had to apply for a license from the government, much less engage in a bidding war with their neighbors. Instead, regulators have set aside special frequency bands for which no license is required. To minimize interference and protect users' safety, the transmission power of devices using these bands is limited to far less than that of a cell phone, restricting their range to, at most, a few hundred meters.

ISM

The ITU has designated several bands for *Industrial, Scientific, and Medical* (ISM) purposes, three of which are within the microwave region used by wireless devices. They were intended mostly for equipment that radiates microwave radiation as a by-product of its main function, not for communications purposes. Nevertheless, many cordless phones and wireless LAN systems have found them convenient.

Though the ISM bands are supposed to be international, the way they are implemented differs between countries. The precise frequencies in Europe and the United States are shown in Table 9.1. Governments anxious to license spectrum for specific services have chipped away at them, usually in different places. For example, the 900-MHz band is used mostly for GSM in Europe, meaning that ISM users need to get a special license.

The only ISM band guaranteed to be available in every country is the one at 2.4 GHz. This is widely used by many devices, including microwave ovens and medical equipment. The interference from these would prevent any government being able to license it for mobile services, so it is free for anyone to use for almost any purpose. This is why it's employed by most wireless LAN technologies, many cordless phones, and Bluetooth.

The ISM-2.4 band is so popular that it has become quite overcrowded, making it unsuitable for high-capacity connections. Because interference is almost inevitable, all communications systems that use it need to be based on some form of spread spectrum, the family of technologies that includes CDMA. Even so, the limit is about 11 Mbps, with higher speed technologies needing to use higher frequencies, usually in dedicated bands.

Table 9.1   ISM Bands Useful for Wireless Communications

Band Name	FCC Frequencies	ETSI Frequencies	Main Use
ISM-900	902–928 MHz	890–906 MHz	Food processing
ISM-2.4	2.4–2.4835 GHz	2.4–2.5 GHz	Microwave ovens
ISM-5.8	5.725–5.850 GHz	5.725–5.875 GHz	Medical scanners

License-Free Radio

With ISM bands subject to interference from all kinds of devices, most governments have allocated bands to specific types of communications services. Echoing their different approaches to cellular licensing, Europe also mandates which technology the services should use; the United States leaves this up to vendors and users.

Though there can be little doubt that Europe made the right decision in mandating GSM for digital cellular, it is questionable whether the same logic applies to wireless LANs. Cellular networks need to cover as wide an area as possible, and the ability to use the same phone while roaming is an obvious benefit. A short-range network is private almost by definition, so most users don't care whether their own is compatible with someone else's.

The most interesting of the specific service bands are allocated to high-speed wireless LANs, shown in Table 9.2. Though several have been set aside for future systems, the only one yet actually in use is at 5.7 GHz, immediately below the higher ISM band. It was first defined by the European Union in 1992, which intended it to be used for a then-future standard called *HiperLan.*

Six years later, the first HiperLan products had still not appeared, and the proposed standard had itself split into two incompatible systems. Despite this apparent failure, the United States and Japan decided to follow Europe's lead in allocating spectrum for high-speed networks, though not in mandating the HiperLan standards. The U.S. band is known as *U-NII* (Unlicensed National Information Infrastructure), Japan's as *HSWA* (High-Speed Wireless Access).

Both the HiperLan and the U-NII bands overlap with the ISM-5.8 band. This is deliberate: There aren't many ISM devices at 5.8 GHz., so they shouldn't cause too much interference—and if they do, devices can change to the interference-free, dedicated band for communications only.

Higher up the frequency chart and further into the future, two other bands have been allocated. *HiperLink* is a European project aimed at longer range links between different rooms or floors within a large building, using spectrum around 17 GHz. A huge chunk in the 60-GHz range has also been given over to the wireless LAN component of *MBS* (Mobile Broadband System), the fourth-generation system already planned by some in Europe.

Though all these bands are designated for communications, they're not reserved for wireless LANs only. Many companies are also interested in using them for long-range outdoor links that require high-power directional antennas. These are discussed further in Chapter 11, "Fixed Wireless Technology."

Table 9.2   *Spectrum Allocation for High-Speed Wireless LAN Systems*

Name	Frequencies	Bandwidth	Available
U-NII	5.15–5.35 GHz, 5.725–5.825 GHz	200 MHz dedicated, 100 MHz ISM	United States
HSWA	5.15–5.25 GHz	100 MHz dedicated	Japan
HiperLan	5.15–5.35 GHz, 5.47–5.875 GHz	455 MHz dedicated, 150 MHz ISM	Europe
HiperLink	17.1–17.3 GHz	200 MHz dedicated	Europe
MBS	57–61 GHz	4000 MHz dedicated	Worldwide

Light

Another unlicensed option for wireless networks is light. Though it requires a line of sight and can cover a comparatively short range, it has some important advantages: higher bandwidth and absolute security. Unlike radio-based systems, there is no chance of a light beam leaking through a wall.

Infrared is the most common type of light used in wireless communications, partly because it can't be seen and partly to avoid possible interference from other light sources. Most televisions have an infrared remote control, and most laptop computers include an infrared data port.

Visible light can be used for some simple wireless communications systems. In particular, a television screen or computer monitor emits light at very high energy, which is easy to pick up with a simple sensor. These have been exploited for decades by *light pens,* devices used to draw on a screen, as well as by toy guns that video game players can fire at a TV. They've even been used in simpler toys; as long ago as 1985, shortly after cartoons began to be tied in with toys, some went further than marketing and design. Mattel sold a toy spaceship that would make different noises, depending on whether it was pointed at the hero or at the villain during a battle scene.

More recently, similar systems have been exploited for more sophisticated data transfer. Timex sells a wristwatch with a built-in contact list, which can be automatically updated from a PC without wires or any special hardware. It incorporates a tiny scanner of the type found at supermarket checkouts, which reads bar codes rapidly flashed up on a screen. The system's weakness is that it works only with cathode ray tube (CRT) monitors, because the liquid crystal display (LCD) screens on mobile devices simply aren't bright enough.

WIRELESS LANS..

Anyone who has tried to connect even two computers knows that cables can be a major problem. Many LANs have such a complex spaghetti structure that some companies need to employ full-time technicians simply to look after cabling. Tracking down faults or loose connectors is so difficult that a billion-dollar industry has sprung up to sell network management tools, databases combined with reporting software that try to give people a better indication of where to look for faults.

For network managers who want an easier life, wireless LANs have always been a tempting alternative. They are far more flexible than wire-based systems and potentially cheaper—as well as eliminating cable, a wireless system can also eliminate *hubs,* the machines that serve as a central meeting point for all data on a LAN segment.

When a wireless LAN needs to be upgraded to deal with the continuing rise in demand for capacity, it is usually a matter of simply replacing the computer interfaces. An upgrade to a wired LAN often means tearing out much of a building's infrastructure.

Unfortunately, wireless LANs have traditionally suffered from an often fatal flaw: They are slow. When the popular Ethernet system first appeared in 1974, it gave users a (shared) capacity of 10 Mbps. The wireless equivalent only reached this speed a quarter-century later, by which time Ethernet's data rate had multiplied a hundredfold and was already being pushed higher. The result was that wireless LANs remained a niche, used only in environments such as warehouses and factories, where mobility is essential.

But things are changing. Four new trends meant that, by the turn of century, local data broadcasting was finally ready for prime time:

- With the rise of the PC and then the Internet, networking is no longer confined to the office. Plenty of households want to connect multiple machines, and home users are often put off by the complexity of wired networking. Although many offices were built with data cables installed alongside the plumbing and electricity, most homes were not. For people who want to share files or access the Internet from any computer in their house, a wireless network can be ideal.

- The popularity of laptop PCs and cellular phones has demonstrated the benefits of mobility, first to executives and then to other employees. People who were once tied to their desks have been freed to move around the building, but wired networks mean they must keep returning to the same place to access e-mail. Wireless LANs would solve this problem, as well as allow access to the network even when visiting other offices.

- Wireless networks have become faster. Though the speed of wired systems is also increasing, many users don't need the 10 Gbps of modern Ethernet. The latest wireless LANs offer shared capacity of up to 54 Mbps, enough for most purposes.

- The IEEE's 802.11b standard meant that products from different manufacturers could all work together. A customer could buy a wireless LAN card for her computer and know that its continued usefulness would not be dependent on the support of one particular company. Competition brought prices down, and economies of scale brought them down still further. By 2002, many computer manufacturers were putting wireless LAN adapters into all of their high-end laptops, so that users didn't even need to buy a separate card.

Wireless LAN Standards

The main problem faced by early wireless LANs was that there were no real standards. Each company produced its own proprietary system, giving customers a confusing choice. Many simply chose not to buy a wireless LAN at all, for fear of being locked into a single vendor's technology.

Standards began to emerge in the late 1990s, but potential customers were again spoiled for choice. Wireless LANs are a young technology, so there are still many competing standards. Most industry players expect some to disappear, just like the Betamax video format. Unfortunately, it is difficult to predict in advance which one will win.

Most wireless LAN standards are spawned by either the IEEE or the European Telecommunications Standards Institute (ETSI). The IEEE is responsible for Ethernet, the dominant wired system, so its recommendations might have more resonance within the networking community. But ETSI has the support of European governments and is respected among many telecom companies for its GSM and UMTS cellular standards. These pedigrees hint at the biases of the two standards bodies: IEEE is more concerned with data and ETSI with voice.

Between them, ETSI and the IEEE have produced several incompatible standards, listed in Table 9.3. The capacity figures are very optimistic, because up to half the bandwidth in most wireless systems is wasted in protocol overhead. Their broadcast nature also means that the figures are only half-duplex. For example, a capacity of 10 Mbps is really only 5 Mbps in each direction.

Table 9.3   *Wireless LAN Standards*

System	Theoretical Capacity	Real Max. Throughput	Spectrum	Air Interface	Status as of 2002
IEEE 802.11 (FHSS)	1 Mbps	0.5 Mbps	2.4 GHz	FHSS	Obsolete
IEEE 802.11 (DSSS)	2 Mbps	1 Mbps	2.4 GHz	DSSS	Obsolete
IEEE 802.11b	11 Mbps	6 Mbps	2.4 GHz	DSSS	Popular
IEEE 802.11g	54 Mbps	31 Mbps	2.4 GHz	OFDM	Near future
IEEE 802.11a	54 Mbps	31 Mbps	5 GHz	OFDM	New
ETSI HiperLan1	23.5 Mbps	Unknown	5 GHz	TDMA	Abandoned
ETSI HiperLan2	54 Mbps	31 Mbps	5 GHz	OFDM	Near future
HomeRF	1 Mbps	0.5 Mbps	2.4 GHz	FHSS	Obsolete
HomeRF2	10 Mbps	6 Mbps	2.4 GHz	FHSS	Endangered
5-WING/5-UP	104 Mbps	72 Mbps	5 GHz	OFDM	Future

There is also a third organization, the HomeRF Working Group, which adds two more standards (incompatible with ETSI's and the IEEE's). The choice can seem confusing, but IEEE 802.11b has emerged as a clear leader. The others are either rapidly becoming obsolete or still in the future. Which of these future systems will ultimately replace 802.11b is still unknown, but the most likely to succeed is its close cousin, 802.11a. This may ultimately converge with ETSI's HiperLan2 in a joint standard known tentatively as *5-WING* or *5-UP*.

Wi-Fi (IEEE 802.11b)

Most wireless LANs to date are based on the IEEE 802.11b standard, better known as *Wi-Fi* or *Wireless Ethernet*. Wi-Fi stands for Wireless Fidelity and is a trademark of a group called *WECA* (the Wireless Ethernet Compatibility Alliance), which tests products made by different manufacturers for interoperability. Those that pass are allowed to carry the Wi-Fi logo, intended to reassure users that they will be able to connect to other systems that carry it.

WECA does *not* set the standards itself, but it does sometimes act as a marketing arm of the IEEE's 802.11 working groups: Though entirely separate organizations, their memberships overlap extensively. Like any effective marketing department, it isn't just focused on telling people how great the product is. It also listens to customer feedback and makes suggestions for improvements. In 2001, the IEEE came under pressure from WECA to improve the security built into 802.11b.

The name *Ethernet* is mostly intended to reassure computer networkers, many of whom are familiar with regular Ethernet, but it also describes the kind of multiplexing scheme that all 802.11 networks use. Ethernet is one of several standards for wired LANs that the IEEE set in the 1980s, officially IEEE 802.3. It proved to be far more popular than the others, thanks mainly to its simplicity: Every computer on a network segment shares a single communications channel, which can carry only one data packet at a time. Rather than try to organize specific time slots for each computer, as TDMA would do, Ethernet simply allows each to transmit data whenever it needs to. If two happen to try to use the channel at once, a collision occurs, and both packets are lost. Both computers then try again, each waiting for a random time interval before doing so.

The wireless version of Ethernet is slightly more complex, trying to anticipate collisions before they occur. Before sending a full packet of data, 802.11 terminals check that the air is clear by transmitting a short test signal. This system is known by the unwieldy acronym *CSMA/CA* (Carrier Sense Multiple Access/Collision Avoidance). This saves on bandwidth by reducing the amount of time that the link wastes on collisions, but is still broadcast in nature: It doesn't reserve a communications channel for any particular user, as do the protocols used for cell phone transmission.

All 802.11 networks use CSMA/CA to share a link among users, but they differ in the type of physical technology used. The original 802.11 specification, set in 1998, called for three different versions, mutually incompatible:

- **Optical**, using infrared transmitters such as the ports built into many laptop PCs. Though proprietary wireless LANs based on infrared were once relatively common, infrared 802.11 networks were never actually built.

- **FHSS** (Frequency-Hopping Spread Spectrum), which rapidly cycles between frequencies many times each second. It has 79 different frequencies to choose from in the ISM-2.4 band, so even though some may be blocked by interference, the theory is that others should be clear. The FHSS version of 802.11 could reach 1 Mbps.

- **DSSS** (Direct-Sequence Spread Spectrum), which is the same as CDMA cellular: It transmits on all frequencies simultaneously, hoping to overcome interference. This increased the capacity to a maximum of 2 Mbps but also used more power. Most people considered a doubled data rate to be worth a slightly shorter battery life, so DSSS became the most popular type of 802.11.

The IEEE later made several enhancements to the physical layer, shown in Figure 9.1. The first of these to reach mass production was 802.11b, based on an enhanced version of DSSS called *CCK* (Complementary Code Keying). This essentially just uses extra CDMA codes, boosting the data rate when reception is clear. It's backward-compatible with the older DSSS systems, automatically dropping down to 2 Mbps to communicate with them if necessary. It is not compatible with FHSS-based 802.11 networks, but backward compatibility with any other type of wireless LAN is not often needed. Most of the 802.11 devices in use (and all of those carrying the Wi-Fi mark) support full 802.11b.

The theoretical maximum capacity of 802.11b is 11 Mbps, which is often quoted by vendors and by groups such as WECA. It pushes wireless LANs through an important psychological barrier, matching the speed of the original Ethernet standard. However, the number is misleading. It refers to the total physical layer capacity, much of which is used by the protocol itself, so it is not actually available for data. The maximum data rate of an 802.11b network is really only about 6 Mbps, and that can be achieved only under optimum conditions—over a short range and with no interference. It quickly drops when packet collisions or other errors occur, as shown in Figure 9.2. A 50% error rate will reduce the real throughput by about two thirds, to only 2 Mbps.

To prevent these errors, 802.11 automatically reduces its physical layer data rate when errors occur, because lower data rates are more resistant to interference. If reception is particularly bad, it will drop down to regular 802.11, at 2 Mbps or

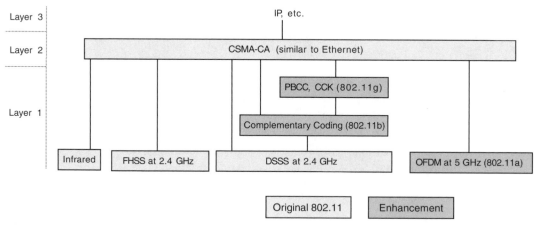

Figure 9.1
IEEE 802.11 protocol stack.

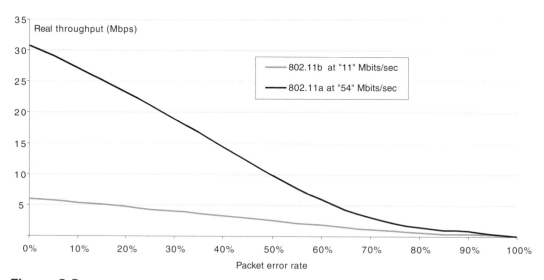

Figure 9.2
Effect of errors on 802.11 throughput.

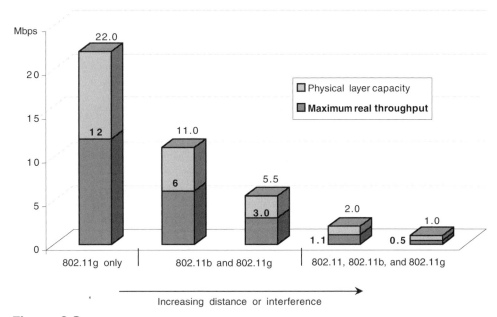

Figure 9.3
Data rates of IEEE 802.11 DSSS technologies in the ISM-2.4 band.

1 Mbps, illustrated in Figure 9.3. Collisions and interference can reduce the real throughput to less than a tenth of the touted 11 Mbps.

Where reception is very clear, it's possible to increase capacity beyond 11 Mbps using a newer system, IEEE 802.11g. Most Wi-Fi equipment does *not* support this, and the standard has been held up by companies arguing over whose proposal should be adopted. The IEEE eventually reached a compromise that includes several modes of operation—rather like IMT-2000, the umbrella name by which all the different versions of 3G cell phones are known.

All 802.11g equipment must support both CCK and *Orthogonal Frequency Division Multiplexing* (OFDM). The latter is the same system as used by the more advanced 802.11a standard but, whereas 802.11a uses a different frequency band, 802.11g operates in the same 2.4-GHz band as 802.11b. As an option, 801.11g can also support *Packet Binary Convolutional Coding* (PBCC), another form of DSSS that uses yet more CDMA codes. Because it's fairly similar to 802.11b's CCK, it should be easier to build into existing designs.

OFDM can theoretically reach up to 54 Mbps, but this would require a very clear channel and break compatibility with existing 802.11b equipment. Instead, most 802.11g hardware will use a combination of CCK and OFDM, which sends some signaling information at the slower speeds. To reach OFDM's full potential, it's necessary to use a new frequency band that's relatively free of interference, the approach taken by 802.11a.

Wi-Fi5 (IEEE 802.11a)

The letters after the number 802.11 aren't chosen at random: They refer to the order in which the standards were first proposed. This means that the first enhancement to 802.11 was actually 802.11a, not 802.11b. Despite being defined first, it's often thought of as a newer standard, because building real products to fit the specification took so long. Whereas 802.11b was a relatively simple upgrade to the existing DSSS system, 802.11a is an entirely new physical layer. It replaces spread spectrum with OFDM and migrates to a new frequency band.

The main benefit of a new physical layer is that 802.11a can reach much higher data rates. Its theoretical maximum is 54 Mbps, the same as that of 802.11g and nearly five times that of 802.11b. As with other wireless standards, real throughput is less than the theoretical maximum, but three features should mean that it can achieve a higher fraction of its maximum than can 802.11b (or 802.11g):

- It operates in dedicated spectrum: the U-NII band in the United States and the HSWA band in Japan. Both of these are reserved for communications purposes, meaning that they should contain less interference than the ISM band that 802.11 uses. There is some overlap of the U-NII band with another ISM band at 5.8 GHz, but few devices actually use this, so it is still relatively interference-free. Domestic microwave ovens, Bluetooth chips, and (in North America) cordless phones are all competing with 802.11b for ISM 2.4, not with 802.11a for ISM-5.8.
- It has seven lower data rates, illustrated in Figure 9.4, compared with 802.11b's three. These mean that, when interference does occur, 802.11a can try sacrificing just a little capacity for better reception, rather than having to halve its data rate as 802.11b does.
- There is much more bandwidth at 5 GHz than at 2.4 GHz, allowing more networks to operate in the same area. The precise amount varies from country to country, because different regulators allocate different amounts for ISM and unlicensed communications use. The FCC, for example, allows 83.5 MHz at ISM-2.4, compared with 300 MHz for U-NII. Each

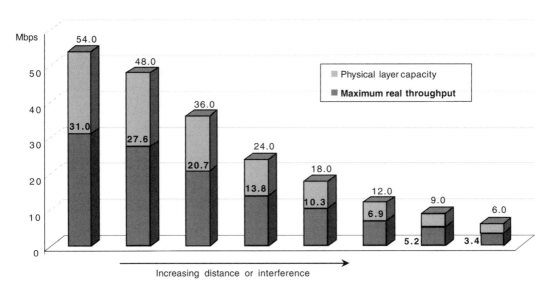

Figure 9.4
Data rates of 802.11a and HiperLan2 systems.

802.11a or 802.11b network requires its own channel of about 20 MHz, with some extra frequencies on either side to guard against interference. As shown in Figure 9.5, this means that only three separate networks can operate at 2.4 GHz, compared with 12 at 5 GHz.

These channels have several uses. The most important is simply to allow different people to operate 802.11 networks without causing interference: Radio waves often leak through walls, and the range of 100 m can extend beyond a home or small office. A large office or public space can be covered with a small cellular network based on 802.11, with adjacent cells using different channels, as described in Chapter 3, "Cellular Systems." The additional channels of 802.11a enable cells to be spaced closer together or for each cell to use more than one channel.

The first 802.11a products support only eight of the channels (those in the part of the U-NII spectrum that isn't shared with ISM-5.8), but this is still enough for most purposes. There's even a (so far) proprietary scheme developed by Atheros (www.atheros.com) called *turbo-mode* that combines two 802.11a channels together, doubling the capacity of 802.11b. Because some of the protocol overhead and signaling doesn't have to be shared, the real data rate is more than doubled—from a maximum of 31 Mbps to 72 Mbps.

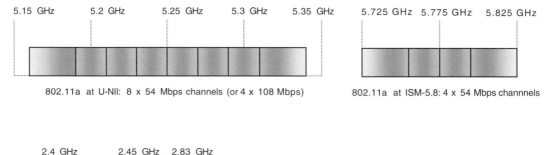

802.11a at U-NII: 8 x 54 Mbps channels (or 4 x 108 Mbps)

802.11a at ISM-5.8: 4 x 54 Mbps channnels

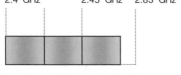

802.11b at ISM-2.4: 3 x 11 Mbps channels

Total 802.11a capacity: 12 x 54 Mbps = 648 Mbps

Total 802.11b capacity: 3 x 11 Mbps = 33 Mbps

Figure 9.5
Channel spacing of IEEE 802.11 networks at 2.4 and 5 GHz.

Of course, 802.11a does have weaknesses. The most obvious is compatibility: The move to higher frequencies means that 802.11a products are not interoperable with the installed base at 802.11b. The only way to get around this is to use dual-mode devices, which support both systems. Many companies are trying to develop these, most of which will also support 802.11g.

Less obviously, the 5-GHz band could result in a shorter range, because higher frequencies are more easily absorbed by air, walls, and everything else between a transmitter and receiver. This effect is partially cancelled out by the use of OFDM, which is designed to take advantage of multipath effects and, thus, can cover a longer distance than 802.11b's DSSS. The ranges of different 802.11 technologies are shown in Figure 9.6. Because 802.11g combines OFDM and the lower frequency band, it can go further than either of the others.

The most serious problem for 802.11a is regulatory, not technical. The system is banned in Europe, which has reserved its 5-GHz band for ETSI's own HiperLan standard. European regulators say they want a system that can be used for voice services, as well as data, which requires better control over who is able to use a channel. ETSI and the IEEE are working to address these issues, intending to produce a single standard that will unify both 5-GHz systems, standardize the dual-channel mode, and gain approval for use worldwide.

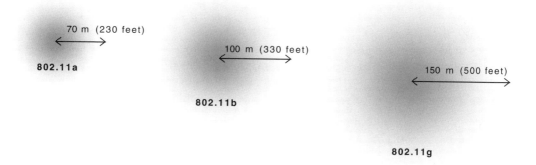

Figure 9.6
Approximate ranges of IEEE 802.11 networks.

ETSI HiperLan

The European Union first recognized the need for high-speed LANs back in 1992, standardizing a system called *HiperLan*, which was based partly on GSM. It also recommended to European governments that they dedicate spectrum to it in the 5-GHz band, a recommendation they accepted. The maximum data rate was supposed to be 23.5 Mbps, but nobody knows for sure what is achievable because no equipment based on the original HiperLan standard actually exists.

Undeterred by the failure of HiperLan (or HiperLan1, as it is now known), ETSI produced a successor standard, HiperLan2. This is almost identical to 802.11a at the physical layer: It uses OFDM to reach a maximum capacity of 54 Mbps and even has the same lower data rates shown in Figure 9.4. The main difference from 802.11a is that HiperLan isn't based on Ethernet. It imposes a more rigid TDMA structure, which is intended to provide better guarantees of service quality. Rather than allowing every computer on a network to broadcast at all times, it imposes a top-down structure that reserves a certain amount of bandwidth for particular users.

Because the original HiperLan never appeared, some people refer to it as "hype LAN" instead. Although this criticism certainly fits HiperLan1, HiperLan2 is more real. Prototypes have already been demonstrated by Ericsson and NTT. However, it has fallen behind 802.11a in real development. Many vendors are lobbying to convince European governments to allow 802.11a in the HiperLan bands, and the IEEE is working to develop a version of 802.11a that will address Europe's concerns.

HomeRF

As the name implies, *HomeRF* was designed for home networking. (The RF is for "Radio Frequency.") It was intended to be a cheap and simple way for people to link together several computers in their homes, so it was designed for price, rather than speed. The first version had a maximum data rate of 1 Mbps, because it was based on the original FHSS 802.11 standard. Thanks to a change in FCC rules regarding FHSS, a newer version, HomeRF2, has a maximum data rate of 10 Mbps.

Despite its intentions, HomeRF was neither cheap nor simple. At the time it was developed, 802.11b cards for laptops still cost hundreds of dollars, and HomeRF's designers expected this to continue. They were wrong, and 802.11b soon became cheaper than many cards based on the slower system. By the time HomeRF2 was announced, 802.11b had already reached critical mass. A home network based on 802.11b enables people to use the same access cards as in the office wireless LAN, whereas HomeRF requires them to buy a new one.

In fact, HomeRF does have some advantages over 802.11b, which ironically might appeal to business users. It includes a better security mechanism and a quality-of-service (QoS) scheme called *Shared Wireless Access Protocol* (SWAP). The big disadvantage is that it's incompatible with Wi-Fi equipment, but businesses wanting to stop eavesdroppers from accessing their networks might not see this as a disadvantage.

For home users, HomeRF's main selling point is that SWAP has built-in support for telephony. This would allow cordless phones and wireless LANs to share the same air waves without interference, overcoming a problem experienced by many users in North America, where cordless phones use the same 2.4-GHz ISM band as 802.11b. However, there are other ways to solve this problem: Europe and Japan already give cordless phones a dedicated wave band so that they don't have to fight for ISM, and many U.S. users might switch their wireless LANs to 5 GHz.

Access Points

Wireless LAN systems can all be used for ad-hoc networking between any two or more users who happen to have a card installed. Areas such as offices or homes can also be fitted with *access points*, which both extend the range of the system and enable it to link to ordinary LANs or the Internet. Figure 9.7 shows these two types of networks.

Private users can create their own miniature cellular network by setting up several access points. All the standards include a handover mechanism, similar to those of public cellular networks. The IEEE 802.11 family inherits the soft handoff system from CDMA cellular, meaning that the mobile unit tries to form a link with a new access point before it disconnects from its previous one. This is illustrated in Figure 9.8. HiperLan systems use a hard handover similar to GSM's, which means that they have to disconnect from one

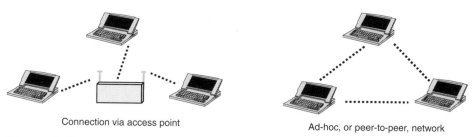

Connection via access point

Ad-hoc, or peer-to-peer, network

Figure 9.7
Wireless LAN with and without access point.

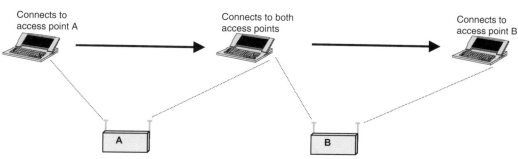

Figure 9.8
Soft handoff in IEEE 802.11 roaming.

access point before reconnecting to another. This is less reliable and results in a short interruption in connectivity.

HiperLan scores over 802.11 in ad-hoc networking, because any machine on a HiperLan network can act as an access point. This is necessary because the TDMA scheme requires that one particular node take charge of the network, assigning bandwidth slots to particular users. It also means that a cloud of HiperLan machines can extend far beyond the range of an individual radio by relaying data from one to another, illustrated in Figure 9.9. If one machine in the cloud has a connection to a fixed or cellular network, the others can also share this.

Figure 9.9
HiperLan machine acting as hub.

Hubs versus Switches

Access points can take two forms, *hubs* and *switches*. A hub is the simplest, simply rebroadcasting everything it receives. A switch is more discriminating, sending transmissions only to smaller subgroups known as *segments*. This improves network performance, because the total capacity is shared per segment.

On a wired network, there is no limit to the number of segments. A switch could put every user on his or her own segment, giving each access to the full capacity all the time. Wireless networks usually can't do this, because each segment needs its own radio channel. However, they do make it much easier to reallocate machines between different segments, a task that would otherwise require rewiring. A wireless network can do this at the push of a button or even automatically.

Figure 9.10 shows the advantage of a switch over a hub as an access point. In both the hub- and the switch-based networks, user A is transmitting to user C. With a hub, users B and D must also receive and decode this transmission; with a switch, they are free to transmit to each other.

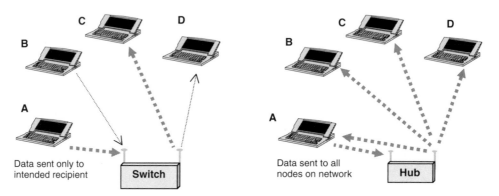

Figure 9.10
Hubs vs. switches as access points.

Security

Most wireless LANs are insecure. This is partly because of weaknesses in the 802.11 standards and partly because LANs have traditionally relied on the difficulty of physical access for security: To get to a LAN based on copper or fiber cable, an intruder first has to get inside a building. With a wireless LAN, this difficulty is eliminated. All data is simply broadcast, enabling anyone to eavesdrop or worse.

Criminals who break into computer networks are often described in the media as *hackers,* a term that annoys many programmers. They prefer to use it as a badge of honor, meaning anyone fluent in computer languages and protocols. Many of the people who connect to someone else's 802.11b network aren't hackers in either sense of the word. To do so requires neither malice nor skill, and can be as simple as switching on a computer and plugging in an interface card.

The security protocol built into all 802.11 versions is known as *Wired Equivalent Privacy* (WEP), but it doesn't actually provide privacy equivalent to a wire. It has several problems, the most important of which is that it is turned off by default. The designers of 802.11b hardware wanted them to be simple to use and thought (perhaps rightly) that people would be put off by having to type in a password, let alone implement more sophisticated security measures. The result is that many access points will allow a connection from anyone who is within range, without actually verifying their identity or encrypting the signal.

Home users who just use an access point to link a laptop to the Internet might not be too bothered by this: It just means that they are sharing their Internet connections with the wider world. (Sharing a connection is often against the terms of a DSL or cable service agreement, but it's not actually dangerous.) Anyone connecting an access point to a private network should be more concerned, especially if the network contains an e-mail system or servers that store sensitive data. Armed only with a wireless LAN card, an intruder could read the data from the server or send spam through the e-mail system.

In 2001, the media occasionally reported stories of *war driving*, which means people driving around with a laptop and an 802.11b card to see how many unencrypted networks they can find. It's also possible to scan them from afar, using powerful directional antennas similar to satellite dishes (which are often illegal), so the lack of a street or public area within a wireless LAN's normal range isn't necessarily a defense. The war drivers usually didn't have to go far, finding so many networks that the only way to keep track of them all was to program a computer to plot their locations automatically. The resulting maps were sometimes published on the Internet, showing hundreds of unsecured networks in many cities. There's one street corner above a major transit station in San Francisco where people had a choice of six different corporate networks, including one belonging to a major bank.

Some of these companies could have official wireless LANs that they have forgotten to secure, but many of them might be unofficial rogue access points. Because they are so cheap and easy to set up, almost anyone who uses a computer at work can buy one and plug it into an office PC, inadvertently exposing the entire network. Sometimes, this is officially sanctioned by managers in departments such as sales or accounting, who don't understand network security.

WEP and TKIP

Even when WEP is switched on, it has severe weaknesses. The encryption algorithm itself is RC4, which is thought to be secure: It's also employed by SSL and TLS, the security systems used by most Web sites, and they have never been cracked. Unfortunately, the way that WEP implements it opens at least three vulnerabilities:

- WEP requires that every user on a network use the same encryption key and provides no easy way for this to be changed: The key has to be shared in advance, for example, on a floppy disk or as a password from which it can be derived. This makes it awkward to use for large networks and means that if one laptop is stolen, the entire network is vulnerable.

- WEP's key is only 40 bits long. This is short enough for many computers to crack through simple trial and error, especially if the key is not changed frequently. Because there is no easy way to change the key, most users keep the same key on a semipermanent basis, leaving plenty of time for a hacker to try every combination.

- The key management system built into WEP allows an attacker to eliminate most possible keys, leaving far fewer to test by simple trial and error. This weakness would normally be quite difficult to exploit and was discovered only after advanced mathematical research by several prominent cryptographers. Fortunately for attackers, they don't need to understand the math: The process of breaking WEP has been automated by a program called *Airsnort*, which is available free from many Web sites. Most dangerous, the length of time that the attack takes scales linearly with key length, meaning that using longer keys doesn't help much. Doubling the key length simply doubles the time taken for Airsnort to crack the code, whereas it would add billions of years to the time taken by a regular trial-and-error attack.

WEP's first two weaknesses have been apparent since it was first developed, so the IEEE is working on a new system, 802.11i, to replace it. Because this takes time to develop and won't be compatible with existing hardware, many vendors are instead pushing an interim solution that used to be known as WEP2. After Airsnort was released, they became so embarrassed by the name WEP that they changed the second version's name to *Temporal Key Integrity Protocol* (TKIP), in an attempt to disguise its ancestry.

Regardless of the name, TKIP is fully backward-compatible with WEP and, thus, vulnerable to the same attacks. It uses 128-bit keys, but this merely means that an attack that once took one second takes three seconds. Some members of the IEEE warn that TKIP may even be more vulnerable than WEP, because it adds support for Kerberos, a password-based authentication scheme. Most passwords are taken from a dictionary, which makes them relatively easy to guess. Other vendors are pushing another authentication protocol, 802.1x, but this doesn't address the core issue of encryption.

Most experts recommend that users treat a wireless LAN in the same way that they would the Internet. For a company running a large network, this means putting a firewall between the network and access point, just as most already use a firewall to protect their networks from Internet intruders. Similarly, all traffic sent over the wireless LAN should be encrypted using a *VPN* (Virtual Private Network), special software running on users' computers and on a server behind the firewall.

VPNs are already used by remote workers who dial in through a modem or a cell phone, so many organizations can reuse the same software for their wireless connections. They can also reuse the same firewall, as shown in Figure 9.11. This protects only the private network, not the Internet connection, but the data in the private network is usually far more valuable than the Internet connection. One possibility is to leave the connection open, sharing it with everyone. Another is to protect it using the imperfect security of WEP, on the basis that few attackers will go to the trouble of breaking this merely to steal Internet access.

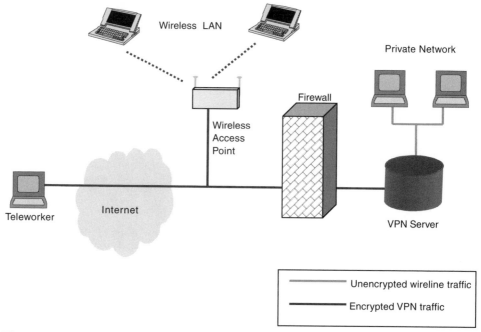

Figure 9.11
Wireless LAN access point protected by firewall and VPN.

For total security, networks should use a second firewall, as shown in Figure 9.12. This places the access point in a region called a *DMZ* (demilitarized zone), which is separate from either the Internet or the private network. The disadvantage of this is that it costs more, and the disadvantage of any firewall and VPN solution is that it doesn't scale well. If a company has several access points, it needs a firewall for each of them or a separate network infrastructure to connect them all securely to a single firewall.

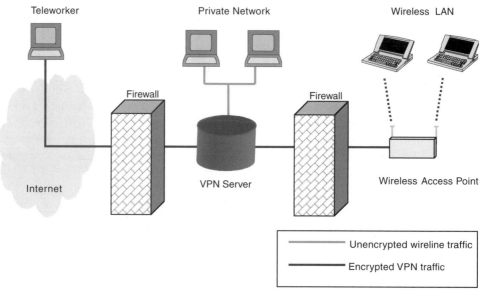

Figure 9.12
Wireless LAN access point in DMZ.

Other 802.11 Standards

The various IEEE 802.11 standards can be confusing, to say the least. In addition to the three extensions that define complete wireless LAN systems (802.11a, 802.11b, 802.11g), the IEEE also has enhancements that mitigate weaknesses in the existing protocols. These are not new wireless LAN systems, but rather extensions that will eventually be applied to one or all of the existing three:

- **802.11c** covers how 802.11 networks interoperate with regular Ethernet and is already included in most products.
- **802.11d** originally aimed to produce versions of 802.11b that work at other frequencies, making it suitable for parts of the world where the 2.4-GHz band is not available. Most countries have now released this band, thanks to

an ITU recommendation and pressure from equipment manufacturers. The only holdout is Spain, but even that may follow soon. However, 802.11d may still be useful in adapting the technology to other applications that use licensed bands.

- **802.11e** will eventually add QoS capabilities to 802.11 networks. It replaces the Ethernet-like multiplexing with a coordinated TDMA scheme and adds extra error correction to important traffic. The technology is very similar to Whitecap, a proprietary protocol developed by Sharewave and used in Cisco's 802.11a prototypes. A standard was supposed to be finalized by the end of 2001 but has run into delays, thanks to arguments over how many classes of service should be provided and exactly how they should be implemented. It could help to persuade European regulators to accept 802.11a in the HiperLan band.

- **802.11f** tries to improve the handover mechanism in 802.11, so that users can maintain a connection while roaming between two different switched segments (radio channels) or between access points attached to two different wired networks. This is vital if wireless LANs are to offer the same mobility that cell phone users take for granted.

- **802.11h** attempts to add better control over transmission power and which radio channels are used in 802.11a. Because 802.11a uses OFDM, each channel is split up into several lower data rate signals as it is transmitted. For example, a 54-Mbps channel is actually made up of 48 separate channels at 1083.3 kbps. Under 802.11h, each of these 48 channels could be assigned to specific users or applications. Like 802.11e, this would help ensure QoS and perhaps secure approval in Europe.

- **802.11i** deals with 802.11's most obvious weakness: security. Rather than an enhancement to WEP, this will be an entirely new standard based on AES, the U.S. government's "official" encryption system. The committee has not yet chosen an authentication protocol: Some members want to use a new algorithm called *Offset Codebook* (OCB), but this is covered by three separate patents, and other members would prefer a system that everyone can adopt royalty-free. There are also ongoing arguments about how (if at all) the new standard should be backward-compatible with WEP and TKIP and whether a transmitter should apply encryption before or after the QoS criteria of 802.11e.

- **802.11j** is so new that IEEE hasn't officially formed a task group to discuss it, let alone produced a draft standard. It's supposed to cover how 802.11a and HiperLan2 networks can coexist in the same airwaves. It doesn't cover the unified standard, which is a joint initiative from ETSI and the IEEE.

CORDLESS TELEPHONY ....

A *cordless* phone, as opposed to a mobile, works with only one specific base station and uses unlicensed spectrum. The base station is known as a *fixed point* because it is connected to the regular fixed phone network. Transmission power is very low, for a range of 100 m or less.

Cordless phones are usually sold for home use in sets of a single phone and base station that can cost under $50. More sophisticated systems are available for businesses, which use several handsets that all work with the same base station. The base station often incorporates a miniature *PBX* (Private Branch Exchange), so that users can dial each other privately, as well as make external calls.

Because cordless phones compete heavily on price, some use the simplest possible technology: analog FM in one of the ISM bands. This results in terrible, often incomprehensible voice quality. Even when users are standing next to their fixed points, interference can make a cordless call sound worse than a GSM where the phone and base station are separated by several miles.

To overcome this problem, an increasing number of users are turning to digital cordless systems. These offer voice quality as good as the fixed network and sometimes even high-speed data. Echoing the situation with HiperLan, Europe and Japan both have government-mandated standards using specific spectrum, whereas the United States allows any system to be used, provided that it meets safety requirements.

Telepoint

The theory behind *telepoint* systems was that they allowed the same phone to be used in both private and public networks. Telepoint operators set up hundreds of cordless fixed points around cities, often in areas such as shopping malls and subway stations, which were originally difficult for true mobile systems to reach. A home cordless phone was an attractive alternative to the long lines that usually formed in front of public payphones.

Telepoint's flaw was that it could be used only to make calls, not receive them. Consumers in many countries couldn't see any benefits over a regular phone box and perceived it as "a poor man's mobile." It was never tried in the United States, and many European networks failed. An ETSI standard known as *CT-2* (Cordless Telephone System 2) was eventually abandoned.

Some telepoint networks did enjoy success in Asia, primarily because they were used for services other than telephony. Japan's system incorporated its own store-and-forward messaging service and eventually allowed people to dial up to an ISP and surf the Web or check e-mail.

Standards

Most American digital cordless systems use proprietary spread spectrum technologies in one of the ISM bands. Europe and Japan have both defined standards, known respectively as *Digital Enhanced Cordless Telephony* (DECT) and *Personal Handyphone System* (PHS).

The standards are very similar. Both use time-division duplexing (TDD) and TDMA, and offer a data rate of 64 kbps one way (or 32 kbps each way). This results in very clear voice quality and Internet access at near ISDN speed. But they have been put to different applications. DECT is still used almost entirely for private cordless systems, whereas PHS was the basis of a very popular telepoint network.

Table 9.4 compares the technical details of the two systems. Because they employ TDD instead of c spectrum, the maximum number of users is only half the number of TDMA slots; each needs at least two slots, one to transmit and one to receive.

Table 9.4   Technical Information about PHS and DECT

	PHS	DECT
Spectrum	1895–1918 MHz	1880–1900 MHz
Modulation	QPSK	GMSK
Channel bandwidth	300 kHz	2 MHz
Gross data rate per channel	384 kbps	1152 kbps
Usable data throughput per channel	128 kbps	768 kbps
TDMA slots per channel	4	24
Maximum users per channel	2	12
Available in	Japan	Europe

Picocells

Some companies are pushing private base stations based on one of the public cellular standards, usually GSM. These should allow people to use the same phone wherever they are, both to make and receive calls. If a cell were placed in the home or office, calls could be routed over the fixed rather than the mobile network, theoretically saving money.

So far, few companies and almost no homes have actually deployed these systems, called *picocells*. But vendors have high hopes. They forecast particular popularity in the

United States, where GSM coverage is poor and big radio-blocking skyscrapers are common. The FCC has even allocated an *unlicensed PCS* spectrum band, meaning that anyone can set up a low-power system. In other countries, they require cooperation from a cellular operator because cellular frequencies have usually been licensed to the operator.

Picocells can be connected to the outside world in two ways, both of which are illustrated in Figure 9.13:

- **Via the public telephone system.** This makes the network truly private, under the full control of whoever set up the base station. It can be the easiest type to set up, but means that advanced mobile services, such as text messaging, are not available. People dialing the mobile number may also fail to get through, unless the mobile is still within range of a public base station or the user has remembered to set up a call divert system.

- **Via the mobile network.** Some operators and companies collaborate on building picocells so that they can also be used by other subscribers to the mobile network. This would seem to be the best solution for everyone, because costs are shared and the network extended, but it does mean that capacity is not dedicated to the company in whose office the fixed point is placed.

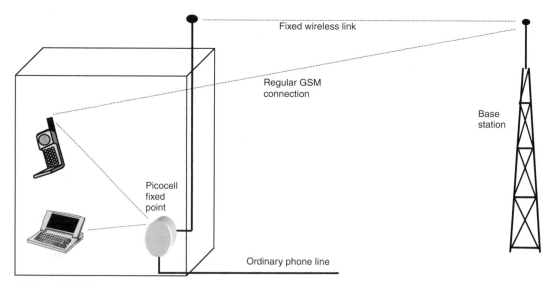

Figure 9.13
GSM picocell within a building.

IRDA ···

If you have a laptop or a PDA, you probably have an infrared port. Named after the *Infrared Data Association*, which oversees the system, IrDA is supposed to be a simple way to replace cables when printing or sending data to another PC. Millions of them are installed worldwide, theoretically making it one of the world's most popular standards. Of all wireless data technologies, its installed base is second only to SMS.

But despite its ubiquity, IrDA is hardly ever used. This is partly because at first it didn't work very well; different companies implemented the system in different ways. Although these early problems have been ironed out, the perception has stopped people from using it, which in turn has stopped vendors from implementing it on more devices. This creates a vicious circle—users won't ask for IrDA unless it's fully supported, and it won't be fully supported until users ask for it.

IrDA's creators envisaged a world where people would print simply by pointing a computer at a printer, or link up to a network by pointing it at an access point. The problem is that few manufacturers have developed these printers or access points, meaning that the only thing many laptops get the chance to connect to is another laptop.

Few people have two laptops, but most laptop owners do have a desktop PC. The most practical application for many users would be to synchronize the two, but so far this has been impossible. Although infrared transceivers cost less than one dollar, almost no companies build them into desktops. A notable exception is Apple, one of IrDA's first adopters. It has been promoting infrared data since the 1980s, using a proprietary system before the standard was defined.

Types of IrDA

Over the years, IrDA has progressed almost unnoticed to increasingly faster speeds. There are now four different versions of it, with no obvious way to tell which is built into a given device. One laptop may be able to send and receive infrared more than a hundred times faster than another, even if they were built at the same time, cost the same, and had similar processor, display, and memory configurations.

Infrared is almost never an issue for people buying a laptop, so manufacturers have no incentive to fit the latest version, even if it would cost no more. Some high-speed transceivers are wrongly configured to run at the lower speeds, meaning that they can often be upgraded with software alone.

The other good news is that the different versions of IrDA differ only in their data rate and are entirely backward-compatible. A new device ought to be able to work with an older one, albeit at the slower speed.

- **SIR** (Serial Infrared) was the original standard and ran at 115 kbps. This is the same speed as a standard serial port, on which the IrDA protocol was based.

- **MIR** (Medium Infrared) runs at 1.152 Mbps, fast enough to transmit or receive television-quality video. It is not widely implemented, with most systems choosing either the serial or fast versions.

- **FIR** (Fast Infrared) offers speeds of up to 4 Mbps. This is built into most new computers and is the standard setting on Windows 98 and 2000.

- **VFIR** (Very Fast Infrared) goes up to 16 Mbps and is not yet widely implemented. Undeterred, the Infrared Data Association is working on even further upgrades and claims it can push the ports up to a blistering 50 Mbps.

Such high data rates may seem like overkill for simple file transfer between computers, but the plan is for IrDA to be incorporated into other devices, such as digital cameras and MP3 players. At the current 4 Mbps, a full CD's worth of music in MP3 format would take longer than six minutes to transfer to a player, compared with less than 30 seconds at 50 Mbps.

Infrared LANs

Although designed only to connect two points together, IrDA can also be used to form complex networks. The principle is the same as for most wired LANS—every computer is connected separately to a central switch through which all data passes.

An IrDA-based LAN isn't as useful as a radio-based one, because the range is usually shorter, and it requires a line of sight between the switch and the terminal. But it has one enormous advantage—the infrared port is already built into many laptops. The port also consumes much less power than a separate plug-in card, and people can't lose it or forget it (unless they lose the entire computer).

Because the data rates available from IrDA vary so much, nearly all these systems are switched. An ordinary hub would try to transmit all data to every computer, which would limit PCs equipped with 16 Mbps VFIR to the 0.1 Mbps of SIR.

BLUETOOTH ....

Bluetooth is one of the most hyped wireless technologies, and justifiably so. It promises to cram an entire wireless system onto a single chip, cheap enough to be built into all mobile phones, PCs, PDAs, and eventually other devices. Rather than a LAN, Bluetooth's advocates describe it as a *PAN* (Personal Area Network).

These PANs will surround everyone, Bluetooth promoters hope, embracing every device that people carry. They will automatically interface with the refrigerator at home, the security system in the office, and mobile phones on the move. As people interact, their PANs will connect to beam over contact details, data files, or even digital cash.

Bluetooth dates back to an Ericsson project in 1994, which tried to find a way for mobile phones to communicate wirelessly with accessories such as hands-free kits. In May 1998, it joined with Nokia, Intel, Toshiba, and IBM to form the *Bluetooth Special Interest Group* (SIG), an alliance aimed at developing an open standard. It was named after Harald Bluetooth, a Viking king who unified Denmark and Norway in the tenth century.

The founding five threw the SIG open to new members, and the results were unprecedented. In less than two years, they were joined by nearly 2,000 others, even winning over initial skeptics such as Microsoft. The main condition of membership is that all members of the SIG must let all others use their Bluetooth patents under reasonable terms, preventing particular companies from getting a lock on the standard.

Technology

Despite such heavyweight backing, Bluetooth has run into problems. Products were originally supposed to appear by the beginning of 2000, but a year later they were still very scant. It is simply such an ambitious project that it has taken far longer than expected.

Bluetooth's stated aim is to create a single-chip radio with a range of 10 m, a peak throughput of 720 kbps, and a cost under $5. Up to eight Bluetooth devices can be directly connected to one another in a *piconet*. Networks with more than eight are possible, but in this case, not every device will be able to transmit to every other—each one can see only eight. A network of more than eight is known as a *scatternet* and must be subdivided into piconets, as shown in Figure 9.14.

The $5 price point is important; Bluetooth will have to reach this level, and ultimately cheaper, if it is to be fitted to all electronic devices. The first chips cost substantially more and were put inside relatively high-priced PC or CF+ cards for existing laptops or PDAs. These are relatively pointless without other Bluetooth devices, because a far higher capacity wireless LAN card can be purchased for around the same cost.

Bluetooth has been criticized for the way it uses the crowded 2.4-GHz ISM band. It is based loosely on the frequency-hopping technique of the original 802.11 standard but cycles through frequencies much faster, hopping up to 3,200 times every second. Some in the wireless LAN industry describe it as a rude radio, because this rapid cycling is almost guaranteed to interfere with other systems. However, this

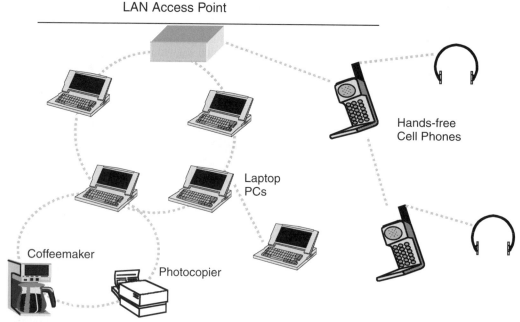

LAN Access Point

Hands-free
Cell Phones

Laptop
PCs

Coffeemaker

Photocopier

Figure 9.14
Scatternet formed from seven piconets.

shouldn't harm Bluetooth itself; 802.11, HomeRF, and Bluetooth are all competing for the same spectrum, and the rapid cycling means that Bluetooth is likely to win a head-to-head battle.

More serious questions hang over interoperability, both at the radio layer and between the applications that will actually be using Bluetooth. In this area, it has learned from some of the mistakes made by IrDA. The Bluetooth SIG will not let any devices use the Bluetooth logo until they have been tested for compatibility with the reference design, and some protocols originally developed for IrDA have actually been licensed for Bluetooth.

To help with interoperability, the IEEE is trying to develop an official standard based on Bluetooth, under the auspices of its 802.15 group. There are four separate sub-standards within this, none of them yet complete:

- **802.15.1** is the standardized system based on Bluetooth, with almost the same capabilities.

- **802.15.2** is an attempt to make 802.15 and Bluetooth radios less "rude," so that they can coexist with 802.11 LANs that use the same 2.4-GHz band. The most likely solution is a dual-standard transceiver, which will co-ordinate transmissions to prevent interference.

- **802.15.3** is aimed at increasing the data rate to at least 20 Mbps. This is necessary for some multimedia applications, which use large files that would take several minutes to transfer over regular Bluetooth.

- **802.15.4** will be an even lower power version, with an unspecified (but probably also low) data rate. The theory is that lower power will mean a battery life of many months or even years, permitting it to be embedded inside smart cards or used as a security tag.

Profiles

Bluetooth is intended to be used for many futuristic applications, but the first draft of the specification specifies nine. Each application is described by a separate set of protocols and procedures called a *profile*. Not every Bluetooth device supports every profile, and the cheapest support only one.

The profile system has attracted some criticism because it means that Bluetooth is effectively nine standards, not one, and the number is likely to grow as more profiles are added. However, the SIG says that it is necessary to ensure interoperability. The profiles share many common protocols, which are illustrated in Figure 9.15. This common ground should make it simple to adapt existing hardware for applications when additional profiles are published.

The first draft includes 13 profiles, listed below. In addition to the nine applications, there are four system profiles (numbers 1, 2, 5, and 10), which include features common to one or more applications.

1. **Generic Access Profile.** This is the core Bluetooth profile, responsible for maintaining links between devices. All Bluetooth devices need to include this profile, but in itself it is not sufficient for any useful applications. It includes functions necessary to use all of the core Bluetooth protocols, shaded light gray in Figure 9.15.

2. **Service Discovery Application Profile.** This profile enables a user to access the Service Discovery Protocol (SDP) directly, to find out which Bluetooth services are available from a given device. SDP is included as part of the core, but without this extra profile it can be accessed only by applications, not by the user directly.

3. **Cordless Telephony Profile.** This is designed for what the Bluetooth SIG calls a "3-in-1-phone," meaning a cell phone with a Bluetooth chip that enables it to be used as a cordless phone. It can also be used for cordless-only phones or for adding cordless telephony functions to any other Bluetooth-equipped device, such as a digital watch. It runs over the Telephony Control Service (TCS) protocol.

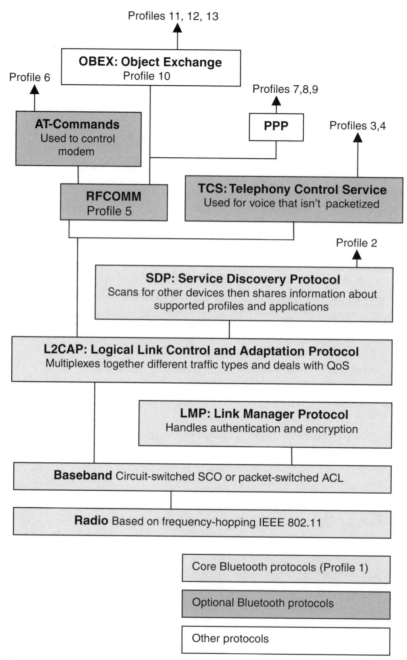

Figure 9.15
Bluetooth protocol stack.

4. **Intercom Profile.** Also based on the TCS protocol, this allows two-way voice communication. It differs from the Cordless Telephony Profile in that it supports only connections between two Bluetooth users within range of each other, not full telephony over the phone system or the Internet. Because Bluetooth has such a short range, it is unlikely to be used extensively.

5. **Serial Port Profile.** This profile allows Bluetooth devices to emulate a PC's serial port, using the RFComm protocol. It can emulate either an older RS232 or a newer USB (Universal Serial Bus) cable and is used by many higher level profiles.

6. **Headset Profile.** This specifies how Bluetooth can provide a wireless connection to a headset containing earphones and perhaps a microphone for use with either a computer or a mobile phone. It uses the serial port profile and the AT (Advanced Technology) commands, which were originally designed to control modems and are so called because they are taken from an IBM computer of the same name.

7. **Dial-Up Networking Profile.** This is designed for computers connecting to the Internet via a cell phone. At present, they have to do this through a special cable or perhaps IrDA, but in the future they should be able to use Bluetooth. It includes the serial port profile and Point-to-Point Protocol (PPP), the same protocol used by ordinary modems connecting to the Internet.

8. **Fax Profile.** This is very similar to the dial-up networking profile. It enables a mobile phone to emulate a fax modem when connected via Bluetooth to a laptop PC with fax software. Like the dial-up networking protocol, it uses PPP and the serial port profile.

9. **LAN Access Profile.** This is potentially the most useful profile. It is intended for IP data networking, enabling Bluetooth-equipped PCs to form a small wireless LAN among themselves or to connect to other LANs via a special access point, as in Figure 9.14. The SIG envisages these access points being placed within companies' own private networks and in public places, so that people with Bluetooth devices will be able to connect to the Internet.

10. **Generic Object Exchange Profile.** This profile controls how Bluetooth uses OBEX (Object Exchange), a client-server protocol taken from IrDA. It allows applications to exchange data directly, without having to use Internet-style packets.

11. **Object Push Profile.** This profile governs the exchange of electronic business cards, short files that contain the same information as a regular business card but can automatically be filed into a device's database.

The "push" in the name refers to the fact that this information must actively be given out by a user; to protect privacy, electronic business cards are usually not just beamed out to every device in range.

12. **File Transfer Profile.** This profile allows a device to access files stored on another. It can be used by any application that needs to transfer files between devices, from one device to another, or directly by users. Apart from linking two computers together, devices that might use this profile include MP3 players and digital cameras, which would transfer music and image files.

13. **Synchronization Protocol.** This helps to keep the data stored on different devices up to date. It is supposed to automate synchronization, so that a computer will automatically synchronize data with a mobile phone or PDA whenever they are within range of each other.

Applications

Some analysts have rightly mocked the more extreme claims made for Bluetooth. It turned the much-maligned Internet toaster from a joke to a serious proposition, as companies known only for kitchen appliances joined the SIG. Other favorites include a refrigerator that users can dial up from the supermarket to check what groceries they need or a trash can that automatically reorders supplies as empty packaging is discarded.

Though these ideas seem over the top, there is definitely a market for some networked appliances. Many people would gladly pay extra for a video recorder that could be programmed remotely over their mobile phones or the ability to access their music collections wherever they are. It could even save lives—doctors are experimenting with Bluetooth pacemakers so that patients' heartbeats can be monitored and even controlled remotely. If a patient suffers a heart attack or other medical emergency, the Bluetooth device could immediately call an ambulance, transmitting the patient's exact location and diagnosis at the same time.

The sheer number of players in the Bluetooth game points toward success; there are few major computer companies on Earth that haven't bet millions of dollars on the technology. Bluetooth will either bring about a revolution in networking or be an even greater embarrassment to the industry than Iridium.

FOURTH GENERATION ....

With 3G still not a reality in most parts of the world, talk of 4G mobile phones can seem premature. But this hasn't stopped visionaries from working on them. Higher data rates generally mean a shorter range, so 4G may have more in common with wireless LANs than traditional cellular networks.

The first 4G research projects took place in Europe in the early 1990s, while few people had a cell phone at all and those that did were still using analog (1G) systems. They resulted in many ideas but no firm standards, which is perfectly normal at such an early stage. The main plan that emerged was to aim for a network called the *Mobile Broadband System* (MBS), tentatively scheduled for 2010. This would use very small cells and high frequencies, probably at around 60 GHz. There is a lot of bandwidth around this frequency, but it also has a very short range, because radio waves at 60 GHz are very easily blocked by oxygen.

The planned data rate of MBS is about 100 Mbps, allegedly enough for telepresence, a type of virtual reality defined as full stimulation of all senses to provide the illusion of actually being somewhere else. Some desktop PCs can already reach 100 Mbps and don't experience anything like virtual reality, but the technology to provide this would presumably be developed by 2010.

Whether virtual reality is ready by 2010, 100-Mbps wireless connections may be here a lot sooner. A regular 802.11a wireless LAN can already reach data rates of 54 Mbps, more than halfway, and Atheros's proprietary two-channel version exceeds MBS, at 104 Mbps. This was first demonstrated in 2001, nearly a decade before the deadline for MBS. In an industry where everything seems to be either too slow or too late, the early arrival of 4G could be cause for celebration.

But there are still obstacles that 802.11a must overcome if it is to rival the cellular systems. It needs better security, because people expect their cell phone conversations not to be overheard. It also needs better power control, because cell phone batteries have to last a long time. Perhaps most importantly, it needs QoS guarantees. Not coincidentally, these features are all built into ETSI's HiperLan and are the subject of the IEEE's 802.11h working group.

When the standards are worked out, potential 4G operators will still face huge costs in actually building a network. The only operator to have tried constructing a network based on small cells is Metricom, and the cost of putting so many tiny base-stations throughout major cities drove it bankrupt. However, wireless LANs don't have to be built by large telecom operators. Anyone can buy an access point and plug it in, providing coverage to a small area. If the spare capacity on corporate or personal wireless LAN Internet connections were either given away or sold, a sizable 4G network could spring up within less than a year. This would be cheap and quick, and would offer a real competitor to 3G.

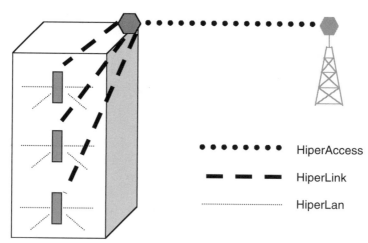

Figure 9.16
Broadband Radio Access Network (BRAN).

BRAN

The *Broadband Radio Access Network* (BRAN), shown in Figure 9.16, is an ETSI project to develop a complete wireless communications system based on HiperLan2. As well as HiperLan2 itself, it includes two other as-yet undefined standards. ETSI hopes that BRAN will help bridge the gap between fixed and mobile networking, enabling high-speed wireless networking everywhere:

- **HiperAccess,** originally called *HiperLan3*, is a variant of HiperLan designed for fixed links to a carrier or ISP. It uses the same spectrum as HiperLan2 and has the same maximum data rate, with a range of up to 5 km.
- **HiperLink**, originally called *HiperLan4*, is an entirely new system. It will use spectrum in the 17-GHz region and provide data rates of up to 155 Mbps. The plan is that it will act as an indoor point-to-point link, connecting HiperAccess antennas on rooftops to HiperLan2 access points below.

Public Access Wireless LANs

Many wireless LANs are left open by mistake, because they're set up by people who don't understand security. There are also idealists, who do so deliberately. They want to share their Internet connections with the rest of the world, either out of pure generosity or because their neighbors help pay for the bandwidth. Residents of apartment buildings can club together to buy a single high-speed Internet connection, and citizens of some towns have set up larger scale networks that cover many blocks.

The most ambitious of these are not merely aimed at connecting to the Internet. They want to replace it entirely, routing all local traffic through the free wireless network. People set up their home computers to act as relay stations, carrying e-mail across town. These networks are currently limited by the range or the availability of the relays, but the visionaries behind them hope that they will eventually be placed everywhere, replicating the Internet but using the public airwaves instead of wires.

Not all public wireless LAN services are free or idealistic. Companies such as Wayport are placing access points in public areas such as airports and hotels, charging customers a monthly subscription for unlimited access. Wayport's coverage is still very poor compared with cellular service providers, but it's much faster, as well as cheaper.

Some businesses are also giving away wireless LAN bandwidth—and not out of idealism. Conference centers and coffee shops sometimes operate open access points as loss leaders, calculating that free Internet access will attract paying customers. Large office buildings may eventually do the same, though perhaps only to certain people. A company could negotiate roaming agreements so that its employees could access the Internet via wireless LAN while in the vicinity of another company's buildings.

WEB RESOURCES

www.bluetooth.com
The Bluetooth SIG, the cross-industry alliance that drives the Bluetooth standard, includes on its site comprehensive technical information, as well as a database of every Bluetooth product.

www.wi-fi.com
This is the site of the Wireless Ethernet Compatibility Alliance, a vendor organization that certifies interoperability between IEEE 802.11b devices.

www.wlana.org
The Wireless LAN Association is a nonprofit consortium of wireless LAN vendors established to help educate the marketplace about wireless LANs and their uses. WLANA develops educational materials about wireless LAN users' experiences, applications, and industry trends.

www.hiperlan2.com
The HiperLan2 Global Forum promotes the HiperLan standard. There used to be a similar forum surrounding the original version of HiperLan, but it's been disbanded and the Web site replaced by porn.

www.homerf.org
The HomeRF working group site aims to introduce home users to wireless LANs.

(continued)

WEB RESOURCES (CONTINUED)

www.ofdm-forum.com
The OFDM Forum is an alliance of vendors set up to promote this technology, which is used primarily in wireless LANs. Its site tries to explain how the system works and the potential applications.

www.consume.net
This is a project to develop an alternative to the Internet, based entirely on wireless LAN technology. It can also form a free access method to the existing Internet.

www.4gmobile.com and www.wireless-world-research.org
There are already two forums trying to develop and promote 4G mobile systems.

http://web.mit.edu/kerberos/www/
This is the official site of the Kerberos authentication protocol, now used in 802.11 (and other) networks. The file called dialogue.html is a particularly good introduction to what is otherwise a very complex topic.

www.comnets.rwth-aachen.de/project/mbs/
This site describes the European Union's original MBS project in detail, along with subsequent work and the results of 1995 tests on a prototype, which achieved a data rate greater than anything for the next few years.

BIBLIOGRAPHY

Flickenger, Rob, and Sue Miller. **Building Wireless Community Networks**. O'Reilly, 2001.
This book explores the benefits of setting up free wireless networks based on the 802.11b standard and shows how to do it. There's some technical information, but it's introduced in a way that should make sense to nonengineers.

Wheat, Jeffrey. **Designing a Wireless Network**. Publishers Group West, 2001.
An instructional guide to choosing, setting up, and administering wireless LANs, with a particular focus on the IEEE 802.11 standards.

SUMMARY ....

- Short-range wireless systems use unlicensed frequency bands. These can either be dedicated to communications or shared with ISM applications.

- There are many incompatible wireless LAN standards, pushed by IEEE (the organization that develops Ethernet) and ETSI (the organization that develops GSM).

- The most popular wireless LAN technology is IEEE 802.11b, which can run at up to 11 Mbps in the 2.4-GHz ISM band.

- Higher capacities need to use higher frequencies. HiperLan2 and IEEE 802.11a both use the 5-GHz band and reach 54 Mbps.

- Digital cordless voice systems provide call quality as good as a regular telephone. Their analog equivalents usually suffer from severe interference.

- Infrared technology is built into almost all portable computing devices and is often more convenient than cables as a method of transferring data.

- Bluetooth is designed for very short-range connections between devices such as mobile phones, headphones, televisions, and even pens. It is not designed for full-scale wireless LANs.

- 4G mobile systems are really just extended wireless LANs. Because their range is so short, many devices may use a combination of 3G, wireless LAN, and Bluetooth.

10 Phones or Computers?

In this chapter...

Internet evangelists once spoke of an "information age" that promised to free us from the tyranny of the physical world. Losing our dependence on corporeal objects and physical travel, we would use wireless networks to access data where and when it suits us.

The reality is slightly different. Just like the paperless office, the wire-free world is further away than ever. Far from freeing their users, mobile networks seem to be giving us an ever-growing electronic burden. It's not unusual to see people carrying around five or six portable devices, each with a different function. As well as a cell phone, many of us need a separate pager, a palmtop, and a laptop. Americans can add another phone or two to deal with the competing standards, and international travelers will also need various adapters and spare batteries if they have a long flight.

This may finally be changing. One of the main trends in communications is convergence, which is often overhyped but really does apply here: Phones are beginning to incorporate more computing features, which may enable them to replace not only laptops and personal digital assistants (PDAs), but personal stereos and eventually even televisions. There will never be one converged device that does everything—the manufacturers still want to sell us plenty of gadgets, after all—but those that we do have may be smaller, lighter, and more tightly integrated with each other.

FUTURE PHONES

The wireless Internet industry is unsure about what types of devices people will want, or more accurately, what they can persuade consumers to buy. The consensus is around *smart phones*, but this is a nebulous term, and nobody is quite sure what it means. Should handsets be more "smart" or more "phone"? Would customers prefer something as easy to carry as a pen or a real keyboard on which they can type?

The most likely answer is both, but even this leads to further questions. There are two competing philosophies about the future of mobile devices:

- **Personal Area Network (PAN).** This assumes a modular system, whereby people continue to carry a plethora of devices, as they do now. The difference is that all are linked together by a short-range radio system, such as Bluetooth, with the cell phone taking the role of central hub and router, as shown in Figure 10.1. When the customer needs to surf the Net on her laptop PC, it connects to the Internet via the cell phone. Her headset does the same when she wants to listen to streaming audio.

- **Integrated Device.** This assumes that people will want to carry only one device but vary it according to the situation. A user might want to travel light and use only voice communication, with a cell phone built into a wristwatch. At other times, he will need to use a full-featured computer

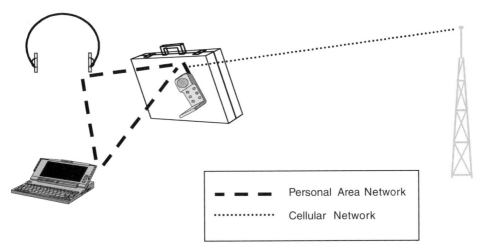

Figure 10.1
PAN: Headset and computer link via a cell phone.

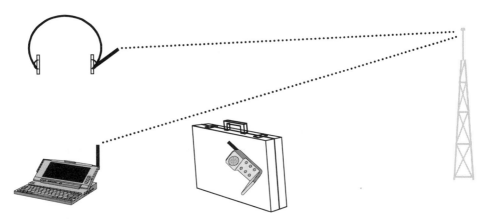

Figure 10.2
Integrated devices: Headset and computer have their own antennas.

with an internal high-speed wireless data connection or a headset for streaming audio. The mobile network automatically detects which terminal is in use at any given time and routes calls accordingly, as in Figure 10.2.

Most companies plan gadgets that will fit into either ideal or both. Many computers and PDAs will have their own internal connection to the cellular network but also be equipped with Bluetooth and wireless LAN technology for shorter-range connections to the likes of printers, refrigerators, and heaters.

If the vendors have their way, the assortment of devices that will ultimately be linked into these short-range networks is infinite. However, all will rely on something similar to a cell phone or a PDA for their long-range connectivity. These future devices can be fitted into five loose categories, each of which contains elements of present-day phones and computers. Listed in order of increasing size, they are wearable computers, smartphones, tablets, clamshells, and subnotebooks.

Wearable Computers

The idea of speaking into a wristwatch or a brooch is straight out of science fiction, but plenty of companies have demonstrated cellular terminals small enough to be worn as jewelry. Most are still just prototypes, though Phillips has shipped a GSM phone that can be worn around the wrist. It is slightly larger than a normal phone and requires headphones. The trend in Japan is toward slightly larger devices called *keitai*, which also incorporate data (usually i-mode) and are worn as a pendant around the neck.

Anything smaller than a telephone will need a headset containing an earpiece and a microphone, so an obvious idea is to build the cellular phone into the headset. This has possible health risks, because it means that people's heads could be in close proximity to radiation sources for much longer periods than at present. One European vendor, Dolfy, is already selling phones that transform into headsets. They're based on the DECT cordless system, which uses much lower-power radiation and so should be safer than a true cellular headset. This also means that people will wear it only around their homes or offices, not in public.

For video on the move, several vendors have proposed putting tiny screens inside sunglasses and even contact lenses. The latter has the potential to immerse users completely in virtual reality, which would be both a risk and a major selling point. Liquid crystal display (LCD) projectors already use transparent screens no larger than the lens in a pair of glasses, so this is a real possibility in the near future. Sony already sells virtual reality goggles designed to produce the same effect as sitting directly in front of a wide-screen TV, which can also show 3D pictures if programmed to. A system like this is really more virtual than reality—it can't reproduce touch, taste, or smell—but it does show what can be done using relatively inexpensive existing technology.

The problem with any very small mobile terminal is that its battery will quickly run down, and batteries cannot be miniaturized in the same way as other devices. The only items of clothing large and solid enough to contain a reasonably sized battery are shoes, which could also be used to generate energy and recharge the battery as the user walks. The cellular terminal itself would also have to be in a shoe, because there is no way to send actual energy wirelessly. Other devices, such as a headset, could communicate with the shoe over a PAN. Bluetooth requires far less energy than a cellular terminal and could run from a battery the same size as that inside a digital watch.

Shoe-based computers equipped with wireless transceivers have actually existed since the 1960s, thanks to Las Vegas gamblers. Led by communications pioneer Claude Shannon, a team of scientists realized that a spinning roulette wheel follows relatively simple laws of physics. By writing a complex program, they were able to simulate the wheel and calculate the winning numbers. Equipped with small computers hidden in their shoes that could accept input after the wheel had started to spin, they successfully beat the casinos.

Very primitive wearable computers enjoyed a surge in popularity in late 2001, thanks to a loophole in security measures that banned bags from many venues such as conference centers. Instead of carrying their mobile devices in bags, people started wearing very bulky clothes with huge pockets across the chest or back. These often resemble lifejackets (but they don't float!) and are large enough to contain a full-sized laptop and a small library of manuals. Some even have cabling ducts linking the pockets, so that people can form a simple PAN without using wireless technology.

Smartphones

A *smartphone* is a mobile phone with some extra computer-type functions, the most obvious being a WAP microbrowser. In some ways, the term is a misnomer because phones are actually fairly dumb; most of the intelligence resides in the mobile network, rather than on the terminal. It's also fairly misleading, because the phone manufacturers plan to make all phones incorporate these features. Every phone is "smart" in some way, compared with those made five years ago.

The name is particularly misleading when related to *smart cards*, a term for any credit card that includes a tiny chip. These are very common in some countries, and the banking industry is moving toward putting chips in almost all credit and debit cards worldwide. There is also one inside every GSM phone in the form of the SIM, which is literally just a smart card without the extraneous plastic that usually surrounds the chip. (New SIMs are actually supplied in a credit card form, with perforations so that the chip can easily be removed and put into the phone.) In this sense, all GSM phones made since 1982 are smart.

Other than mobile data capabilities, features generally regarded as smart include location-based services and sophisticated address books that can interface with a computer. The smartest phones are now able to change into PDAs, offering capabilities that do not depend on the availability of a cellular signal.

Tablets

A *tablet* PDA is one that doesn't have a keyboard and relies on a touch-sensitive screen for input. The theory behind tablets is that users can take notes in the same way as on a paper notepad but can also access information, such as a calendar and address book.

The most well known tablet is the Palm series, which began life in 1996 as the PalmPilot. But the concept predates this. It was popularized by the TV series *Star Trek: The Next Generation* in 1988, and the first attempt to produce one was Apple's Newton MessagePad in 1993. Though very advanced for its time, Apple's device failed because it was too expensive and relied on an ineffective handwriting recognition technology.

Palm Computing learned from Apple's mistakes, and the Palm has been phenomenally successful. Palm Computing, spun off from 3COM in 2000, says that its device has been taken up faster than anything else in the history of technology. Its user base grew at a rate faster than TV, the Internet, or even the mobile phone.

Because tablets are so popular, mobile phone manufacturers and network operators believe that they will be the initial type of terminal used to access 3G wireless services. The companies envisage a device about the size of an ordinary phone but with a high-resolution screen where the keypad is presently located. If the data rate is high enough, this can be used to surf the Web, watch TV, or conduct videoconferences.

Back in reality, Palm has been saying for two years that it is about to equip all its tablets with mobile data capability, and rivals Microsoft and Symbian have also produced tablet operating systems for PDAs. The PalmOS has been licensed to several mobile phone manufacturers, the first of which was Qualcomm. Its pdQ series of phones has a hinged keypad that flips down to reveal a Palm-style tablet screen through which the user can access the wireless Web. Later Palm-based phones, such as Handspring's Trëo, dispensed with the keypad altogether, reasoning that a touch-sensitive screen could display a "virtual keypad."

Most tablets are small enough to fit comfortably into one hand, hence names such as *Palm* and *Pocket PC*. They're designed to be carried around and used to store information such as a phone book or appointment list. For Web surfing, most people prefer a larger device about the size of a book or magazine. These giant PDAs are known as *Web pads*. They're often functionally identical to the smaller versions but cost more because of the need to produce a large, flat screen.

In November 2001, Microsoft announced its *Tablet PC* initiative. Tablet PCs are the size of Web pads, but they're full-featured PCs rather than PDAs: They include hard disks (most PDAs don't) and are based on Windows XP, the same operating system that Microsoft is pushing for desktop and laptop PCs. This makes them heavier and more expensive than Web pads, and means that their batteries have a much shorter life. The advantage is that they can run regular Windows applications, not the cut-down versions found on PDAs, though people may find these hard to use without a keyboard. For this reason, some Tablet PCs are laptops with touch-sensitive screens that can flip over to cover the keyboard.

Clamshells

Before the arrival of large, touch-sensitive screens, nearly all PDAs used the same *clamshell* design as laptops, where the screen folds over the keyboard. For a long time, the most successful company in this market was Psion, which started life as a software firm but is commonly credited with inventing the PDA.

Released in 1984, the original Psion Organizer was essentially a glorified pocket calculator. Its unique feature was a slot for cartridges containing programs. Psion supplied software for scientific, financial, and database applications, and users could write their own, using a variant of *BASIC* (Beginners' All-purpose Symbolic Instruction Code) called *POPL* (Psion Organizer Programming Language).

The first clamshell PDA to achieve widespread popularity was Psion's Series 3, released in 1991. It had a tiny keyboard but a screen large enough for a graphical user interface and useful programs, such as a word processor and spreadsheet. Other companies, such as Casio and Tandy, quickly released similar organizers of their own, each based on a different device-specific operating system.

Noticing the booming market, Microsoft released its Windows CE software for organizers in 1997. With the exception of Psion, most companies duly replaced their own systems with Microsoft's.

Clamshell PDAs began to wane in popularity when the PalmPilot was launched, but there is still a market for them. The most interesting are hybrid devices, which look and act as ordinary cell phones when closed but can open up to reveal a small PDA. The first of these was Nokia's Communicator, released in 1988. It was considered a toy for very rich executives, but three years later similar devices were becoming mainstream. Clamshell phones seem to be most popular among children, perhaps because adults find their very small keyboards awkward to use.

Subnotebooks

Subnotebooks sit on the borderline between PDAs and full-fledged laptop computers. They have been dreamed of for decades, and the first serious design was produced in 1968 by computing pioneer Alan Kay. He proposed a system simple enough for children to use, cheap enough for everyone to own, and weighing less than 1 kg.

Lacking the technology for a working prototype, Kay built a model from cardboard and lead—the *Dynabook*, so called because it was intended to be the size and weight of a book but adaptable to different applications. The graphical software he designed for it at Xerox's PARC (Palo Alto Research Center) lab was too sophisticated to fit into a portable computer at that time. It instead had to run on a desktop machine called the *Alto*, inspiring both the Apple Macintosh and Microsoft Windows.

The first true subnotebook was Atari's Portfolio, released in 1989. It was designed to be IBM-compatible, running MS DOS on an Intel 80C88 processor, a similar configuration to the original IBM PC. Windows machines soon followed, such as the Toshiba Libretto and the Hewlett-Packard Omnibook. These were real PCs, with the same advantages and drawbacks as a laptop (or a Tablet PC). They could run any program designed for a desktop but suffered from short battery life because they had hard disks and PC-class processors. They also tended to be more expensive than standard desktops or laptops.

Rather than scaling down a PC, some subnotebooks scale up a clamshell PDA. These devices are quite rare in Europe and America, though most people who have used one love them. They look like ordinary laptops, usually with a full-size screen and keyboard, but are much lighter because they don't include components such as disk drives. They are also cheaper and have battery lives long enough for an intercontinental flight.

According to processor manufacturer Intel, subnotebooks are being squeezed from either side of the market by full-featured laptops and smaller, cheaper clamshells or tablets. It says that people always indicate in polls that weight and battery life are the most important features when choosing a laptop, but when actually buying one they opt for fast processors, big screens, DVD-ROMs, and sound cards.

Japan has been much more receptive to subnotebooks than Europe or the United States because of space constraints. Intel believes that they will eventually become more popular worldwide as customers buy their third or even fourth computer. It hopes that people will want to own a desktop, a laptop, a subnotebook, and a smaller mobile device.

MOBILE OPERATING SYSTEMS ....

Although Microsoft dominates the computer desktop, there is much more competition among PDA operating systems. Two other companies are fighting with Microsoft for leadership in this market, and they have managed to push it into third place in terms of the number of users. Manufacturers are also interested in producing PDAs based on Linux, the free and open-source software, and many companies have responded with versions of Linux optimized for these. The largest Linux company, Red Hat, has even produced an entirely new Linux-style system called *eCos*, intended for small devices. Table 10.1 shows the names of the operating systems produced by these companies for different classes of device.

Table 10.1   Operating Systems for Different Device Families

Device/ Company	Symbian	Microsoft	Palm Computing	Red Hat
Smartphones	Symbian OS Crystal	Stinger or Mobile Explorer	PalmOS	Red Hat eCos
Handheld Tablets	Symbian OS Quartz	Pocket PC (Windows CE Mercury)	PalmOS	Linux
Clamshells	Symbian OS Pearl	Windows CE Mars	N/A	Linux
Subnotebooks	Symbian OS Pearl	Windows CE Jupiter or Windows XP	N/A	Linux

Symbian

As phones began to incorporate computer-type features and customers demanded wireless Internet access, the mobile industry feared that it would be dominated by Microsoft. To resist the software giant, the leading cell phone vendors formed a joint venture with Psion in 1998. Known as *Symbian*, the new company intended to build on Psion's EPOC operating system and to license it for both phones and PDAs.

With Nokia, Ericsson, Motorola, and Toshiba all owning a stake in Symbian, its operating system is destined to be widely adopted by mobile manufacturers. But the alliance is uneasy. The four companies are fierce competitors and may not be committed to working together. The operating system for tablets and phones also took longer to develop than planned, as is usual for software projects. By 2000, the company could display only dummies, and tablet PDAs based on the system were still not shipping at the end of 2001.

Two versions of EPOC for clamshells exist, known as EPOC16 and SymbianOS (formerly called EPOC32). The former is designed for older, 16-bit processors and is used only in very low-cost organizers from Psion and a few other companies. The latter is a modular 32-bit system containing a variety of optional applications. The plan is to adapt this for other types of devices, focusing on three reference designs. Each is named after a crystal and includes different hardware and software components optimized for what Symbian sees as the three main market segments: clamshells, tablets, and phones.

PalmOS

Palm Computing was the success story of the late 1990s, its growth paralleling that of the Internet—though at first there was little connection between them. By 2000, only four years after its launch, the PalmPilot and its successors had captured 80% of the American PDA market. Only a tiny proportion included their own wireless link to the Internet, though all do now have the capability to send e-mail and read "clipped" Web sites if they're connected to a cell phone.

Despite its popularity, Palm's dominance is not assured. The company is losing money, and its stock price fell by more than 95% during the dot-com crash of 2000 and 2001. It suffers from the same problem as Apple: It manufactures both hardware and software, a situation Psion avoided by spinning off its software side into Symbian. Palm says that it will do the same, eventually separating its hardware and software businesses.

The PalmOS has been licensed to several other companies. A few, such as IBM, actually commission Palm to develop hardware for them as well, then add some extra software of their own. Customized versions exist for professional groups as diverse as doctors and realtors. Most just buy the software, putting it into their own hardware. Handspring, Qualcomm, and Sony have all followed this route, producing cell phones that run PalmOS. There is always the suspicion that Palm favors its own hardware division over its competitors, hence the plan to split it in two.

Palm is focused on small, handheld tablets: It has no operating system for computers that have a keyboard but may release one in the future. Palm bought the assets of Be, a desktop operating system company, in 2001. Though Palm has no plans to continue selling Be's operating system—BeOS, which was used by several companies, including Sony—it does plan to integrate some features of the system in future releases of PalmOS. This may include support for larger devices. Palm has also acquired ThinAir-Apps, a company producing gateway software for wireless access to corporate e-mail. Like Be, its technology will be incorporated into PalmOS.

Windows CE and Pocket PC

By 1995, Microsoft had a near-monopoly on operating systems for PCs. The success of companies such as Psion led it to believe, correctly, that PDAs would eventually become a bigger market than computers. Its response was Windows CE, an operating system that looked just like the popular Windows 95 and even included cut-down versions of Microsoft's Office applications.

Despite the support of every major manufacturer except Psion, some of whom added features such as color screens and music playback, CE initially failed to win a strong following. Users criticized its lack of compatibility with non-Microsoft applications and said that the Windows user interface was too cluttered. It also suffered from bad timing—as Windows CE and Psion battled over the clamshell market, Palm's tablets were becoming enormously popular.

Microsoft tried again in 1998, with a version of Windows CE for palm-size devices that it optimistically dubbed the PalmPilot killer. User reaction was again unfavorable. The Windows clutter made even less sense on an even more compact screen. The interface was improved over two versions until, by 2000, many analysts believed that Windows CE had finally got it right. But its competitors had a head start, and it still trailed both Palm and EPOC in the PDA market.

Microsoft offers several versions of CE, four of which are aimed at mobile devices. Three are intended for different types of PDAs and named after planets; the fourth is designed for smart phones and known as *Stinger*. The most popular runs on small tablets that compete directly with the Palm (though they're more powerful and more expensive), called *Pocket PCs*. The operating system for these is also sometimes called *Pocket PC*, but at its core it is Windows CE. The latest upgrade is Pocket PC 2002, which adds some more programs for applications such as playing audio files but is still Windows CE underneath.

In response to competition from free and open-source software, Microsoft decided in 2001 to publish the full source code for Windows CE, though not necessarily all the components of the latest version. This is semi-free, meaning that people are allowed to download and copy it freely but only for noncommercial use. Companies producing PDAs and phones still have to pay Microsoft royalties, as do programmers who download it for business purposes.

Linux

Linux is a *free* and *open-source* operating system, which means that it is produced by many programmers who work independently, then share their work. The original program listings are free for anyone to download and change as they see fit—in contrast to proprietary software, which is produced by companies that usually keep the listings a closely guarded secret.

Some people claim that because people can obtain Linux without payment, it is dependent on the generosity of programmers. This isn't true: Although many programmers do work on Linux or other open-source projects for fun or out of altruism, the system no longer depends on this. Linux did require idealists to get started, but it is now self-sustaining, thanks to the way it is licensed.

Instead of simply being released into the public domain, Linux is licensed under the *General Public License* (GPL). This means that whenever it is sold or given away, users are free to adapt it for their own needs (free as in speech) and to make as many copies as they want (free as in beer). The only thing they're not free to do is incorporate it into a proprietary, closed-source product. This prevents a company such as Microsoft taking the Linux code, making alterations, then selling it back at a fat profit.

Although the GPL means that few software companies want to work on Linux, many other companies do. They calculate that it is cheaper to adapt a free system than to buy a proprietary package or write their own program from scratch. This calculation is particularly attractive to hardware vendors who want to ship machines with preinstalled software, which is one reason why IBM has become Linux's largest advocate. PDAs are cheaper than most hardware, so the proportionate saving from using free software is greater.

The GPL only requires that improvements be shared if the software is sold on or given away: People are free to adapt Linux for their own use (commercial or otherwise) and keep their changes secret. However, putting the software on a piece of hardware and selling that does count as redistributing the software, so all PDA manufacturers who use Linux will effectively be contributing to its development. The more companies and programmers who work on the system, the more attractive it is to others, so a virtuous circle is set up.

Low cost is only one of Linux's benefits. Because its source code is free and open, users are not dependent on a single company for technical support. If the software vendor shuts down (as Be did when it sold its assets to Palm) or abandons a system (as Microsoft has done with some early versions of Windows), other programmers can pick up where it left off. This also makes it easier to fix bugs and repair security weaknesses, which is one reason why Linux systems are less vulnerable to viruses and other attacks than those based on Windows. (To be fair to Microsoft, it isn't the only reason: People who use Linux tend to know more about computers than people who use Windows, and so are less likely to download and run a virus by mistake.) Perhaps most important for small platforms like PDAs, it's infinitely customizable. Manufacturers can cut out as much of it as they want, keeping only the routines absolutely necessary for a particular device.

Of course, most of these benefits directly affect only programmers: The vast majority of users are not going to view the source code, let alone try to fix bugs themselves and release their own versions under the GPL. This is why Linux has traditionally appealed more to experts, such as the people who run computer networks, than to regular users. Most Web sites are hosted on Apache, a free and open-source Web server, while most surfers that visit them use Microsoft's Internet Explorer. However, Linux is not intrinsically any more difficult to use than other operating systems, and the benefits pass indirectly to users through lower costs and better reliability.

Linux has the potential to overtake Microsoft, Palm, and Symbian, but it has some weaknesses to overcome. The people promoting it frequently argue over semantics, such as what to call the system. Technically, Linux is just the name of the *kernel*—

the program at the core of an operating system. The bundles of software sold or given away by companies such as Red Hat combine this with various other programs necessary for a complete operating system, most of which were developed by a group called the Free Software Foundation and also licensed under the GPL. The Foundation originally intended these programs to be used in a system called *GNU*, so the complete package is sometimes called *GNU/Linux*.

There are also arguments over whether to say *free* or *open source*. The Foundation prefers free, because it reminds people of freedom. Many companies prefer open source, because it describes a major business advantage. Both terms are open to misinterpretation, or *FUD* (fear, uncertainty, and doubt) from companies such as Microsoft. Free is often used to describe programs that can be downloaded at no cost, although they don't allow users to see the source code or make changes. Likewise, open source is sometimes used to describe programs that allow users to see the source code but don't allow them to make changes or copies.

Linux and other free/open-source programs also face external threats. They don't get as much attention from the press as proprietary systems for several reasons. Some are comparatively trivial: Editors like to spell out abbreviations and, thus, often question the awkward phrase *GNU* (a recursive acronym, "GNU's Not Unix"). More problematic, lazy journalists would rather reprint a slick press release than hunt down a free program that emerges gradually and without fanfare. The nearly annual Windows upgrade is a big "event," carefully orchestrated to fit the news agenda. It easily drowns out the daily incremental improvements to the Linux kernel.

Worse, Linux is under attack from laws that restrict its use and development in the United States. The most serious such law to have passed so far is the *Digital Millennium Copyright Act* (DMCA). This forbids research into any encryption or compression algorithm used to restrict the use of copyright material and was first used to prevent Web sites from even linking to a program that lets Linux users play DVDs. It was later used to prevent a Princeton professor from giving a lecture and to arrest a graduate student who wrote a program that enabled Adobe's "electronic books" (encrypted files) to be transferred to a PDA.

Lobbyists are attempting to pass even more restrictive legislation. The *Uniform Computer Information Transactions Act* (UCITA), already law in two U.S. states, allows software companies to ban reverse-engineering of any file format, preventing compatibility across different types of hardware or operating systems and protecting monopolies. The proposed *Consumer Broadband and Digital Television Promotion Act* (CBDTPA) is even more draconian, requiring all hardware and software to include an unspecified copyright management system set by a cartel of media companies. Legislation such as this would effectively make Linux and most other free/open-source software illegal in the United States, though it would still be an important force in other parts of the world.

Real-Time Operating Systems

Most cell phones don't yet run Linux, PalmOS, Symbian, or any form of Windows. The main advantage of all these systems is that they allow users to run programs, and phones don't really need this capability: They're used mainly to make phone calls or to send simple messages, not for complex computing tasks.

Instead, phones run *real-time* operating systems, which require far less processor or memory capacity than most of the larger systems. The name comes from their ability to time operations to the exact nanosecond, which in turn derives from their simplicity: They don't need to stop doing everything while waiting for a user input, and they don't allow rogue programs to take over and slow down the rest of the system.

Real-time operating systems are used in all kinds of household appliances, such as washing machines and alarm systems, which many users don't even realize contain computers, let alone operating systems. As processing power increases, devices such as cell phones may grow to incorporate more visible operating systems that allow programs to be run. But real-time systems will remain important for mobile data, because many of the gadgets that may ultimately connect to mobile networks don't need the overhead of a large operating system.

About half of all devices that contain real-time operating systems use one written by the hardware manufacturer itself to save on licensing costs and because the manufacturer often understands the hardware better than an outside company. However, a growing number are based on other systems. Linux is becoming more popular, thanks to its low cost and customizability: Several companies, such as Lineo, have already adapted the system to make it real-time. Microsoft is also adding real-time capability to Windows CE. Among the others:

- **VxWorks** from Wind River is the most popular real-time operating system. It's used in some phones and in many other embedded applications, from spacecraft to digital watches.

- **Neutrino** from QNX Software is designed to be similar to UNIX, the server operating systems that inspired Linux. Like VxWorks, it's used in a wide range of applications, such as nuclear reactors and TV sets, as well as phones. Much of the source is available at no charge for noncommercial use.

- **eCos** is an open-source operating system produced by Red Hat, the company behind the most popular version of Linux. Though Red Hat is also pushing an embedded version of Linux, it says that eCos is necessary for smaller devices that aren't yet able to run the full system. It is distributed under a license similar to Linux's GPL, but a bit more liberal: Manufacturers can adapt parts of it to run on their own hardware without having to release every change to the community.

Microbrowser Wars

The wired Web saw a fierce browser war between Microsoft and Netscape, as each side tried to give away its browser software in the hope that it would entice customers to use them. Microsoft eventually won by integrating its browser with the Windows operating system, a practice that was at the heart of the antitrust actions brought against it by the U.S. Department of Justice, individual states, and the European Commission.

Part of the motivation for both Netscape and Microsoft was the ability to control the *home page* that users see when they first start up their browsers, as well as to provide built-in links to other features, such as search engines and online shopping. This is much less important on the wireless Web, because home pages and other links are usually determined by the mobile operator, rather than the software company, but there is still a battle between several different microbrowsers.

Most microbrowsers interpret the standards in slightly different ways, which means that sites need to be tested individually with each one. If one becomes dominant, site designers might decide to support just that one, giving the company behind it a chance to move away from the standards and toward its own proprietary system, as Microsoft is already doing with the PC-based Web. Fortunately, there are so many different microbrowsers that this seems unlikely to happen.

Each of the largest phone manufacturers has developed its own microbrowser, but there are also several produced by software companies. In addition to Microsoft, which does sells its Mobile Explorer browser without the Windows CE operating system, the most important are:

- **NetFront** from Access Systems is the mostly widely used microbrowser, because it is built in to most i-mode phones. The original version supports only Compact HTML (C-HTML), but Access has announced a new version that adds support for XHTML Basic.

- **Opera** supports more operating systems than any other browser. Though most of its users are running desktop PCs and surfing regular HTML, it has been ported to several mobile systems and adapted to support WAP and C-HTML. Opera is included as standard on some PDAs running Symbian and Linux and can also run under QNX's real-time operating systems.

- **Openwave** invented HDML, the language on which WAP 1.2 is based, and has become the leading supplier of WAP microbrowsers. It has also released a version that supports XHTML Basic and C-HTML.

PDA HARDWARE ....

PDAs are essentially very small computers. As such, they require the same type of hardware that a computer needs: a processor, memory, and interfaces to connect to the outside world. Unlike in a traditional computer, all this has to be designed to consume as little power as possible so that the device's battery doesn't run out.

Processor

The processor is far less important in a mobile device than in a PC. Although desktop PCs are frequently marketed with a large number of GHz as their main selling point, it can be very difficult to discover the speed and even the make of the processor inside a PDA or phone.

The reason is that there is no single common hardware or software platform, so it is harder to make comparisons. The Palm and the Pocket PC devices offer comparable performance, but the extra complexity and added features of the Windows CE operating system means that the Pocket PC demands more computing power. Even for users who have settled on an operating system, Windows CE alone has been ported to more than 10 different types of processor. Each has its own unique characteristics, making it hard to compare them using only one measure. Nevertheless, clock rate can serve as a rough guide to the power of a system.

All PalmOS devices so far use Motorola's DragonBall chip, a variant of the M68000 used in the original Apple Macintosh. The DragonBall runs at only 33 MHz. This would be too slow for Windows CE, which most users agree feels rather sluggish at anything below 100 MHz.

The Symbian system is more modular, so its processor requirements vary, depending on which components are installed—Psion's product range alone spans 8–133 MHz. The most powerful processor inside PDAs at present is the StrongARM, originally designed by Digital Equipment Corporation but now built by Intel. It can run at up to 200 MHz and uses far less electricity than the x86 chips inside PCs. Microsoft has announced that all future Pocket PCs will be based on the StrongARM.

The predicted boom in mobile computing has led many companies to develop small chips with a low electrical appetite. The most well known is Transmeta, a Silicon Valley startup that counts Linux father Linus Torvalds among its founders and has several heavyweight backers, including PC giant Gateway. Its Crusoe processors are able to run a variety of operating systems by emulating the x86.

Memory

Memory has a greater impact than processing power on most computer users. Even in the PC domain, nearly every computer would see greater benefit from a memory expansion than from a processor upgrade. Memory is even more crucial for PDAs, because they have no disk drives. A PC can store most of its data on hard disk and even use part of the drive as *virtual memory* if its real memory does run low. (Virtual memory takes a comparatively long time to access, which is why PCs often slow down when users rapidly switch between several applications.) A PDA has to keep literally everything within memory, including its store of contacts and appointments, every spreadsheet or word processor file, and even programs that the user decides to install.

As with the processor, different types of PDA require different amounts of memory, though in every case, more is obviously better. The Palm can get by with only 4 MB, whereas Windows CE machines need at least 32 MB. Again as with the processor, EPOC's requirements vary between these two extremes. The memory and processor requirements of each operating system are summarized in Table 10.2.

Like all computers, PDAs have two types of memory:

- **ROM** (Read-Only Memory) stores the operating system and any other programs that the manufacturer has preinstalled. This differs from the architecture of a PC, which has only a very basic ROM telling the computer to load (boot) an operating system from a disk drive. The advantage is that a PDA can be used almost immediately after it is switched on, whereas a PC can take a minute or more to start up. The disadvantage is that upgrading the software is difficult or impossible.

- **RAM** (Random Access Memory) holds all information specific to the user. Most RAM is *volatile*, meaning it loses all data when switched off. To avoid such a disaster, PDAs and phones are never switched off completely. Though they may look inactive to the user, there is still a tiny current flowing through the memory. Many even contain a small backup battery to keep the memory active while the main battery is being replaced. This often fails to work or has a very short life, so PDA data should always be backed up on a PC.

There are several different types of RAM available, though exactly which kind is installed really makes a difference only with a fast processor and a memory-hungry operating system, such as Windows CE. Three have found their way into phones and PDAs so far, and two more look promising:

- **DRAM** (Dynamic RAM) is the cheapest and is used in most mobile devices.

- **EDO** (Enhanced Data Output) is more expensive but offers a speed increase of about 30% over DRAM. It is used by some Windows CE handhelds, such as Compaq's Aero.

- **SDRAM** (Synchronous Dynamic RAM) offers a further 50% speed increase and is the standard on PCs. It's used by some higher-end Windows CE and Linux PDAs, such as Compaq's iPAQ and Sharp's Zaurus.

- **DDR** (Double Data Rate) SDRAM is, as the name suggests, twice as fast as regular SDRAM. It is used in some very high-performance PCs but not yet in PDAs. Some Intel-based PCs use a system called *Rambus*, which is similar to DDR but plugs into the computer's circuit board using a proprietary interface.

- **OUM** (Ovonics Unified Memory) is still experimental. It's no faster than the other memory types, but it does allow a lot more storage to be packed into a given area. A small OUM chip in a handheld PDA could hold 500 MB, enough to store several full-length movies. Because it's based on the same material as rewritable CDs, it could also retain data even when switched off, saving power and allowing it to be used for removable storage.

Table 10.2 Hardware Requirements of Mobile Operating Systems

Operating System	Typical Processor Speed	ROM	Minimum RAM
EPOC 16	7.7 MHz	2 MB	2 MB
Symbian OS (EPOC 32)	36 MHz	6 MB	6 MB
PalmOS 3.x	16 MHz	2 MB	2 MB
Windows CE (Pocket PC)	133 MHz	32 MB	16 MB
Linux	133 MHz	16 MB	16 MB

Interfaces

Despite the ideal of a wireless world, mobile devices still require physical interfaces for cables and expansion modules. In particular, most need some way to connect to a computer so that data can be backed up. Many PDAs still don't have a built-in cellular terminal or even a modem, so linking to a computer can also be the only way to install new software, whether from CD-ROM or the Internet.

Most phones still have only one proprietary expansion plug, used to connect to accessories such as a hands-free kit or to a computer for wireless data. PDAs tend to offer a greater choice of options. Many have a *Universal Serial Bus* (USB) port, a small jack on the back that can be used to connect to most computers built after about 1998. Some also have an infrared port and interfaces for other equipment, such as a standard keyboard or mouse.

Palm pioneered the idea of a *sync cradle*, which other manufacturers are now copying. This is a small box that can be left connected to a PC, with the device simply dropped into it for automatic updating. Such things should be unnecessary once Bluetooth is ubiquitous, but manufacturers are already finding other uses for them. Well-designed sync cradles act as battery chargers too, providing a permanent home for the Palm when it isn't in the user's pocket.

The latest trend among tablets is for the manufacturer to sell a variety of proprietary plug-in cartridges, which offer extra functions or expansion ports. They say that this keeps the basic specification light, but it also locks customers into that particular manufacturer's equipment. Such a system was first tried by Psion for its original Organizer, released back in 1984. It was abandoned but resurrected 15 years later by Handspring and then Compaq. Known as Springboards, Handspring's expansion modules include a modem, a pager, and even a golf game.

There are also two industry-standard expansion systems found in many PDAs and some phones. Both consist of small slots into which the user can insert one or more cards. Each card can be a complete device in itself, such as a hard disk drive or RAM pack, but they usually involve connecting to something else and, thus, have either a wire or an antenna sticking out.

- **PC cards** were developed in 1990 by the PCMCIA (Personal Computer Memory Card International Association), under whose name they were known until 1995. They can be used in almost all notebook computers, some PDAs, and occasionally in other devices, such as digital cameras. As the name suggests, they were originally intended as an easy way to expand a computer's memory but are now used for all types of interfaces. The most common PC cards are modems, network interfaces, and interfaces for mobile phones.

  All PC cards are the same shape as credit cards, 86 mm × 54 mm. There are three different thicknesses (3, 5, and 10 mm), but all use the same kind of interface. The only difference is how much space is needed to accommodate them. Many PDAs do not have room for the thickest, known as *Type III*, but this is rarely used except by high-capacity hard disk drives.

- **CF+ cards** are a miniaturized version of the PC card. They are available in only two thicknesses (3 and 5 mm) and measure 36 mm × 43 mm—about the size of a credit card broken in two. CF+ (Compact Flash) slots are found in many PDAs and some cell phones, and are used for much the same applications as their larger ancestor. The first commercially available Bluetooth products were CF+ cards.

It's possible to put a CF+ card in a PC card slot by sheathing it inside an adapter. This allows people to use the same cards in all their mobile devices and makes it easier for manufacturers to support both.

Power Consumption

For laptop computer users, battery life is the single greatest limitation. Despite advances in battery technology, faster processors and extra features, such as CD-ROM drives, mean that most still need a recharge after two hours or less. Mobile phones and PDAs last longer, but the increased power consumption of high-speed data services and the planned convergence of phones with computers threaten to change this.

Phone manufacturers quote highly exaggerated battery lives based on how long the phone can remain on standby. Users need to look instead at the length of *talk time*, unless they intend never to make or receive calls. Most modern phone batteries have several hours of talk time, enough to last for a full calendar day, provided they are not in constant use. Power consumption also depends on signal strength; the further a digital phone is from its base station, the louder the broadcast must be.

Battery capacities are measured in *watt-hours*, which means the number of hours for which the battery could supply a power of 1 watt. This is a very small unit by the standards of electricity. A typical light bulb requires 60 watts, so a watt-hour is enough to keep it going for only a minute. In human metabolic terms, it's less than the nutritional energy contained within a can of diet soft drink. Most mobile phone batteries have a capacity of less than 10 watt-hours, barely enough to heat the water for a lukewarm cup of espresso.

Table 10.3 shows the typical battery capacity needed for some applications. It is only a rough guide. Different brands of battery have different capacities, and many are available in several sizes. Some phone manufacturers give users a choice: a slimline battery that has to be recharged frequently or a large, bulging one that can last for many days. But in every case, higher capacities mean a bulkier and heavier battery.

Because battery life is so important, mobile devices are typically very energy-efficient. Though this may seem to be a good thing from a cost or environmental point of view, the amounts of energy concerned are too small to be significant. It may be more important when considering the health effects of mobile phones, because the human body could be sensitive to smaller changes.

Table 10.3   Battery Capacities

Device	Battery Capacity	Lifetime	Usual Type
Electric Car	1,000 watt-hours	1 hour	Lead-Acid
Laptop PC	50 watt-hours	2 hours	Li-ion
Mobile Phone	10 watt-hours	10 hours talk	NiMH
PDA (AA battery)	2 watt-hours	20 hours	NiCad or Alkaline
Digital Watch	0.1 watt-hours	2 years	Zinc Carbon

Batteries

Almost all batteries built into mobile equipment are known as *secondary* power cells, which means that they can be recharged. There are five main types:

- **Lead-acid** batteries were used in some very early mobile phones but are now reserved mainly for vehicles and industrial applications. They are relatively cheap and can be recharged an indefinite number of times, but the ingredients are quite dangerous.

- **NiCad** (nickel cadmium) batteries are the cheapest type of rechargeable battery. They can be recharged up to 1,000 times but need to be completely discharged each time. If not, they can suffer from a *memory effect*. At its most extreme, this memory effect means that devices can access only the electricity put into the battery during its last charge, not any left from previous charges. NiCad batteries used to be very common in all kinds of devices, but thanks to the memory effect are now rarely fitted as standard in computing or communications equipment. Their main use is as a replacement for disposable batteries, and they are usually the type supplied with home battery chargers. Environmental groups have criticized NiCad batteries because they contain the pollutant cadmium, though they are still considered far more environmentally friendly and cheaper than disposable batteries.

- **NiMH** (nickel metal hydride) batteries are slightly more expensive than NiCad batteries but have up to 25% more energy capacity for the same size and weight. Their main advantage is that they don't suffer from the memory effect. A user can top up the battery whenever convenient, even if it has just been charged a few minutes ago. They are found in most mobile phones and in some laptop PCs.

- **Li-ion** (lithium ion) batteries also resist the memory effect and provide higher capacities than other types. They are also more expensive, so many manufacturers of phones and laptops give their customers a choice: If long battery life is important, they can pay about $50 extra to have a Li-ion battery.

- **Li-Po** (lithium polymer) batteries are similar to Li-ion batteries in energy capacity but cost about three times as much. Their chief advantage is in the physical density of the material used: A Li-Po battery weighs only a quarter as much as a Li-ion battery of the same capacity and dimensions, which makes devices based on them easier to carry.

Smart Batteries can be based on either Li-Po, Li-ion, or NiMH technology and include a built-in power meter. This is used by power management features in mobile devices and by chargers so that they know when to stop.

Ordinary nonrechargeable batteries are known in the jargon as *primary power cells* and come in two main variants: *Alkaline* and *Zinc-Carbon*. Of the two, alkalines offer the highest capacity and are more expensive. The most common are the AA size, used by many Palm and Psion PDAs.

Nonrechargeable batteries are not normally used in mobile phones, though kits are available that enable them to act as an emergency power source. The theory is that, if a user is stranded away from a power source, she will be able to buy a relatively cheap disposable battery that gives the phone a few minutes of talk time. Another emergency power option is the *Zinc-Air* booster, a small device kept in a sealed foil pack that reacts with oxygen to provide a full power charge.

A better solution than spare batteries may be a hand- or foot-cranked generator, which allows a phone's own battery to be recharged without external power. Cell phones use relatively little energy, compared with most electric appliances, and it's possible to generate enough electricity to power them through relatively little work. Although some pampered users in the West might object to expending any physical effort at all, these systems could prove invaluable in areas of the world where a reliable electricity supply is simply not available.

At least two companies are developing human-powered battery chargers. Freeplay, which produced the first clockwork radio in 1991, sells a device called the Freecharge, which weighs 230 g (8 ounces) and is about the same size as a small cell phone. It claims that winding the Freeplay's crank for 30 seconds generates enough power for a 10-minute call or several hours of standby time. For laptops, which have a higher power consumption, Aladdin Power sells a foot-operated charger. By tapping one foot on a small pedal while they type, users can keep their computers running indefinitely.

USER INPUT ···

The trouble with miniaturization is that input can be difficult without a proper keyboard. This has been a problem for PDAs ever since they first appeared, and it gets worse as devices become smaller. A typical mobile phone may have no more than 12 small buttons, and tablet devices could have none at all. These are supposed to rely on handwriting or (in the case of Microsoft's Tablet PC) voice recognition, but this rarely works perfectly.

Many applications and operating systems spurn the keyboard in favor of the mouse, which is sensible for desktop users. Tests carried out by Apple in the 1980s consistently showed that, if a mouse is available, it is actually a more efficient input method. (People tend to *think* that the keyboard is faster, but according to Apple, that's just because the act of typing distracts them for long enough that they don't notice the time passing.)

Unfortunately, a mouse is difficult to implement without a desk to roll it over. Even laptops large enough to accommodate a comfortable keyboard usually rely on touch-sensitive pads or small sticks instead. These can slow down laptop users significantly, because they are much harder to use than a mouse, negating the benefits that Apple found. To cater to the increasing number of laptop users, applications need to provide better keyboard support.

Keyboards

The keys on a full-size, typewriter-style board measure 19 mm square and can be pressed down at least 3 mm, shown in Figure 10.3. This means that the keyboard needs to be at least 200 mm wide for the QWERTY layout alone—and more if function keys are included. Most PDAs and all mobile phones are substantially smaller than this.

All clamshell PDAs include their own built-in keyboard, though there is always a trade-off between usability and portability. The big Jupiter-class Windows CE sub-notebooks do have room for a real keyboard, but smaller devices have to compromise.

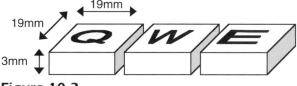

Figure 10.3
Full-size keys.

A few manufacturers, such as Psion, have developed fold-out keyboards, which can be slightly larger than the device itself. Psion's largest model so far is the Series 7, which has fairly usable keys measuring 17 mm square.

Tablet PDAs and phones with larger screens sometimes offer a virtual keyboard, so that the user can type on a touch-sensitive screen. A less awkward solution is an external plug-in keyboard. Palm Computing has a full-size keyboard that folds into four, making it the same shape as the Palm device itself—though slightly thicker and heavier. Ericsson's Chatboard plugs into many of its mobile phones; it uses calculator-style keys and isn't foldable, but it's still an improvement on a phone's keypad.

Predictive Text Input

Entering text on a mobile phone's keypad can be a difficult and laborious task. To make it simpler, many companies implement a system known as *Predictive Text Input*. The most common is *T9*, which is licensed from AOL subsidiary Tegic Communications by all the major phone manufacturers.

T9 technology was first developed in 1987 as a communication system to aid people with disabilities. Using a specially engineered pair of glasses, a person could type text using eye movements. The major obstacle to developing such a system was that the human eye can target only eight clear areas, and the computer processing needed to be fast. T9's inventors solved these problems by grouping letters onto fewer target areas and by creating a compressed linguistic database that recognizes commonly used words. In 1995, the T9 team noticed that their target groups of letters corresponded to the keypad of a phone, which also uses eight keys to represent every letter of the alphabet, as illustrated in Figure 10.4.

Under the T9 system, users need to press each button only once, even though it could represent up to four different letters. The phone compares the key presses with its own dictionary to work out which word is being typed. Where more than one is possible, it presents a choice, with the most likely highlighted.

For example, the key sequence 263 could represent 27 different combinations of three letters, but only two of them actually correspond to English words: *and* and *cod*. The first of these is most commonly used, so this would be the default.

T9 has become particularly popular in Europe, even though Europeans are not used to phones with letters on the keys. Many fixed-line phones in Europe still show only numbers, and no telephone numbers are advertised as words (which is very common in the United States).

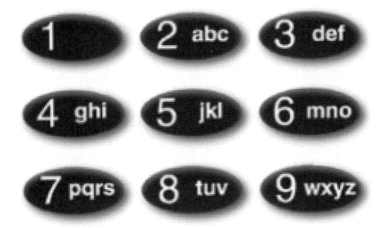

Figure 10.4
Telephone key layout.

Handwriting Recognition

Because tablets lack a keyboard, they need to incorporate some kind of handwriting recognition. This is notoriously difficult because everyone's writing is slightly different. Even the advanced mainframe computers used by post offices to sort mail have problems reading some people's writing, and the limited power of a PDA makes the problem much worse.

Nonetheless, handwriting recognition is making great progress. It improves with every version of Windows CE and has gotten to the stage where people can use it for serious note taking. With an autocorrect feature in most Microsoft programs, many users find that they rarely need to make corrections—provided that they write carefully.

To get around the difficulty of trying to recognize everybody's scrawl, PalmOS devices use their own special code called *Grafitti*. This is supposed to be easier to recognize than regular writing and also faster for the user to scribble. Though learning this special type of shorthand intimidates many users, most find it is surprisingly easy, because the code amounts to a simplified version of existing characters. Computer magazine reviewers regularly say that the Grafitti system is faster, easier, and more accurate than the natural handwriting recognition of Windows CE devices, though it still isn't perfect. Palm claims a maximum speed of only 30 words per minute, which is less than even many two-finger typists can manage.

For technophobes, the company Anato is producing the ultimate handwriting recognition device: an ordinary pen. It automatically senses the movements of the pen across paper and transmits them to a nearby PC using Bluetooth. The PC recognizes the characters and responds using synthesized speech, allowing the user to send e-mail or access text-based Web sites without ever pressing a button or seeing a screen.

WEB RESOURCES

www.pdabuzz.com
This site has discussion boards and daily news about all kinds of PDAs.

www.geek.com/pdageek/
More daily news, plus reviews and tips for PDA users are featured on this site.

www.the-gadgeteer.com
News and reviews of PDAs, mobile phones, and other gadgets are available on this site.

www.nearlymobile.com
Aimed at beginners, this site introduces PDAs with a particular emphasis on the Palm Computing platform.

3lib.ukonline.co.uk
This is a frequently updated amateur site, dedicated to Psion and Palm devices.

www.media.mit.edu/projects/wearables/
This site contains information about the wearable computer project, aimed at producing PDA-like devices that can be used while walking around or performing other tasks.

www.fsf.org and www.opensource.org
The Free Software Foundation and Open Source Initiative both aim to educate users on the benefits of free and open-source software, such as Linux.

www.linuxdevices.com
A portal to many articles and whitepapers covering embedded Linux.

www.asktog.com/TOI/toi06KeyboardVMouse1.html
Think that the keyboard is faster than the mouse? It probably is on a laptop using a mouse replacement but not on a desktop PC.

BIBLIOGRAPHY

Brown, Glenn. **Palm Computing Bible.** Hungry Minds, 2000.
A comprehensive introduction to using devices based on the PalmOS, covering both the system itself and some popular third-party software.

Ferguson, Derek. **Mobile .Net.** APress, 2001.
Though aimed at programmers, this book is a good description of how the Pocket PC fits into Microsoft's .Net strategy and how the other platforms don't.

Winton, Greg, and Troy Mott. **PalmOS Network Programming.** O'Reilly, 2001.
An introduction to writing programs that can run on the Palm platform, used by organizers and, increasingly, cell phones.

Torvalds, Linus, and David Diamond. **Just for Fun: The Story of an Accidental Revolutionary.** Harper, 2001.
The creator of Linux explains his philosophy of free and open-source software.

SUMMARY

- Phones and computers are converging, but no one knows exactly what the result will be.

- Three large companies are vying to produce operating systems for these future devices: software giant Microsoft, 3COM spin-off Palm, and mobile phone consortium Symbian.

- So far, PDAs fall into two main categories: clamshells, such as the Psion and tablets, such as the Palm.

- Computers may eventually become wearable, but several problems will have to be overcome first. These include battery life and user input.

11 Fixed Wireless Technology

In this chapter...

Compared with mobile technology, fixed wireless can seem rather unexciting. In some respects, this skepticism is justified: It doesn't involve fancy gadgets, revolutionary applications, or anything that tracks a user's location. Fixed wireless is used for exactly the same applications as wireline technology, competing directly with it and offering the same high data rates. This does make it less exciting, but also means that fixed systems can provide 1 Gbps or more, capacity that will never be available with mobile.

Over long distances, there is no doubt that wires have won. A single strand of fiber-optic cable can carry many petabits of data per second, covering hundreds of miles before it needs to be amplified. It's a different story in the local loop. Though fiber networks are being constructed beneath major cities, these usually serve just the financial center. Outside of these small areas, analysts estimate that most customers will have to wait until 2020 or later before it reaches their homes.

Broadband wireless systems are here now and expected to become widely available within the next few years. Whether bringing telephone service to remote villages or competing with cable TV in the suburbs, carriers usually find it easier and cheaper to set up transceivers than to tunnel through the ground. They also have uses outside the local loop, in private and mobile networks. Cellular base stations are already positioned for optimum radio coverage, so fixed wireless provides an easy way to link them together.

Many in the networking industry believe that, within 10 years, fixed wireless will be how most desktop computers (as opposed to mobile devices) are connected to the Internet. Also, although wireless will never be as fast as fiber, new laser systems are pushing the boundaries even further.

WIRELESS LOCAL LOOP.....................................

The greatest potential for fixed wireless is in the local loop, or *last mile*, the link from a customer's home or office to an Internet Service Provider (ISP). It is the most efficient way to roll out communications services quickly. Transceivers can be installed in as little as an hour, compared with the several weeks taken to dig the ground and lay fiberoptic cable.

Fixed wireless comes in two broad varieties: *point-to-point* and *multipoint*, shown in Figure 11.1. Of the two, the latter is overwhelmingly the most useful for wireless local loop (WLL). It enables many customers to be connected to a single central transceiver, just like a mobile system. Some multipoint technologies are even deployed in a cellular pattern, though they usually save spectrum by putting gaps between cells. They can do this because every user has his or her terminal pointed permanently at one base station,

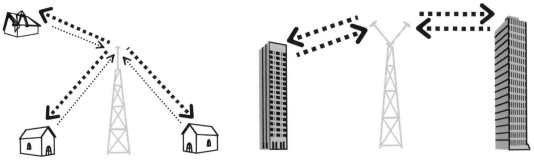

Multipoint: One antenna at ISP site
provides multiple asymmetric links.

Point-to-point: ISP requires separate
microwave or laser transceiver for each
customer.

Figure 11.1
Point-to-point and multipoint fixed networks.

removing the need for handoffs. Dead zones are also less important. People buying a WLL system care only whether it reaches their homes or offices, not whether it can be used worldwide.

The disadvantage of a multipoint system is that, as in a mobile network, the total bandwidth is shared between all users in a cell. A point-to-point system provides a dedicated link, equivalent to a wire. Multipoint also tends to be asymmetric because some systems were originally developed for television broadcasting, whereas point-to-point links are always symmetric.

The systems described here and summarized in Table 11.1 are all digital, aimed at providing high-speed Internet access. However, multipoint wireless over the local loop is not a new idea. Analog radio systems have been around for decades and are still used in many parts of the world. In the late 1990s, Eastern European governments installed them as a temporary measure, because they could not keep up with the demand for new telephone lines.

Table 11.1   *Multipoint Wireless Local Loop Technologies*

System	Frequencies	Shared Capacity	Licensed?	Cell Radius
Spread Spectrum	2.4 GHz	11 Mbps	No	8 km
MMDS	2.1–2.7 GHz	36 Mbps	Yes	45 km
LMDS	28–31 GHz	155 Mbps	Yes	8 km

Though the United States is famously backward in mobile technology, it leads the world in WLL. In part, this is because it's a large, sparsely populated country that has traditionally relied on fixed wireless to reach remote areas. Another reason is Americans' love for TV, a primitive but popular type of fixed wireless. Perhaps most important, the FCC has placed a greater emphasis on local loop access, a policy also apparent in the U.S. government becoming the first to pass laws requiring that telcos let competitors use their copper networks. There is only a limited amount of radio spectrum available, and some of what Europe uses for mobile the United States uses for fixed.

Spread Spectrum

The most popular wireless local loop systems use the Industrial, Scientific, and Medical (ISM) frequencies around 2.4 GHz, the same as many wireless LANs. Indeed, some systems are actually based on the IEEE 802.11b standard, using DSSS and CDMA.

The advantage of the ISM band is that no license is required, theoretically enabling anyone to set up a network. The disadvantage is that everyone else might do the same, producing a lot of interference.

The 802.11b standard is supposed to offer up to 11 Mbps but was designed for relatively controlled, indoor environments, not for the wide area. As well as other 802.11 networks, long-distance links using ISM are subject to interference from HomeRF, Bluetooth, microwave ovens, and other users of the band.

To improve quality and reduce interference, many manufacturers of spread spectrum equipment add their own proprietary twist to the 802.11 standard. This means that the equipment sold by different companies is often incompatible—every node of a network must use the same type.

Proprietary systems are usually undesirable in the telecom and computer industries because they lock customers into a specific vendor, but this is less important for fixed wireless. A point-to-point link has only two ends anyway, and receivers for multipoint systems are usually bought in bulk and installed by operators.

Although unlicensed worldwide, most governments do still place controls on ISM radiation for health and safety reasons. The limits are less strict for equipment designed to be installed on a pole outdoors than that kept inside and near people, so the 802.11b-based local loop systems have a longer range than wireless LANs that use the same technology. Some can reach up to 8 km under ideal conditions.

The further a signal has to travel, the more likely it is to encounter interference or simply be blocked somewhere along its path, so most operators use cells smaller than the maximum size. There is no real minimum, so they can be made smaller indefinitely as operators sign up new customers.

Most people who use ISM spread spectrum systems find the actual throughput to be about 2–6 Mbps, which for a multipoint system is shared between all users in a cell. This might seem to cut capacity drastically, but operators have found that they can still offer high-speed Internet access. A typical system might aim to give each user 256 kbps, which is 10 times the speed of a dial-up modem. Even under the worst case (2 Mbps), up to eight customers could simultaneously download files at this speed, and far more could be online.

MMDS and 802.16a

Multipoint Multichannel Distribution System (MMDS) was developed in the 1970s as a television broadcast system. It was intended to compete with cable TV, carrying analog channels over a distance of up to about 45 km. This was shorter than the usual UHF and VHF channels, supposed to allow more local programming of the type that is sometimes carried by cable operators.

The FCC originally licensed only two 6-MHz channels, at frequencies starting from 2,150 MHz, the same part of the spectrum that the ITU later wanted to use for 3G mobile. It later added another 31, from 2,500 to 2,672 MHz. Only 11 of these have actually been auctioned. The remaining 20 were retained by the FCC for what it calls the *Instructional Fixed Television Service* (ITFS).

The channels are shown in Figure 11.2. They are grouped into quartets (with one triplet), and the FCC originally planned to sell each group to a separate operator. However, it eventually auctioned all 13 as a single lot. ITFS was intended for public service broadcasting but is often leased to TV companies on the condition that they broadcast at least 40 hours of educational programming per week.

MMDS proved unpopular as a television technology in the United States, though it is used for this purpose in many other countries, including Mexico and Australia. Its deployment further afield was held back by the incompatible television systems of many countries. For example, Europe's analog TV channels use a system called *Phase Alternating Line* (PAL), which has a higher resolution picture than the

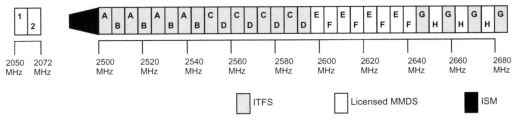

Figure 11.2
FCC spectrum allocation for MMDS.

National Television Systems Committee (NTSC) standard of North America. The better quality images require 8 MHz of spectrum and won't fit into the 6-MHz MMDS bands.

In 1998, the FCC approved MMDS use for two-way Internet access. The failed TV companies holding licenses were immediately snapped up by several carriers, including WorldCom and Sprint, whose Sprint Broadband service was the first to enter commercial operation. Designed for Web access, it is highly asymmetric. It initially offered download speeds of up to 5 Mbps and uploads at up to 256 kbps.

The main advantage of MMDS over spread spectrum is simply that its spectrum is licensed, so operators can be sure that no one will (legally) interrupt their services. Licenses also permit higher power transmitters, similar to a cellular base station. This similarity has encouraged some companies to experiment with limited mobility. It really works only while stationary, because there is no handoff mechanism, but most people access the Internet while sitting at a desk anyway.

If mobility can be provided, operators' licenses will seem an incredible bargain. United Kingdom operator Zipcom acquired its MMDS license for only $150 million, compared with the $9 billion paid by Vodaphone Airtouch for only a third as much Universal Mobile Telecommunications System (UMTS) spectrum. The frequencies are similar, so if MMDS is not successful, some countries may reallocate it to 3G. The U.S. has already taken a step in this direction.

Until 2001, MMDS lacked open standards, which was a major impediment to any moves toward making it a mobile technology. The IEEE has an ongoing project to develop standards, under the auspices of its 802.16 working group. This does *not* yet cover mobile operation but does try to make equipment from different vendors interoperate. The standard is still evolving and at present is a bit of a fudge: To avoid conflicts between vendors who use different technologies, it simply specifies various "options" corresponding to each of the technologies. This differs from the approach taken by the writers of the very popular 802.11b and GSM standards, which select one particular technology.

Various vendors have also formed a consortium to improve interoperability, independently of the IEEE. To get away from MMDS's connotations as a failed cable replacement, the alliance has renamed the technology *WDSL* (Wireless Digital Subscriber Line). This is a rather confusing and inaccurate name, because it has nothing to do with the existing alphabet soup of DSLs, technologies used for sending high-speed data through ordinary phone lines.

LMDS and 802.16

Local Multipoint Distribution System (LMDS) is the highest capacity multipoint technology yet devised. By using high frequencies and small cells, it can compete with expensive leased lines and provide all the fully integrated communications services traditionally associated with fiber. It has a peak data rate of around 155 Mbps, which leaves plenty of capacity to spare, even if providing telephone, Internet, interactive television, and other services.

As the similar names suggest, LMDS and MMDS have much in common. The main difference is that LMDS uses higher frequencies, around 30 GHz. This means that more spectrum is available but reduces the range and makes the signal more susceptible to fading. Whereas other systems can be blocked only by severe rain or snow, LMDS requires an exact line of sight and is subject to interference from many weather phenomena, especially rain. This makes the cell size dependent on the climate—8 km is possible in ideal conditions, but operators in Northern Europe and many United States cities cannot make them much larger than 1–2 km.

Each LMDS cell uses between four and six directional transmitters, each of which can provide a shared capacity of many megabits per second. The exact figure depends on how much spectrum the operator has been licensed, with some of the FCC's very generous assignments giving each sector up to 30 Mbps. With a distance of only 2 km, this means it can serve either densely populated areas, such as a city center, or a few customers with very high bandwidth demands. Figure 11.3 shows a typical cell, with a total capacity of 150 Mbps.

Like MMDS, LMDS was pioneered and first licensed in the United States. In an attempt to promote competition in the local loop, the FCC offered a total of 1,300 MHz

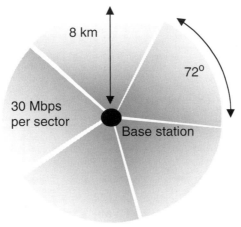

Figure 11.3
Five-sectored LMDS cell.

for the services, more spectrum than it has licensed to any other single technology. Even more remarkable, 1,150 MHz of this was reserved for a single operator in each of the 493 regions. Incumbent telephone and cable operators were forbidden to bid for these, though they could buy the remaining licenses of only 150 MHz. The reduced spectrum means that they offer much lower capacity, similar to MMDS.

There was less spectrum available for LMDS in Europe, because many of the frequencies proposed for it were already used for satellite systems. Most countries did eventually license it, though in far smaller blocks than the United States. As Figure 11.4 shows, the United Kingdom split its LMDS band into three equal chunks of 224 MHz each, which all together are less than the single A license in the United States. It also specified paired spectrum (112 MHz in each direction), which means that services have to be symmetric. This is unusual, because most U.S. operators are choosing to deploy asymmetric technology suitable for Web surfing.

Both are available from vendors because, like MMDS, LMDS suffered from a lack of standards until recently. The IEEE's 802.16 standard aims to solve this problem. The name is just plain "802.16" without any following letters, because it is the first and simplest standard produced by the 802.16 working group.

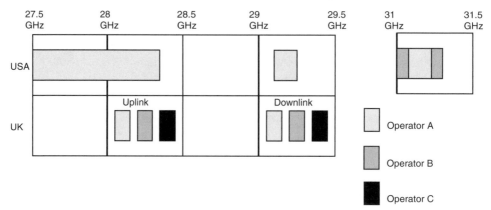

Figure 11.4
Spectrum allocation for LMDS.

Competing Technologies

Although mobile networks are by definition wireless, WLL has to compete with several wireline technologies, listed in Table 11.2. In most parts of the world and even the United States, customers don't yet see this competition—many people would be grateful for any affordable way to access the Internet at high speed, regardless of the technology behind it.

Competition still exists but at the operator level. ISPs that want to provide high-speed access without expensive leaded lines need to decide how they are going to reach their customers, which means evaluating the costs and benefits of each technology:

- **Fiber** is the last-mile technology of choice for most people. Depending on the type and what is at the other end, it has a maximum data rate of anything from 2 Mbps to 10 Gbps, all of that two-way and dedicated to an individual customer. The actual glass cable is extremely cheap, but the tiny lasers needed to send and receive wavelengths of light are not. Still, where fiber is available and priced reasonably, there should be no need to consider WLL or anything else.

  The problem with fiber is that for most customers it is not available. Negotiating rights of way is very expensive, and actually laying the cable is a disruptive and labor-intensive process. This pushes up prices to end users, making it cost-effective only for very heavy business users.

- **DSL** sends high-speed data through ordinary copper phone lines. Voice calls use only relatively low frequencies, leaving a lot of spare bandwidth for other services. Many types of DSL are available, each of which offers a different capacity and distance. The most common is the relatively long-range *ADSL* (Asymmetric DSL). Most leave the lower frequencies alone so that they can coexist with regular phone service and even ISDN. It really does appear to offer something for nothing, but of course there are drawbacks.

  The biggest barrier to DSL is that the copper lines are owned by phone companies, which would rather charge for expensive leased lines or fiber than offer cheap high-speed data to everyone. The United States passed laws in 1996 that forced the incumbent companies to let competitors offer service over their copper, a process called *unbundling*, but other countries have been much slower to do so. Even where unbundling has taken place, there are frequent disputes over charges, interference, and *colocation*, which means putting a competitor's equipment inside a telephone exchange. Some even use the threat of terrorism as an excuse to maintain a monopoly, claiming that they can't let competitors inside their facilities for security reasons.

  Like wireless local loop, DSL is highly distance-dependent: As distance increases, capacity goes down. However, the actual range of DSL can often be less than the stated maximum, because phone lines do not necessarily use the most direct route. Whereas LMDS signals travel in a straight line from the user to the base station, DSL usually follows the paths of streets or overhead cables.

- **Cable Modems** are sometimes offered by cable companies along with their TV service. They typically use the equivalent of one channel for data, with a maximum downstream capacity of 36 Mbps under NTSC and 48

Mbps under PAL. Upstream is around a tenth of this, and both are shared between all cable subscribers.

The similarities between cable modems and MMDS are entirely deliberate. Before the WDSL moniker caught on, MMDS was sometimes referred to as "wireless cable," and some of the underlying standards are the same. In an attempt to create an open standard, the WDSL consortium has borrowed the *Data Over Cable Systems Interoperability Standard* (DOCSIS), a protocol for encoding data into NTSC television signals.

- **Powerline Networking** is a new system that sends data through the electricity supply. Electricity is far more ubiquitous than telephony, so it offers even greater potential than DSL. Many areas of the world that don't yet have phones do have electricity, and most homes and offices in the West have many more electricity outlets than phone sockets. Another advantage over DSL is that the power cables are usually owned by companies who don't have a vested interest in preventing telecom competition.

  Unfortunately, powerline network is still in its infancy. One unresolved problem of particular interest to the wireless industry is interference, caused by the powerline's electrical and magnetic field. All wires carrying AC electricity emit some kind of radiation, but traditional power lines are at a very low frequency, and data wires are at a low voltage. A powerline network combines high voltages with high frequencies, turning the electric grid into a high-energy radio transmitter.

  Despite frequent claims that in the future we will think no more about interacting with the Internet than with the electricity supply, this scenario is still many years away. For the foreseeable future, networking will remain more difficult than plugging in a computer.

Table 11.2   Competing Local Loop Technologies

Technology	Uplink	Downlink	Range
Fiber	622 Mbps	622 Mbps	100 km
ADSL	384 kbps	2 Mbps	6 km
ADSL	2 Mbps	24 Mbps	0.6 km
Cable Modem	384 kbps (shared)	48 Mbps (shared)	No limit
Powerline	2 Mbps	2 Mbps	No limit
LMDS	8 Mbps (shared)	155 Mbps (shared)	8 km
MMDS	1 Mbps (shared)	36 Mbps (shared)	45 km

So far, broadband wireless hasn't done too well against its competitors. In the United States, home to both the technologies themselves and the largest market for broadband, it's still behind everything except fiber. The FCC publishes precise statistics of broadband deployment each year, some of which are illustrated in Figure 11.5. Wireless trails both DSL and cable modems in the residential and small business market. In the large corporate market, it's behind all competitors—even cable, which is considered a consumer technology.

Despite this, WLL may yet become more popular. The failure of unbundling in the United States means that DSL customers are forced to buy their connections from an expensive monopoly provider, just as the 802.16 standard will make MMDS equipment cheaper. Cable and DSL are less widespread outside of the United States, so the opportunities for wireless are even greater.

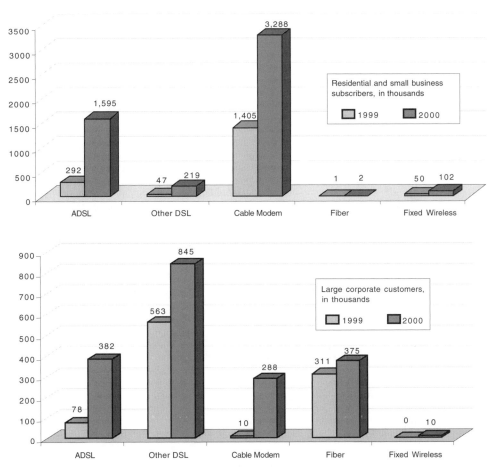

Figure 11.5
Popularity of broadband access technologies in the United States.

POINT-TO-POINT MICROWAVE...............................

Point-to-point microwave links are rare in the local loop because operators would require a separate base station unit for each customer. They provide higher capacities than multipoint systems, so are occasionally used to connect customers who would otherwise need fiber, but their main application is for private networks.

The classic example of a private point-to-point network is between skyscrapers in a city. If a company has two offices with a clear line of sight between them, it can save on call costs and leased line charges by installing microwave transceivers on each. This type of setup, illustrated in Figure 11.6, is called a *wireless bridge*. Typical systems have a range of up to about 20 km, so the offices could be in different states or even different countries. For example, some United States companies avoid expensive calls to and from Mexico by setting up a wireless bridge with one node in San Diego and the other in Tijuana. These systems can operate in both licensed and unlicensed bands. The most important are listed in Table 11.3.

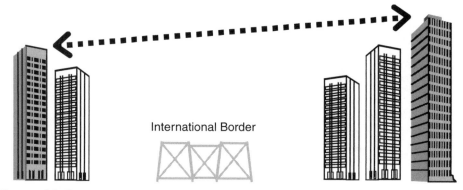

Figure 11.6
Private point-to-point network (wireless bridge).

Table 11.3   Point-to-Point Microwave Bands

Band Name	Actual Frequencies	Used	Max. Capacity	Licensed?
ISM	2.4–2.483 GHz	Worldwide	11 Mbps	No
U-NII	5.725–5.825 GHz	U.S.	108 Mbps	No
HiperAccess	5.47–5.725	Europe	108 Mbps	No
18 GHz	17.7–19.7 GHz	World	155 Mbps	Yes

Table 11.3   Point-to-Point Microwave Bands (Continued)

Band Name	Actual Frequencies	Used	Max. Capacity	Licensed?
23 GHz	21.2–23.6 GHz	World	155 Mbps	Yes
26 GHz	24.5–26.5 GHz	Europe	155 Mbps	Yes
28 GHz (LMDS)	See Figure 11.4	World	155 Mbps	Yes
38 GHz	37–39.5 GHz	Europe	155 Mbps	Yes
38 GHz	37–38.4 GHz 38.6–40 GHz	U.S.	155 Mbps	Yes
60 GHz	55.78–64 GHz	U.S., Japan	1,000 Mbps	No
94 GHz	92–96 GHz	None yet	1,000 Mbps	Undecided

Licensed

Most microwave radio systems operate at frequencies between 18 and 38 GHz, where relatively large slices of bandwidth are available. They generally offer throughput of up to 155 Mbps, the same as LMDS. The advantages are that this capacity is two-way: It is dedicated to a single user, rather than shared by an entire cell, and the range is increased by focusing the beam on a specific recipient.

Spectrum between 18 and 38 GHz always requires a license, though some vendors and user groups are pushing for this requirement to be removed. Because point-to-point links confine their beams to a very narrow area, there is little risk of interference, though it's still a possibility. Recognizing this, many governments have adopted rather liberal licensing policies, so in some countries, it is little more than a formality.

Different parts of the spectrum are available for point-to-point wireless in different parts of the world. North America and Europe have agreed on four bands: 18, 23, 28, and 38 MHz. Europe has an additional band at 26 MHz, which cannot be used in the United States. Their characteristics are very similar, and most equipment vendors sell transceivers for all of them; some can even be adapted, depending on which part of the world they are in.

The 28-GHz band is the same as that used for LMDS, meaning that licenses to use it have already been allocated. This may make it seem rather pointless, but some LMDS operators do find it useful. They can use point-to-point links for customers who require higher capacity than LMDS can offer, as well as to link together their base stations.

Unlicensed

Point-to-point links can also be set up in unlicensed parts of the spectrum, although their performance will not be as good as their licensed counterparts. One option is the familiar ISM band, using IEEE 802.11 or similar equipment. It offers the same 11-Mbps capacity as in multipoint links, but this is dedicated to one user instead of shared over a cell.

For higher capacity links, the FCC's U-NII (Unlicensed National Information Infrastructure) band can be used for unlicensed point-to-point microwave. It's at frequencies of 5.8 GHz, which it shares with 802.11a wireless LANs—the theory being that, because the point-to-point systems are outside, they won't interfere with wireless LAN systems inside.

Using proprietary systems, vendors such as Proxim and Western Multiplex sell equipment that can send and receive at up to 100 Mbps in this band. There are also plans to adapt the 802.11a standard itself for fixed access, just as 802.11b has already been adapted. As with 802.11b, the outdoor version will be allowed to transmit at higher power and, thus, have a longer range than its indoor counterpart. This new standard will be known as 802.16b.

The disadvantage of the U-NII band is that it has been granted only by the United States, not internationally. Some other countries may decide to adopt it, but Europe will not—it has already granted the same spectrum to the HiperLan wireless LAN standard. The European Telecommunications Standards Institute (ETSI) is trying to develop a higher power version of HiperLan that can be used for local loop and building-to-building applications, but this isn't ready yet.

Known as *HiperAccess*, this local loop version of HiperLan was originally supposed to offer two-way links at 20 Mbps. The final standard may eventually be faster than this, because technology has advanced in the years since HiperAccess was first proposed. Because HiperLan 2 and 802.11a are so similar, HiperAccess may eventually be almost identical to 802.16b.

The W-Band

Some newer point-to-point systems use the very high 60-GHz band, parts of which most countries have dedicated to unlicensed communications. Its advantage is the huge amount of bandwidth available: The FCC, for example, allows 5 GHz, which is more than the entire spectrum used for cell phones, wireless LANs, and broadcasting put together. This allows very high data rates: Harmonix produced a 60-GHz system in 2001 that offered speeds of 1 Gbps, and other companies are working on even faster systems.

All this speed comes at a price, of course. The main reason that there's so much bandwidth around 60 GHz is that this band has traditionally been useless for communications purposes. Waves at that frequency are easily absorbed by oxygen, making them unable to pass through more than a very thin layer of air. During the twentieth century, the only application for 60 GHz was in secure links between military satellites, shielded from eavesdroppers by the atmosphere.

Harmonix developed a new modulation technique that was able to reduce the absorption problem, but its first 60-GHz systems still have a shorter range than either laser or licensed microwave. The largest and highest power units can transmit only 1,400 m (less than 1 mile). Several other companies are working on ways to push this further, but oxygen absorption will remain a problem.

There is some debate over how to use the 60-GHz band. Not all of it is available everywhere: Europe is considering parts of it for 4G cellular systems, and there are also proposals to use it for wireless LANs. It's possible that 4G will simply be a combination of wireless LANs and point-to-point links, so the different ideas may not be incompatible. The short range also means that indoor LANs could share the same frequencies as outdoor point-to-point links in the same way that they already share the worldwide 2.4-GHz ISM band and will probably share the American U-NII and European HiperLan bands.

T-Rays

There is more spectrum beyond 60 GHz, which opens up the possibility of even higher capacity links: Industry and government representatives are currently making plans for the 94-GHz band, and scientists are investigating even higher frequencies at around 140 GHz and 220 GHz. Endwave, a company that makes high-frequency transceivers, believes that these will enable speeds of up to 100 Gbps, which is more than enough for any application yet developed.

Such links depend on frequencies beyond what is traditionally regarded as radio, in the *near-infrared* or *T-ray* part of the spectrum (the *T* is because their frequencies approach 1 THz). The only current use for T-rays is radar, though there are other applications emerging: They can pass through flesh but not metal, so they could become a safer alternative to X-rays. (They are safer because X-rays are a form of ionizing radiation, discussed further in Chapter 13, "Do Wireless Devices Fry Your Brain?", whereas T-rays are non-ionizing.) There are even suggestions, made *before* the post-September 11th obsession with airport security, to T-ray all passengers getting on to planes.

These other uses mean that there may be objections to communications systems based on T-rays, but there is so much spectrum in this region that there should be enough for everyone. Frequencies above 300 GHz have traditionally been left unregulated, meaning that anyone is free to use them for any purpose.

Network Architecture

Although point-to-point radio is not usually thought of as ideal for WLL, some operators have tried to use it. Instead of trying to connect all customers to their own central sites, these companies connect each customer to another, a process known as *daisy chaining*.

The customers can't actually access each other's data or communicate directly (unless they want to); the intention is simply to extend the range of the system. Despite the limit of about 20 km, a customer could be much further away than this, using multiple hops to reach the operator. These extra hops make the system less reliable, because they introduce extra points of failure, so extra redundant links are sometimes added to compensate.

The largest network to be designed in this way was built by Advanced Radio Telecom (ART). It covered large parts of the United States, using 38-GHz radios that connected customers in a series of interlocking rings. However, there weren't enough customers, and ART closed down in 2001. Vista Broadband is trying something similar, but using MMDS instead. This should be cheaper to build out than ART's system, because it is a point-to-multipoint system: Each new link will require only one new antenna, not two.

RINGS OR STARS?

In general, networks of all types can be arranged in three different ways, known as topologies. Real networks are usually a mixture, but the "ideal" cases serve to illustrate the point. The three topologies are shown in Figure 11.7.

Star networks connect every user to a central site, such as a cellular base station. This is the typical setup for most wireless networks, including mobile systems and multipoint fixed wireless. It's also the most common type of LAN, with each computer connected to a hub. Star networks are often hierarchical. In a cellular network, many base stations are connected to an MSC; in a LAN, many hubs may be connected to a switch.

Ring networks have no central site, instead connecting each user to another. Rings have the advantages that a network can be built up from many short links and that they are resistant to a single failure—though not to more than one. They are popular among long-distance fiber networks, which may cross an ocean in two separate places or even encircle the entire world.

RINGS OR STARS? (CONTINUED)

Mesh networks connect every node to many others. A fully meshed network links each node to every other, but these are rare. The only real fully meshed networks are Bluetooth PANs, ad-hoc wireless LANs, and occasionally groups of Private Mobile Radio (PMR) users. More usual is for extra links to be placed in ring networks, both for redundancy and so that the ring doesn't have to be reordered when new nodes are added. The Internet backbone is the best example of a partially meshed network.

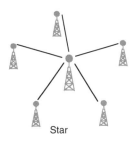

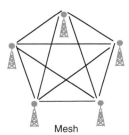

Star   Ring   Mesh

Figure 11.7
Network topologies.

FREE SPACE OPTICS......................................

The idea of sending data through a beam of light is not new. It was first suggested in 1880, by telephone pioneer Alexander Graham Bell. Shortly after inventing the phone itself, he patented the *photophone*: a mobile phone that relied on light to connect to a base station. Because of the need for a line of sight, it was never actually used, and the mobile telephone had to wait for the invention of radio.

A century later, several companies developed systems that could send data through a modulated laser beam. These were little more successful than the photophone: The beams had to be so tightly focused that even buildings swaying in the wind could dislodge them, and customers feared being zapped by a misconfigured ray gun.

These problems have now been solved, but because laser has such negative connotations, most of the companies selling such systems prefer to describe them as *FSO* (Free Space Optics). There are even some FSO systems that are technically not lasers, instead using wider beams that cannot travel as far but are more tolerant of obstructions.

Optical Networking

Fiber networks are able to reach such high capacities because they use spectrum at much higher frequencies than radio. The term *optical* is slightly misleading, as these bands are in the *far-infrared* part of the spectrum, rather than the visible part (which is even higher). Their frequencies are measured in hundreds of terahertz, so a very small part of the spectrum can offer a higher bandwidth than the entire radio region.

With bandwidth to spare, optical networking does not yet need OFDM, Ultra-Wideband, or other complex technologies. Optical channels intended for different users are separated by simple FDMA, just like analog cell phones, except that it's called *Wavelength Division Multiplexing* (WDM) instead. Wavelength and frequency are different ways of referring to the same property, so the difference is just due to the culture of the engineers. The usual description of WDM is that it uses different colors of light for different beams of information—the difference being that all these "colors" look the same (pitch black) to people because they're infrared rather than visible.

Though our everyday experience of light is that it behaves rather differently from radio, the principles remain the same. As frequencies increase, signals are more easily blocked, so the distance that they can travel decreases. Light is at much higher frequencies than radio, so this blocking is a major issue. A light beam quickly becomes fainter as it passes through the air and is stopped entirely by almost all solid objects.

Optical networking has traditionally solved the blocking problem by using glass fiber, which conducts light in the same way as wire conducts much lower frequencies. Only certain wavelengths are able to pass through glass for long distances, so if demand for network capacity continues to increase, optical networks may eventually run out of bandwidth and have to turn to the modulation and multiplexing techniques developed in the wireless industry. However, there is little chance of this in the immediate future: The Internet bubble led to many companies laying long-distance fiber cables in the ground, often going bankrupt before they could afford the lasers needed to "light" them, let alone connect them to end users. This fiber will eventually be used, but only when high-speed local loop technologies, such as WLL and DSL, become more widespread.

Despite the *fiber glut* in the Internet backbone, there is still a lot of hype around the optical networking industry. Part of this is because advances in physics at the end of the twentieth century made it possible to switch light beams using mirrors and prisms, rather than electronics and lasers. Another reason for the hype is that some companies decided they could eliminate the fiber entirely.

Laser

Modern laser networks use infrared radiation, usually at a frequency of around 380,000 GHz. This is well below the visible spectrum, partly to keep interference to a minimum but mostly so that people can't see them. The sight of brightly colored laser beams firing between buildings would provoke understandable complaints and make covert communication impossible.

Compared with other wireless systems, the great advantages of lasers are their high bandwidth and the absence of licensing laws. Whereas radio spectrum is tightly governed, few countries have laws on light emissions. There is no possibility of interference, so any number of people could use lasers at exactly the same frequency. Users can even avoid planning restrictions on rooftop antennas—because light travels through glass, the laser units can be placed inside and pointed through a window.

Capacity varies, depending on the manufacturer. Most systems can comfortably reach 622 Mbps, beyond any microwave system, but some companies claim higher rates. Experiments have used lasers with ranges less than 1 km to send up to 10 Gbps, the same as some fiber systems.

Because they need to be highly focused, lasers are always point-to-point. A few companies sell "multipoint" units, but these are just several independently targetable transceivers stacked on top of each other. Most have built-in electronic tracking systems to keep the two transceivers pointed at each other as buildings sway or atmospheric conditions bend the light beam.

Laser technology used to be the victim of safety fears, thanks to its popularity as a weapon in science fiction movies. However, the industry believes that the widespread use of lasers in devices such as CD players has helped to allay these concerns. It is even ready to exploit scares about microwaves; one manufacturer points out that its system delivers data only to where it is supposed to go, rather than "irradiating an entire area." Its main differences from microwave and T-ray are listed in Table 11.4.

Table 11.4   *Laser vs. Point-to-Point Microwave*

	Laser/FSO	**T-Ray/W-band**	**Microwave**
Max. Data Rate	2.5 Gbps	1 Gbps	155 Mbps
Max. Range	4 km	1 km	45 km
Licensing	Unlicensed	Unlicensed	License needed
Uptime	99.7%	99.8%	99.9%
Frequency Range	300–400 THz	50–1000 GHz	2–50 GHz

Table 11.4   *Laser vs. Point-to-Point Microwave*

Beam Width	0.5 degrees	1 degree	2 degrees
Blocked by	Fog, Snow	Air	Rain
Typical Cost	$40,000	$20,000	$10,000

Wireless Circuit Boards

Lasers may eventually eliminate wiring within computers. The problem with wires, including circuits printed on a board or a chip, is that changing currents always generate some kind of radiation. As computers get smaller, their circuits become closer together, making them more susceptible to interference from their neighbors. Within the next few years, electronics will reach a limit beyond which the interference between circuits prevents further miniaturization.

Light doesn't suffer from this effect. Two laser beams can pass straight through each other and be completely unaffected. Another possible solution is to use fiberoptic cables, but the short distance should make them unnecessary. Fiber could also slow a computer down. Despite hype about "networking at the speed of light," the speed of light is actually reduced when passing through glass.

An electromagnetic wave moving through a fiberoptic cable travels about a third *slower* than one in air or even wire. This adds a slight extra latency to fiber networks, compared with their copper or wireless equivalents, though it is usually more than compensated for by the elimination of complex TDMA and CDMA processing. But as computers get faster, this latency will become more significant.

WEB RESOURCES

http://wirelessman.org/
This site is run by the IEEE 802.16 committee and explains its standard for wireless Metropolitan Area Networks (MANs).

www.etsi.org/bran/
ETSI's site has the latest details on the development of HiperAccess, the standard for high-speed, unlicensed networks in the 5-GHz band.

www.watmag.com
The online magazine **Wireless Access Technologies** is dedicated to wireless and satellite local loop solutions.

www.lightreading.com
This site provides regular news and analysis of optical networking, mostly fiber-based but also including wireless.

www.bwif.com
The Broadband Wireless Internet Forum promotes MMDS and OFDM as last-mile technologies.

BIBLIOGRAPHY

Clark, Martin P. **Wireless Access Networks**. Wiley, 2000.
A mildly technical guide to choosing and setting up fixed wireless systems, both for private networks and WLL applications.

Smith, Clint. **LMDS: Local Multipoint Distribution Service**. McGraw-Hill, 2000.
So far, the only reference work on LMDS, the most advanced of the fixed wireless technologies. It's aimed mainly at engineering students and people working for network service providers, not at end users.

SUMMARY ....

- Fixed wireless technology can be a simple and inexpensive way for operators to reach customers.

- Unlicensed systems can use the international ISM band and are usually based on the IEEE 802.11 wireless LAN standard.

- MMDS and LMDS are multipoint systems that can be used to form fixed cellular systems. MMDS has a long range but relatively low bandwidth. LMDS has a shorter range and higher bandwidth.

- Laser beams do not require a license and offer far higher capacity than other types of fixed wireless, but they can cover only short distances.

12 Internet in Space

In this chapter...

In 1945, science fiction writer Arthur C. Clarke published an article called "Extra-Terrestrial Relays" in the magazine *Wireless World*. He described almost everything necessary to build a satellite network, including the radio spectrum needed, the solar panels to power the satellites, the geostationary orbits they would travel in, and even the type of rocket needed to launch them.

Clarke himself was afraid that his ideas were "too farfetched to be taken very seriously," but less than 50 years later, they had gone from speculation to a multibillion-dollar industry. This progress was largely due to the invention of the transistor and later to computer technology. Transceivers in the 1940s relied on valves, which needed to be replaced frequently, so Clarke's "relays" would have required astronauts to perform maintenance. Transistors meant that radios could be made smaller and more reliable.

Communications satellites, often called simply *comsats* or "birds," were for a long time the main means of transporting intercontinental phone calls. Satellites were owned by government agencies or specialized corporations, and dishes were owned by the phone companies. Ordinary phone users had no contact with the technology, though they sometimes noticed a slight delay in conversations because of the time taken for a signal to get into space and back.

All that changed with the growth of the Internet and advancements in fiberoptics. A single strand of fiber can carry more information than every satellite ever launched, making it more economical to use cables. By 2000, several international consortia were planning to ring the world in fiber. With their traditional role gone, satellites seemed to be in danger of obsolescence.

In the twenty-first century, the biggest application for satellite communications is as a local loop technology, similar to fixed wireless but covering a much larger area. Data is beamed directly to and from users, bypassing the phone company altogether.

There are also plenty of satellite-based mobile systems under construction, though these are running into difficulties. Constructing a phone that can find a satellite in the sky is a technical challenge. Most satellite antennas use a dish that is manually pointed toward the satellite and focuses its signals to a point. Satellite phones have to do without this but still need a large antenna that makes them bulkier than regular cell phones.

The economic case for satellite-based mobile has also been undermined by the very thing that it hoped to cash in on—the popularity of mobile communications. With earthbound cellular networks so widely available, there are few major business areas where a satellite-based system is necessary. They are useful mostly in poorer countries, where few people are able to afford them.

ORBITS ....

Orbits are in general elliptical, but nearly all artificial satellites aim for one as circular as possible so that they can remain at the same height. They generally fall into three categories, classified as *Low, Medium,* and *Geosynchronous Earth Orbits.* The last category has traditionally been the most useful for communications, though some newer systems have used others.

Each of the orbits illustrated in Figure 12.1 and listed in Table 12.1 has slightly different properties. Higher orbits require more powerful rockets and take longer to reflect a signal back to Earth. Lower orbits cover a smaller area per satellite and fall back to Earth more quickly because of *atmospheric drag:* A very thin atmosphere extends thousands of kilometers into outer space, and friction from air molecules eventually makes low orbits decay.

The orbital period of a satellite depends only on its distance from Earth, and increases as it gets higher. The closer a satellite is to the ground, the faster it moves. For example, the space shuttle uses a relatively low orbit of no more than 400 km, circling Earth in around an hour and a half. The moon is a thousand times more distant and takes nearly a month to make one complete circuit.

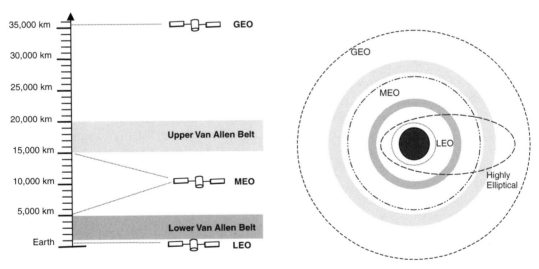

Figure 12.1
Satellite orbits around Earth.

Table 12.1   Communications Satellite Orbits

Orbit	Altitude	Latency	Min. Number of Satellites for Global Coverage
GEO	35,785 km	0.5 s	3
MEO	5,000–12,000 km	0.1 s	10
LEO	100–1,000 km	0.05 s	48
Highly Elliptical	500–27,000 km	variable	15

Geostationary

The *Geosynchronous Earth Orbit* (GEO) was proposed by Arthur C. Clarke at the same time as he outlined the principles of satellite communication. Clarke calculated that at 35,784 km, the orbital period is exactly 24 hours. This means that if a satellite is placed at precisely this altitude above Earth's axis of rotation—the equator—it should not drift east or west at all.

The *geostationary* orbit, another of Clarke's ideas, is a special and very useful case of the geosynchronous orbit. It has to be perfectly circular so that the satellite doesn't drift north and south or bob up and down. A geostationary satellite appears to hang in the sky, so people don't have to track orbits or worry about them disappearing over the horizon. A User simply points her dish at a fixed spot and leaves it there. With only three satellites in geostationary orbit, an operator can cover the entire planet.

The first satellite to reach geostationary orbit was Syncom 3, launched by NASA (the National Aeronautics and Space Administration) in 1964. Positioned above the Pacific, it carried live television pictures of the Tokyo Olympic Games to American viewers before being commandeered by the U.S. military for use in the Vietnam War. Since then, an increasing number of mainly communications satellites have joined it. They are too high to experience atmospheric drag, so old geostationary satellites remain in space, slowly drifting into more inclined orbits as a result of the moon's gravity. Over the years, they have formed an artificial ring of space junk round Earth, called the *Clarke Belt*.

The main problem with geostationary satellites is that they must be positioned over the equator, making it difficult for people to use them at latitudes in the far north or south. The dish requires a clear line of sight to the satellite, which can be blocked by buildings if it lies low on the horizon. For example, a geostationary satellite can't reach many parts of Manhattan unless the dish is placed high up on a skyscraper. In the Antarctic, even low-lying hills can block the field of view.

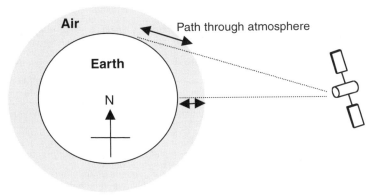

Figure 12.2
Longer path through atmosphere at high latitude.

The dish size increases with latitude, because the signal strength is made much weaker the further north or south the antenna is positioned. This happens for the same reason that less heat from the sun reaches the poles than the tropics—it loses energy passing through the atmosphere. As Figure 12.2 shows, the amount of atmosphere blocking its path is thicker at higher latitudes.

GEO users far from the equator are also more likely to suffer from *sun outages* when satellites literally fly too close to the sun. During the March and September equinoxes, the sun passes behind the satellite, as seen from the dish, temporarily drowning out the signal with its own radiation. These outages occur up to five times each equinox, lasting between 1 and 10 minutes, depending on the location and dish size. The bad news is that they're unavoidable, but the good news is that they're entirely predictable, so users can plan ahead. Many say that, despite these outages, satellites are still more reliable than terrestrial networks. They don't suffer from power failures or fiber cuts when someone inadvertently chops through a cable.

The orbit's other disadvantage is its great height. Even at the speed of light, signals take a fraction of a second to get to the Clarke Belt and back, producing a noticeable delay in conversation and playing havoc with Internet protocols. They also require powerful rockets to launch and are too far away for a malfunctioning satellite to be repaired in orbit or brought back to Earth.

Medium Orbit

Medium Earth Orbit (MEO) satellites are those at an altitude of between about 5,000 and 15,000 km, above the atmosphere and the most dangerous of the Van Allen radiation belts that encircle the Earth. MEO allows the wider area to be reached with relatively few satellites compared to lower orbits, as shown in Figure 12.3. It usually requires around 10 to cover the whole world, with the exact number depending on the altitude. Its advantage over GEO is reduced latency, enabling conversations without noticeable delay.

The MEO region technically extends right out to 35,000 km or more, but few satellites use non-geosynchronous orbits above about 10,000 km. Although it is perfectly possible to put one higher than this, there is little reason to do so. Apart from the Clarke Belt, these higher orbits offer few advantages but require more powerful rockets and radio equipment. Below 5,000 km, the Van Allen radiation is so strong that it will quickly destroy a satellite.

The best known users of the MEO region are the *Intermediate Circular Orbit* (ICO) phone system and the Global Positioning System (GPS) satellites, both of which can be picked up with a nondirectional antenna.

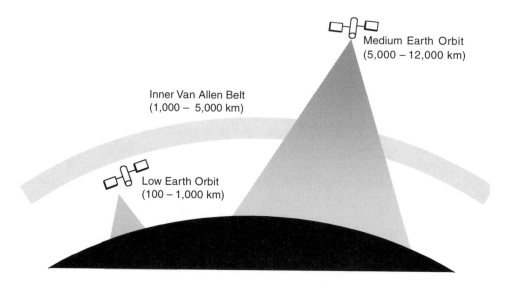

Figure 12.3
Higher satellites can "see" more of the Earth's surface.

Low Orbit

The *Low Earth Orbit* (LEO) region extends from about 100 km to 1,000 km. Any higher would put a satellite inside the deadly Van Allen belt, and any lower would locate it inside the thermosphere, the part of the atmosphere where friction burns meteors up.

Low orbits are the most common kind because they are so easy to reach. The earliest communications satellites, the *Echo series*, used them from 1960 onward. Essentially just balloons coated in silver foil, they could reflect television transmissions across America. They needed powerful tracking equipment and giant antennas the size of houses, so sensitive that two AT&T engineers trying to find a satellite picked up radiation from the Big Bang instead. Their accidental discovery was rewarded several years later with a Nobel Prize.

This complicated tracking meant that low orbits fell out of favor for communications purposes, but they enjoyed a revival in the 1990s. When a satellite is only a few hundred miles up, its transmissions are much easier to pick up. By the late 1990s, advances in technology had enabled receivers for these satellites to be made no larger than mobile phones of a decade earlier, and many companies planned cellular networks based on satellites. The best known of these is the ill-fated Iridium, but its failure has not put off others who plan similar schemes.

LEOs do have some disadvantages. Though huge by the standards of terrestrial cellular networks, their coverage is smaller than higher satellites. The number needed to cover the whole planet varies with altitude, but is generally a lot; proposed systems have required between 40 and 1,000. They also need to be replaced every few years because of atmospheric drag. Most include small boosters to lift them back up, but unlike the solar-powered batteries that run satellites themselves, these require actual rocket fuel. When it runs out, they fall to Earth.

The loss of satellites to drag can be significant, not to mention dangerous for anyone living underneath. If a network of 200 has a lifetime of four years, a new one needs to be launched every week. Modern rockets have a tendency to explode, thanks to cost-cutting, so operators need to keep some spares in orbit.

The lowest orbits of all are used mostly for scientific and military purposes, because they are the easiest and safest for human engineers to reach. With the exception of the Apollo program, few astronauts have ever ventured beyond the LEO range. A mission lasting only a few days doesn't have to worry about being dragged back to Earth, and a space station can be brought supplies of rocket fuel along with food or replacement crews. Unique satellites, such as the Hubble telescope, are regularly saved from burn-up and carried up a few miles by the space shuttle, but doing this is so costly that communication satellites are cheaper to replace than to salvage.

Elliptical

A newer approach is to use highly elliptical orbits, which deliberately vary their altitude from a few hundred to several thousand kilometers. The plan is that these will combine the low latency of LEO with the stability of GEO. The satellites will swoop up and down, seeming from some parts of Earth to hover for long periods in the same position.

Highly elliptical orbits are so complicated that the company Virtual Geosatellite LLC has been granted U.S. patents on the equations needed to describe them. (Whether these patents will stand up in court is questionable, because mathematical formulas are not supposed to be patentable.) The idea is that, like geostationary satellites, they permit a dish to point continuously in the same direction. By the time one satellite has moved away, another will have taken its place.

The orbits can be arranged so that this "virtual geostationary" satellite appears to be anywhere, not just directly over the equator. This should make them more convenient for most areas and means that they can use existing frequencies without interfering with transmissions to the already-crowded Clarke Belt.

VSATS..

With fiber taking over their traditional role in intercontinental links, satellites must compete by reaching customers directly. The innovation that made this possible was the *directional antenna*, first implemented in 1975 by a satellite called *Satcom*. It enabled satellites to focus their beams on one particular area of Earth's surface, usually North America or Western Europe. Newer satellites launched from 2000 onward incorporate even narrower beams, which can switch rapidly between hot spots, such as individual towns.

With a well-focused beam, dishes can have a diameter of one meter or less, a small fraction of the earlier systems'. These are known as *VSATs* (very small aperture terminals). All VSATs use geostationary satellites, so just how small they can be depends on the latitude, as well as on how close they are to the center of the beam's target.

Dish size also depends on the frequency used. Higher frequencies have shorter waves, permitting a smaller dish. Most commercial satellites broadcast at substantially higher frequencies than mobile systems, usually in the *K* part of the microwave spectrum, from 10.9 to 36 GHz For satellite purposes, this is subdivided into the *Ka-* and the *Ku-*bands. The *a* and *u* stand for *above* and *under*, so the Ka-band is the higher of the two.

Higher frequencies also permit higher bandwidth, though increased interference can negate this. Shorter waves are more easily blocked by particles of dust, rain, and even mist, as shown in Figure 12.4. Like terrestrial fixed wireless equipment, a good vendor or operator will ensure that the equipment has enough spare capacity to cope with adverse weather, so that in most conditions, performance should actually be better than stated. The exception is a blizzard—no satellite receiver will work if the dish has filled with snow.

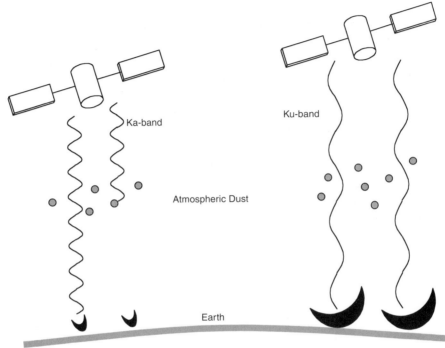

Figure 12.4
Shorter wave Ka-band signals are more easily blocked by dust and rain-drops.

The VSAT Industry

Geostationary satellites are operated by one of a very few specialized corporations or international organizations. The largest and first was *Intelsat*, the International Tele-communications Satellite Organization, created by various governments and companies in 1964. Cold-War politics prompted several rivals to be set up, including the maritime-focused Inmarsat and the European Union's Eutelsat.

Despite the apparent competition between them, these groups all have the same owners, namely, the major telecom companies in each country. The exception is the United States, where the government was in the middle of an antitrust battle with its major operator, AT&T, at the time the satellite industry began. Rather than hand it even more power, the government created and then privatized a satellite-only company, Comsat Corporation.

Some of the companies that design and launch satellites also operate them. Hughes Network Systems, for example, runs several satellites and plans many more. Boeing, more famous for aircraft, also has major investments in several satellite firms. The reason is that the satellite industry has become one of its biggest customers. Airlines each buy only a few jumbo jets, but satellite operators have a near-limitless demand for rockets.

These groups rarely deal with customers directly. Instead, they lease capacity to satellite service providers, in units called *transponders*. These originally represented physical devices, each of which would send and receive at a slightly different frequency, but have become shorthand for blocks of bandwidth.

The satellite industry is obviously more international than other types of wireless communications, so it is particularly important that regulators cooperate internationally. Rather than national governments, nearly all regulation is handled by the International Telecommunications Union (ITU). It allocates satellite frequencies on a worldwide basis and governs positions in orbit, a role that has caused some controversy.

Because of interference problems, only a limited number of satellites can use the same spectrum within a given part of the sky. To keep their signals separate, geostationary comsats need to be separated by at least two degrees, meaning there is room for a maximum of only 180. The ITU originally allocated orbital slots on a first-come, first-served basis, a process that upset the countries underneath the equator. They demanded that orbital slots over their nations should be given to them, not mainly to foreign countries.

National jurisdiction doesn't normally extend into space, a precedent set in the early days of the space race, when no country dared challenge the superpowers' right to overfly them at much lower orbits. Nevertheless, the ITU decided that geostationary orbits are a special case and allocated the equatorial nations slots of their own. Few could actually afford to develop space programs of their own, so the slots went unused until the ITU began to demand that everyone with a slot either launch a satellite or relinquish it.

The slots most in demand are above very poor parts of Africa and South America, because they can cover the lucrative European and North American markets. The obvious solution is for satellite operators to pay these countries a share of their revenue in rent, with many economists proposing a market mechanism similar to spectrum auctions. So far, arguments over international trade have prevented such a system being set up.

Traditional VSAT Architecture

A VSAT system is usually configured in a star or mesh topology around a central master Earth station known as a *hub*. This has a giant dish up to 10 m in diameter, together with routing equipment and a fast terrestrial connection, usually over fiber.

For a corporate system, this is connected to the company's headquarters; for Internet access, it's connected to the Internet backbone.

The hub is connected via satellite to any number of *client installations*, which can be based over a wide region and may span many countries. The remote client sites use VSAT dishes, which are much smaller than the hub's and can even be portable. A portable VSAT doesn't provide the full convenience of genuine mobile communications, but it allows all the equipment for emergency communications to be stored inside something no larger than a briefcase.

Such a setup is useful for any application that needs to connect a large number of users in a private network, especially those in remote areas. Common applications include file transfer, credit card authentication, telemetry, and distance learning. Even in heavily populated areas well-served by terrestrial communications, VSATs are still popular. For example, around 20% of lottery terminals in the United Kingdom use satellite technology because it is faster and cheaper than using British Telecom's fixed network.

The disadvantage of a traditional VSAT system is that all data has to go through the hub. This doesn't matter if most people are communicating with land lines, but it does make a difference when two VSAT terminals need to connect with each other. As shown in Figure 12.5, data has to make two trips to the satellite and back, doubling latency. This is fine for something such as e-mail, but it leads to very noticeable delays with real-time interactive applications, such as voice.

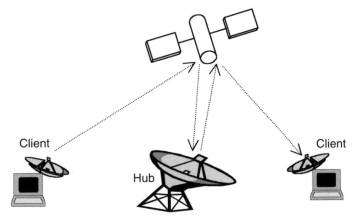

Figure 12.5
VSAT transmissions routed via a hub.

One-Way Data Systems

The growth of the Internet created a huge demand for high-speed data services, often among people who could not afford a full VSAT system. Canny satellite operators realized that they didn't really need one. In Web activity, most traffic flows from a Web server to a user, with only a small amount going the other way. If this small amount could be reduced to zero, customers could access the Internet over the same type of cheap dish that many already use to watch TV.

The first system to take advantage of this idea was *DirecPC,* released by Hughes in 1996. It didn't supply a complete Internet connection, just a downlink. Customers needed to have some other type of connection, usually an ordinary phone line and modem. Mouse clicks were sent via the phone line, with Web pages coming back by satellite. This makes the system very cheap but only suitable for Web surfing, not any application that requires sending large files. Its other weakness was that it tied up the user's phone line, unlike true broadband technologies.

DirecPC was very successful, leading to plenty of copies from rival operators. They have proven most popular in the United States, for the same reason as ordinary ISPs—unmetered local telephone calls. Europeans are less eager because they have to pay for the uplink phone call, as well as for the downlink satellite. Many companies also have "enterprise" versions of DirecPC-style systems. These do have a satellite uplink but differ from traditional VSATs in that they are highly asymmetric. A typical system might transmit at 256 kbps and receive at 4 Mbps.

There are also some two-way satellite services aimed at consumers. The largest of these is Starband, a joint venture between Gilat and satellite TV operator Echostar, which provides coverage across the continental United States (called the *Conus* region in the satellite industry). Customers can use the same dish for both TV and Internet, because the satellites that serve both are very close together. Its price and performance is supposed to be comparable to DSL or fixed wireless but without the requirement that customers live near a telephone exchange or base station.

Internet by Satellite

The geostationary orbit's high latency has traditionally been a problem for Internet protocols, leading some operators of lower satellites to claim that the Internet simply didn't work over GEO networks. Although these claims used to have some basis in reality, there are now several standards and proprietary systems that adapt Internet protocols to work over satellite.

The most serious problem is with TCP, the protocol used by most Internet applications to ensure that data has been received correctly. TCP usually waits for an acknowledgment that one batch of IP packets has been received before it sends the next. These acknowledgments usually take less than a tenth of a second but can take up to an entire second in a high-latency satellite network. The time spent waiting reduces throughput to a small fraction of the real link speed or even breaks the network entirely if the delay is so long that the sending node times out and resends the packets.

Cellular networks also suffer from high latency, so the original designers of WAP and i-mode simply abandoned TCP in favor of other protocols. Satellite networks took a different approach. Their solution is to increase the size of the "window," the amount of data that TCP can send before pausing for an acknowledgment. Known as *TCPSat*, this results in a greater loss of data if errors do occur, but errors are less likely on a satellite link than with most other types of connection. An alternative is to use a different protocol and send *spoofed* (fake) acknowledgments, as shown in Figure 12.6.

The other problem is with HTTP, the protocol used to load files into a Web browser. Most Web pages are made up from many different files, with a separate one needed for every picture, Java application, or piece of data that the page contains. Browsers first load the main HTML file, then request each of its subsidiary style sheets, images, and other files in turn. Each request entails a separate round trip to the server.

This actually makes sense over a narrowband link, because most people want to read the text in a page without having to wait for images to load, but it isn't necessary with broadband. To speed up the process, some satellite networks run special servers that scan HTML code for embedded images and other objects, requesting them before the page is sent. Some people confuse this with HTTP1.1, a newer version of the protocol that many Web servers and browsers now support. HTTP 1.1 does allow several objects to be sent at once, but the browser still needs to request each one separately.

To reduce latency to nearly zero, some satellite companies use *caches*. A cache is simply a hard disk that stores Web pages closer to the user to improve performance and reduce bandwidth consumption. Every Web browser has its own small cache within a PC, usually a directory called *Temporary Internet Files*, for users of MS Internet Explorer. Many companies, universities, and ISPs have special appliances or even entire server farms dedicated to caching. If everyone in a building is accessing the same site, a lot of capacity is saved by fetching the pages only once and storing them locally.

A satellite cache uses the same principle, with a relatively inexpensive hard disk sitting between the user's PC and satellite dish. The satellite automatically broadcasts popular Web sites to everyone so that they will already be stored on this hard disk when the user wants to access them. Back at the main hub, the satellite operator checks these sites for changes, broadcasting them to every user's cache to ensure that content is up to date.

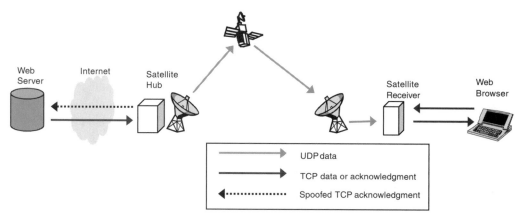

Figure 12.6
Web servers and browsers see regular TCP, though the satellite link doesn't use it.

Onboard Switches

The next generation of VSAT systems transfers the hub's intelligence to the satellite itself, meaning that customers can be connected directly. Some of these are listed in Table 12.2, along with other GEO satellites that aim to provide portable or mobile access.

The best known example of such "switching in the sky" is Hughes's Spaceway constellation, due for completion in 2004. By eliminating the ground-based hub, it frees up more bandwidth for individual VSAT users and cuts latency in half. Hughes plans to reduce latency even further by giving Spaceway a MEO component, though this will be further in the future.

Another innovation under development by Spaceway and its competitors Loral and Gilat is the switchable directional antenna. This is very highly focused, perhaps even onto a particular user, and moves depending on where it is needed. This is similar to cell phone base stations that use Space Division Multiple Access (SDMA), but it's easier to implement because the users aren't moving. The switching is handled electronically, rather than by physically rotating the satellite, allowing capacity to be deployed very efficiently.

Systems based on this new technology are touting spectacular data rates. For example, a company called *V-Star* claims that it will be able to deliver capacity of OC-12 (622 Mbps). Such speeds are normally achievable only through fiber or laser links and even then over distances far less than the thousands of miles between Earth and the GEO orbit.

Table 12.2   Advanced GEO Satellite Systems

System	No. of Satellites	Main Backer	Data Rate		In Service	Market
			Up	Down		
Astrolink	9	Lockheed Martin	20 Mbps	155 Mbps	2003 (US, Europe), 2004 (world)	Fixed
Euro Skyway	3	Alenia Spazio	2 Mbps	32.8 Mbps	2003 (Europe, Africa), 2004 (Asia-Pacific)	Fixed
Spaceway	8	Hughes	16 Mbps		2002 (US), 2004 (world)	Fixed
Inmarsat M	3	Inmarsat	64 or 432 kbps		2001 (64 kbps), 2004 (432 kbps)	Portable
Aces	2	Lockheed Martin, Ericsson	16 kbps		2002 (Asia only)	Mobile

Super VSATs

Some companies are planning huge geostationary satellites equipped with transmitters so powerful that they can be accessed via a nondirectional terminal no larger than a mobile phone. Inmarsat's "M" (Mobile) series can already be used through a portable antenna weighing only 3 kg, about the size of a laptop computer. These aren't really practical for regular business travelers or tourists, but they are useful for some specialized applications in regions where no other network infrastructure is available.

The Inmarsat-M devices have been used extensively by war correspondents in Afghanistan, often described as "videophones" by the TV stations that broadcast their reports. This isn't entirely accurate: Most people think of a videophone as a small gadget that's essentially just a phone (cellular or otherwise) with a screen on it. The Inmarsat "videophones" are really just professional-quality TV cameras connected to a ground unit.

The briefcase-sized units have a capacity of 64 kbps, which is why the live reports often seem quite jerky: There isn't enough bandwidth to transmit broadcast-quality video in real time. The codec tries to save on network capacity by sending only the parts of an image that change between frames, so presenters have learned to stand very still. The less they move, the more detail the viewer gets. (Prerecorded video can be made using a higher quality codec, of course, provided that the show's deadline allows time for it to be sent.) Inmarsat has plans for more powerful satellites, which will boost throughput to 432 kbps and make terminals small enough for travelers to carry in a pocket.

Aces (Asia Cellular Satellite) was the first company to launch satellites powerful enough to be reached through a terminal the size of a of a cell phone. It covers only Asia and is intended to provide better roaming for GSM users through dual-band terminals that support both GSM and satellite connections.

MOBILE (LEO) SATELLITE SYSTEMS........................

In the early 1990s, many companies began to dream of mobile voice and data networks that would span the entire Earth. Cell phones had already been inspired by the flip-top communicators of *Star Trek*, so the thought of being able to beam a message up to space was a marketer's dream. All would use low or middle orbits, eliminating the latency of VSATs and the problems of coverage at high latitudes. The first planned systems are summarized in Table 12.3.

Table 12.3 Mobile Satellite Networks

System	Data Speed (kbps)		Orbital Altitude	No. of Satellites	Frequency (GHz.)		Routing	Latency (seconds)	Service Available	Bankruptcy Status as of January 2002
	Up	Down			Up	Down				
Iridium Satellite	2.4	2.4	780 km (LEO)	66	1.62	1.62	Intersatellite	0.1	Now	New company, owns assets of bankrupt Iridium.
Globalstar	9.6	9.6	1,410 km (LEO)	48	1.62	2.49	Terrestrial	0.1	Now	Solvent
Orbcomm	2.4	9.6	820 km (LEO)	48	0.149	0.138	Terrestrial	400	Now	Emerged from Chapter 11 protection in 2001.
Leo One	9.6	24	950 km (LEO)	48	0.149	0.401	Terrestrial	60	2003	Solvent
New ICO	64	64	10,390 km (MEO)	10	2.19	2.00	Intersatellite	0.2	2003	New company, owns assets of bankrupt ICO.
Skybridge	2,000	20,000	1,469 km (LEO)	80	13.6	11.7	Terrestrial	0.1	2005	Solvent
Teledesic	2,000	64,000	1,350 km (LEO)	288	28.9	19.1	Intersatellite	0.1	2006	Solvent

With so many competing technologies on Earth—at the time, it was far from clear that GSM would emerge the winner, and CDMA was still in its experimental stages—satellite phones also had the potential to create a proper global standard. Why buy different phones for New York, Los Angeles, and Paris when one could work in all three, as well as in the Sahara Desert and at the South Pole?

By the time these networks were ready for launch, many had already been overtaken by terrestrial mobile systems. Cell phones became cheaper and lighter, whereas satellite phones were very bulky and cost thousands of dollars, with call charges to match. An early advertising slogan for one system was "If you can see the sky...," which inadvertently emphasized what it couldn't do—namely, work inside. That system, along with others, later filed for bankruptcy.

It might seem that mobile satellite services have no future, but investors are undeterred. Though business travelers might not need satellite phones, most people on the planet have still not made a phone call, so there is a compelling social case. There is also a large untapped market even in the richer countries. America is big, and nearly 50% of the United States is not yet covered by cell phone networks. The collapse of early systems is put down to financial errors and a failure to anticipate the demand for high-speed data brought about by the Internet.

Mobile Satellite Telephony

Three schemes originally promised worldwide satellite telephony. They are sometimes referred to collectively as *big LEOs*, somewhat inaccurately because one used higher MEO orbits. Two of them went bankrupt in 1999, the main reasons being the huge expense and complexity of the networks, coupled with very low data rates.

Iridium was the most spectacular failure, finally shutting down in March 2000. It was supposedly dreamed up by a Motorola executive in 1987 when his wife complained that her U.S. cell phone didn't work in the Bahamas. It aimed to provide voice service literally everywhere and actually achieved this goal a decade later. But by then, the market had moved on: Regular cell phone networks covered all of the richer parts of the world, including the Bahamas, and the growth of the Internet meant that more people were demanding data. Few people wanted a voice service that charged $7 per minute and worked only outside.

Many users who had paid thousands of dollars for handsets were cut off, including aid workers in Kosovo and an Iridium-sponsored expedition to prove that the system worked at the South Pole. Its 89 satellites, each the size and weight of a car, were scheduled to be "deorbited"—fired into the Earth's atmosphere at a shallow angle to ensure that they burn up safely. However, the network was too valuable to be destroyed in this way. It was eventually purchased by a new company, which restarted the service. Free of the original Iridium's debt, *New Iridium* might be able to operate the system profitably.

Rival ICO was luckier. It filed for Chapter 11 protection before it had even launched its satellites, enabling something to be salvaged. With new investment that enabled its satellites to be refitted for higher data rates, it emerged in July 2000 as *New ICO*, promising broadband services. It is also the only satellite system yet built that uses the 2-GHz spectrum proposed by the ITU for IMT-2000 services, so it may eventually interoperate with 3G standards such as UMTS and CDMA2000.

The most successful so far has been *Globalstar*, which is an intrinsically simpler system. As shown in Figure 12.7, it routes all calls via ground stations, whereas Iridium and ICO used ISL (Intersatellite Links). This means that Globalstar doesn't work everywhere, because it needs a ground station to be in range of the satellite, but the savings in cost and simplicity seem to be worth the reduced coverage. Each station has a range of several hundred miles, so a station in Paris can cover the Irish Sea and one in Miami, the Caribbean. When every station is operational, the system should cover nearly everywhere except the Antarctic and the middles of the oceans.

Globalstar can't compete with Iridium on coverage, but it does provide higher data rates, which mean better quality voice: 9.6 kbps is enough for a codec similar to that of a regular cell phone, whereas 2.4 kbps sounds very patchy. It's also more reliable where coverage is available, because it's based on a CDMA system with soft handover. Each Globalstar phone maintains a link with several satellites simultaneously, meaning that a connection is unaffected if one satellite moves out of range or passes behind a tree.

The financial problems of Iridium, ICO, and Globalstar haven't stopped other companies from planning even more ambitious networks. The most elaborate is Teledesic, which was originally planning to use nearly a thousand satellites to provide broadband data everywhere. It has since reduced it scope to "only" 288 satellites.

MSS and IMT-2000

Back in 1992, the ITU decided that 3G mobile networks should include a satellite component. It recommended that these satellites use spectrum at exactly 2 GHz, right in the middle of the band that it wanted for 3G cellular services. The theory was that if cellular and satellite systems used similar frequencies, it would be easier for manufacturers to produce dual-mode phones and data terminals that could be used for both kinds of access.

Asian and European regulators quickly rubber-stamped the ITU's proposals. The FCC took longer but did finally agree to the ITU's proposed *MSS* (Mobile Satellite Services) band in 2001. As explained in Chapter 5, "Third-Generation Standards," it did *not* agree to the rest of the ITU's recommendations. The result is that satellite access could be the only type of 3G that will work in both the United States and the rest of the world.

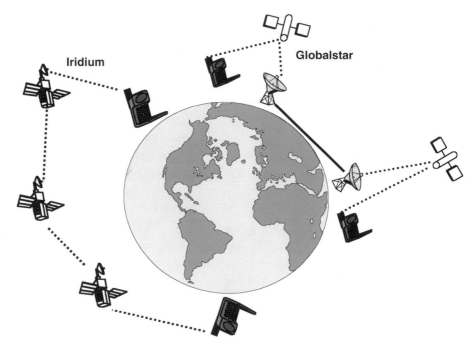

Figure 12.7
Intersatellite Links, pioneered by Iridium.

Whereas 3G cellular aims for data rates of at least 144 kbps, the satellite version is less ambitious. It's targeting data rates of up to 100 kbps, perhaps with voice and video. This will still be quite impressive, if the networks ever get built.

The FCC has issued a total of eight licenses for MSS services in the IMT-2000 band. Three went to the existing satellite mobile phone companies, but only ICO intends to use the band immediately. Globalstar and Iridium are both based on other frequencies, so they will require new satellites for MSS. Many analysts believe that neither company will be able to afford these.

Of the other five licenses, two went to regional geostationary providers, which plan to cover the United States with systems similar to Aces. Two more went to new players, Mobile Communications Holdings and Constellation Communications, both of which want to build MEO networks but have not announced any definite plans. The eighth license was issued to Boeing, which plans to build a specialized network aimed at air traffic control.

Navigation

Satellite-based navigation has become very popular over the last decade, thanks mainly to the U.S. Air Force's GPS network. The first civilian users were shipping and aviation companies, which were soon joined by individual explorers as pocket-sized receivers containing digital maps became available. GPS receivers are now being built into cell phones as the main component of location-based technology.

The GPS system is intended primarily for the U.S. military, which reserves the right to encrypt the signal or switch it off entirely in certain parts of the world. This worries some users, particularly those outside of the United States, because many civilian applications have become totally dependent on it. Air traffic control has largely abandoned its older terrestrial systems, so most planes would be grounded if GPS were switched off. All narrowband CDMA cell phone networks would also shut down, because they require timing signals from the atomic clocks on board the satellites.

To allay fears about the U.S. military's control, some users are looking at other satellite navigation systems. There are really only two alternatives: one that doesn't exist yet and another that may be nearing the end of its life. Both are based on MEO satellites, as is GPS itself.

- **GLONASS** was built by the Soviet Union in the 1980s and is now controlled by Russia's Ministry of Defense. At the time, it was more advanced than GPS, because its satellites were maneuvered into very precise orbits that allowed receivers to be comparatively simple. (This is because the U.S.S.R. led the world in space science but was behind the U.S. in electronics.) There are currently 12 operational GLONASS satellites, but its future is uncertain.

- **Galileo** is a system planned by the European Space Agency (ESA). It will use 30 satellites and broadcast on frequencies very close to GPS so that dual-mode receivers are easy to manufacturer. A dual-mode system would provide a backup in case one system was switched off or failed and enable increased accuracy. Many people question the need for Galileo, but the European Union says that it does not want to be dependent on the United States. Galileo will also be the only positioning system intended primarily for civilian rather than military use. If all goes according to plan, it should be operational by 2008.

Non-Space Networks

Satellites aren't the only way to put a wireless system in the sky. A company called *Sky Station International* plans to avoid the risk of rockets altogether by going back to a far older technology: balloons. Instead of orbiting Earth, its "satellites" will be suspended from huge, unmanned blimps floating on the edge of space, above the weather and all but the highest flying jets.

A stratospheric balloon should be able to hold a steady position, with virtually no latency and a much stronger signal than any satellite. Being open to the air puts the equipment more at risk from the elements than satellites preserved in a vacuum, though it should be easier to repair if a fault does occur. The biggest drawback is that thousands would be needed to cover the whole world, which is why Sky Station is initially concentrating only on urban areas.

HALO (High Altitude Long Operation) uses a similar concept, with planes instead of balloons. This doesn't even make a pretense of global coverage but focuses exclusively on cities, with initial rollout planned in California. The planes fly around all day in a tight circle, landing to refuel at night when the demand for capacity is lower. Burning jet fuel over Los Angeles's crowded skies doesn't help the city's smog problem, but supporters say it is no more expensive or polluting than launching rockets into space.

Mobile Satellite Telemetry

Though not as exciting as the big LEO projects, so-called *little LEO* constellations have proved more successful. They use as few as two satellites to offer narrowband data services, such as telemetry, short messages, and nonurgent paging. They do not offer voice or interactive data, keeping costs down. Most offer only partial coverage and can have latency of several minutes as a transmitter waits for a satellite to appear overhead.

The most successful so far is Orbcomm, which has launched 26 satellites and plans 10 more to achieve greater coverage and lower latency. Analysts say that it has proved that there is a sustainable business case for little LEO schemes. The costs are low, and the potential market is quite high. This has encouraged many other companies to follow it, the most ambitious being *Leo One*, planning 48 satellites. Around 20 other systems plan to use fewer satellites to focus on specific parts of the Earth, mostly in the United States.

MARS ONLINE ....

The satellite industry began as science fiction, and visions of the future have always been an important part of it. With Earth so well covered, visionaries are now looking to other planets. NASA has already committed itself to permanent communications satellites around Mars, and even more exciting schemes exist on paper.

The ability to send data all around the solar system will have important scientific applications and possible long-term benefits, but there are also plans to use it for shorter term financial returns. During the dot-com bubble, some entrepreneurs even hoped to fund space exploration through advertising on Web sites. The Pathfinder landing on Mars in 1997 generated nearly a billion page views per month for NASA's Web site, traffic which would have been worth many millions of dollars a year or two later.

That opportunity has now passed, but other companies have business plans that might be more sustainable. Lunacorp plans to send a remote-controlled rover to the Moon, charging people for the chance to drive it by remote control—either in specially built virtual reality machines or over the Internet. The same principle can be applied to controlling a camera on a satellite or even to a spacecraft itself, if it used a propulsion system that didn't rely on precious rocket fuel.

Rival Advanced Space Research (ASR) plans to go further. There's a burgeoning black market for moon rock, though most of the stuff for which collectors pay up to $2 per gram has no guarantee of authenticity. ASR's founders calculate that a robotic probe to the Moon could make money simply by selling samples of the lunar soil that it brought back. This strategy could also work for a mission to Mars, pieces of which would be far more than simple trinkets. Even scientists will pay millions for samples of Martian soil, and its value would multiply if, as many believe, it does contain fossilized alien life.

Vinton Cerf, co-inventor of TCP/IP, has long been planning what he calls an *Interplanetary Network* (IPN). Working with NASA, he hopes to put seven Internet-enabled communications satellites around the planet Mars by 2010, with the network extended to the rest of the solar system in the following decades. The first such satellite is already under construction and scheduled for launch in 2003. NASA believes that the network can be used to control future probes and, some day, allow space explorers to call home.

WEB RESOURCES

www.ee.surrey.ac.uk/Personal/L.Wood/constellations/
This professional-looking amateur site contains detailed information about all types of communications satellites. Its archive of news about MSS is particularly interesting.

www.trimble.com/gps/
This is an excellent tutorial on satellite navigation, from GPS receiver manufacturer Trimble.

www.tbs-satellite.com/tse/
This site contains a comprehensive encyclopedia of satellite communications, including information on every satellite ever launched. A trial version is available for free download, in either HTML or Windows .hlp format.

www.msua.org
The Mobile Satellite Users' Association aims to promote all the LEO systems, while standing up for users faced with confusing price plans and an uncertain future.

www.gvf.org
The Global VSAT Forum, made up of satellite manufacturers and operators, details on its site the benefits of satellite services and campaigns on issues such as regulation.

www.gpsworld.com/gpsworld/
This is the online version of a magazine covering the GPS technology and its applications.

BIBLIOGRAPHY

Clarke, Arthur C. **The Exploration of Space.** Harper, 1951.
The inventor of communications satellites explains how they work and (very accurately) predicts their applications.

Roddy, Denis. **Satellite Communications.** McGraw-Hill, 1995.
A textbook aimed at engineering students. It's very technical but doesn't assume any previous knowledge of satellites or communications.

SUMMARY ....

- Satellites have traditionally been used for intercontinental backbone networks, but this role has been usurped by fiber.
- Direct satellite-to-user broadcasts, pioneered by TV stations, are increasingly being used to access the Internet.
- Most communications satellites use geostationary orbits, which are so far from Earth that they result in a noticeable latency.
- New lower orbits have been tried with mobile networks. Iridium casts a shadow over their economic case, but compared with the cost of 3G licenses in many countries, a satellite network can seem inexpensive.
- Balloons and airplanes are possible alternative technologies that would provide many of a satellite system's benefits at lower cost.
- Communications satellites may ultimately extend the Internet throughout the solar system.

13 Do Wireless Devices Fry Your Brain?

In this chapter...

$\mathbf{A}$s cell phone use has increased, so have worries about the safety of wireless devices. Several lawsuits are making their way through the U.S. courts, filed by people alleging that their cell phones have contributed to cancer. The British government requires that all terminals include a tobacco-style health warning on their packaging, advising people to limit the time they spend on calls. Some countries in otherwise mobile-mad Scandinavia are considering a ban on wireless devices intended for children, while communities across the world have rallied to oppose new base station towers.

Despite many studies, scientific opinion is still divided. Even discounting obvious scaremongers on one side and industry shills on the other, there is a real debate about whether the widespread use of wireless devices constitutes a threat to public health. The researchers who warn us of risks aren't all conspiracy theorists or Luddites. Likewise, those who reassure us of safety aren't equivalent to the paid lobbyists who deny the dangers of global warming or second-hand smoke. Their only point of agreement is the obvious hazard of driving while talking or dialing.

There *is* evidence that the U.S. mobile industry once tried to prevent research into the health effects of cell phones and even to cover up potential risks. There's also evidence that the energy blasted out by antennas does affect the human body in measurable ways, which aren't yet understood but may be harmful. However, no scientist has yet demonstrated a link between mobile phones and brain cancer, the problem for which they are most often blamed.

One thing is certain, without any scientific tests: If wireless devices do cause problems, these are going to get a lot worse. The higher data rates of 2.5G and 3G technologies are achieved in part by using higher energy transmissions, magnifying whatever effects exist. Worse, there's a loophole in U.S. law that allows data devices to avoid the relatively strict safety standards applied to phones.

This is sensible in some cases: If a device is designed to be mounted on a table or a wall, far from a user, there's no reason to hold it to the same standards as one held up to a person's head. But many data devices aren't mounted on a table or a wall. They're placed in a user's lap, right next to the most sensitive organs of all.

THEORY ....

Electromagnetic waves are well understood, but their effects on the human body are not. This is because the physics of electromagnetism is relatively simple, described by equations that may seem baffling to most of us but contain very few variables: They have a clear solution, which can be found by anyone with a degree in advanced calculus (or more usually, a computer). In contrast, a human body contains thousands of different chemicals, each of which can affect it in a slightly different way. Radio waves interact with all of these, causing effects that may be trivial or may cascade into something more serious.

Everyone agrees that very high doses of radio waves can be dangerous. A mobile phone uses exactly the same type of radiation as a microwave oven, so enough of it would have the same effects. This doesn't mean that using a phone is equivalent to sticking your head in the microwave, because the phone transmits at a much lower power: typically less than 1 watt, compared to a microwave oven's 650 watts or more. Even if the phone somehow malfunctioned and boosted its power output, there simply wouldn't be enough energy in its battery to cause widespread heating.

Rather than literally frying the brain or other organs, two mechanisms have been proposed for possible cell effects of cell phone radiation. The most widely (but by no means universally) accepted is *localized heating*, which would cook only a few cells. More controversially, some scientists believe that microwave radiation could cause as-yet unexplained *nonthermal* effects.

Many people might be more concerned with *whether* wireless devices can affect their health than with the precise biological details of *how*, but scientific theory does matter. Until the effects are understood, cell phone users won't know how to mitigate them. Several companies sell devices that claim to make cell phones safer, but most of these have no effect, and some may even make things worse.

Microwave Heating

Opponents of cell phones often say that they are sources of radiation, whereas the industry prefers to use the almost-as-vague term RF waves. ("RF" is for radio frequency, including all the different wave bands used in wireless systems.) The reason is obvious: Most people associate radiation with danger and death. Many assume, falsely, that exposure to any type of radiation is automatically bad and that it will cause cancer or other health problems.

Though other types of radiation—including RF waves—may pose some risk, the reflex against radiation should really apply only to the ionizing kind. Ionizing radiation refers to any electromagnetic wave that has a high enough frequency to knock electrons out of atoms and generally means a frequency of at least 1,000 THz. As explained in Chapter 2, "Radio Spectrum," all frequencies used for communications purposes are way below this. Unless they work at a nuclear power plant or have an X-ray, the only type of ionizing radiation that most people encounter is ultraviolet, from the sun. This means that sunbathing should be more likely than cell phone use to cause cancer, a theory borne out by statistics.

Ionization is by far the most dangerous effect of radiation, but it's not the only one. Cell phones radiate energy in the microwave band, which, as many people know, is a very efficient way to heat things. Microwave ovens are particularly good at cooking food with high water content, and the human brain is about 80% water. Combined with a peculiar property of microwaves, this leads to understandable fears.

Microwaves are not alone in their heating effects. All types of electromagnetic radiation (ionizing or not) carry energy, and can increase the temperature of anything or anyone that it strikes. The type of electromagnetic wave we are most familiar with is infrared radiation, which is given off by all hot objects. A radiator works by emitting infrared rays, which we can feel. As the temperature of the hot object increases, the atoms within it vibrate faster, so the frequency of radiation also increases. "Red hot" objects emit red light (the lowest frequency in the visible band), and "white hot" objects (such as light bulbs) radiate all colors.

If we stand next to a radiator or underneath a spotlight, we feel hot. This is because the radiation is absorbed mainly by our skin, which contains lots of nerve endings. Unfortunately, the same isn't necessarily true for microwave radiation. It is so low in frequency that much of it passes straight through our skin, as shown in Figure 13.1. The microwaves are instead absorbed by internal organs and bones, which don't contain many nerve endings. This is how microwaves were first discovered: In 1946, a researcher noticed that a chocolate bar in his pocket had melted during an experiment, even though he hadn't been aware of any heat.

The painless heating effect of microwaves does have some benefits. It's used in a medical procedure called diathermy, which produces heat deep inside the body without hurting the skin. It can also cause health problems. A microwave transmitter can injure us just as much as a hotplate or a fire, but since we don't feel the heat, we aren't aware of damage being done. A high-power microwave source can cook our brains or boil our blood, burning us from the inside out before we realize that anything is wrong.

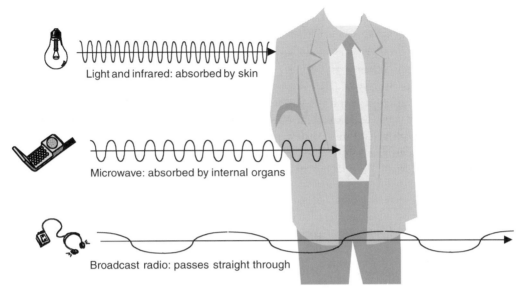
Light and infrared: absorbed by skin

Microwave: absorbed by internal organs

Broadcast radio: passes straight through

Figure 13.1
How nonionizing radiation interacts with the human body.

Power Density

Because of microwaves' proven burning effects, most governments enforce guidelines for human exposure. Unlike guidelines for exposure to ionizing radiation, the theory is that, below a certain threshold, microwaves can do *no* harm. After all, a small amount of heat is not intrinsically bad. People often absorb infrared radiation and don't worry about burns. The only difference is that, because we can't feel microwaves, we need to trust devices not to burn us unwittingly. The limits are set so that, in theory, heating occurs so slowly that the body has plenty of time to disperse the heat. Blood circulation should cool internal organs faster than microwaves can heat them.

The regulations are based on *power density*, which means the intensity of radiation reaching a given area. They also depend on frequency, because different frequencies are absorbed in different ways. For example, the FCC mandates that at the 1,900 MHz PCS frequencies, people should avoid microwaves with a power density of more than 1 mW/cm^2. The limit for 800-MHz cellular is about half this, because the lower frequency is even better at passing through the skin. Its limits for the entire radio spectrum are shown in Figure 13.2, along with the mathematical formulas used to calculate them. Most other countries have similar rules.

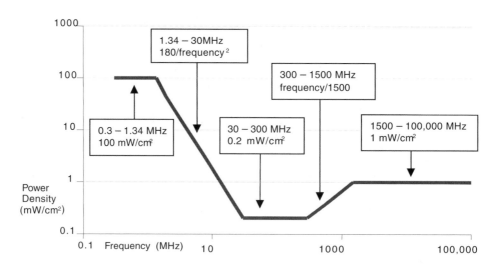

Figure 13.2
The United States' limits on radio-frequency radiation exposure for the general population.

Other radio waves use even lower frequencies than microwaves, so in theory these could have similar effects. However, their frequencies are so low that they often pass straight through the human body. In general, the FCC considers microwaves to be less safe than other types of RF radiation, hence the relatively high limits for high frequencies. Microwaves have just enough energy to cause heating but not enough for us to feel it.

The Inverse-Square Law

Power density around a transmitter decreases with distance, because radiation spreads out over a wider area. This seems obvious, but few people understand its consequences properly, perhaps because these involve some math. Specifically, power density follows an *inverse-square law*: If a person doubles her distance from a transmitter, the power density received is decreased by a factor of four. If she moves 10 times further away, the power density drops to a hundredth of what it was. These figures include only signal spreading: The actual effect of distance is even more extreme when a signal is passing through air (as opposed to empty space), thanks to atmospheric attenuation.

This inverse-square law means that a person's distance from a transmitter is a lot more important than the transmitter's own power. A high-power transmitter can be relatively safe, provided that people keep away from it. Conversely, a relatively low-power transmitter can be dangerous for someone who is very close to it.

Cellular base stations are high-power transmitters, so safety restrictions are usually met simply by keeping people away from them. The exact size of this exclusion zone varies depending on the power output, but because power density falls off so rapidly with distance, it usually doesn't need to be very large. Most base stations have an output power of about 50 watts, with some larger cells transmitting at up to 100 watts. Table 13.1 lists the power density at various distances from both these types of base stations, with densities that exceed the FCC's limit for PCS in bold. It assumes omnidirectional transmissions; a directional antenna will produce a higher density in one direction and a lower one in another, with both still subject to the same inverse-square law.

As the table shows, the power density is very high at distances of only a few centimeters from a base station but not at distances of 1 m or more. If the FCC's limits are right, it is safe to be 90 cm away from a high-power PCS base station or 70 cm from a medium-power one. Most base stations are surrounded by fences to prevent anybody except a radio engineer from getting anything like this close. They're also mounted on poles several meters high, which should mean that even people standing directly below are not exposed to excess heat.

Cell phones transmit at a lower power than do base stations but are usually held very close to the head. Table 13.1 also shows the power density around a phone, assuming that its output is about 0.25 watts. (The actual power varies, but 0.25 watts is about average.) To meet the FCC's safety restrictions, people would have to keep their cell phones at least 5 cm away from the body. This is clearly not possible: Mobile phones are often used in noisy environments, requiring that they be pressed right up against the ear. The antenna is sometimes only 1 cm from the loudspeaker, resulting in a power density about 20 times the limit.

Although base stations are very visible, calculations of power density show that cell phones themselves expose people to higher levels of radiation. Modern phones adjust their transmission power depending on their distance from the base station, increasing it when far away and decreasing it when closer. This leads to the counterintuitive conclusion that, if cell phones pose a hazard, the *safest* place for cell phone users to be is very close to a base station.

Of course, all this doesn't mean that opposition to cellular towers is always unjustified. Base stations irradiate everyone, whereas cell phones affect only those who choose to use them. Radio engineers who complain about base stations may have a particularly strong case, because their job means that they sometimes enter the exclusion zone.

Table 13.1   *Power Density Around Omnidirectional Transmitters*

Distance	Cell phone: 0.25 W	Small base station: 50 W	Large base station: 100 W
1 cm (0.4 inches)	19.9 mW/cm^2	3,979 mW/cm^2	7,958 mW/cm^2
2 cm (0.8 inches)	4.97 mW/cm^2	995 mW/cm^2	1989 mW/cm^2
3 cm (1.2 inches)	2.21 mW/cm^2	442 mW/cm^2	884 mW/cm^2
4 cm (1.6 inches)	1.24 mW/cm^2	249 mW/cm^2	497 mW/cm^2
5 cm (2.0 inches)	0.80 mW/cm^2	159 mW/cm^2	318 mW/cm^2
10 cm (3.9 inches)	0.20 mW/cm^2	39.8 mW/cm^2	79.6 mW/cm^2
50 cm (1.6 feet)	0.01 mW/cm^2	1.59 mW/cm^2	3.18 mW/cm^2
60 cm (2.0 feet)	0.01 mW/cm^2	1.11 mW/cm^2	2.21 mW/cm^2
70 cm (2.3 feet)	0.004 mW/cm^2	0.81 mW/cm^2	1.62 mW/cm^2
80 cm (2.6 feet)	0.003 mW/cm^2	0.62 mW/cm^2	1.24 mW/cm^2
90 cm (3.0 feet)	0.002 mW/cm^2	0.49 mW/cm^2	0.98 mW/cm^2
100 cm (3.3 feet)	0.002 mW/cm^2	0.40 mW/cm^2	0.80 mW/cm^2
1,000 cm (32.8 feet)	0.00002 mW/cm^2	0.004 mW/cm^2	0.008 mW/cm^2

Absorption in the Body

If regulations on power density were strictly enforced, cell phones held next to the head would be illegal. Instead, phones must conform to alternative rules that measure how much radiation is actually soaked up by the body, a quantity called the *SAR* (Specific Absorption Rate). This is in some ways a more rigorous (and more accurate) standard, because it also takes account of heating caused by the phone's own electric and magnetic field, not just its radiation. These fields can be significant within about 20 cm of a phone.

Determining the SAR for a specific phone is a very complicated process. It requires a mixture of computer simulations and experiments using *phantom heads*, temperature sensors that have a similar chemical composition to a human brain. The phone has to be moved around to different positions, because absorption can depend on such factors as how it is held. The peak SAR produced by each phone has to be under certain limits, which are listed in Table 13.2. The United States has slightly stricter regulations than Europe, meaning that some GSM phones used elsewhere cannot legally be sold in America.

Some scientists say that the peak SAR levels for different phones should be published side by side, so that people can choose a phone with a relatively low radiation output. Others say that this could be misleading, because the actual SAR experienced by a user can vary so much. The peak level is just that—an absolute maximum—and a phone with a low peak does not necessarily have a low average. If effects on health are eventually proven, a "low-SAR" phone could be the equivalent of a "low-tar" cigarette, lulling people into a false sense of security.

Governments already keep records showing the SAR for each phone, and some manufacturers also make them available. However, these records are not always easy to find. Manufacturers do *not* publish them on the phones themselves or their packages, and governments don't usually make them easily accessible. The FCC actually publishes them on the Web but not in a very user-friendly form.

Data equipment is *not* subject to the same strict tests as phones. Though all of it does have to meet either the SAR or the power density regulations, manufacturers are allowed to assume that devices will be kept away from a human body. This sometimes makes sense: Many wireless LAN access points are designed to be mounted on ceilings, so it's reasonable to expect that people will not come into very close contact with them. Some ship with warnings saying that they should be kept several centimeters from any person and have their power density measured at that distance.

However, a loophole allows the same assumptions to be made for devices that people might hold right next to their bodies. For example, the 128-kbps wireless modems sold by Metricom included a warning that the devices be kept at least 20 cm (8 inches) away from any part of the body. This wasn't possible, because the modems were designed to be attached to a computer on the outside. Even Metricom's own FCC filing admitted that the distance between the modem and the user might be only 5 inches. Because the modems were usually used with laptops, many people kept them perched on their legs or in a shirt pocket.

Table 13.2   *Legal Limits on SAR at Microwave Frequencies*

Body Location	International SAR Limits	United States SAR Limits
Average over Whole Body	0.08 W/kg	0.08 W/kg
Head	2 W/kg	1.6 W/kg
Limbs	4 W/kg	4 W/kg

Nonthermal Effects

Campaigners have criticized the power density and SAR limits because they consider only large-scale heating. They don't take account of nonthermal effects, on which any possible problems caused by cell phones would depend. The nature of these effects is vigorously debated, with many scientists denying that they exist at all.

The most likely "nonthermal" effects are actually thermal but on a much smaller scale than the regulations were designed to protect against. Many phones don't spread their signal evenly through space: They transmit in one particular direction, trying to reach the base station. If a person's head gets in the way, this could produce heating in a very concentrated area, perhaps destroying a single cell. Time Division Multiple Access (TDMA) phones could cause a further risk, because they concentrate their energy into short pulses, rather than one continuous transmissions. A phone based on GSM (a type of TDMA) that has an average output of 0.25 watts is actually transmitting short bursts at 2 watts, but only for one-eighth of the time.

At the atomic level, there is no difference between thermal and nonthermal effects. All heat is really just random motion of atoms. The hotter something is, the faster the atoms are moving, and the more force with which they will crash into things. When we touch something and think it feels hot, we're really feeling the collisions of fast-moving atoms with our skin. When microwaves heat something, they are giving a push to its atoms, making them bounce around faster.

This means that even if there isn't enough radiation to cook a cell, it could still have an effect by accelerating the movement of some atoms. This might alter the way that hormones pass between the blood and the brain, or cause red blood cells to release certain chemicals that they would otherwise store. One popular theory is that microwaves cause increase in production of heat shock proteins, substances used by the body to repair damage caused by heat. This is sometimes used to explain results from Bristol University that showed radiation from cell phones improving human reaction time, though the scientists who performed the research prefer a simpler explanation involving slight rises in temperature that stimulate blood flow.

More controversially, some people have suggested that radio waves are actually used within the brain and that some effects could be due to interference. It's known that powerful magnets can affect the brain, producing an effect similar to hallucinogenic drugs, but the fields associated with microwave radiation are thought to be too weak for this. Extensive research has been carried out on the effects of low-power fields, mainly related to the safety of electrical wires, and they have been shown to cause no direct increase in cancer or any other illness.

EXPERIMENTAL RESEARCH ....

Theories about the biological effects of radiation are hard to test. They usually involve looking for tiny variations in large quantities, variations that may occur over a very long period of time. Results are often disputed, and a lot of research is funded by companies with an interest in its outcome.

So far, there are no conclusive results about the direct effects of cell phone radiation on the human body. Researchers in 1990s did discover that GSM phones could interfere with some pacemakers and hearing aids, but these have now been redesigned with shielding to protect against such interference. Driver distraction is a greater threat, but that's nothing to do with the radio signals. The only effect demonstrated more than once is a very slight reduction in reaction time.

Though this is interesting, most people are more concerned about cancer. The good news is that nobody has yet shown a link between cell phones and cancer. The bad news is that this could just mean that not enough research has been done or that the research has focused on the wrong area.

Cancer is a particularly difficult disease to study, because it takes so long to develop, and its causes are inherently probabilistic or even random. For example, some estimates say that people who live with a heavy smoker are about twice as likely to develop lung cancer as people who don't. This means that if a nonsmoker who lives with a smoker suffers from lung cancer, there is a 50% chance that it was caused by the smoke and a 50% chance that they would have caught it anyway. There is usually no way to isolate an exact cause. This is one reason why tobacco took decades to be recognized as a killer, even though it causes thousands of deaths each day.

Some scientists say that research into mobile phones is now at the same state as research on smoking was in 1950: There are fears but no hard evidence. However, similar fears have existed about technologies later shown to be harmless; many people were afraid to allow electricity into their homes in 1900, and some scientists back then agreed with their fears. It could be 2050 before we know for sure which comparison is most accurate.

The Scientific Method

Most scientists try to be objective, and the scientific process is designed to weed out the less scrupulous. For example, clinical trials of new drugs follow the "double-blind" principle: Neither the patient nor the doctor prescribing a pill knows whether it is the real drug or an inactive placebo, protecting against even unconscious bias.

Results are then subjected to peer review before publication, a process during which experts check for errors and again try to weed out bias. In theory, anyone reading a scientific paper (and with the necessary expertise to understand it) should be able to repeat the process. When several teams do so and see a similar outcome, the experiment is considered "replicated," and a theory becomes accepted. If they get different results from those predicted, the theory is said to be "falsified" and abandoned.

The science surrounding cell phones doesn't always work like this. Even respected scientists disagree over what constitutes replication. For example, some believe that different kinds of phones or frequencies of radiation should be used, and others say that a replication is valid only if it tries to repeat the original experiment exactly.

There are also ways in which companies that pay for research can affect the outcome. Every scientist will say, correctly, that funding an experiment does not mean dictating its results. The double-blind and peer-review processes are supposed to avoid this. For example, many drugs fail clinical tests, though the tests are paid for by drug companies that have a great interest in the new drug passing and gaining approval.

However, companies can affect results in more subtle ways. They can prevent publication of unfavorable findings or control the way that results are presented. Most importantly, they choose just *what* the research is supposed to study. The U.S. cell phone industry was once quite adept at this, setting its own program of research under a director who (by his own admission) knew very little about microwaves or cancer but had previously worked for the tobacco, dioxin, and asbestos industries.

In his work for Philip Morris, this meant looking at physicians' *attitudes* toward cigarettes, rather than the actual health risks, in the hope that this could be used to claim that doctors were prejudiced against smoking. In his work for the cellular industry, it meant announcing results before experiments were performed. This proved too much for him, and he eventually "defected," writing a book (see the bibliography at the end of this chapter) alleging that the industry had tried to prevent research into cell phones' health effects.

Known as *Wireless Technology Research* (WTR), the industry's program culminated in a lawsuit filed against it, the Cellular Telephony Association of America (CTIA), and several other companies (*Busse v Motorola*). The plaintiffs included WTR's own director, as well as "all subscribers in the United States of America of cellular telephone services" from November 1993 to December 1998. It reached a partial settlement in 2001, with WTR admitting that it had infringed on cell phone users' privacy by sharing information about their health problems, but not admitting that cell phones were responsible for cancer.

Test Results

Researchers use three main types of study, but all have flaws.

- **Animal Experiments.** These are used extensively to test possible carcinogens under laboratory conditions. Most use genetically engineered rodents, bred to have an increased susceptibility to cancer so that anything that multiplies this susceptibility will show a more apparent effect. The problem is that they don't necessarily extrapolate to humans. Even if they do, both sides in any controversial issue will *claim* that they don't whenever results go against their opinions. For example, one famous study found that microwaves caused DNA damage in rat brain cells. Although human brain cells are thought to behave in the same way as rats'—we just have more of them—the industry tried to stress the difference between rats and humans.

- **Epidemiological Studies.** These aren't really experiments at all but do provide an efficient way to examine a large number of human subjects. Researchers simply give questionnaires to cancer patients or look at medical records, both of which can be biased. People with health problems often want to blame them on something, and brain cancer patients may exaggerate their cell phone use when asked. Conversely, the doctors who write medical records may have firm opinions about their patients, blaming their cancer on some other lifestyle factor.

- **Human Experiments.** These are very expensive and raise obvious ethical issues but are otherwise the most reliable source of information. The problem is that they can test for only short-term effects. The greatest fear is that radiation will cause brain cancer, something that might become apparent only after many years. Mobile phones are so new that their long-term effects are still unknown and could remain that way for a generation. The only way to be sure that *anything* is entirely safe is to wait until a large number of people have used it for their entire lives.

Despite these flaws, some results have become apparent. In the short term, the only measurable effect of microwave radiation seems to be stimulation. This is manifested both in improved reaction times (demonstrated by A. Preece of Bristol University in 1999, then by M. Koivisto of Helsinki University in 2000) and as increased brain action (measured by A. Borbely and P. Ackerman at the University of Zurich in 2000). Radiation from both analog and digital cell phones can shorten reaction time, and a half-hour phone call can increase brain activity for up to 50 minutes afterward.

This effect is mild, compared with better known stimulants such as coffee, but it does suggest that microwaves do affect the brain. This has led the Independent Experts Group on Mobile Phones (IEGMP), a committee set up by the British government, to propose a precautionary approach. It recommends that children under 16 use cell phones only in emergencies, because their thinner skulls and developing brains could make them more vulnerable.

Not all health campaigners agree with this. Britain's largest antitobacco group, Action on Smoking and Health, believes that even if wireless devices are dangerous, kids should still be encouraged to use them. The theory is that cell phones satisfy many of the same needs as cigarettes and that many would-be smokers can't afford to buy both. Because the risk is probably so small, compared with that of smoking, phones are considered the lesser evil.

Protection

As people became more concerned about cell phone radiation, many charlatans began selling devices that they claimed could protect against it. According to tests carried out by the Consumers' Association, a nonprofit group based in Britain, most of these don't work. Even when they do provide effective shielding, they're often a waste of money: Anything that blocks the radio waves from leaving a cell phone will also prevent it from functioning. If they merely weaken the signal, rather than block it entirely, the cell phone will increase its power, providing no net effect except a shorter battery life.

The opinion on hands-free headsets is more mixed. Two 2000 reports from the Consumers' Association found that some actually *increased* the radiation reaching the head. This was enough to persuade the British government to remove an endorsement of headsets from its health warnings, but the FCC disagrees. It still recommends that people use a headset if they are concerned about radiation.

Though the Consumers' Association's reports have not gone through the usual scientific channels of peer review, headsets have few defenders except the FCC. The main reason is that they are sold by the phone manufacturers, who are obviously reluctant to stress safety fears as a selling point. Instead, the companies talk about how they are more convenient, enabling people to send text messages or access Web sites at the same time as speaking on the phone.

If the Consumers' Association is right, nobody knows for sure why. Its theory is that the wire between the headset and the phone actually channels energy directly into the ear, instead of letting it spread out in space. This would mean that any potential danger depends on the length of the wire, as shown in Figure 13.3, and perhaps on how close it is held to the phone's antenna. If the wire is the wrong length, it may act as a conduit for a standing wave. This means that the wire can hold an exact integer or half-integer number of wavelengths, trapping the radiation. The phone boosts its output because less energy is reaching the base station, which increases the intensity reaching the user yet further.

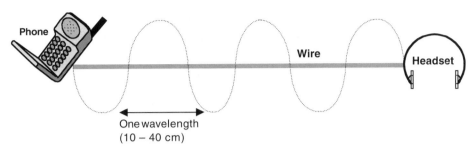

Figure 13.3
Standing wave in wire leading to hands-free headset

Future headsets shouldn't have this problem, because they won't rely on wires. The Bluetooth technology was originally designed to connect headsets to phones without a wire, and some companies already sell phone/headset systems that use this or a proprietary radio technology. Because Bluetooth has such a short range, it can transmit with less than a millionth the volume of a cell phone, reducing any risk by the same factor. Despite this, some people might resist using another wireless gadget as a solution to a problem caused by wireless gadgets.

OTHER WIRELESS HAZARDS ....

Although everyone worries about radiation, this isn't the only (or even the largest) risk that cell phones and other wireless data devices pose, both to their users and to the world at large.

Every new technology attracts some criticism, much of it justified. People worried that the telephone would destroy the art of letter writing, then that e-mail would do the same to the art of conversation. They were right, though few people would deny that these technologies brought great benefits. Similarly, wireless communication has its dark side. In some cases, the problems that it causes are merely inconvenient. In others, they can be deadly.

Don't Talk and Drive

Driving while using a cell phone can kill. Although researchers hotly debate the effects of radiation, the effects of driver distraction are much clearer. The U.S. National Highway Traffic Safety Administration estimated that they were implicated in up to 30% of vehicle accidents in 2000, a figure that can only grow as car phones become more popular.

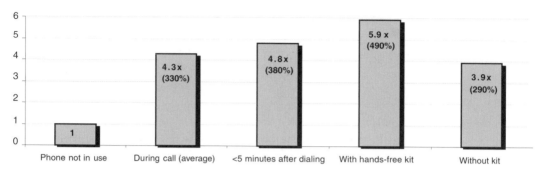

Figure 13.4
Increased risk of motor vehicle accident when driver is using cell phone.

Many states, cities, and countries have responded by passing laws that require drivers to use hands-free kits. But surprisingly, these don't make driving while on the phone any less dangerous. A study at the University of Toronto found that these actually add to the risk, perhaps by lulling drivers into a false sense of safety. As Figure 13.4 shows, a driver using a hands-free kit is more than five times more likely to crash than one not using a phone at all. In comparison, driving with a blood alcohol level at just above the legal limit increases the risk fourfold, suggesting that cell phones are an even worse menace than drunk drivers.

Cell phones are not the only distractions that drivers face, of course, but they do cause unique problems. Unlike a passenger in the car, someone on the other end of a call is not sensitive to the road, and, unlike tuning a radio, dialing a phone is a process that has to be repeated many times. The Toronto study also found an increased risk within the first five minutes of a call, suggesting that dialing caused extra distraction.

Many automakers are already building wireless data capabilities into cars, suggesting that the problem is going to get worse. However, some of this may be used to enhance safety by warning drivers of problems ahead. There are even long-term plans to have vehicles controlled remotely by a central traffic computer. NTT DoCoMo says that this is one of the applications it envisions for 3G and 4G, and the Federal Highway Administration (FHWA) in the United States has planned a very high data rate in-vehicle information system based on the 802.11a wireless LAN standard.

These may eventually free drivers from the need to actually drive, enabling them to concentrate entirely on their phone conversations. Until then, motorists should switch off their phones while in the car and stop if they do need to make a call. If you're still tempted, there's another risk. A metal box on wheels reflects radiation just like a microwave oven's walls, reflecting it straight back to the driver's head.

Know Where You Are

When someone calls the emergency services from a land-line phone, the person who answers the phone knows the exact location of the caller. The often distraught or injured caller doesn't have to waste time describing his location, or worry about giving directions. Whether at someone's home or a pay phone, the phone's location appears on a screen in front of the operator, allowing emergency services to be dispatched efficiently.

None of this happens when the caller is using a cell phone. Indeed, emergency calls from a mobile can be more of a nuisance than a lifesaver. Car crashes are often reported by hundreds of passing drivers, jamming the switchboard and risking further accidents as the drivers who make the calls are distracted—both by the act of making the call and by looking around to find out where they are. Mountain rescuers complain that wireless networks have encouraged foolhardy climbers to carry a cell phone instead of real safety equipment, endangering the team sent up to find them when they call for help.

Cell phones also make hoax calls easier, because hoaxers can simply steal a phone, then throw it away before anyone can track them down. Even worse, they allow these phone thieves to pretend to be in situations where use of a land line is impossible. Life boats have been sent to search for nonexistent drowning sailors, and the Air Force has scrambled to force down planes that someone on the ground pretended had been hijacked.

The solution to all of these problems is location technology. It may or may not have a commercial business case, eventually offering advanced mapping and location-based services, but there is a clear public safety case for it to be built into all cellular networks. The United States is ahead of Europe here, thanks to a mandate issued by the FCC in 1999.

Known as *Enhanced 911* (E-911), the mandate is a two-part order intended to make all cellular network operators supply location information to emergency services. Phase I came into effect immediately and was easy to comply with. It says that operators must reveal which base-station a caller is closest to, data that all cellular networks already track in their location registers, so that they are able to route calls. This helps somewhat, but one cell can cover an area of up to 4,000 square km, so a more precise system is needed.

Phase II says that operators must provide specific latitude and longitude coordinates. The allowed margin of error depends on the type of location technology used, as shown in Table 13.3. Systems that include a GPS receiver on the phone are assumed to be twice as accurate as systems that rely on triangulation by the network of base stations alone.

The companies were supposed to comply with Phase II by October 2001, but all either applied for a waiver or simply failed to meet the deadline. Nonetheless, the FCC is already considering a third phase. Under E-911 Phase III, the location technologies would also have to include a way to determine vertical coordinates, so that they know the altitude of an airliner or even which floor of a building a user is on.

Table 13.3   *Accuracy Requirements of E-911 Phase II*

Type of system	67% of location fixes must be accurate to within:	95% of location fixes must be accurate to within:
Network-based	100 m (328 feet)	300 m (984 feet)
Handset-based (GPS)	50 m (164 feet)	150 m (492 feet)

Vertical measurements are fairly easy to make using GPS, because this system is already designed for three-dimensional location fixes. They're harder using base stations alone, as each extra dimension requires extra fixed points, and there often simply aren't enough cellular base stations within range of a phone. For this reason, some companies have proposed systems that build a TV receiver into a phone, using the television transmitter as another point of reference. This has the added benefit that the phone can double as a portable TV or even use part of the TV signal to carry data.

Stay Out of Touch

Nearly every movie theater now shows a warning asking patrons to please turn off their cell phones and pagers. Railroad companies have introduced "quiet carriages," where mobile phones are banned. Some nightclubs even search their patrons for phones, confiscating them along with drugs and weapons.

There's no doubt that a ringing cell phone can be annoying, but there are several ways to prevent this. The most obvious is simple courtesy, but many people forget to switch off their phones or set them to vibrate mode and don't know how to use features that can block all calls except the truly urgent. Others don't realize that they are shouting when they speak into a cell phone, a problem caused by the lack of any feedback. Fixed phones allow us to hear almost instant echoes of our own voices, so that we can adjust the volume if we are too loud. Cell phones don't, because the latency of a mobile network means the echoes could be received a noticeable time after we speak.

Some of these problems could be solved by technology. There are already attempts to add pseudo-echoes to phones, so that people will know when they are shouting. For areas where total silence is best, an enhancement to the Bluetooth specification could allow Bluetooth access points to issue special "quiet" instructions. These would prevent the phone from ringing and display a warning when the user tried to make a call. This could be over-ridden in genuine emergencies.

Jamming devices can blanket an entire area in artificial interference, over-whelming any cell phone signals. However, these are banned in most countries. A legal alternative is a *Faraday cage*, a fine metal mesh that literally traps microwaves inside. There is one embedded within the glass (or plastic) in the doors of every microwave oven, where it is used to prevent the radiation escaping and heating up the room rather than the food.

The same principle can be used to keep cell phone signals out by surrounding a whole room or even an entire building with the cage. The problem here is that the gaps in the mesh have to be smaller than the cell phone's wavelength, as shown in Figure 13.5. Wavelength decreases as frequency increases, so a Faraday cage designed to protect against radiation in the cellular band will not always work against that in higher bands used by wireless LANs.

A large part of the problem is that people haven't yet become used to cell phones and other mobile communications devices. As well as disturbing everyone else in the vicinity, a phone has a sense of urgency that often forces the phone's owner to answer it, putting any other activity aside. This is a holdover from the days when phone calls were a rare and expensive luxury, only possible to and from restricted locations. As wireless communication becomes ubiquitous, we will no longer treat it with such reverence.

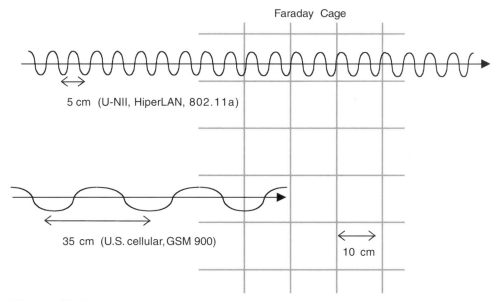

Faraday Cage

5 cm (U-NII, HiperLAN, 802.11a)

35 cm (U.S. cellular, GSM 900)

10 cm

Figure 13.5
Short wavelengths can pass through the holes in a Faraday cage.

WEB RESOURCES

www.electric-words.com/

Run by Australian journalist and campaigner Stewart Fist, this site has the Internet's most comprehensive archive of research into cell phones, with free summaries or abstracts of many studies and explanations of what they mean.

www.prwatch.org

This features a look at how industry tries to manipulate science and public opinion, updated daily.

www.fcc.gov/oet/rfsafety

The FCC has guidelines on radiation safety and an online database of SAR levels for every device approved in the United States, but this is deliberately difficult to access. First, you need to find the device's FCC ID number, which is often hidden inside its battery compartment in very small print. Next, enter this number into the FCC's Web server, and accept the popup warning that continuing may infect your PC with a virus. Finally, download several PDF files and manually search each one for the SAR. As an additional barrier, the site uses a nonstandard protocol that most Internet firewalls reject, meaning that it can't be accessed from many corporate networks.

www.iegmp.org.uk/

The Independent Experts Group on Mobile Phones was a committee set up by the British government to produce safety guidelines about cell phone use. Its complete report is available for free download.

www.mcw.edu/gcrc/

Dr John Moulder, professor of radiation biology and the Medical College of Wisconsin, maintains several skeptical FAQs on cellular base station safety and related topics.

www.newscientist.com

British science weekly **New Scientist** keeps an archive of articles relating to mobile phone safety on its site.

Bibliography

Carlo, G. **Cell Phones: Invisible Hazards in the Wireless Age.** Carroll & Graf, 2001.
The WTR director's own account of the cell phone industry's attempt to manipulate research into the health effects of cell phones.

Levitt, Blake B. **Electromagnetic Fields: A Consumer's Guide to the Issues and How to Protect Ourselves.** Harvest Books, 1995.
A nontechnical handbook covering all kinds of electromagnetic waves, including microwaves.

Rampton, Sheldon and John Stauber. **Trust Us, We're Experts: How Industry Manipulates Science and Gambles With Your Future.** Madison, WI: Tarcher/Putnam, 2001.
An excellent description of how powerful interests can claim fake scientific expertise.

SUMMARY

- Cell phones generate the same kind of radiation that microwave ovens use to cook food. This can't cause ionization, the damaging effect of nuclear, X-ray, and ultraviolet radiation, but can cause heating.

- Unlike conventional heat sources, people don't always feel hot when exposed to microwaves, even though their temperatures may rise.

- When calculating your exposure to a transmitter, your distance from it is more important than its power output.

- The only reproducible effect of cell phone radiation on the human brain is a slight improvement in reaction times, demonstrated by researchers in the United Kingdom and then in Finland.

- There is no evidence that cell phones cause cancer, though this doesn't guarantee that they are safe.

- The greatest danger that cell phones pose is driver distraction. Most researchers believe that even if wireless devices are shown to increase the risk of cancer, the number of people killed by wireless-related cancer will be fewer than those killed by drivers who use cell phones.

Glossary

1xEV-DO
(Enhanced Version—Data Only)

Narrowband CDMA system that offers data speeds of up to 2.4 Mbps, relying on $1 \times MC$ for voice. Also known as HDR.

1xEV-DV
(Enhanced Version—Data/Voice)

Narrowband CDMA system that may offer data speeds of more than 5 Mbps and increased voice capacity.

1xMC
(Multi-Carrier)

Narrowband CDMA system that offers data speeds of up to 384 kbps and compatibility with existing cdmaOne (IS-95) networks. Also known as *1xRTT* (Radio Transmission Technology).

1Xtreme

Narrowband CDMA system promoted by Motorola and Nokia, offering data rates of up to 5.2 Mbps.

2.5G

Digital cellular networks that have been upgraded to allow packet switching and data rates comparable to those of an analog modem.

3G
(third generation)

Generic name for mobile systems that aim to offer performance similar to an ISDN line, the first two generations being the existing analog and digital cellular networks, respectively.

3G lite

Name given either to 2.5G networks that can be upgraded to 3G or to 3G networks that do not yet reach the target data rate of 144 kbps.

3xMC
(Multi-Carrier)

Proposed wideband CDMA system offering data rates of up to about 4 Mbps and compatibility with existing cdmaOne networks. Also known as *3xRTT* (Radio Transmission Technology).

802.11

IEEE committee responsible for setting wireless LAN standards. Also the name of a family of standards that uses a CSMA/CA access control layer, and either FHSS, DSSS, infrared, or OFDM physical layers.

802.11a

A wireless LAN standard that uses OFDM to provide 11 separate 54-Mbps channels in the 5-GHz band, inheriting the CSMA/CA access control from IEEE 802.11. Also known as *Wi-Fi5*.

802.11b

The most popular wireless LAN standard, which upgrades the DSSS version of IEEE 802.11 to provide three separate 11-Mbps channels in a 2.4-GHz band. Also known as *Wireless Ethernet* or *Wi-Fi*.

802.15

IEEE committee responsible for setting an official Bluetooth-like standard.

802.16

IEEE committee responsible for setting wireless local loop standards.

AAA
(Authentication, Authorization, and Accounting)

The way in which a telecom or computer system keeps track of which users are accessing it for security and/or billing purposes.

air link

The physical layer protocol used to send information over radio waves, including the multiplexing and modulation schemes.

AM
(amplitude modulation)

Method of encoding data onto a wave by varying its transmission power.

AMPS
(Advanced Mobile Phone System)

The analog mobile phone standard used in North and South America and some parts of Asia.

ANSI
(American National Standards Institute)

Body that formally approves standards in the United States.

ANSI-136

Narrowband TDMA standard that uses the same frequency as the analog AMPS system and, hence, is also known as *D-AMPS*.

antenna

Electrical conductor used to transmit and/or receive radio waves.

architecture

A description of the different interfaces, protocols, and topologies used by a network.

ASP
(Application Service Provider)

Company that hosts applications on its own servers for customers to access via the Web.

asymmetric

A two-way communications link that offers higher data rates in one direction than in the other. Many wireless technologies are asymmetric, because receivers are smaller than transmitters and require less power. Asymmetric systems are useful for Web surfing, where most data flows from server to client.

asynchronous

A communications system that does not require both ends of a link to have their clocks precisely synchronized.

ATM
(Asynchronous Transfer Mode)

A packet-switched technology that uses fixed-length (48-byte) packets and offers QoS guarantees. Often utilized at the core of carrier networks to combine voice, IP, and other types of traffic.

bandwidth

The amount of radio spectrum (in Hz) used by or available to a service. Can also refer to the data rate of a link (in bits)

baud
(or baud rate)

The number of modulation symbols transferred per second. A modulation symbol may represent one or more bits.

bit
(binary digit)

The smallest unit of information, a single 0 or 1.

Bluetooth

Initiative from more than 2,000 companies to set a standard for ubiquitous wireless networks. It aims to fit a 1-Mbps transceiver onto a single chip priced at $1.

BRAN
(Broadband Radio Access Network)

European project that aims to create wireless local loop and LAN standards, including HiperLan, HiperLink, and HiperAccess.

bridge

A device that passes data between separate networks without examining or processing it.

broadband

Originally meant a system with a broad spectral bandwidth but now used to mean any communications link that can offer high data rates. In its original meaning, it has largely been replaced by *wideband*.

broadcast

Transmission sent to many recipients. Most radio transmissions are broadcasts, so senders must use encryption to protect privacy, and receivers must use fine tuning to ensure that they do not pick up the wrong signal.

BSC
(Base Station Controller)

Device that converts signals to and from the format used when they are transmitted over the air. One BSC may control several base stations.

BTS
(Base Transceiver Station)

Powerful radio equipment that cellular operators need to place at the center of each cell, usually called simply a *base station* or *cell site*.

byte

A group of bits, usually 8, that represents a character and is handled as a unit. An 8-bit byte is often referred to as an *octet*.

capacity

The raw data rate of a communications link, measured in bits per second.

carrier frequency

A wave form that can be modulated to carry information.

CBS
(Cell Broadcast Service)

A messaging system built into GSM networks that can send messages to all phones within a cell.

CDMA
(Code Division Multiple Access)

A method of sharing frequency among many users by encrypting each user's signal using a different code. Despite the name, it does not by itself provide any security, as the decryption keys are included with all hardware.

CDMA2000

A group of technologies that upgrade cdma-One networks to data rates of at least 2 Mbps, including 1×MC and 3×MC.

cdmaOne

A brand name of the CDMA Development Group, an industry association, for the present CDMA standards IS-95a and IS-95b.

CDPD
(Cellular Digital Packet Data)

A way to send data packets over one channel in an AMPS network.

cellular

Any wireless network made from overlapping radio cells, especially the older analog mobile phone systems.

CEPT
(Conference of European Post and Telecommunications Authorities)

Former intergovernmental body that designed the GSM system.

channel

A communications path between two or more points.

circuit-switched

A type of network that temporarily creates an actual physical path between parties while they are communicating.

CLEC
(Competitive Local Exchange Carrier)

A company that runs telecommunications networks in competition with the local phone operator, often over the operator's own copper network.

client

A computer that accesses resources on a network—as opposed to a *server*, the computer that provides them. In a wireless data network, almost all end-user devices are clients.

C-Netz

An analog cellular system used in Germany and other central European countries.

codec
(coder/decoder)

Software used to convert analog signals, such as voice, to digital data.

compression

A technique that eliminates redundant information to increase data throughput.

connectionless

A protocol or service that does not require a logical connection and does not send automatic acknowledgements when data is received.

connection-oriented

A protocol or service that sets up a logical (but not necessarily physical) connection between communicating parties.

cordless

A private wireless system that provides short-range mobility.

core network

The physical infrastructure that links together all the radio transceivers in a cellular network. Existing core networks are circuit-switched and will have to be replaced by IP backbones for data services.

CSMA/CA
(Carrier Sense Multiple Access/Collision Avoidance)

The method by which 802.11 devices decide who can access the airwaves. The device that wants to send a packet first broadcasts a very short test signal and continues its transmission only if this receives no interference from other devices.

CSMA/CD
(Carrier Sense Multiple Access/Collision Detection)
The method by which 802.3 Ethernet networks decide who can access a wire. Each device simply broadcasts packets whenever it needs to and tries again if it detects a collision.

CT-2
(Cordless Telephone System 2)
A mobile technology developed in the United Kingdom that allowed people to make calls but not receive them. Also known as *telepoint*.

daisy chaining
The connection of multiple devices serially, often in a ring topology.

D-AMPS
(Digital AMPS)
Narrowband TDMA standard that uses the same frequencies as the analog AMPS system, also known as *ANSI-136*.

datagram
A unit of data that can be delivered independently of others, used in connectionless services.

DECT
(Digital European Cordless Telephony)
A cordless standard designed to work alongside GSM.

de facto standard
A system that has become widely used, although not ratified by any standards body. Examples include WAP, the QWERTY keyboard, and Microsoft Windows.

DSL
(Digital Subscriber Line)
A family of technologies that transmit data over unused frequencies in ordinary copper phone lines.

DSP
(digital signal processor)
A high-speed processor designed for digitizing analog signals and vice versa, used in all mobile phones.

DSSS
(direct sequence spread spectrum)
A spread spectrum system that transmits on many frequencies simultaneously.

Echelon
A spy network run by the United States, United Kingdom, Canada, Australia, and New Zealand, intercepting radio transmissions and Internet traffic around the world.

EDGE
(Enhanced Data Rates for Global Evolution)
An advanced upgrade to GPRS systems that uses improved modulation to triple data capacity.

encryption
The process of encoding data before transmission so that an eavesdropper cannot decipher it.

Enhanced Messaging Service
Smart Message System developed by Ericsson and ratified by 3GPP that adds color and other gimmicks to SMS messages but requires no new infrastructure in a cellular network. Functionally almost identical to (but incompatible with) Smart Messaging.

ERMES
(European Radio Message System)
A paging standard used in Europe.

Ethernet
An industry standard LAN system that follows the IEEE's 802.3 protocols and uses CSMA/CD. It operates across copper or fiber wires at 10, 100, 1,000, and 10,000 Mbps.

ETSI
(European Telecommunications Standards Institute)
Europe's main standards body, whose projects include GSM, UMTS, and DECT.

extranet
A network using Internet protocols, usually including the World Wide Web, to communicate with select individuals outside an organization.

FCC
(Federal Communications Commission)
A government agency responsible for licensing spectrum and regulating telecommunications in the United States.

FDD
(Frequency Division Duplex)
The allocation of one frequency to the uplink and another to the downlink, allowing simultaneous transmission and reception. Also known as *paired spectrum*.

FDMA
(Frequency Division Multiple Access)
A method of sharing spectrum between users by dividing it into discrete channels.

FHSS
(frequency-hopping spread spectrum)
A spread spectrum system that rapidly switches between seemingly random frequencies.

fiber
Strands of glass used to carry optical signals.

firewall
Device or program that separates a network or computer from a potentially hostile network, usually by blocking access to certain types of TCP or UDP traffic.

Flex
A popular paging system developed by Motorola.

FM
(frequency modulation)
A method of encoding data onto a wave by varying its transmission frequency.

FOMA
(Freedom Of Mobile Multimedia Access)
NTT DoCoMo's brand name for its W-CDMA system. The first version is not compatible with UMTS, but later versions will be.

"free as in beer"
Something given away at no cost. In particular, the right to make unlimited copies of a piece of software.

"free as in speech"
A license agreement that does not restrict people's rights. In particular, software that users can edit and do with as they wish.

FSK
(frequency-shift keying)
A type of FM that uses discrete tones to represent symbols in a data stream.

gateway
A device that converts voice or data traffic from the format of one network (e.g., the Internet) to that of another (e.g., the cell phone system).

geostationary
A perfectly circular orbit exactly 35,785 km above the equator, in which a satellite will remain stationary with respect to the Earth's surface.

geosynchronous

An orbit of average height 35,785 km above the equator, not necessarily exactly circular. Geosynchronous satellites may move north or south and up or down, but not east or west.

GGSN
(Gateway GPRS Support Node)

An interface between a GPRS network and an external network, such as the Internet.

GMSC
(Gateway Mobile Switching Center)

The interface between a mobile network and the PSTN.

GMSK
(Gaussian minimum shift keying)

A phase modulation technique that encodes 1 bit per waveform symbol, used in GSM.

GPRS
(General Packet Radio Service)

An upgrade to GSM networks that offers each user up to eight 14.4-kbps channels and employs packet switching to use bandwidth more efficiently.

ground station

Radio equipment designed to track and control satellites.

GSM
(Global System for Mobile Communications)

A wideband TDMA standard originally developed in Europe but used worldwide.

Handheld PC

Microsoft's name for small devices that run Windows CE and have a keyboard.

Handoff

The transfer of a mobile terminal from one base station to another as it moves between cells, also called *handover*.

HDR
(High Data Rate)

A narrowband CDMA system developed by Qualcomm that offers high-speed data, but not voice, now known as *1×EV-DO*.

HiperAccess

A proposed future wireless local loop technology using the 5-GHz band, which it shares with HiperLan. Also called *HiperLan3*

HiperLan1

A proposed (but never built) wireless LAN system that would have operated in the 5-GHz band and provided data capacity of up to 23.5 Mbps.

HiperLan2

A wireless LAN specification set by ETSI, which operates in the 5-GHz band and provides data capacity of up to 52 Mbps.

HiperLink

A proposed future wireless LAN or local loop system using 17-GHz spectrum. Also known as HiperLan4.

HLR
(Home Location Register)

A database that keeps track of all the mobile terminals that usually reside within a group of cells.

HomeRF

A wireless LAN standard designed for consumer devices operating in the 2.4-GHz ISM band.

HSCSD
(High-Speed Circuit-Switched Data)

A software upgrade to GSM networks that gives each user up to four 14.4-kbps circuits.

HSDPA
(High-Speed Downlink Packet Access)

An upgrade to UMTS networks that increases the maximum data rate to 10 Mbps but only from the base station to the cell site.

HTML
(Hypertext Markup Language)

A programming code used to describe Web pages and interpreted by a browser.

HTTP
(Hypertext Transfer Protocol)

A protocol used to transfer Web pages from servers on the Internet to users' computers.

iDEN
(integrated Digital Enhanced Network)

A digital PMR system developed by Motorola and operated in the United States by Nextel.

IEEE
(Institute of Electrical and Electronic Engineers)

A professional society responsible for many networking standards, notably, Ethernet and its wireless derivative, 802.11.

IEGMP
(Independent Experts Group on Mobile Phones)

A commission set up by the British government to produce guidelines for mobile phone safety. Its main recommendations, published in 2000, were that cell phones not be advertised to children, that drivers refrain from using phones (even with a hands-free device), and that stricter planning controls on base stations be implemented.

IMT-2000
(International Mobile Telecommunications)

An ITU initiative to create a global standard for third-generation wireless data networks, providing 2 Mbps when stationary and 384 kbps when mobile. Includes three modes of operation: UMTS/WCDMA, EDGE/UWC-136, and CDMA2000.

i-mode

A very popular service offered by NTT DoCoMo over its PDC network. The original version uses SMS messaging and C-HTML browsing, but new versions include support for XHTML and multimedia messaging.

infrared

Light with frequencies just below the visible spectrum, used by lasers and for simple cordless networking.

interconnect agreement

Contract signed by two or more telecommunications companies that allows one to carry or terminate calls that originate on another's network.

Internet

A network of networks, linking together nearly all computers that use the IP networking protocol.

IP
(Internet Protocol)

The protocol governing how data packets are routed across the Internet.

IP Address

A unique number of either 32 or 128 bits that specifies a device on the Internet or other IP network.

IrDA
(Infrared Data Association)

A consortium governing the standards supported by the infrared ports fitted to many laptops and PDAs.

IS-54

An older version of the ANSI-136 or D-AMPS standard, lacking its text messaging features.

IS-95a

The first CDMA standard, better known under the brand name *cdmaOne*. It offers high-quality voice and data at up to 14.4 kbps.

IS-95b

A software upgrade to IS-95a, which increases the maximum data rate to 115.2 kbps.

IS-95c

Another name for 1×MC, the upgrade to IS-95b that increases maximum data rate to 384 kbps.

ISDN
(Integrated Services Digital Network)

A fully digital communications network, providing channels of 64 kbps each.

ISP
(Internet Service Provider)

A company that provides access to the Internet. Measured by number of customers, the world's largest is NTT DoCoMo.

ITU
(International Telecommunications Union)

An agency of the United Nations that covers worldwide communications regulation and allocates radio spectrum.

Java

A programming language developed by Sun Microsystems and usually interpreted within a Web browser.

jitter

Variation in latency that, in extreme cases, can cause packets to arrive in the wrong order.

Kbyte
(Kilobyte)

1,024 bytes. The capital *K* refers to the fact that it is a power of 2 (binary), not a power of 10 (decimal, as in kbit).

Kerberos

An authentication and key exchange protocol that depends on a password that has been previously shared with a central server. Used in the TKIP wireless LAN security protocol.

key

A code used to encrypt and/or decrypt messages.

LAN
(Local Area Network)

A data network connecting nearby devices, usually within the same building or office.

latency

The time taken for a unit of information to pass through a part of a network, such as a wire or router.

leased line

A dedicated circuit that permanently connects two or more locations and is for their sole use.

LMDS
(Local Multipoint Distribution Service)

High-speed, short-range wireless local loop technology.

local loop

The portion of a telephone network that runs from the telephone exchange to the user's premises, also known as the *last mile*.

lossless compression

Compression that allows the original file to be reconstructed exactly, used for data. The best known types of lossless compression are the GIF image format and the ZIP file format.

lossy compression

Compression that introduces some errors into the file when it is reconstructed, often used for voice and photographs. The best known types of lossy compression are the MP3 music format and the JPG image format.

MAN
(Metropolitan Area Network)

A high-speed communications network operating within a city, usually based on fiber or microwave radio.

MBS
(Mobile Broadband System)

A proposed future 4G mobile system promising multimegabit capacity by 2010.

MCDN
(Micro Cellular Digital Network)

A proprietary mobile data network developed by Metricom. It uses a mixture of licensed and unlicensed frequencies and is marketed as Ricochet.

m-commerce
(mobile e-commerce)

Any kind of business where a buyer and seller are connected through a mobile data link.

MExE
(Mobile Execution Environment)

European standard for wireless devices that include WAP and Java.

MMDS
(Multipoint Multichannel Distribution System)

A television broadcasting system adapted for use as a wireless local loop technology.

MMM
(Mobile Media Mode)

A branding mark that appears on some WAP-compatible hardware and services.

MMS
(Multimedia Messaging Service)

Advanced messaging and e-mail system designed for packet-switched mobile networks. Built into UMTS but can be added to GPRS or other systems by replacing their SMS gateways.

mobile network

A wireless network that allows users to move around freely and remain connected.

Mobitex

A packet-switched mobile data network designed by Ericsson and operated in the United States by Bell South.

modulation

A technique for encoding a user's information into a carrier signal.

MS
(Mobile Station)

A mobile terminal, such as a phone, PC card, or PDA.

MSC
(Mobile Switching Center)

The telephone exchange that aggregates and switches voice calls to and from a mobile network.

multicast

A message transmitted separately to several recipients but not broadcast to an unlimited number.

multimedia

A combination of two or more media, usually including video or sound.

multipath

A type of interference caused when a signal takes different paths to the same destination. "Ghost" images on an analog TV with an indoor antenna are the best examples that most people encounter.

multiplexing

Division of a channel into two or more subchannels so that it can be shared by more than one user or application.

multipoint

A base station that can connect to several subscribers at once, either by blanketing an entire area or by targeting them with individual antennas.

MVNO
(mobile virtual network operator)

A mobile operator that does not actually own a network of its own but instead leases capacity from another.

NIC
(Network Interface Card)

A circuit board placed inside a computer to connect it to a network, usually including either an antenna or the end of a wire. Many computers now have built-in NICs for Ethernet, Bluetooth, and/or IEEE 802.11b.

node

Anything connected to a network.

NTSC
(National Television Systems Committee)

An analog TV broadcasting system using 525 picture lines and a refresh rate of 60 Hz, used in North America and Japan.

OEM
(Original Equipment Manufacturer)

A company that builds devices that then appear inside others. The term is also used as a verb, meaning to buy a product from another manufacturer, stick a new label on it, then sell it under the new label. Many name-brand electronics are actually OEM'd from less well-known manufacturers.

OFDM
(Orthogonal Frequency Division Multiplex)

A system that divides a high-capacity data stream into multiple streams of lower capacity and sends each separately.

packet

A datagram that is routed between an origin and a destination, both of which are encoded into the packet itself, rather than into the route.

packet-switched

A type of network in which small units of data are routed through a network based on the address contained within each packet. Packets may take different routes to the same destination, where they will be reassembled.

paging

A radio system for transmitting short text messages, usually only one-way.

PAL
(Phase Alternating Line)

TV broadcasting system developed in Germany and the United Kingdom that uses 650 picture lines and a 50-Hz refresh rate.

PAN
(Personal Area Network)

A very short-range data network that connects all the gadgets carried by a person, interacting as necessary with those of other people.

PCN
(Personal Communications Network)

Another name for GSM, particularly systems based on frequencies in the 1,800-MHz band.

PCS
(Personal Communications Services)

A generic name for any digital mobile voice or data service, especially those that use the 1,900-MHz band in the United States.

PCU
(Packet Control Unit)

A device that must be added to older GSM base stations if they are to carry GPRS traffic.

PDA
(personal digital assistant)

A pocket-sized computer typically used to store names and addresses but increasingly incorporating wireless communications applications.

PDC
(Personal Digital Cellular)

A TDMA digital standard used only in Japan, based on D-AMPS but adding packet switching for data.

phase modulation

A method of encoding data onto a carrier by varying the phase of its waves.

PHS
(Personal Handyphone System)

A Japanese telepoint standard that allows users to make calls while roaming but not to receive them.

PMR
(Private Mobile Radio)

A cellular system that allows direct communication between two terminals when out of range of a base station. Examples include iDEN and TETRA.

point-to-point

A direct link between two nodes.

PQA
(Palm Query Application)

A small program that runs on a Palm device and is required to access some sites encoded using the Web Clipping system.

protocol

A set of rules governing the format and transmission of data.

PSK
(phase-shift keying)

A type of phase modulation that uses preset phase changes to represent digital symbols, rather than relative changes of phase.

PSTN
(Public Switched Telephone Network)

The regular nonmobile telephone system.

PTMSC
(Point-to-Multipoint Service Center)

A server that handles QoS issues in a GPRS network.

QAM
(quadrature amplitude modulation)
A combination of amplitude and phase modulation used in many mobile systems.

RBOC
(Regional Bell Operating Company)
One of the local telcos spun off from AT&T in 1984, also known as *Baby Bells*.

RC4
A popular symmetric encryption algorithm used by WEP, SSL, and TLS.

roaming
The movement of a mobile terminal outside its home cell or group of cells, especially to another network in another country.

routing
Decisions regarding the communications path taken by a message or telephone call.

satellite
An orbital communications relay station, usually placed in a geostationary position.

server
Computer that responds to requests from others on a network, usually storing data and transferring it when asked.

SGSN
(Serving GPRS Support Node)
A computer that routes data between a GPRS backbone and a mobile terminal via a base station.

SIM
(Subscriber Identity Module)
A smart card that fits inside digital phones or wireless data devices and contains all information particular to a mobile subscriber, including phone number, network operator, and the user's phone directory.

smart antenna
An antenna that can focus its beam on one particular area to reduce interference, increase spectral efficiency, and reduce power consumption.

Smart Messaging
System developed by Nokia that adds color and other gimmicks to SMS messages but requires no new infrastructure in a cellular network. Functionally almost identical to (but incompatible with) EMS.

smartphone
A cell phone that includes some computer functions, such as a Web browser.

SMS
(Short Message Service)
A feature available with some mobile phones that allows users to send and receive short alphanumeric messages. They are usually carried over the signaling channel, so users can talk on the phone at the same time as messages are transmitted or received.

spam
Unsolicited commercial or bulk e-mail, usually advertising pornography or fraudulent get-rich-quick schemes. The name comes from a Monty Python sketch about a brand of tinned pork.

spread spectrum
A radio technology that spreads a signal over a wider bandwidth than it really needs, to overcome interference.

SSL
(Secure Sockets Layer)
An encryption protocol designed by Netscape for secure transactions over the Internet and the i-mode system. Still in use by most sites but officially replaced by the almost identical TLS.

symmetric

A two-way communications link that offers the same data rate in each direction. Most telephone lines (wireless or otherwise) are symmetric.

synchronous

A communications system that requires both ends of a link to have their clocks precisely synchronized.

Tablet PC

A full-featured PC that includes a hard disk and an operating system similar to a desktop PC but uses a touch-sensitive screen for input.

**TACS
(Total Access Communication System)**

An analog cellular system used in Europe and Africa but being phased out in favor of GSM.

**TCP
(Transport Control Protocol)**

A connection-oriented protocol used on the fixed Internet to verify that sent data has been received.

**TDD
(Time Division Duplexing)**

The sharing of a frequency band between the uplink and downlink, so that a user cannot transmit and receive at once.

**TDMA
(Time Division Multiple Access)**

A method of sharing one frequency between several users by dividing it into discrete time slots; often used to refer to the D-AMPS system.

telco

Telephone company (one that operates a phone network, not one that makes phones).

telepoint

A cordless system that allows a phone to make calls by connecting to low-power base stations in public places, such as railway stations, airports, and shopping malls.

**TETRA
(Terrestrial Trunked Radio)**

A European standard for digital PMR, offering data rates up to 28.8 kbps.

**TKIP
(Temporal Key Integrity Protocol)**

A new name given to WEP2, in the hope that people will not associate it with WEP.

**TLS
(Transport Layer Security)**

The encryption protocol built into WAP 2.0 and fully compatible with SSL, the protocol used by most e-commerce sites.

**UMTS
(Universal Mobile
Telecommunications System)**

A European standard for 3G wireless networks, using WCDMA and new spectrum in the 2-GHz band.

**U-NII
(Unlicensed National Information
Infrastructure)**

Spectrum set aside by the FCC for unlicensed data links in the 5-GHz band.

**USSD
(Unstructured Supplementary
Services Data)**

A protocol for two-way alphanumeric messaging over a digital mobile network, allowing users to interact in real time with a remote server, such as a WAP gateway.

UWC-136
(Universal Wireless Communications)

Another name for EDGE, the TDMA-based 3G network.

videophone

A futuristic dream that has been possible for many years but never manufactured widely, due to low customer demand. Most wireless videophones are simply PDAs with small cameras stuck on top.

voice portal

An attempt to transfer Web content through a voice interface.

VoIP
(voice over IP)

The transmission of telephony through the Internet or other networks based on IP. (Speech-based Internet radio stations are generally not considered VoIP.) Many analysts believe that all voice will eventually be carried over IP, and it is a requirement in version 6 of UMTS.

WAN
(Wide Area Network)

A network that connects users over a range of 1 km or more, especially between different cities.

WAP
(Wireless Application Protocol)

Stack of protocols designed for sending simplified Web pages to wireless devices. It replaces Web protocols with its own and requires that pages be written in WML instead of HTML.

WAP gateway

A device that converts Internet protocols to and from WAP protocols. It does not convert HTML Web pages themselves to WAP's more limited WML.

WASP
(Wireless ASP)

A company that offers m-commerce or remote access services. The most common such services are wireless access to corporate e-mail and WAP site hosting. Many WASPS have found that their business model doesn't work and tried to become software companies instead.

W-CDMA
(Wideband CDMA)

A CDMA system that uses 5-GHz channels and can hand calls over to GSM.

Web Clipping

A proprietary system developed by 3COM that delivers Web content to Palm devices.

WEP
(Wired Equivalent Privacy)

The encryption protocol built into 802.11 networks. It uses 40-bit RC4 keys, which must be shared between all users and is easily cracked.

WEP2

An enhanced version of WEP that uses 128-bit keys and Kerberos authentication. Also known as *TKIP*.

wideband

A communications channel that requires a large amount of spectrum. The term is relative: GSM is considered wideband, because its minimum spectrum requirement (200 kHz) is more than that of other TDMA technologies, whereas cdmaOne is not because its minimum bandwidth (1,250 kHz) is less than that of most CDMA systems.

Wi-Fi
(Wireless Fidelity)
A mark given by WECA to wireless LAN equipment to certify that it follows the 802.11b standard and can interoperate with other equipment from different manufacturers.

Wi-Fi5
Similar to Wi-Fi but for 802.11a instead of 802.11b.

WLAN
(Wireless LAN)
A short-range wireless system designed to link computers (usually laptop) to each other or to an access point on a fixed network.

WML
(Wireless Markup Language)
A programming language used to specify Web pages optimized for small wireless devices, such as mobile phones.

WScript
A simple programming language used in WML pages, which is compiled by a WAP gateway and sent in binary form to a WAP terminal

WTLS
(Wireless Transport Layer Security)
The encryption scheme added to WAP with version 1.2, which is incompatible with the Internet's SSL and TLS.

Index